THE MAKING OF ENGLAND
To 1399

A HISTORY OF ENGLAND

General Editor: Lacey Baldwin Smith

THE MAKING OF ENGLAND: TO 1399

C. Warren Hollister
Robert C. Stacey
University of Washington, Seattle
Robin Chapman Stacey
University of Washington, Seattle

THIS REALM OF ENGLAND: 1399–1688

Lacey Baldwin Smith
Northwestern University

THE AGE OF ARISTOCRACY: 1688–1830

William B. Willcox
Walter L. Arnstein
University of Illinois, Urbana-Champaign

BRITAIN YESTERDAY AND TODAY: 1830 TO THE PRESENT

Walter L. Arnstein
University of Illinois, Urbana-Champaign

THE MAKING OF ENGLAND
To 1399

Eighth Edition

C. Warren Hollister
University of California, Santa Barbara

Robert C. Stacey
University of Washington, Seattle

Robin Chapman Stacey
University of Washington, Seattle

HOUGHTON MIFFLIN COMPANY   BOSTON   NEW YORK

Editor-in-Chief: Jean Woy
Associate Editor: Leah Strauss
Associate Production/Design Coordinator: Lisa Jelly
Senior Cover Design Coordinator: Deborah Azerrad Savona
Manufacturing Manager: Florence Cadran
Senior Marketing Manager: Sandra McGuire

Cover design: Walter Kopec
Cover art: *Sir Lancelot vowing to seek the Holy Grail.* Bibliothèque
    Nationale, France

Printed in the U.S.A.

Library of Congress Catalog Card Number: 00-133911

ISBN: 0-618-00101-8

6789-QF-09 08 07 06 05

In Memory of
C. Warren Hollister
Teacher and Scholar

Contents

Illustrations

Maps

Genealogical Charts

Foreword

Carl Becker once complained that everybody knows the job of the historian is "to discover and set forth the 'facts' of history." The facts, it is often said, speak for themselves. The businessperson talks about hard facts; the statistician refers to cold facts; the lawyer is eloquent about the facts of the case; and the historian, who deals with the incontrovertible facts of life and death, is called a very lucky fellow. Those who speak so confidently about the historian's craft are generally not historians themselves; they are readers of textbooks that more often than not are mere recordings of vital information and listings to dull generalizations. It is not surprising, then, that historians' reputations have suffered; they have become known as peddlers of facts and chroniclers who say, "This is what happened." The shorter the historical survey, the more textbook writers are likely to assume godlike detachment, spurning the minor tragedies and daily comedies of humanity and immortalizing the rise and fall of civilizations, the clash of economic and social forces, and the deeds of titans. Anglo-Saxon warriors were sick with fear when Viking "swift sea-kings" swept down on England to plunder, rape, and kill, but historians dispassionately note that the Norse invasions were a good thing; they allowed the kingdom of Wessex to unite and "liberate" the island in the name of Saxon and Christian defense against heathen marauders. The chronicler moves nimbly from the indisputable fact that Henry VIII annulled his marriage with Catherine of Aragon and wedded Anne Boleyn to the confident assertion that this helped produce the Reformation in England. The result is sublime but emasculated history. Her subjects wept when Good Queen Bess died, but historians merely comment that she had lived her allotted three score years and ten. British soldiers rotted by the thousands in the trenches of the First World War, but the terror and agony of that holocaust are lost in the dehumanized statistic that 765,399 British troops died in the four years of war.

In a brief history of even one "tight little island," the chronology of events must of necessity predominate, but if these four volumes are in any way fresh and up-to-date, it is because their authors have tried by artistry to step beyond the usual confines of a textbook and to conjure up something of the drama of politics, the humdrum of every day life, and the pettiness, as well as the greatness, of human motivation. The price paid will be obvious to anyone seeking total coverage. There is relatively little in these pages on literature, the fine arts, or philosophy, except as they throw light on the uniqueness of English history. On the other hand, the complexities, uncertainties, endless variations, and above all the accidents that bedevil the design of human events — these are the very stuff of which history is made and the "truths" that this series seeks to narrate and preserve. Moreover, the flavor of each volume varies according to the tastes of its author. Sometimes the emphasis is political, sometimes economic or social, but the presentation is always impressionistic — shading, underscoring, or highlighting to achieve an image that will be more than a bare outline and will recapture something of the smell and temper of the past.

Even though each book was conceived and executed as an entity capable of standing by itself, the four volumes were designed as a unit. They tell the story of how a small and insignificant outpost of the Roman Empire hesitantly, and not always heroically, evolved into the nation that has probably produced and disseminated more ideas and institutions, both good and bad, than any state since Athens. Our hope is that these volumes will appeal both individually, to those interested in a balanced portrait of particular segments of English history, and collectively, to those who seek the majestic sweep of the story of a people whose activities have been wonderfully rich, exciting, and varied. In this spirit this series was originally written and has now been revised for a seventh time, not only to keep pace with new scholarship but, equally important, to keep it fresh and thought-provoking to a world becoming both more nostalgic and more impatient of its past.

Time has not left this series untouched since its inception in 1966. As the four volumes have changed over seven revisions, so also have their authors. William B. Willcox of the University of Michigan and Yale University, a decade before his death in 1985, turned responsibility for revising volume III, *The Age of Aristocracy*, over to Walter L. Arnstein of the University of Illinois, and now, five revisions later, this volume belongs to him although Willcox's name still appears on the title page. In September of 1997 C. Warren Hollister, the author of volume I, *The Making of England*, died, and the series has been fortunate in persuading Robin and Robert Stacey of the University of Washington to take on the revision of the volume. A new generation is emerging to keep our four volumes abreast of the changing needs and interests of educators and students.

The writing of history is always a collective enterprise, and so the authors of this series would like to thank the following reviewers who made valuable suggestions for the eighth edition: Lorraine Atreed, Holy Cross College; Joel D. Benson, Northwest Missouri State University; Katherine French, SUNY–New Paltz; Amy M. Froide, University of Tennessee–Chattonooga; Helen Hundley, Wichita State University; Susan K. Kent, University of Colorado; Newton Key, Eastern Illinois University; Fred M. Leventhal, Boston University; Muriel C. McClendon, University of California–Los Angeles; and Joseph P. Ward, University of Mississippi.

Lacey Baldwin Smith

Preface

The first edition of *The Making of England* appeared in 1966. Through thirty years and six subsequent editions, Warren Hollister diligently revised and updated this volume to take into account the ever-increasing flood of new scholarly work on the history of medieval England. As he himself remarked in the preface to the seventh edition (1996) of this book: "Most authors, when revising their textbooks, are torn between introducing important changes, at the risk of irritating teachers who have grown accustomed to the materials in the book over a period of years, and making only cosmetic changes, at the risk of permitting the book to fade off into the sunset as exciting new archaeological evidence emerges and historical scholarship marches on. I have regularly chosen the first alternative, and I firmly believe that it is the wiser course." We trust, therefore, that in revising this book for a new, eighth edition, we have done so in a spirit that Warren Hollister would have approved.

Much has changed in the recent scholarship on medieval England, and we have tried to reflect those changes in this new edition. The book now begins, not with the Romans, but with the Celtic-speaking peoples who settled the British Isles before the Romans came, whose existing patterns of settlement and land-use would structure Romano-British and Anglo-Saxon life for centuries to come. Roman Britain is another subject on which recent historical work has shed remarkable new light. To take into account this new work, we have completely rewritten chapter one. With this new understanding of Roman Britain, the transition from Romano-British to Anglo-Saxon rule also appears as quite a different process from the one historians envisioned just a few years ago. Along with much else, the treatment of the so-called "Celtic" church in chapter two will also be very different from the one that may be familiar to long-time users of this book.

As we move into the later Anglo-Saxon and Anglo-Norman period, we enter territory over which Warren Hollister was an acknowledged master. We have tried in these chapters to update without fundamentally altering the picture Hollister painted. We've reduced the attention Hollister paid to some of the technical aspects of administrative history (the development of the great offices of state, the mechanics of writs and seals), while continuing to stress the profound impact the precociously powerful Old English state had upon its people. We have tried to explain the consequences of these developments in this section for "the making of England" and for the emergence of a distinctively English nationalism. We have modified the treatment of feudalism without abandoning the term altogether. We have also tried in chapter seven to emphasize the impact of economic change in shaping the new society of twelfth-century England.

In the high and late medieval sections of the book, readers will find a significantly revised account of Henry II's legal and administrative reforms, and a new chapter on the reign of King Henry III. We have also tried to emphasize more clearly the creative and dynamic elements of fourteenth-century English culture, as English men and women struggled to adjust to the new world created by the Black Death.

Throughout the eighth edition we have tried to better integrate social, economic, and political history without losing sight of the book's traditional strengths: its strong narrative line and its focus on the development of the English state. We are well aware that a very different and no less valuable book (or indeed, series of books) could be written that would privilege social, cultural, and religious history over political history, and that would shift the focus away from a history of England towards a history of the British Isles and Ireland. But although recent historical scholarship has shown many similarities and parallels between the history of England and the rest of Britain, we believe it has also validated the wisdom of the presumptions upon which Warren Hollister began writing this book nearly forty years ago: that the history of England is in many ways a peculiar one, different in fundamental ways from the history of Scotland, Wales, Ireland or France; that the origins of this peculiarity are very early; and that explanations for the uniqueness of England's history must always and inevitably lead us back to the history of the English state. As we enter a new century, we have tried to honor these presumptions in revising this book for a new generation of students and scholars.

That England's medieval history could have turned out differently is indisputable. From the standpoint of England's neighbors, this would almost certainly have been desirable. In no sense, therefore, does our emphasis upon the peculiarities of England's history imply any endorsement of English triumphalism, past or present. Difference is not superiority. It is merely difference. But the differences between England and its neighbors are fundamental to the subject of this book, which is the making of England as a distinctive political, social, and economic entity, and that is why we emphasize them here. These are the themes Warren Hollister set out in the first edition of *The Making of England*. They remain its themes as the eighth edition goes to press.

Robert C. Stacey
Robin Chapman Stacey

About the Authors

C. Warren Hollister (1931–1997) was Professor and Chair of Medieval Studies at the University of California, Santa Barbara. He earned a Ph.D. from the University of California, Los Angeles. His twelve books include *Anglo-Saxon Military Institutions on the Eve of the Norman Conquest* (Oxford, 1962) and most recently, *Monarchy, Magnates, and Institutions in the Anglo-Norman World* (London, 1986).

Robert C. Stacey is Professor and Chair of the History Department at the University of Washington in Seattle, where he teaches medieval English history and Jewish history. He is the author of two previous books: *Politics, Policy, and Finance under Henry III, 1216–1245* (1987), and *Receipt and Issue Rolls, 26 Henry III* (1992), and more than twenty scholarly articles. A B.A. graduate of Williams College and Oxford University, he received his Ph.D. from Yale University in 1983. He has held fellowships from the John Simon Guggenheim Foundation and from the American Council of Learned Societies, and is a Fellow of the Royal Historical Society. He serves on the editorial boards of *The Medieval Review* and *Jewish History*, and is a member of the Council of the Pipe Roll Society. He has also been honored with two prizes for Distinguished Undergraduate Teaching, one from Yale University, where he taught from 1984 to 1988, and the other from the University of Washington.

Robin Chapman Stacey is Associate Professor of History at the University of Washington in Seattle, where she teaches medieval history and Celtic history. A B.A. graduate of Colorado College, she holds a Master's Degree from Oxford University and a Ph.D. in Medieval Studies from Yale University. Her work has been supported by fellowships from the John Simon Guggenheim Foundation, the American Council of Learned Societies, and the Fulbright Fellowship Program. Her first book, *The Road to Judgment: From Custom to Court in Medieval Ireland and Wales* (1994), received both the John Nicholas Brown Prize from the Medieval Academy of America, and the Hywel Dda Prize from the University of Wales for the best work on Welsh law and history published in 1994 and 1995. A past President of the Celtic Studies Association of North America, she is a member of the Editorial Board of the *Law and History Review* and of the *Celtic Studies Association of North America Yearbook*.

THE MAKING OF ENGLAND
To 1399

PART ONE

THE BIRTH OF
THE REALM

To 1066

CHAPTER 1

Celtic and Roman Britain

When Julius Caesar's Roman legions landed on the beaches north of Dover in 55 B.C.E.,[1] they were invading a land that had already been densely settled and intensively cultivated for many centuries. Human occupation of the island of Britain dates back to at least the seventh millennium B.C.E. and may be far older than that. Despite the best efforts of archaeologists, however, knowledge about these early peoples is meager; and although more is being learned all the time, it is doubtful we will ever know enough about them to evaluate fully their contributions to the basic patterns of settlement and land use that appear in more recent (and better recorded) periods of British history.

Britain Before the Romans

Massive stone circles — most famously, of course, at Stonehenge — give some hint of the difficulties of trying to interpret these early centuries. These enormous monuments were constructed at various dates between approximately 3000 and 1500 B.C.E., to serve purposes at which we can now only guess. Their size and alignment testify to the inhabitants' knowledge of engineering and astronomy, as well as to their possession of the social, economic, and political capital necessary to carry out such enormous construction projects. But virtually nothing is known about how the social, economic, religious, and political systems that produced these monuments actually functioned. Historians can only infer the existence of such systems, and admire the surviving evidence of their accomplishments. It is impossible to assess the social structures that lay behind their constructions or the human costs these constructions entailed.

About the history of Britain during the first millennium B.C.E. somewhat more is known.[2] Ironworking begins to appear in Britain before the

---

[1]This book will use the dating system B.C.E. ("Before the Common Era," equivalent to the Christian dating system B.C., i.e., "Before Christ") and C.E. ("Common Era," equivalent to the Christian dating system A.D., i.e., "Anno Domini," "in the year of the Lord").

[2]Barry Cunliffe, *Iron Age Communities in Britain*, 3rd ed. (London, 1990), is an excellent recent guide to this period.

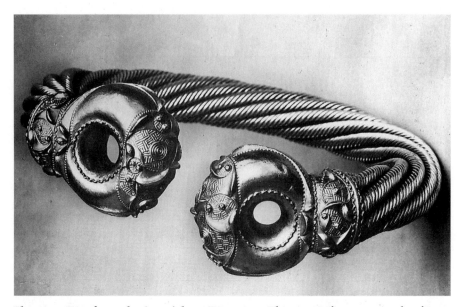

Electrum Torc from the Snettisham Treasure   This magnificent example of Iron Age metalwork dates from the first century of the Common Era. Such torcs, frequently fashioned out of solid gold, were worn by both men and women in the pre-Roman period as a sign of their high status. *(The Granger Collection)*

end of the seventh century B.C.E., along with evidence of locally produced and imported metalwork in iron and bronze. By the third century B.C.E., British artisans were producing elaborate metal craftwork comparable in design and execution to the highest quality contemporary metalwork on the European mainland. Close connections between Britain, Ireland, and the Continent are further suggested by linguistic evidence. Somewhere between the seventh century and the third century B.C.E., the Celtic languages spoken on the European continent became the dominant languages in Britain and Ireland also. We do not know how this important change occurred. Only rarely do artifacts reveal anything directly about the language their users spoke; and even when the production of a specific type of artifact can be identified with a specific linguistic group, it must always be kept in mind that artifacts can travel. Toyota cars, for example, are obviously a Japanese product. But it would be foolish indeed for archaeologists of the future to presume that wherever Toyota cars are found on late twentieth-century sites, their drivers must have spoken (much less been) Japanese.

How Celtic languages became the predominant languages of Britain and Ireland during this period is a mystery. Although historians once were inclined to connect ironworking specifically with the Celts — whoever, precisely, the Celts might have been in this period — and to imagine that a massive Celtic invasion of Britain and Ireland brought both ironworking and the Celtic languages to the islands around the middle of the first millennium B.C.E., few historians today would accept such a claim. To date, there simply isn't enough evidence for such a mass migration of peoples in this period. There is good evidence, however, of accelerating economic and cultural contacts between Britain and the Continent during the last half of the first millennium B.C.E.; and it seems likely that such contacts would have led to a certain amount of immigration, especially by elites. We suspect, therefore, that the immigration of Continental, Celtic-speaking elites may be part of the process by which the Celtic languages traveled to Britain. By the late second century B.C.E., such immigration is almost certain, as we begin to be able to trace connections between the Celtic-speaking peoples of modern-day northern France and Belgium and the Celtic-speaking peoples of Britain. Even here, however, there are difficulties. A branch of the Parisi, for example, resided in northern Britain, but lent their name to Paris, the future capital of France. Yet it remains fiendishly difficult to date this connection with any precision; "sometime between 200 B.C.E. and 400 C.E." is likely to be right, but is not very informative.

Patterns of settlement in pre-Roman Britain were governed by the island's geography. Britain is divided into two major districts: a lowland area in the southeastern half of the island, with rich, heavy soil and extensive river systems; and a highland zone in the north, west, and southwest, rich in mineral resources but with thinner and less fertile soils and fewer alluvial plains. The agriculturally wealthier southeast would, under the Romans, prove capable of supporting quite large urban communities, and it has remained the most densely populated region of England until the present day. Prior to the first century B.C.E., however, the only permanent urban settlements in Britain took the form of hillforts.

Hillforts were large, usually circular enclosures bounded by earthen walls. As their name implies, they were located at the tops of hills, usually in such a way as to overlook (and so to be seen by) the surrounding lowland areas. Hillforts could serve as defensive strongholds, and even as centers of authority, without being occupied year-round. But from the middle of the first millennium some hillforts, especially in the south and west, did become sites of intensive, year-round settlement. These hillforts show evidence of central planning in their design and construction, of craft manufacturing within their walls, and of regional and long-distance trade passing through them. All this suggests that such hillforts served as centers of authority for tribal elites. But beyond this observation, historians' confidence quickly breaks down. Political and religious power were closely intertwined in this society, but only rarely can the archaeological remains of a temple be distinguished from those of a residence or a storehouse. Evidence for crafts manufacture and long-distance trade is much clearer; but in emphasizing the role of hillforts in manufacturing and trade, it must be kept in mind that most of the population of

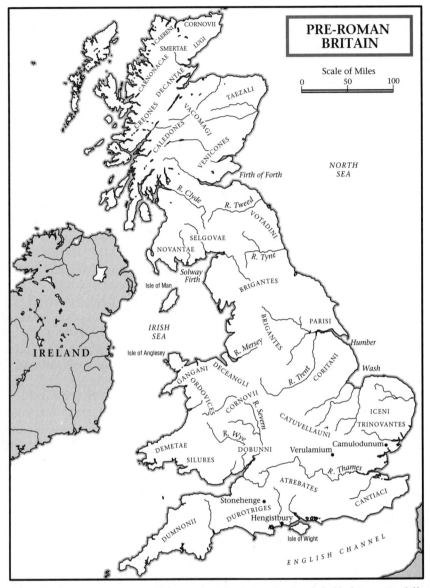

PRE-ROMAN BRITAIN

Scale of Miles

0   50   100

Reproduced with permission of Curtis Brown Ltd., London, on behalf of Barry Cunliffe. Copyright © 1978.

Britain during the first millennium B.C.E. were farmers and herders of cattle and sheep, who lived either in villages or else in scattered, individual houses of stone, wood, or mud surrounded by enclosures. Little is known about the lives they led and even less about how tribal elites extracted from them the agricultural surpluses upon which these elites must have lived.

Little is known about the religious practices of the British Celtic peoples, although the sources do mention religious leaders called druids.[3] Greco-Roman accounts of druids on the Continent portray them as a learned elite, concerned with philosophy, theology, and divination, who were charged with keeping many of the traditions of their people. They presided over judicial matters, punishing wrongdoers who refused to come to law by ostracizing them from public ceremonies and sacrifices, and they maintained the calendar, keeping track of auspicious and inauspicious days for human activities. Druids certainly existed in Britain: Tacitus reports a Roman attack on a druidic stronghold on the island of Anglesey in northern Wales, where Roman soldiers were met by screeching druids and wild-haired priestesses raising their hands to heaven and calling down curses on their enemies. The terrified soldiers at first retreated, but were later rallied by their leader and ultimately advanced to destroy the sacred groves of the druids, said to be drenched with the blood of sacrificed victims.

This last speaks to perhaps the most mysterious aspect of druidism — the role druids are said to have played in human sacrifice, a practice attested in various parts of the Celtic-speaking world. Especially intriguing is a body found recently in Lindow Moss, a peat bog in Cheshire. Known to archaeologists as Lindow Man (or, more informally, Pete Marsh), the body is that of a well-fed, apparently upper-class man of about twenty years of age, who probably died during the first century C.E. His death was clearly deliberate and achieved in a manner that suggests a ritual killing of some sort. He had been hit on the head several times with an axe; he had been garrotted; and his throat had been cut. In his stomach were the remains of a special type of griddle bread, along with grains of pollen from mistletoe, a plant associated by the Roman author Pliny with druidism. Lindow Man's fingernails, hairstyle, and body condition show signs of an upper-class lifestyle. It has been suggested that he may have been not merely a victim of the druids, but himself a member of the druidic priesthood chosen for ritual sacrifice. Another body found recently in the same marsh, dating to about a century later than Lindow Man, also showed signs of a ritual death.

The pace of economic change seems to have increased during the final two centuries before the Common Era. Coinage began to circulate within Britain during the second century, and there is evidence of a lively trade by the first century not only between Britain and Gaul, but also between Britain and the Mediterranean. Britain exported silver, tin, lead, and copper from the rich mineral deposits of Wales and the southwest. It

---

[3]A good popular account of druidism is Miranda J. Green, *The World of the Druids* (London, 1997). A more cautious look at British religion during this period is Ronald Hutton, *The Pagan Religions of the Ancient British Isles: Their Nature and Legacy* (Oxford, 1991; repr. 1996).

Lindow Man   The body of Lindow Man as it emerged from a peat bog in Lindow Moss, Cheshire. (© *British Museum*)

also exported hides, meat, probably grain, and very likely slaves. It imported gold, wine, pottery, glasswork, and figs (among much else) from Gaul and the Mediterranean. Much of this trade passed through Hengistbury Head in Dorset, near the present-day harbor of Christchurch. Control over this important trading site must have been one of the central political facts of second and first century B.C.E. British life, but the artifacts themselves tell little about who profited from them.[4]

Settlement evidence suggests, however, that important political changes were occurring around this time throughout southern Britain. Hillforts were being abandoned and replaced by large, lowland settlements located in river valleys and surrounded by dykes, such as we find at Camulodunum (near modern-day Colchester) in Essex. Coins were being struck in these new lowland settlements, and the long-distance trade in luxury goods was being rerouted through them. Behind these changes probably lay a process of political consolidation by which smaller tribes were being amalgamated or engulfed by larger ones. "All in all, the rise of these huge sites seems to mark a decisive stage in the development of late Iron Age society. A break was made with the clannish, familiar past and an era of centralized tribal monarchy began."[5]

---

[4]Barry Cuncliffe, *Hengistbury Head, Dorset I* (Oxford, 1987).

[5]Malcolm Todd, *Roman Britain*, 3rd ed. (Oxford, 1999), pp. 26–27.

The Roman Invasions of Britain

This was the world into which the Roman military leader and statesman Julius Caesar led his invading legions in 55 B.C.E. Caesar was a man of remarkable military skill and boundless confidence. He was also one of the great self-promoters of his age. Never a man to leave publicizing his exploits in the hands of others, Caesar himself wrote an account of his invasion of Britain in his *History of the Gallic Wars.* Caesar's conquests in Gaul were of enormous consequence. By extending Roman control throughout Gaul, Caesar's campaigns brought Roman civilization and government into the heartland of what would later become western Europe. His invasion of Britain, by contrast, was a failure, which even Caesar's own prose could not entirely obscure. Although Caesar's disciplined infantry won a crushing victory over the Britons and their war-chariots, Caesar had no cavalry with him, and his fleet — his sole means of escape — was seriously damaged in a storm. In the end, Caesar contented himself with unenforceable promises of tribute from the Britons and returned with his army to Gaul and ultimately to Rome, where he had more important business to attend to. Caesar's justification for this unauthorized invasion — that it was necessary in order to secure Roman control over Gaul — is belied by the facts. No Roman army returned to Britain for a hundred years, while Roman control over Gaul went from strength to strength. The truth is simpler. Caesar invaded Britain in search of glory and plunder. Finding little of either, he withdrew and went home.

The Roman conquest of Britain[6] may, nonetheless, be said to have begun with Julius Caesar, for from his time on, Roman influence within Britain steadily grew. Caesar's imperial successors in Rome, Octavian/Augustus and Tiberius Caesar, maintained diplomatic and commercial relations with a number of British tribes, accepting some British rulers as Roman client-kings and channeling valuable trade and treaty contacts through them. Connections with Rome strengthened these rulers enormously, reinforcing the importance of kingship in Britain at a time when kingship in Gaul was already in decline. But Rome benefited from this strengthening of British kingship also. Kings whose power depended upon their contacts with Rome had a strong motivation to prevent piracy along their coasts, an important objective of Roman policy. Through such contacts, Rome was also learning far more about the island of Britain than it had known a century before. This knowledge would prove invaluable in any future invasion.

When, in 43 C.E., the emperor Claudius decided to emulate the accomplishments of his hero and model Julius Caesar by launching a new invasion of Britain, his armies enjoyed not only a secure base in Gaul but

---

[6]The standard works on this subject are Malcolm Todd, *Roman Britain* (Oxford, 1999); Peter Salway, *Roman Britain* (Oxford, 1981); and Graham Webster, *The Roman Invasion of Britain* (London, 1980).

The Emperor Claudius
(c.e. **41–54**) *(The
Granger Collection)*

also reliable knowledge of the geography of southern Britain. A century
before, Caesar had had neither. Still, the campaign was not expected to be
easy. Forty thousand Roman troops, most of them seasoned veterans
from the German provinces, were sent with the expeditionary force.
Even so, the emperor had to send his personal emissary to persuade them
to set sail toward so remote an island. Once landed, however, the Roman
army required only six months to fight its way across the River Thames,
secure its control over the southeast, and capture the important British
center at Camulodunum. Thereafter, the question, both for the Romans
and for the remaining British tribal leaders, was where the Roman conquest of Britain would stop. Over the following decade, Roman campaigns brought most of the southwest under Roman control; but the
southwest could not be held until Wales, too, was in Roman hands, and
that campaign would last until the year 60, when the island of Anglesey,
the granary of Wales, finally fell to the invading Romans.

In the midlands and East Anglia, several British leaders attempted to
strike alliances with the invading Romans, in the hope that by so doing
they could retain a degree of independence. Cartimandua, queen of a
northern British tribe known as the Brigantes, ultimately divorced her

anti-Roman husband in order to ally herself with Rome. The tactic succeeded, insofar as she could now count on the intervention of Roman
armies to keep her on the throne, but the price was high. It was Cartimandua who handed over to the Romans Caratacus, the leader of the
British forces fighting against the Romans. Her policy of accommodation
split the tribe (which may have been not so much a single tribe as a confederation in the first place), and in the resulting disorder, the Brigantes
fell further under the control of Roman generals and administrators.

In East Anglia, Prasutagus, king of the Iceni, ruled his kingdom as a
Roman client until his death in 60. When he died, he left his kingdom to
his two daughters but granted a portion of his estates to the emperor, "a
common device by which wealthy Romans ensured the secure carrying-
out of their wills."[7] Prasutagus no doubt hoped that his daughters would
be able to maintain the same client relationship with Rome that he had
enjoyed. Roman administrators, however, immediately claimed the entire province for Rome and began mistreating the Iceni. When Boudicca,
Prasutagus's queen, objected, she was flogged and her daughters raped by
Roman soldiers.

The resulting rebellion, led by Boudicca, came near to driving the Romans out of Britain. The newly established Roman settlements at Camulodunum, London, and Verulamium (near modern-day St. Albans, in
Hertfordshire) were burned to the ground, but in a climactic battle near
Verulamium, the Roman legions defeated and massacred the British
forces, including the women and children who had accompanied them to
the battlefield. Roman historians claimed 80,000 British casualties. Although the exact number may not be reliable, the impression of an enormous slaughter must be correct. Nor did the slaughter end on the battlefield. British territories that had joined the rebellion or remained neutral
were now systematically devastated. Crops and herds were destroyed,
settlements burned, and civilians sold into slavery throughout southern
and southwestern Britain. A savage lesson was learned by the conquered
Britons. No further rebellions would occur in the south for the next three
hundred years.

The role of Cartimandua and Boudicca in the political and military
affairs of their kingdoms raises large questions. A number of British
tribes worshipped female tribal deities; the Brigantes, indeed, took their
name from the goddess Briganti. British queens may have been able to
draw upon such associations, especially in emergency conditions, to take
on political and military roles that would in ordinary circumstances have
been denied them. But the extraordinary power of queens like Cartimandua and Boudicca reveals little about the position of ordinary women in
British (much less Irish) society. There is no evidence for the claim, occasionally advanced in nonscholarly circles, that "Celtic" (i.e., British and
Irish) societies were matriarchal in nature, and little to suggest that

---

[7]Salway, *Roman Britain*, p. 114.

Celtic women exercised significantly more independent power within their societies than did Roman women within theirs.

It should be remembered that sources of information on these British queens are largely Roman and so reflect the highly gendered presumptions of their Roman authors. The rape of Boudicca's daughters makes brutally clear the extent to which Roman power rested not only upon armies, but also upon gendered presumptions about masculine, Roman strength and female, British weakness. The relentless and at times inefficient straightness of Roman roads — going straight over steep hills at impossible grades, instead of going around them — reflects the same gendered ideas about the dominance of masculine Roman might over a feminized natural world (in Latin, *natura* is a feminine noun). Roman roads were constructed to move troops marching on foot and to allow couriers to travel quickly with messages. But they were also powerful symbolic statements about the way the Romans saw their relationship to the non-Roman world. Domination was no less essential to the Roman arts of government than was law, and Roman domination rested upon the gendered relationships that extended from the upper-class Roman household all the way up to the relationships between Rome, its conquered peoples, and the natural world of rivers, hills, and valleys.

The Conquest of the North

The two decades after Boudicca's rebellion witnessed the consolidation of Roman rule over southern Britain. Then, between 78 and 84 C.E., in a series of brilliant military campaigns, the great Roman governor Agricola conquered the rest of Britain, strengthening Roman control over Anglesey and extending his conquests to the northern tip of Scotland. Soon after Agricola's governorship ended, however, the legions dismantled their fortifications in northern Scotland and withdrew to a new frontier drawn between the Solway Firth and the mouth of the River Tyne. Further fighting in the north during the early second century persuaded the emperor Hadrian (117–138) to establish this line as a permanent frontier by constructing a wall, ten feet wide and fifteen feet high, across the entire seventy-three mile stretch of countryside between the Tyne and the Solway. This great barrier, the largest in the Roman Empire, included fortresses at every mile (known, appropriately, as milecastles), which housed about one hundred soldiers each, with much larger garrisons stationed along the wall at Chesters, Housesteads, and (later) Wallsend. A V-shaped ditch ten feet deep and nearly thirty feet wide ran along the northern side of the wall, and a similar ditch, known as the vallum, was constructed along its southern side. Much of Hadrian's Wall still stands today, attracting tens of thousands of visitors annually.

The purposes for which Hadrian erected his famous wall have been much debated. The wall was not well designed to serve as a defensive fortification, and it seems doubtful that any Roman government would

Hadrian's Wall *(The Granger Collection)*

have invested such huge amounts of money in a construction designed merely to stop cattle-raiders from driving their captured herds north across the border. "Wall studies" are among the liveliest areas of Romano-British archaeology; any conclusions, at this stage of research, can only be provisional. It seems likely, however, that the primary purpose of Hadrian's Wall was to create and define a northern frontier beyond which Roman Britain would not extend, but from which Roman armies could strike as necessary to control the potentially hostile peoples north of the wall. The vallum may have served a similar "marking" function, defining a military zone immediately south of the wall within which civilian access and travel would have been severely restricted.

Creating such a defined and definite frontier line was not a popular decision, especially because Hadrian combined it with withdrawals from other conquered territories on the eastern borders of the Roman Empire. The Roman army preferred to think of itself as a conquering force, not a garrisoned one; and later emperors, most notably Antoninus Pius (138–161), would abandon Hadrian's Wall and send the army north again to try to conquer the peoples of modern-day Scotland. But all these attempts were unsuccessful. During the 150s, Antoninus built another wall, further north, between the Firth of Forth and the Firth of Clyde, but the new wall proved impossible to hold. By the end of the second century, the Antonine Wall had been abandoned, reoccupied, and abandoned again. By the year 200, Hadrian's Wall once again marked the northern boundary of Roman Britain; but after fifty years of war, it was a boundary much less securely held than it had been when Hadrian constructed it.

The years between 150 and 200 are exceptionally poorly documented, but they appear to have been marked by incessant warfare in northern Britain. More than 50,000 Roman troops were stationed in Britain by the end of the second century, making the province one of the most heavily garrisoned territories in the empire. This was a fact of political as well as military significance. During the 190s, some of these troops were withdrawn when the Roman governor of Britain, Clodius Albinus, was proclaimed emperor by his soldiers and then went to the Continent to fight for the throne. He failed and was killed in battle by the ultimate victor in the civil wars, Septimius Severus. The incident is important, however, not only because it marked the first (although by no means the last) time British troops would attempt to seat their leader on the imperial throne, but also because it focused the attention of Septimius Severus on the dangers that the military situation in Britain might pose to his own control over the empire.

In 208, Severus took steps to resolve the problems on the northern British frontier. Taking with him his sons, Caracalla and Geta, Severus strengthened and rebuilt the fortifications along Hadrian's Wall and then launched a three-year campaign to subdue the peoples north of the wall. When Severus died in 211, that project remained incomplete. Caracalla, his eldest son, quickly wound up the campaign so that he could return to Rome to become emperor. Before he departed, however, he signed a series of treaties with the northerners, offering them subsidies in return for peace. Remarkably, these hastily arranged treaties held. Roman subsidies flowed north, and trade increased. For the next seventy years, Roman Britain was at peace, and gradually in the north a unified, semi-Roman society began to emerge on both sides of the boundary demarcated by Hadrian's Wall.

The Romanization of Southern Britain

In southern Britain, the processes of Romanization proceeded much more quickly. After Boudicca's revolt, the south enjoyed unbroken peace and considerable prosperity for the next three hundred years. By the end of the second century, most of the cities of Roman Britain had attained their greatest physical size, and British nobles were beginning to move into them in numbers. Most of the public buildings essential to Roman civic life had also been constructed by this date, including baths, temples, theaters, and public *fora* (the plural of *forum*: in America, a term for sports arenas, but in Roman days, the central public area within which Roman political life was carried on). The Romans introduced building in stone into southern Britain; and they did quite a lot of it, especially in the

ROMAN BRITAIN

Military occupation

Not permanently occupied

Extent of conquest, A.D. 140

Roman roads

SCOTLAND

NORTH

SEA

ANTONINE WALL   *Firth of Forth*

HADRIAN'S WALL A.D. 123

Carlisle

Solway Firth

Isle
of Man

York

IRISH SEA

R. Humber

IRELAND

The Wash

Anglesey

Lincoln

Chester

Wroxeter

High Cross

Severn R.

Avon R.

Gloucester

Vérulamium (St.
Albans)

Colchester

Caerleon

Cirencester

London

Thames

Canterbury

Bath

Silchester

Dover

Salisbury

Winchester

Lymme

Chichester

Pevensey

Exeter

Dorchester

Isle of Wight

Axminster

English Channel

FRANCE

first and second centuries. By the end of the second century, the physical structures of Roman life were largely in place.

Roman cities in Britain were of three basic types: (1) the *colonia*, usually a newly established urban center occupied by a colony of retired legionaries and their families (this is what Camulodunum had become, just before Boudicca's rebels destroyed it); (2) the *municipium*, normally a previously existing town whose inhabitants received from the imperial government a charter conveying certain important privileges; and (3) the *civitas*, an older tribal center that developed urban institutions in imitation of the *colonia* and *municipium*. The inhabitants of *coloniae* and *municipia* were Roman citizens; those of the *civitates* were not, or at least not automatically so, until the third century, when the emperor Caracalla extended the privileges of citizenship broadly to the male residents of the Roman provinces. But all three types of cities enjoyed a degree of local self-government and exerted political control over the territory surrounding them. All were governed by local senates composed of wealthy townspeople and by annually elected magistrates who supervised finances, the construction and upkeep of public buildings, and the law courts.[8]

Only four British cities are known to have possessed *colonia* status: Colchester (as Camulodunum was renamed), Gloucester, Lincoln, and York. Only Verulamium is known to have been a *municipium*, although other cities (Leicester, for example) may have been. *Civitates* are more difficult to count, but probably numbered between twenty and forty. It is a telling sign of how little is really known about the governance of Romano-British cities that London's constitutional status remains unknown, even though it was clearly the foremost city of Roman Britain. The Romans founded London, and it was they who made it the major trade center it has remained ever since. Whereas most of the chief British cities of the Roman era covered between 100 and 200 acres, London by the end of the second century occupied some 325 acres. It was situated on the River Thames at a crucial point where the river was broad enough to accommodate ocean-going ships but narrow enough to be bridged — precisely analogous to Rome's own position on the Tiber. It was also well located to act as the nexus of the very important trade that passed between southeastern Britain and northern Gaul. But was it founded as a *colonia* or a *civitas*? We simply do not know.

---

[8]Membership in local civic councils was open only to men who met certain property qualifications. By the end of the second century, these councils were generally chosen by co-optation (i.e., existing members chose new members) rather than by election. In the fourth century, much of the authority (and almost all of the financial resources) of these councils was taken over by the imperial government. But in Britain, these councils retained some influence; and when Britain seceded from the imperial government in the early fifth century, these civic councils probably took over such governmental functions as continued to be exercised.

In view of its commercial and administrative importance, especially in the first and second centuries, it was natural that London should also have been the focal point of the Roman road system in Britain. Stretching from London far and wide across the land, the Roman roads formed a five-thousand-mile system of paved thoroughfares running in nearly straight lines over the countryside. Roman roads were constructed principally for military and administrative purposes. They were not well suited to the transport of bulk goods by horse — or ox-drawn wagons — one reason for the ruinously high cost of transporting such goods by land in the Roman Empire. In later centuries, unpaved wagon roads often developed alongside the Roman roads; these other roads were wide enough to accommodate large freight wagons and more forgiving to the hoofs of the draft animals and the spines of their drivers than were the narrower, paving-stoned Roman roads. Nevertheless, Roman roads remained in use for many centuries after the Roman legions had departed, serving as avenues for people and goods, and sometimes as boundary lines between territories.[9]

Agricultural Prosperity in the Third and Fourth Centuries

In Roman Britain, as elsewhere in the empire, farming was the basic economic activity. The fundamental agrarian unit was the small family farm, a few acres in extent, consisting typically of a couple of houses, a number of pits for storing grain, and farmlands laid out in small, rectangular fields. Farms of this type abounded in both pre-Roman and Roman times. Villages too were common, but large agrarian villages of the high medieval type, with houses clustered together and surrounded by common fields, were probably unknown in Roman Britain. In Britain as elsewhere in the empire, the Roman conquest seems to have had little impact on native agricultural methods and practices. Rome had always lagged in agrarian technology, and it contributed little to existing British farming practices because it had little to offer. During the Roman period, further progress was made toward the clearing of forests and draining of swamps: the Fenlands along the Cambridgeshire/Lincolnshire border were an early Roman public drainage project. Primarily, however, it was the achievements of the pre-Roman British farmers that enabled Roman Britain to export agricultural products in quantity to the Continent during the prosperous years of the third and fourth centuries.

Perhaps the most striking change the Romans brought to the British countryside was the construction of villas. A villa was a country house. Many such houses served as centers of agricultural exploitation for the surrounding countryside. A villa might, therefore, be a source of income

---

[9]When King Alfred signed his famous peace treaty in 886 with the Viking leader Guthrum, the line between their respective territories was defined by the old Roman road known as Watling Street.

The Great Roman Villa at Chedworth, Gloucestershire, as Reconstructed by A. Forestier   This villa, which seems to include two distinct residences with shared workshop and storage facilities, may have been owned and operated by two separate families in joint proprietorship. *(Mansell/Time)*

as well as a residence. Wealthy individuals might own many different villas in several provinces. Indeed, it was not unknown for the owners of villas in Gaul or Britain to reside in Rome. Some of these villas were very grand examples of Roman provincial architecture, with elaborate mosaics, rich furnishings, glass windows, and underfloor heating. But villas like these constituted only a small fraction of the total, and in Britain, most achieved such grandeur only from the later third century on. Most British villas were far more modest establishments, consisting of a timber or stone house, some outbuildings, and huts for the slaves or hired laborers who worked the fields and vineyards. The earliest villas in Britain were constructed in the southeast, near estuaries that offered access by sea to the grain markets of northern Gaul and Belgium. But villas also played an important role in provisioning the growing towns and cities of southern Britain. By the middle of the third century, there were hundreds, possibly thousands, of villas scattered across the southern half of Britain.

The great days of villa culture in Britain began in the last half of the third century, and continued until the end of the fourth. The extraordinary prosperity of rural Britain during these years was partly a consequence of the natural productivity of the land, helped also by the fact that these years came at the end of a several-hundred-year climatic warming cycle that made Roman Britain a land of vineyards as well as grainfields. To a great extent, however, the rural prosperity of late third- and fourth-century Britain was a consequence of political factors over which Britain itself had no control. Between 235 and 284, the Roman Empire was wracked by succession disputes and civil war. Twenty-six emperors were declared, deposed, and replaced during these years by competing factions of the Roman army, each intent upon installing its own general on the imperial throne. In the resulting chaos, frontier defenses deteriorated while subsidies to the peoples beyond the frontiers went unpaid. The result was a devastating series of invasions by these cross-frontier peoples, affecting both the eastern and the western empire. The nadir came in 259–260, when the emperor Valerian was captured and humiliatingly executed by the Persians, revolts erupted along the Danubian frontier, and invading armies from Germany swept across the Rhine into Gaul and ultimately Spain.

The great villas of Gaul never fully recovered from the damage caused by these mid-third-century invasions. Britain, by contrast, remained at peace until the mid-fourth century. There were apparently some difficulties on the northern frontier around the year 300, and there were recurrent troubles with pirates along the eastern coast; but these were not sufficient to disturb the general prosperity of Britain, which now became a principal supplier of agricultural products to the rest of the western empire. Between the mid-third and the mid-fourth centuries, exports of grain, meat, hides, and even wine traveled from Britain to Gaul and Belgium in enormous quantities, making the villa owners and merchants of Britain rich. The evidence of their wealth is to be found in the extraordinary mosaics and wall paintings adorning the palatial residences they built in the towns and countryside of southern Britain, and in the astonishing quantities of silver they hid in the ground when, in the late fourth and early fifth centuries, their world collapsed around them.

The Fracturing of the Western Roman Empire

The prosperity of late-Roman Britain, combined with the political chaos in Rome itself, accelerated a developing sense of regional and provincial autonomy in Britain that would ultimately contribute to the dissolution of the western Roman Empire. The empire was much too large to be governed effectively from a single center. Nevertheless, the imperial government became progressively more centralized and autocratic. The result was the emergence, during the third century, of a series of regional capitals, from which military and civil governance was organized. For Britain, as for the other western provinces of the empire, this regional capital lay at Trier, a legionary center in east-central Gaul just west of the Rhine. When imperial governance from Rome collapsed with the defeat and capture of the emperor Valerian, Britain joined with Germany, Gaul, and Spain in a self-declared *Imperium Galliarum* ("Gaulish empire") with its headquarters at Trier. Under a series of usurping imperial claimants, this Gaulish empire lasted from 260 until 273. Resentment toward the ineffectiveness of Roman central authority in defending the western provinces continued, however, even after the emperor Aurelian put an end to the *Imperium Galliarum*. Between 286 and 293, Britain was again in rebellion, this time led by a dissident Roman naval officer named Carausius, who had been sent to the northwestern coast of Gaul to control Saxon and Frankish pirates, but who quickly fell out with his superiors and then declared himself the emperor of Britain. Although Carausius was overthrown by one of his own supporters in 293, Britain did not return to the imperial fold until Constantius, then second-in-command for the western empire under the great soldier-emperor Diocletian, led a military expedition to Britain in 296 to recover the province for Rome.[10]

Efforts to improve the coastal defenses in southeastern Britain had already begun before Constantius's arrival — in the fourth century, this coast would be known as the Saxon Shore (*Litus Saxonum*), and would have its own military leader appointed to defend it from Saxon and Frankish sea-raiders. Constantius pushed these fortification efforts forward. He also initiated an important rebuilding campaign along Hadrian's Wall, which had not been well maintained during the long years of peace after 211. By the 290s, however, a new and potentially hostile confederation of northern peoples, known collectively as the Picts, had taken shape beyond the wall. By 305, the Pictish threat was so severe that Constantius, now in charge of the western empire, returned to Britain to lead a military expedition against them. When Constantius died at York in 306, his troops proclaimed his twenty-year-old son Constantine to be his successor as the western emperor. Six years of civil war followed, but in 312 Constantine finally made good his claim to the western empire by defeating his western rival, Maxentius, at the battle of the Milvian Bridge.

Just before this battle, the still-pagan Constantine had seen a Christian symbol in the sky, and in a dream had been instructed, "In this sign, conquer." At the Milvian Bridge, he did. Soon thereafter, he became a Christian and made Christianity, for the first time, one of the officially tolerated religions of the Roman Empire. Lavish imperial patronage for the Christian churches quickly followed. In 325, he presided over the famous council of Christian bishops held at Nicaea, at which the Nicene Creed, a fundamental statement of Christian belief, was declared. A year earlier, he had finally reunited the eastern and the western halves of the empire. In 330, he moved the capital of this reunited empire to the east, to the ancient city of Byzantium, which he renamed Constantinople.

---

[10]In an attempt to end the succession disputes that had created such chaos in the third-century empire, Diocletian had established a system whereby two emperors (each called an Augustus) ruled the empire jointly, one in the east, one in the west, with each Augustus assisted by a second-in-command, called a Caesar. The idea was that each Augustus would be succeeded by his respective Caesar, who, upon becoming Augustus, would name a new Caesar. Constantius was the Caesar for the western empire; the western Augustus was Maximian. Technically, Diocletian was the Augustus for the eastern empire only. But he was so much the dominant figure of the two Augusti that we feel justified in describing Constantius's position in the slightly simplified way we have done above.

Constantine's career is a reminder of the large and cosmopolitan world of which fourth-century Britain was still very much a part. Regionalism was a potent force in the later Roman Empire, but the empire remained, despite its divisions, an interdependent cultural and political unit. Disasters on the eastern borders quickly brought pressure on the western borders, but military help from the east continued to come west right up until the end of the fourth century. Administrative and military assignments continued to take men from the borders of Persia to the northern frontiers of Britain, and usurpers proclaimed in York might still hope to rule as emperors in Rome or Constantinople. The failures of imperial pretenders like Carausius should not blind us to the scale of their ambitions or to the possibility of their success. Late-Roman Britain was not an impossible place from which to launch a successful bid for the imperial crown, as Constantine's own career so dramatically demonstrates.

Constantine's Christianity also illustrates the important cultural forces at work in fourth-century Britain.[11] About the spread of Christianity in Britain prior to Constantine's reign as emperor, we are almost wholly ignorant. Legend has it that at some point in the third century, St. Alban and two of his fellow Christians were martyred at Verulamium, but although there was a late Roman shrine to the saint at Verulamium, the medieval monastery of St. Alban never claimed to have descended uninterruptedly from that earlier shrine. It is therefore not certain that there was a continuous tradition of devotion to St. Alban at Verulamium. The name of another semilegendary martyr, Aaron of Carleon, suggests the presence of a Jewish element in the population of third-century Britain, providing a hint of at least one of the avenues through which Christianity in pre-Constantinian Britain probably spread. But beyond these scraps of information, almost nothing is known about Christianity prior to Constantine.

There is more evidence about Christianity in fourth-century Britain. In 314, three British bishops, a priest, and a deacon are recorded as being present at the Council of Arles in southern Gaul, suggesting that some kind of diocesan structure was already in place. Archeologists have unearthed a pre-350 hoard of Christian silver liturgical vessels at Water Newton in Huntingdonshire. At Lullingstone in Kent, a mid-fourth-century villa has been discovered; its impressive Christian wall paintings suggest its use as a place of worship. From approximately the same date, we also have the extraordinary mosaic floor from Hinton St. Mary in Dorset, containing the first pictorial representation of Christ to survive from Roman Britain. Similar mosaics, somewhat less elaborate, have also been discovered at the nearby villas of Frampton and Fifehead Neville, also in Dorset.

By the end of the fourth century, however, Christianity in Britain had progressed far enough to have generated its own heretic, the British priest Pelagius, who had the distinction of having his theological views at-

---

[11]Charles Thomas, *Christianity in Roman Britain* (London, 1981), is the standard account.

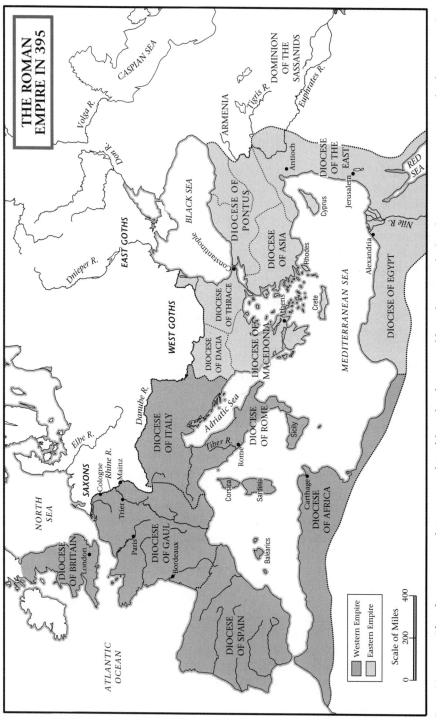

THE ROMAN EMPIRE IN 395

CASPIAN SEA

DOMINION OF THE SASSANIDS

Volga R.

ARMENIA

Tigris R.

Euphrates R.

Don R.

DIOCESE OF PONTUS

DIOCESE OF THE EAST

Antioch

RED SEA

EAST GOTHS

BLACK SEA

DIOCESE OF ASIA

Cyprus

Jerusalem

Dnieper R.

Constantinople

Rhodes

Nile R.

DIOCESE OF THRACE

Athens

Crete

Alexandria

WEST GOTHS

DIOCESE OF DACIA

DIOCESE OF MACEDONIA

MEDITERRANEAN SEA

DIOCESE OF EGYPT

Danube R.

Adriatic Sea

DIOCESE OF ITALY

DIOCESE OF ROME

Sicily

Elbe R.

SAXONS

Cologne

Rhine R.

Mainz

Tiber R.

Rome

Corsica

Sardinia

Carthage

DIOCESE OF AFRICA

NORTH SEA

Trier

DIOCESE OF GAUL

Paris

Balearics

DIOCESE OF BRITAIN

London

Bordeaux

ATLANTIC OCEAN

DIOCESE OF SPAIN

Western Empire

Eastern Empire

Scale of Miles

0   200   400

From Mortimar Chambers, Raymond Grew, David Herlihy, Theodore K. Rabb, and Isser Woloch, *The Western Experience*, 6th ed., © 1995 The McGraw-Hill Companies. *Reprinted by permission of The McGraw-Hill Companies.*

The Hinton St. Mary (Dorset) Mosaic This elaborate mosaic floor, now in the British Museum, is divided into two parts. The lower, square section centers on a male figure with the Christian chi-rho monogram behind his head, probably (though not certainly) intended to represent Jesus, and surrounded by figures in the corners representing the four winds. The upper, rectangular section depicts Bellerophon slaying the Chimaera, perhaps a Christian allegory for the triumph of good over evil. The entire mosaic measures 28 × 15 feet, and illustrates the levels of luxury in which some of the villa owners of fourth-century Britain lived. *(© Crown copyright NMR)*

tacked by the greatest of all the western Christian theologians, St. Augustine of Hippo. Pelagius left Britain as a young man and seems to have spent most of his life in Rome, but his teachings became popular enough among the British upper classes to provoke preaching tours against Pelagianism by orthodox continental churchmen visiting Britain a generation later. By this date, Christianity had spread deeply enough into the British countryside to produce St. Patrick, whose autobiography and *Letter to Coroticus* are the only first-person accounts we have of British Christianity that may date to this period.[12] The writings of the British priest

---

[12]Although St. Patrick's missionary work was done mainly in Ireland, he was born in Britain, possibly in the northwest near Carlisle. Captured as a youth by slavers, he spent some years as a captive in Ireland before escaping to Britain and then returning to Ireland. Patrick's dates are hotly disputed. The majority of historians have favored a death date of c. 461, suggesting that Patrick must therefore have been born in the late fourth century. But powerful arguments have recently been made for a death date about thirty years later, moving his probable date of birth into perhaps the 420s. On the dating of Patrick, see David Dumville, *St. Patrick, AD 493–1993* (Woodbridge, Suffolk, 1993), esp. pp. 51–57.

Gildas leave no doubt that by the sixth century, the British were securely (if still inadequately, in Gildas's view) Christian.[13] It seems probable, therefore, that by the early fifth century, Britain had become a largely Christian country. The steps by which this occurred, however, are almost entirely obscure.

The End of Roman Britain

Fourth-century Britain[14] presents a picture of increasing prosperity in the midst of growing threats to its security. Knowing, as we do, that Britain's connection to the Roman Empire would be permanently severed in the early fifth century, it is understandable that historians have emphasized the political, economic, and military difficulties fourth-century Britain faced. There is no doubt that these difficulties were real. In the north, the Pictish confederacy had already shown itself capable of launching devastating attacks across Hadrian's Wall. In the east, sea-borne Saxon raiding parties were a cause for serious concern. In the west, Irish raiders had been attacking the Welsh coast since the late third century, and by the end of the fourth century they had settled the area in significant numbers. Imperial taxation in fourth-century Britain was heavy, and inflation was a significant problem. Mining continued, as did large-scale pottery manufacturing, both under the control of the Roman army. But no new coins were minted in Britain after 326. Thereafter, the coinage that circulated in Britain came from abroad, principally from Gaul, in exchange for British exports, and in the pay packets of British soldiers. Should the inflow of coin from either of these sources cease, the British economy would be in dire straits.

For all its difficulties, however, fourth-century Britain does not present itself as a society under siege. The country villas were now in the midst of their greatest period of expansion. So too were the smaller towns and cities, which reflected most directly the prosperity of their surrounding countryside. London was shrinking, but other southeastern ports appear to have been growing, as was York, now the site of the largest legionary fortress in western Europe. Towns and cities were building defensive walls, but their very willingness to do so speaks not only of threats, but also of their citizens' capacity to carry out such expensive building projects. Assimilation between Roman and British elites was

---

[13]See Gildas, *The Ruin of Britain and Other Works,* ed. and tr. Michael Winterbottom (London, 1978); and *Gildas: New Approaches,* ed. Michael Lapidge and David Dumville (Woodbridge, Suffolk, 1984).

[14]On this period, the standard works (in addition to those cited in note 6 above) are A. S. Esmonde-Cleary, *The Ending of Roman Britain* (London, 1989); John Matthews, *The Roman Empire of Ammianus* (London, 1988); and John Wacher, *The Towns of Roman Britain,* 2nd ed. (London, 1995). There are also a great many ideas in *The Anglo-Saxons,* ed. James Campbell (London, 1982).

also continuing. Celtic languages were probably spoken by the majority of the population — which may have numbered as many as four million people — but knowledge of Latin went quite far down the social scale, particularly in towns. Many town-dwellers were probably bilingual. One wonders, indeed, whether any sensible distinction could have been made by the mid-fourth century between "native" Britons and "immigrant" Romans. The more salient distinction was more likely between the Romano-British natives and the imperial officials from elsewhere in the empire who filled the top spots in Britain's military and civilian administration.

Renewed succession disputes, this time between the sons of the emperor Constantine (d. 337), brought Britain once more into the thick of imperial politics. Initially, these three sons divided their father's empire between them, with Constantine II holding Britain, Gaul, western Germany, and Spain. But when Constantine II invaded Italy, he was killed by his brother Constans, who now took control of the entire western empire. Even under Constans, however, the four northwestern provinces continued to be administered as a unit known as the Gallic Prefecture. Under this new name, the third-century "Gaulish Empire" lived on throughout the fourth century. In 350, however, Constans was killed — perhaps by unreconciled supporters of his brother Constantine II — and the army proclaimed a man named Magnentius the new emperor in the west. Magnentius's support came almost entirely from the Gallic Prefecture, including Britain. When Constantius II, the last of Constantine's sons, defeated Magnentius in 353, he undertook severe reprisals against Magnentius's British supporters. These measures probably undermined even further British support for the imperial government based in Constantinople.

In 355, Constantius appointed his cousin Julian to rule Britain, Gaul, and western Germany. Julian's success was immediate. He brought the reprisals in Britain to an end and won the support of his troops by leading a successful military campaign to restore the Rhineland frontier — an expedition made possible by massive shipments of provisions Julian brought from Britain to Germany. In 360, when Constantius II tried to move against him as a potential rival, Julian's troops proclaimed Julian emperor. Julian marched east against Constantius, but Constantius died before the two armies clashed. Julian thus became emperor. Throwing off the Christianity traditional to his family, Julian now returned to the traditional religion of Rome. To the Christian historians of the Roman Empire, Julian therefore became known as Julian the Apostate. As it turned out, he was the last non-Christian emperor of Rome. His death in 363, in battle against the Persians, was a turning point for the empire, which thereafter became increasingly authoritarian about its Christianity and increasingly unwilling to tolerate diversity of religious practice.

Julian's death may also have been a turning point for Roman Britain. In 367, the hitherto divided enemies of Roman Britain — Picts, Irish, and Saxons — united in a massive series of attacks by land and sea. Continuing western disaffection toward the government at Constantinople is suggested by reports that these attacks were assisted by intelligence provided to the attackers by the Roman army in Britain. At the very least, the army proved itself completely incapable (and perhaps even unwilling) to engage the attackers seriously. The new Roman emperor, Valentinian, was at that moment in Trier, trying to suppress related attacks by the Alamans along the Rhineland frontier. He quickly sent a detachment of troops, led by Theodosius (the father of the emperor Theodosius I), to drive the barbarians back out of Britain. Theodosius did so, although the effort — along with the rebuilding of the fortifications along Hadrian's Wall — took him two full years.

In 378, the emperor Valens (brother of Valentinian, who had died in 375) was defeated and killed by the Goths at the Battle of Adrianople. His death cleared the way for Theodosius's son, also named Theodosius, to ascend the imperial throne. Of necessity, Theodosius I's primary concern was to protect the eastern half of the empire. With the attention of the central government directed to the east, Britain once again emerged as a hotbed of imperial separatism. In 383, the army in Britain declared one of its officers, a Spaniard named Magnus Maximus, to be the new western emperor. Accompanied by a sizeable portion of the Roman army in Britain, Magnus proceeded to take over the rest of the Gallic Prefecture and succeeded in winning the grudging acceptance of Theodosius for his position until 388, when Theodosius defeated and killed Magnus. But between 392 and 394, Britain was yet again in the hands of an imperial usurper.

Events in Britain now moved swiftly toward the end. Theodosius the Great died in 395 and was succeeded by his two young sons, who divided the empire between them. In 398, the western imperial court sent a major military expedition to northern Britain (authorized, and perhaps even led, by the chief Roman general during these years, a German named Stilicho) to restore the Hadrianic frontier. The strength of the garrisons along the wall had already been depleted by the continental campaigns of Magnus Maximus. In 401, however, many of the remaining troops were transferred by the imperial court to Italy to defend it against Alaric's invading Goths. Some Roman troops still remained in Britain, but after 401 Hadrian's Wall ceased to exist as a meaningful military fortification. Pottery production (which had been organized by the army) ceased, and coin finds come to a sudden end. Some individual fortresses along the wall would be reoccupied and reused by local potentates over the following two centuries. Urban life in some northern cities (Carlisle and Chester, for example) would also continue. But after 401, the Roman history of the wall was over.

By the winter of 406–407, when the next great invasions of the western empire came pouring across the frozen Rhine into Gaul, Britain was once again in the hands of an imperial usurper. In response to this new invasion, Constantine III (for so the usurper was called) led what remained of the Roman army in Britain to Gaul, where he proceeded to re-establish, yet again, the Gaulish Empire. When Saxon invaders attacked Britain in 408, Constantine was abroad, and Britain had already been in rebellion against the Roman Empire for several years. The task of defense therefore lay entirely with the Britons themselves. They seem to have performed creditably. The sixth-century Greek historian Zosimus (who based his account on fifth-century sources that are now lost) writes that "the Britons took up arms, and, braving danger for their own safety, freed their cities from the barbarians threatening them."[15] In 410, when the western emperor Honorius wrote his famous letter to the British *civitates*, telling them to look after their own defense, he was thus trying to put a good face, retrospectively, on the fact that the province of Britain had already chosen to go it alone by seceding from his empire. As Malcolm Todd has remarked, "Rome did not withdraw from Britain: she was ejected."[16]

Britain in the Fifth and Sixth Centuries

"What happened during the next fifty years in Roman Britain?" is a question we cannot satisfactorily answer. After 410, Britain recedes from the consciousness of historians working at the imperial courts; and while there is no shortage of more local accounts, the reliability of the information these provide is uncertain to say the least. A biography of St. Germanus of Auxerre, composed in Gaul shortly after the saint's death, recounts that Germanus visited Britain in 429 and again in the 430s to preach against the Pelagian heresy and that while there he not only refuted the Pelagians at a conference at Verulamium, but also led the Britons to military victory over an invading army of Picts and Saxons by teaching his followers to terrify the enemy by shouting out the Christian war cry, "Alleluia!"[17] Also from the fifth century, we have the autobiography of St. Patrick, written to defend himself against charges relating to his mission in Ireland, along with a letter Patrick wrote to a local British ruler named Coroticus. From a somewhat later date comes the moralizing tract *On the Fall of Britain*, written by a British priest named Gildas, probably in the mid-sixth century but possibly in the fifth.[18] Gildas's account is a bitter outcry against the moral shortcomings of contemporary British Christians, for whose failings the Anglo-Saxon invasions were, in Gildas's view, a deserved retribution. Gildas makes reference to a

---

[15]Cited in Campbell, *The Anglo-Saxons*, p. 16.

[16]Todd, *Roman Britain*, p. 209.

[17]Michael Jones, "The Historicity of the Alleluia Victory," *Albion* 18 (1986): 363–373; Ian N. Wood, "The Fall of the Western Empire and the End of Roman Britain," *Britannia* 18 (1987): 251–262.

[18]Ian N. Wood, "The End of Roman Britain: Continental Evidence and Parallels," in *Gildas: New Approaches*, ed. Lapidge and Dumville, pp. 1–25.

number of past events that must have been familiar to the people of his own day; unfortunately, he provides not a single verifiable date that would establish when his own day actually was. We also have some British heroic poetry written in Welsh, as we may now call the vernacular language of the majority of the British population.[19] The most famous of these works, the *Gododdin*, is a collection of eulogies for heroes slain in a disastrous battle in northern Britain. Composed at an uncertain date, the *Gododdin* recounts events that probably took place around the year 600.

As for works more obviously intended as histories, there is the great *Ecclesiastical History of the English People,* written in the early eighth century by an English monk named Bede.[20] We also have a collection of annals — accounts of events organized year by year — and some genealogical material that purports to tell about the fifth and sixth centuries, but it comes from the ninth-century *Anglo-Saxon Chronicle.* Some of this material parallels Bede's account; some of it seems incompatible with Bede. There are also some British annals and legends preserved, with much else, in an anonymous compilation entitled *History of the Britons (Historia Brittonum)* and ascribed to a ninth-century Welsh monk named Nennius. Archaeology has, of course, added greatly to knowledge of these centuries, but it has not yet succeeded in producing a narrative that can stand on its own apart from the evidence of written sources. In short, we have just enough information to construct narratives of the events of this period, but not enough to allow us to choose with confidence between the various narratives we can construct.

What is clear, however, is that Roman Britain did not simply disappear. Its cities had exercised substantial powers of self-government for centuries. There had even been a council of British cities, largely powerless in the fourth century, that may have re-emerged in the early fifth century to provide a degree of central government to the province. Urban life certainly continued after 410. Some British cities may even have had a continuous history throughout the fifth century and into the sixth. At Verulamium, archaeologists have discovered a mid- to late-fifth-century timber water pipe, newly laid, suggesting that at this date the Roman public water system was still functioning. A similar situation may have existed at Bath, where the Roman baths may still have been operating when the city fell to the invading Saxons in the late sixth century. Canterbury, the capital of the Romano-British *civitas* of Kent (*Cantia*), is another probable example of urban continuity. It retained not only its British name, but also its role as the capital of the Anglo-Saxon kingdom of Kent. At Lincoln too, evidence suggests continuity of some kind from

---

[19]Along with Welsh, a Latin-based vernacular language also continued in use in western Britain until around the year 600. See Thomas Charles-Edwards, "Comment," in *The Anglo-Saxons from the Migration Period to the Eighth Century: An Ethnographic Perspective,* ed. John Hines (Woodbridge, Suffolk, 1997), p. 96.

[20]Bede's work is described in Chapter 2.

the British to the Anglo-Saxon city.[21] And at York, although the city may have been abandoned, the headquarters building of the legionary fortress was kept in repair throughout the fifth century.

In most of the cities of Roman Britain, however, organized civic life collapsed during the fifth century. This was more likely a result of economic changes, however, than of large-scale Germanic invasions and sieges. In the year 400, Britain was still a place in which large quantities of Roman coinage circulated freely, despite the fact that no coins had been struck in Britain itself since 326. The final secession of Britain from the empire, combined with the chaos of the barbarian invasions in Gaul, brought the flow of coins into Britain to a sudden end during the first decade of the fifth century. As a result, the British economy quickly demonetized. "By about 425 at the latest, coinage had lost its function as a means of exchange, and there is no evidence either for circulation or for hoarding [of coins] after this time."[22] Centralized pottery manufacture also came to an end around this date, as does evidence for large-scale mining. Only the production of bronze hanging bowls, something of a British specialty, seems to have continued much beyond 425. Some British cities survived as centers of local authority during the fifth and sixth centuries, but as centers of population, trade, and manufacturing, the cities of southeastern Britain had largely ceased to exist by the mid- to late-fifth century.

In these circumstances, political leadership quickly shifted away from the administrators of the Roman *civitates* (who were presumably still in charge when the emperor Honorius addressed them in his letter to the Britons in 410) and into the hands of local or regional leaders whom Gildas terms "tyrants," but whom we should probably regard as kings. One of these fifth-century British kings, Vortigern, is said to have invited a detachment of German warriors to Britain, offering them lands in Kent in return for their military assistance. We do not know who Vortigern was or from whence his power derived. "Vortigern," in Welsh, means "High King" or "Over King," suggesting that it may be his title rather than his given name. Archaeological evidence, largely in the form of burials, confirms the presence of detachments of Germanic soldiers in East Anglia, Essex, and northern Lincolnshire during the first two decades of the fifth century, with similar evidence appearing in Kent and Yorkshire about a generation later. These dates would support Bede's claim that Vortigern's Germanic allies arrived in Kent in the 440s. Gildas, characteristically, gives no dates at all, although he sermonizes at length on Vortigern's folly in introducing "the ferocious Saxons (name not to be spoken!), hated by man and God . . . into the island like wolves

---

[21]Janet Nelson, "Anglo-Saxon England, c. 500–1066," in *The Oxford Illustrated History of Medieval England*, ed. Nigel Saul (Oxford, 1997), p. 29.

[22]Todd, *Roman Britain*, p. 224.

into the [sheep]fold."[23] But Gildas notwithstanding, the number of Germans who settled in Britain before the mid-fifth century appears to have been small. Bede claims that under their leaders, Hengest and Horsa, Vortigern's Germanic allies came to Kent in only three ships. The number "three" is likely to have been symbolic rather than precise, but the implication of quite limited Germanic settlement prior to about 450 is consistent with the current archaeological evidence.

One of the most striking features of fifth-century Britain is the speed with which pre-Roman patterns of authority re-emerged in this post-Roman world. Cities were abandoned, hillforts reoccupied, new defensive dykes constructed; and a host of local and regional kings suddenly reappeared, all in the first half of the fifth century. Roman influence did not end, of course. Some of the new kingdoms carved out in the fifth century seem to have been continuations of existing Roman *civitates*. In western Britain, Latin land charters from the sixth century continued to employ Roman measurements to define estate boundaries. Latin inscriptions continued to be erected: in Wales and the northwest, more such inscriptions survive from the fifth and sixth centuries than from the third and fourth. But the re-emergence of kingship during the fifth century and the reoccupation of hillforts speak eloquently of the extent to which Roman Britain, throughout its history, had continued to rest on its British foundations.

Fifth-century Britain also retained many of its traditional links with Gaul. Between 446 and 454, the British even sent a letter to the Gallo-Roman military leader Aetius, begging for his assistance against their Pictish, Irish, and German enemies. Representatives from the British church attended the 455 ecclesiastical council of Arles in Gaul, where they continued to worry about Pelagianism in the British Church.[24] Around the same time, British settlers were also emigrating to the Continent in large numbers, both as refugees and as invaders. By the 460s, indeed, Britons had largely taken over the Gaulish province of Armorica, eventually changing both the name of the province (to Brittany) and its language (to Breton, like Welsh a linguistic descendant of the early British vernacular). Britons also settled in Galicia in northwest Spain, where they had their own bishop as late as the 570s. There are even claims that a British king named Riothamus (which means, in the British vernacular, "supreme ruler") led a military campaign against the Goths in Gaul in the late 460s. The date corresponds suggestively with references in Gildas and the *Historia Brittonum* to a period of successful British resistance against Germanic attacks, which the *Historia* places in the late fifth and early sixth centuries. The *Historia Brittonum* connects this resistance with a British leader named Arthur, not a king but a war

---

[23]Gildas, *The Ruin of Britain and Other Works*, p. 26.

[24]J. M. Wallace-Hadrill, *Bede's Ecclesiastical History of the English People: A Historical Commentary* (Oxford, 1988), p. 27.

leader, a *dux bellorum*, whose triumph over the Anglo-Saxons at the battle of Mount Badon brought peace for a generation to the Britons.

Arthur, of course, became the inspiration for the richly elaborated Arthurian romances of the twelfth and thirteenth centuries. But except insofar as these later legends testify to a continuing interest in the Arthurian legend, these high medieval tales have little connection to the events of the fifth and sixth centuries. A great deal of scholarly ingenuity has been applied nevertheless to identifying and locating a historical, British King Arthur in the scraps of evidence that survive. The materials, however, are not promising. In the *Gododdin*, a hero is described as brave, but "not Arthur." This reference may be a later interpolation, but if it is not, it could date from the seventh century, when the earliest parts of the poem were probably composed. The *Historia Brittonum* contains a list of twelve battles fought by Arthur. Those we can locate are mostly in the north of Britain, where the *Gododdin* and several other early Welsh battle poems are also set. Appended to the *Historia* is a set of "Welsh Annals," written in Latin, which date the battle of Mount Badon to 516 and record Arthur's death at the battle of Camlann in 537. Gildas, by contrast, does not mention Arthur at all, but he does ascribe military victories of comparable effect (that is, they brought peace for a generation) to a Roman-descended king named Ambrosius Aurelianus, who also appears in the *Historia Brittonum*. And finally, we have some eighth- and ninth-century Welsh poetry in which Arthur leads an expedition to the underworld, and in which the tradition that Arthur's gravesite is unknown first appears.

With evidence like this, it would be as foolish to declare that Arthur did not exist as it would be to declare that he did. What seems clear at the very least is that whatever historical reality he may have had, Arthur was already a figure of legend among the Welsh by the time the first references to him appear. Ambrosius Aurelianus was probably another such heroic figure, whose legend, for some reason, did not catch on to the degree that Arthur's did. To climb farther out on a scholarly limb, we might wonder whether the Arthur story perhaps began as a northern British legend, which spread somewhat later to the west and south, picking up geographical associations as it traveled. If Gildas could be connected with southwestern Britain, as has sometimes been argued,[25] it might be possible to speculate that Ambrosius's legend may also be localizable to this

---

[25]K. R. Dark, *Civitas to Kingdom: British Political Continuity, 300–800* (Leicester, 1994), pp. 258–266, reviews the evidence (which is far from conclusive) for a southwestern Gildas. N. J. Higham, *The English Conquest: Gildas and Britain in the Fifth Century* (Manchester, 1994), sees Gildas as a fifth-century author writing in south-central Britain. David Dumville, *Gildas: New Approaches* (Woodbridge, Suffolk, 1984), has argued for a northern Gildas; Patrick Sims-Williams, "Gildas and the Anglo-Saxons," *Cambridge Medieval Celtic Studies* 6 (1983): 1–30, is not persuaded by the evidence for a northern Gildas, and doubts it is possible to localize Gildas at all.

area, where it eventually became merged into the Arthur story at some later date. But by now, we have long since left our evidence behind.

Such speculations may, however, explain the Arthurian associations at a much later date in southwestern Britain, in such places as Tintagel, Glastonbury, and South Cadbury. At Tintagel, an ancient stronghold at the extreme southwest tip of Cornwall, recent archaeological excavation has unearthed a sixth-century inscription, *Pater coliavificit Artognov* ("Arthnou, father of a descendant of Coll, has had this built").[26] The temptation to turn Arthnou into Arthur is great — but to do so would violate all the basic principles of historical linguistics. They simply are not the same name, much as they may look alike to Arthurian enthusiasts.

Among these southwestern Arthurian sites, South Cadbury (in Somerset) is particularly interesting because of speculation that it might have been King Arthur's headquarters, the fabled Camelot. An important, well-populated political center in pre-Roman times, South Cadbury was stormed, demolished, and abandoned by the conquering Romans. Like many other hillforts, however, South Cadbury was reoccupied and refortified during the fifth and sixth centuries. Archeologists have found a great embankment of rubble dating from about 500 C.E., strengthened by wooden beams and provided with two sizeable wood-and-timber gatehouses. Behind the embankment stood a great timber hall some sixty feet long. The entire fortress complex covers eighteen acres, and the site enjoys spectacular views of the surrounding countryside, including, off in the distance, the ancient monastery of Glastonbury, whose monks would claim, in the twelfth century, to have discovered the tomb of Arthur and his wife Guinivere on their property. But at neither of these sites is there any surviving evidence to connect them with Arthur.

It would be wrong to leave Arthur on this negative note, however. Whether or not the Arthurian legend has a real historical core, the image he represents, of successful British resistance against their enemies, is not misplaced. As James Campbell has remarked,

> Britain in the face of the crisis of the fifth century proved not the weakest, but the strongest, part of the Empire. In this sense; by 500 control of every part of the western Empire had passed to barbarian rulers, even if some of these sometimes left considerable power in the hands of the Roman ruling classes. There was one exception, Britain. There, although large areas of the island had passed under barbarian control, at least half was still under British rule. And although in the end none of Britain was left under British rule, the defeat of the Britons took a very long time. When Edward I defeated Llewellyn, Prince of Gwynedd, in 1282, and subjugated his principality, this marked the loss to a foreign ruler of the last piece of the Roman Empire in the West which was still in the hands of rulers of the race which had inhabited it before the Romans came.[27]

---

[26]*National Geographic* 196:3 (September 1999), p. xi.

[27]Campbell, *The Anglo-Saxons*, p. 19.

The Anglo-Saxon Conquest

Bede writes that the Germanic warriors Vortigern introduced into Kent were Jutes, from modern-day Jutland in northern Denmark. There is archaeological evidence to support this claim and to suggest that this same group also settled on the Isle of Wight, just as Bede claimed they did. The majority of the Germanic invaders of Britain during the fifth and sixth centuries were not Jutes, however, but Angles (from southern Denmark and some of the Danish islands) and Saxons (initially from the German province of Saxony, but by the fourth century settled broadly along the coast of the North Sea). Other peoples came also, including Frisians, Franks, and Danes; and here too, archaeology supports the outlines of the story Bede tells, including his claim that some of the areas from which these peoples had departed for Britain remained empty of people for centuries thereafter — a phenomenon to which fifth-century flooding along the North Sea littoral must also have contributed. There is no reason to insist too firmly, however, on the distinctions between Jutes, Saxons, Angles, Frisians, and Franks. All these peoples had mixed freely for several centuries on the Continent before they began their emigration to Britain. And all had been in contact with the Roman world for centuries before they came to Britain. The British regarded them as barbarians, and one can understand their point of view. But the material level of their civilization was not decisively different from that of their British enemies.

In bringing Germanic fighters into Britain, Vortigern may have been following a long-established Roman policy of recruiting Germanic warriors to defend the empire against the attacks of other invaders. He may also have intended this force to assist him in his own designs against competing British leaders. But whatever his intentions, his plans backfired. More Germanic settlers quickly arrived, and by the third quarter of the fifth century, significant parts of southern and eastern Britain had passed into Germanic hands. Further immigration followed. "Recent calculations based on the size of excavated boats indicate that several hundred thousand people could have crossed to England between the mid-fifth and the mid-sixth centuries."[28]

During the last half of the sixth century, a new surge of Germanic conquests followed in the north, the midlands, and the west. By 597, when St. Augustine and his missionaries arrived from Rome to convert the Anglo-Saxons to Christianity, British political authority had been relegated to Wales, the southwestern counties of Devon and Cornwall, and the border country between modern-day England and Scotland (Galloway, Strathclyde, Rheged). Nor were Germans the only invaders. Irish invaders established kingdoms in Dyfed (in modern-day Wales) and in southwestern Scotland (the kingdom of the Dal Riada). Both these

---

[28]Nelson, "Anglo-Saxon England, c. 500–1066," p. 28.

THE EARLY
ANGLO-SAXON KINGDOMS
ABOUT A.D. 600

KENT: Kingdoms ruled by
Anglo-Saxons

DYFED: Kingdoms ruled by
Celtic-Speaking Peoples

Northern
Picts

Southern
Picts

Iona

STRATHCLYDE

*NORTH
SEA*

GODODDIN

Lindisfarne

Old
Yearvering

Bamburgh

BERNICIA

GALLOWAY

NORTHUMBRIA

Carlisle

RHEGED

IRELAND

IRISH SEA

DEIRA

York

Chester

Lincoln

GWYNEDD

LINDSEY

Lichfield

MERCIA

POWYS

EAST
ANGLIA

Sutton Hoo

DYFED

GWENT

Gloucester

ESSEX

London

KENT

Canterbury

WESSEX

Salisbury

SUSSEX

DUMNONIA

Exeter

English Channel

FRANCIA

kingdoms would survive for several centuries. By the end of the sixth century, Roman Britain was thus effectively divided into two separate cultural and economic zones: a Christian, Celtic world around the Irish Sea that extended also to Brittany and Galicia; and a Germanic, largely pagan world around the North Sea that included the Christianized Frankish kingdoms of Gaul.[29]

By the year 600, political control over most of the territory of modern-day England had thus passed from British to Anglo-Saxon rulers. The population over whom these new Anglo-Saxon kings ruled, however, remained overwhelmingly British. In the year 400, the population of Roman Britain was probably around four million people: approximately the same number of people as lived in England and Wales around the year 1500. Archaeology is beginning to confirm what common sense should always have suggested: it is simply impossible to imagine so many people being pushed by the Anglo-Saxon invasions into Wales, Devon, and Cornwall. The British population had almost certainly declined by 600 from its levels in 400. Emigration to Brittany and Galicia, warfare, and a devasting mid-sixth-century plague had all taken their toll. To what extent British losses might have been offset by Anglo-Saxon immigration we cannot begin to know. What is clear, however, is that by the year 600, across much of Anglo-Saxon England, a relatively small group of Germanic warriors ruled a much larger group of subject, and sometimes enslaved, Britons.[30]

Most of what is known about the Anglo-Saxon conquerors during these years comes from the archaeological excavation of cemeteries and gravesites. Christians, however, did not generally bury grave goods with their dead; as a result, there is far more material evidence about the non-Christian Anglo-Saxon minority than about the British majority. Some Christian churches survived the Anglo-Saxon conquests. When, for example, the Frankish Christian princess Bertha married the pagan King Ethelbert of Kent, probably in the early 580s, the church of St. Martin in Canterbury was quickly refurbished for her use. But although the church building had survived, it was clearly disused and abandoned. Outside Wales, the organizational structures of British Christianity seem to have collapsed by the end of the sixth century. A degree of residual Christianity could have survived nonetheless among the British population of England, but at present, there is little solid evidence to demonstrate that this was the case.

---

[29]James Campbell, *Essays in Anglo-Saxon History* (London, 1986).

[30]The Anglo-Saxon word for slave, *wealh*, is the word from which modern English derives "Welsh," i.e., "British." We cannot, however, infer anything directly about the status of the subject Britons from this linguistic fact. Even as an element in place names, *wealh* can be placed probably not earlier than the eighth century — too late to tell anything about the fifth and sixth centuries. See the following note.

The Britons remained, but the British vernacular languages, both Celtic and Latin-based, eventually disappeared from the territories conquered by the Anglo-Saxons. This shift in language, from Welsh and Latin to Anglo-Saxon (also known as Old English), was once regarded as proof that the British population had indeed been swept westward into Wales by the Anglo-Saxon invasions, leaving an empty countryside behind them. In recent years, however, historians and linguists have concluded that linguistic change on this scale more likely reflects the respective power and wealth of the competing language groups than their respective numbers. In other words, Old English could (and we now believe did) triumph over Welsh and Latin despite the fact that the British population of England greatly outnumbered the Anglo-Saxon population during the fifth and sixth centuries.[31]

Intermarriage is another probable route through which such a change in language could have occurred. This may also help to explain the intriguing number of British names in the early genealogies of several Anglo-Saxon royal dynasties. There is also some archaeological evidence for such relationships. One fifth-century Hampshire cemetery, for example, has revealed a population of tall men and small women, suggesting that intermarriage between Anglo-Saxon men and British women was common in this area.[32] But ethnic divisions between Britons and Anglo-Saxons were probably quite malleable, even apart from the effects of intermarriage. By the seventh century, and probably earlier, individuals who spoke Old English, bore an Old English name, and worshipped as did their Anglo-Saxon neighbors were probably regarded by their neighbors as Anglo-Saxons. "Englishness" and "Britishness" were cultural identities much more than they were descriptions of biological descent.

Anglo-Saxon cemeteries also suggest that a quite rapid differentiation of wealth and status took place within this new society. In the earliest phases of the Anglo-Saxon conquest, the political units carved out by the conquerors were often very small (fifteen to twenty square miles), and a rough equality seems to have been preserved among the conquerors. In the sixth century, however, marked differences in the graves and grave goods of certain individuals begin to appear, signaling the emergence of princes or kings exercising more extensive lordship. By the end of the sixth century, a set of powerful regional kingdoms had come into existence, each identified with a specific people — the East Saxons (Essex), the West Saxons (Wessex), the South Saxons (Sussex), the North

---

[31]We cannot date this change in language with any precision. But the emergence during the eighth century of place names ending in *-wealh* (an Anglo-Saxon word meaning "British," from which the term "Welsh" is derived) may suggest that the majority of the population under English rule had by this date ceased to speak a British language, making those communities that did remain British-speaking particularly notable. For discussion, see Hines, *The Anglo-Saxons*, p. 76.

[32]Nelson, "Anglo-Saxon England, c. 500–1066," p. 29.

Folk and the South Folk (who together made up the kingdom of East Anglia), Lindsey (which was eventually absorbed by its neighbors), the people of Kent, the Middle Angles (who formed Mercia), and, north of the Humber estuary, the Deirans and the Bernicians, who together became the kingdom of Northumbria. The earlier, small kingdoms did not necessarily disappear, however. As administrative units absorbed into these larger kingdoms, some would survive until the end of the Anglo-Saxon period and beyond.

Undoubtedly, the most striking example of the increasing wealth and status of these late-sixth- and early-seventh-century Anglo-Saxon rulers is provided by the Sutton Hoo treasure.[33] This remarkable site, first excavated in 1939 and re-excavated during the 1960s and again in the 1980s, was a ship burial of a kind familiar in eastern Sweden but unknown in England outside east Suffolk. Beneath the burial mound, within the body of the buried ship, archaeologists discovered the remains of a coffin; within the coffin and surrounding it they found an elaborate, late-Roman-style helmet; a splendid shield; spears; a belt buckle made of gold with garnet inlays; a sword and sword belt, also with gold and garnet fittings; a purse containing thirty-seven Merovingian gold coins and ingots; a balance; bronze and silver bowls of various sizes, including one Byzantine bowl manufactured around the year 500; a large bronze cauldron; a lyre; and various apparently ceremonial items, including a whetstone (perhaps a scepter?) and an iron stand that might have been intended to display a banner. Recent excavations have revealed a number of additional burials surrounding the main burial mound. These surrounding burials include a horse sacrifice and a number of human burials, possibly sacrifices, but more likely executions. These discoveries have confirmed what had long been suspected — that this is indeed a pagan burial site, despite the presence within the treasure of a set of Christian "conversion" spoons, one labeled "Saul," the other "Paul." Recent work has also lent additional support to the traditional dating of the main ship burial to the first third of the seventh century. But it has not confirmed or disproved the suggestion that this might be the burial site of King Redwald of East Anglia (d. 627), whom Bede described as keeping "in the same temple . . . one altar for the Christian sacrifice and another small altar on which to offer victims to devils."[34]

The Sutton Hoo treasure is now on permanent display in the British Museum in London. Seeing it, one also sees early Anglo-Saxon kingship in a new light. We do not know whether the individual buried at Sutton Hoo was a king or not. In a certain sense, it doesn't matter. By the year 600, the political chaos of the fifth and sixth centuries had given way to

---

[33]On Sutton Hoo, see Martin Carver, *Sutton Hoo: Burial Ground of Kings?* (Philadelphia, 1998).

[34]Bede, *The Ecclesiastical History of the English People,* ed. Judith McClure and Roger Collins (Oxford, 1994), II.15, p. 98.

The Sutton Hoo Helmet
This extraordinary helmet, found in the Sutton Hoo ship burial, is modeled on late Roman parade helmets. The design derives ultimately from Sassanian Persia, but the closest similarities to the Sutton Hoo helmet are with helmets found in Sweden. *(The Granger Collection)*

more stable regimes dominated by well-organized and potentially powerful Anglo-Saxon kingdoms. The splendor of Sutton Hoo demonstrates that these early Anglo-Saxon rulers already commanded quite remarkable resources of wealth and craftsmanship and were in every respect the equals of their continental competitors. What set them apart from their fellow kings in the former Roman Empire was their paganism. But that too was shortly to change. In the seventh century, the Roman Church would return to England, gradually winning the allegiance of the Anglo-Saxons and profoundly shaping their historical development. It is to these developments that we now turn.

CHAPTER 2

Conversion and Unification: Anglo-Saxon England to the Death of King Alfred (899)

By the year 600, Roman political authority had collapsed almost everywhere in the western Roman Empire. Roman political institutions survived, however, in altered but recognizable form, in the organization of the Catholic Church. Indeed, many historians regard the Church as a kind of transfigured empire. Its administration paralleled the old Roman civil administration, with dioceses, provinces, parishes, and even claims to central authority in Rome. Only centuries later would the papacy become a powerful international political force. But already Roman popes claimed responsibility for the immortal souls of the inhabitants of western Europe, much as Roman emperors had once exercised political authority over their bodies.

The Church has been termed by some the "ghost" of the Roman Empire. And although the ghost metaphor belies the tangible and effective organization of the early medieval Church, there is still some value in regarding the Church as an institutional legacy of the defunct empire. In England, the Church's Roman past was to prove crucial in constructing the future, for it was from within the Roman Catholic Church that a sense of "Englishness" would first emerge among the politically divided peoples of early Anglo-Saxon England.

The "Celtic Church"

In England, Christianity was swamped by the Germanic migrations. Some local churches may have continued to serve the remaining British population for a generation or two, but Christianity as an organized institution quickly receded into the lands of Cornwall, Wales, and the British-speaking north. In these lands, the Britons found sanctuary against the military thrusts of the Anglo-Saxons, and here the British Church endured. Even in the midst of these disasters, however, fifth-century British

39

missionaries were actively spreading the faith to other regions. St. Patrick was a Briton, whose missionary efforts in Ireland were likely overseen by the native British Church. Ninian was another British missionary, active in Galloway (southwestern Scotland). Other British missionaries were active on the Continent, in Brittany, and in northern Spain. Strikingly, however, British missionaries made no efforts to convert the pagan Anglo-Saxons, a fact for which they would later be condemned by the English historian Bede.

Although Christianity seems from the historical record to have disappeared from England with the Anglo-Saxon conquest, it flourished in the lands that bordered upon the Irish Sea: Cornwall, Wales, Cumberland, Galloway, Ireland, and Brittany. In each of these areas, however, Christianity assumed a distinctively different organizational and institutional shape. Linguistically, these areas all spoke one of the several Celtic languages. But they were not united by any common form of "Celtic" Christianity. Research over the past twenty years has made clear that the religious customs and practices of these areas were simply too diverse for any such common label as the "Celtic Church" to make sense. As a result, it is now necessary to rethink much of what we once thought we knew about the differences between the "Celtic" and the "Roman" churches.[1]

Previous generations of historians (and previous editions of this book) emphasized the distance between the Celtic and Roman churches, especially the manner in which the Celtic Church stubbornly maintained its independence from Rome with respect to important matters of religious practice and organization. Chief among these differences were the "Celtic" method of calculating the date of Easter, which differed from that in use in Rome at that time, and the all-important matter of ecclesiastical organization. St. Patrick, it was argued, had originally envisaged a church divided into dioceses, each ruled by a bishop as was the norm on the Continent. In Ireland, however, the diocesan structure never took hold, and Christianity developed its own distinctive organization based on great, autonomous monastic federations. Bishops existed, but exercised no real administrative power, keeping instead strictly to sacramental affairs and living in monasteries under the authority of an abbot. So significantly was the "Celtic Church" believed to deviate from the Roman norm that many books, including an earlier edition of this text, spoke of them as "two historically distinct Christian traditions."

It is now widely recognized, however, that there was no single "Celtic Church"; rather, there were many Celtic churches, each with its own differing customs and practices. With respect to Easter, for example,

---

[1]Kathleen Hughes, "The Celtic Church: Is This a Valid Concept?" *Cambridge Medieval Celtic Studies* 1 (1981): 1–20; Wendy Davies, "The Myth of the Celtic Church," in *The Early Church in Wales and the West*, ed. Nancy Edwards and Alan Lane (Oxford, 1992).

while it is true that some churches (most notably the important monastery of Iona) continued until the eighth century to cling to older methods of calculating Easter, many other churches in Wales, Ireland, and Brittany had adopted the newer procedures long before this time. Variety was also the rule with regard to other issues on which the "Celtic Church" was once believed to dissent from the Roman norm, such as the shape of the monastic tonsure and aspects of the liturgy. Even the idea that the "Celtic Church" was organized around monasteries rather than bishops has been revised in recent scholarship. Large monastic federations did exist, particularly in Ireland, where there were no Roman cities around which to organize dioceses. But bishops were also a basic feature of the Irish Church and exercised significant administrative functions within it. In Wales, the evidence suggests even more clearly the existence in the fifth and sixth centuries of a church governed by bishops ruling dioceses whose origins lay in the late Roman period.

It is important to set this variety in its proper historical context. Historians now realize that "Roman" tradition was no less heterogeneous: the Continent also knew tremendous variety in ecclesiastical matters. Popes may have claimed supreme authority over the Church, but they were in no position to enforce uniformity in religious life. Sixth-century Europe saw several different conceptions of the monastic life enshrined in the form of monastic rules: not for several centuries would the Benedictine idea of monastic life come to be the dominant form. Similarly, the Irish were not the only ones to deviate from Rome in the dating of Easter — churches in Gaul were also using different Easter tables (to calculate the date of this moveable festival). Indeed, it is now recognized that the so-called "Celtic Easter" was not Celtic in origin at all. The tables used by the dissenting Irish churches in fact had their origins in a high-status circle of Gaulish clerics that included Sulpicius Severus, the biographer of the unquestionably "Roman" St. Martin.[2]

But if our picture of the "Celtic" churches has changed, our appreciation of their influence has only increased. The contribution of the Irish Church to English and continental Christianity has long been recognized by both the popular and academic press. Irish monasticism was one of the great energizing forces of the early medieval church. During the sixth and seventh centuries, Irish monks traveled widely, founding monasteries wherever they went. Many important religious houses in Gaul and Italy, among them Luxeuil and Bobbio, owed their foundation to Irish missionary activity. Celtic monastic practices exerted a particularly strong influence on the Franks, who often adapted Irish customs in modified form for the governance of their own monastic communities. Among their European contemporaries, the Irish were known and praised

---

[2]Daniel McCarthy, "The Origin of the *Latercus* Paschal Cycle of the Insular Celtic Church," *Cambrian Medieval Celtic Studies* 28 (1994): 25–49.

for the rigor of their scholarship, the depth of their sanctity, and the austerity of their lives. Irish monastic schools were the best in western Europe for the teaching of the Latin language, and a rich artistic tradition culminated in the illuminated manuscripts and intricately styled metalwork of the eighth and ninth centuries. These works of art were the wonder of their age and continue to excite admiration in our own.

From the English perspective, the most significant of these Irish missionary monks was St. Columba (d. 597), who worked with great success toward the conversion of northern Britain. In about 565, Columba founded a monastery on the island of Iona, off the west coast of Scotland, and his monastery quickly became a fountainhead of missionary activity among the Picts of Scotland and the English of Northumbria. From Iona, the work of converting the Anglo-Saxons began in earnest. As it happened, the spiritual penetration of Anglo-Saxon England from the north anticipated an entirely separate Christian missionary endeavor from the south. In 597, the very year of St. Columba's death, a large band of Christian missionaries sent to England by the Roman pope St. Gregory the Great and led by the monk St. Augustine made contact with King Ethelbert of Kent. So it was that the seventh century saw Anglo-Saxon paganism under spiritual assault from both north and south.

The Roman Church and Continental Monasticism

As England was recovering from the chaos of the Anglo-Saxon conquests, much larger Germanic kingdoms were forming on the Continent. The Franks had established a kingdom in Gaul and the Rhineland that came to be known as "Francia"; their great warrior-king Clovis (d. 511) renounced paganism and adopted Catholic Christianity under the influence of his Christian wife Chlotilde. The Visigoths founded a kingdom in Spain that would be overwhelmed in the early eighth century by the advancing Muslims. Italy, after a series of upheavals, was ruled in part by the Byzantine Empire and in part by a Germanic people known as the "Long Beards"or Lombards. In Rome itself, the papacy, under nominal Byzantine jurisdiction, maintained a precarious independence against both the Byzantines in the south and the Lombards in the north. But everywhere in continental Europe, Germanic cultures and institutions were in the ascendant.

In the ecclesiastical life of western Europe, however, Rome lived on through the influence of two remarkable institutions: monasticism and the papacy. Christian monasticism emerged in Egypt in the third century, and by the fourth it had become a significant institution in the life of the Church. After the conversion of Constantine and his rise to power in 312, Christianity became not only a legally tolerated religion, but the favored religion of the imperial family. Profession of the Christian faith was no longer the perilous and heroic act it had been in the days of the martyrs. As converts poured into the now-respectable fold, men and women of unusual piety began to seek a more rigorously Christian way of life — one that would enable them to withdraw from the world and devote all their energies to communion with God. Many of them found this new life in monasticism.

Traditionally, Christian monasticism was of two types: eremitic (hermit monasticism) and cenobitic (communal monasticism). During the fifth and sixth centuries, increasing numbers of fervent believers, men and women alike, adopted some form of monastic life. The lives of the hermit monks were especially bewildering in their variety. Some established themselves atop pillars and remained there for many years — to be revered as wise and wonder-working "holy men" by their surrounding communities. Others retreated to the desert, living in uncompromising austerity. Both hermit monks and cenobitic monks often carried the mortification of the flesh to extreme lengths, indulging in severe fasts, going without sleep for prolonged periods, wearing hairshirts, and whipping themselves.

In the course of the fifth century, eremitic monasticism began to give way in western Europe to more ordered religious communities in which monks or nuns governed their lives by written rules of conduct. In the west, the most influential of these monastic rules was composed by St. Benedict of Nursia (c. 480–544), a well-born Roman who stressed the practical Roman virtues of discipline and organization. St. Benedict founded many monasteries in his lifetime, the most important of which was Monte Cassino, built on a mountaintop between Rome and Naples. Used as German military headquarters in World War II, Monte Cassino was demolished by the United States Air Force in 1943, but it has since been rebuilt.

Benedict's rule was characterized by Pope Gregory the Great as "conspicuous for its discretion." Benedict himself described it as "a little rule for beginners" in the monastic life. Both comments speak to the essential moderation of the rule's requirements. The lives of Benedictine monks and nuns were austere, but not excessively so. They ate, slept, and dressed simply but adequately. Their day was divided into a regular sequence of activities: there was a time for eating, a time for sleeping, a time for prayer, and a time for work. The Benedictine order had no central organization. Each monastery and nunnery was autonomous (subject to the jurisdiction of the local bishop), and each was under the full authority of its abbot or abbess. On important matters, the heads of Benedictine houses might consult with the whole community, but they were not bound by the majority opinion. Still, St. Benedict cautioned his abbots to respect the views of their monks, not to "sadden" or "overdrive" them or give them cause for "just murmuring." This combination of moderation and organization was the chief reason for the rule's success. St. Benedict's monks had to submit to the discipline of their abbot and the authority of the rule; they had to practice poverty and chastity; they had to work as well as pray. Yet the life St. Benedict prescribed was not for spiritual superstars alone, but rather one that any dedicated Christian might hope to follow.

Benedictine monasticism has shaped the lives of countless English monks and nuns from the seventh century until the present day. Throughout the seventh and eighth centuries, increasing numbers of monasteries and nunneries adopted the Benedictine Rule, both in England and on the Continent. Benedictine monasteries housed many of the most prominent individuals of their day and operated the best schools of the period. Their extensive estates — the gifts of generations of pious donors — often served as models of the most efficient agricultural techniques known in their time. It is difficult to imagine how early medieval Europe might have looked without them. But it is important to remember nonetheless that there were many other monastic rules that monks and nuns might follow in the early Middle Ages. The Benedictine Rule became the standard for English monastic life only in the tenth and eleventh centuries, as a result of the monastic reform movement sponsored by King Edgar of Wessex.

The other great institution in the early medieval Church was the papacy. For centuries, the popes, as bishops of Rome and heirs of St. Peter, had claimed spiritual dominion over the Church, but they had seldom been able to exercise it until the pontificate of St. Gregory the Great (590–604). A man of humility, piety, and genius, St. Gregory was the most powerful pontiff of the early Middle Ages. He had been a monk before ascending the papal throne and had personally founded the Roman abbey of St. Andrew's. Although neither Gregory nor his abbey were Benedictine, he was an enthusiastic admirer of St. Benedict and was the author of his earliest biography. Like St. Benedict, he was a gifted administrator as well as a sensitive pastor. He was a notable scholar, too, and is traditionally grouped with the great fourth-century intellectuals — St. Ambrose, St. Jerome, and St. Augustine of Hippo — as one of the "Doctors" of the early Latin Church. His *Pastoral Care*, a handbook on the duties of bishops and priests, is a work of extraordinary practical wisdom, which became one of the most admired and widely read books of the Middle Ages.

The Mission to England

Gregory never set foot in England, but he is one of the central figures of early English history, because it was through his influence that the first papally sponsored effort to convert the Anglo-Saxons to Christianity was begun. His first exposure to the country came before he was pope, when Gregory encountered a group of fair-haired English boys being sold on the Roman slave market. Asking the name of their race, he was told that they were Angles. "That is appropriate," he replied, "for they have angelic faces, and it is right that they should become fellow heirs with the angels in heaven."[3] It was this desire, claimed Bede, that induced Pope

St. Martin's Church, Canterbury   This is the oldest church in England still in use today. Both the nave (left) and the chancel (right) were built in the seventh-century, using Roman bricks and masonry blocks. The chancel, however, most likely incorporates the Roman chapel used by Queen Bertha before the arrival of St. Augustine in 597. *(E. T. Archive)*

Gregory to send a band of missionaries to work among the English. Gregory's devotion to the monastic ideal prompted him to entrust the hazardous task to a group of forty monks from his own monastery of St. Andrew's led by a monk named Augustine.[4] The ultimate effect of Augustine's mission was not only to win England to the Christian faith but also to enlarge enormously the scope of monastic missionary activity and the authority of the papacy within western Europe.[5]

In 597, St. Augustine's army of monks arrived in Kent, which was the closest Anglo-Saxon kingdom to the Continent. Its king, Ethelbert, was at the time the preeminent monarch of England. His queen, Bertha, was a

---

[3]Bede, *The Ecclesiastical History of the English People,* ed. Judith McClure and Roger Collins (Oxford, 1994), p. 70.

[4]Later canonized as St. Augustine (d. 604), and sometimes referred to as "St. Augustine the Less," to distinguish him from the renowned North African theologian, St. Augustine of Hippo (d. 430).

[5]On the process of conversion, see Henry Mary-Harting, *The Coming of Christianity to Anglo-Saxon England,* 3rd ed. (University Park, Penn., 1991); James Campbell, *Essays in Anglo-Saxon History* (London, 1986); and Richard Fletcher, *The Barbarian Conversion from Paganism to Christianity* (New York, 1997; paperback ed., Berkeley, 1999).

Christian and a member of the Frankish royal family. As a condition of the marriage, a Frankish bishop accompanied Bertha to Kent and resided in King Ethelbert's household. Ethelbert gave him the abandoned Christian church of St. Martin's in the royal capital of Canterbury, where he celebrated Mass for the queen and her household.

As a result of his connections with the Frankish court, King Ethelbert was thus already familiar with Christianity before the papal mission arrived. He received Augustine's mission courteously, permitted the monks to establish themselves in Canterbury, and quickly became a convert to Christianity himself. Many of Ethelbert's Kentish subjects followed him into the new faith — ten thousand were baptized at one time, we are told — and Christianity began spreading into the client kingdoms of Essex and East Anglia. Returning briefly to the Continent, Augustine received consecration by papal order as "archbishop of the English peoples." He thereby became the first in the line of archbishops of Canterbury that has continued unbroken to the present day.

With conversion and the Church's emphasis on the Bible came literacy. It is probably no coincidence that Ethelbert of Kent, the first Anglo-Saxon monarch to become a Christian, was also the first to issue a series of written laws, or "dooms" (literally, "judgments"). Although they are mainly concerned with recording Germanic custom, Ethelbert's laws were likely committed to writing at the instigation of the Church. Indeed, the first law in Ethelbert's list provides explicitly for the protection of ecclesiastical property. Other provisions define the compensation payments perpetrators would owe their victims for a variety of offenses. Should a man cut off another's ear, for example, he must pay twelve shillings; he must pay fifty shillings for an eye, six shillings for a front tooth — rather along the lines of modern insurance schedules for accidental death or dismemberment. Such lists of compensation payments are found in a number of Germanic law codes from throughout early medieval Europe. What makes Ethelbert's laws remarkable is that they were apparently written in English. In continental Europe, barbarian law codes were invariably written in Latin, as were the laws of Rome, which in some sense these barbarian codes sought to imitate. England, Ireland, and Wales are the only early medieval cultures in western Europe to preserve any significant amount of vernacular law or vernacular literature — evidence of the remarkably fruitful encounter between Latin Christianity and native culture in these insular lands.

The Conversion of Northumbria

In accordance with the instructions Augustine had received from Pope Gregory, the early archbishops of Canterbury permitted their English converts to retain those aspects of their former customs and rites that were not inconsistent with Christianity. Old temples were neither abandoned nor destroyed but were converted to Christian use. However, at the death of Ethelbert in 616, Kent, Essex, and East Anglia underwent a pagan reaction. Political hegemony passed briefly to East Anglia whose king, Redwald, so Bede reports, hedged his bets by keeping in the same temple "an altar to sacrifice to Christ and another, smaller one to sacrifice to devils." Redwald is often suggested as a potential candidate for the king buried in pagan splendor — but with Christian cult objects — at Sutton Hoo (see discussion in Chapter 1).

While paganism rallied in the southeast, the center of Christian missionary activity shifted to remote Northumbria. The Anglo-Saxon kingdom of Northumbria emerged shortly after 600 through the unification of two smaller and mutually hostile northern kingdoms, Bernicia and Deira. The founder of Northumbria was a Bernician warrior-king named Ethelfrith (d. 616) who through a series of military victories established himself as the dominant power in the north and brought the kingdom of Deira under his sway. The Deiran heir, a young warrior named Edwin, went into exile for a time at the East Anglian court, but in 616 Edwin's forces defeated and killed Ethelfrith, and Edwin became king of Northumbria (616–633). Now it was the Bernician royal heirs who were driven into exile. They found refuge in Scotland, where they forged a relationship with the monks of Iona.

Edwin proved himself a monarch of rare ability. He maintained a firm peace in Northumbria, led a highly successful military expedition against the Welsh, and even took his army on a triumphant campaign southward across the midlands into Wessex. One of his royal capitals was Edinburgh, formerly the home base of the British people commemorated in the early Welsh poem the *Gododdin*. Another royal center was located at Yeavering, high in the Cheviot Hills, to the south of Edinburgh and some forty miles north of Hadrian's Wall. In 1949, an aerial photograph of the Yeavering site disclosed outlines in the earth of extensive ancient and early medieval buildings, which were afterwards subjected to meticulous archaeological investigations — with dramatic results. These excavations revealed numerous graves from across many centuries (the site had been a British political center before falling into Bernician hands), a large and well-defended cattle corral dating from the British Iron Age, and several impressive plastered-timber structures that appear to date from the reign of Edwin. The most spectacular among Edwin's buildings was a great royal hall over eighty feet long and nearly forty feet wide. Its timber supports were set as much as eight feet into the ground, suggesting that the hall was also of considerable height. It reminds one of the description in the celebrated Anglo-Saxon poem *Beowulf* of the hall of King Hrothgar, called "Heorot," which is said to have had a gilded roof. Perhaps Edwin's hall at Yeavering was also named and gilded; there is no way of knowing. But that Edwin held court and feasted in great splendor at Yeavering is beyond doubt. Most remarkable of all, archaeologists working at Yeavering located what appears to be an important "constitutional" artifact —

An Artist's Reconstruction of Yeavering under King Edwin   Yeavering was an important Northumbrian royal vill, which had been under British control prior to its conquest by the Anglo-Saxon rulers of Bernicia. The scene is dominated by Edwin's great hall, measuring appproximately eighty by forty feet. Behind the hall sits the amphitheater where Edwin addressed his great men. In the foreground is a portion of the fence that surrounded the large cattle enclosure. *(English Heritage Picture Library)*

the outline of a grandstand with a seating capacity in Edwin's time of some 320, with a platform at the front on which Edwin might have stood to address and consult his great men.

In the pages of Bede, Edwin's prowess as a warrior acquires a fundamental historical significance because of his conversion to Christianity. Like Clovis, king of the Franks, and Ethelbert of Kent, Edwin had a Christian wife. He had married a daughter of Ethelbert himself, Ethelberga, who brought with her to Northumbria a Christian chaplain named Paulinus. King Edwin was thus subject to Christian lobbying from several quarters: from his devout wife, from Paulinus, and from the papacy. In one of his letters to Ethelberga, the pope gave this counsel: "Persist, therefore, illustrious daughter, and to the utmost of your power endeavor to soften the hardness of his [Edwin's] heart by insinuating the divine precepts." To King Edwin, the pope wrote urging his conversion so that he might, having been "born again by water and the Holy Spirit . . . dwell in eternal glory with Him in whom you shall believe."

After a time, Edwin succumbed. At a royal council in 627, he and his councilors accepted Christianity. In a beautifully lyrical passage, Bede tells of an episode in this council that, whether authentic or not, has become one of the most famous anecdotes in English history — as familiar to English schoolchildren as the story of George Washington and the cherry tree is to Americans. According to Bede, one of Edwin's councilors, asked to consider whether the king and his people should convert to Christianity, advised his monarch as follows:

> This is how the present life of man on earth, O king, appears to me, in comparison with that time which is unknown to us. You are sitting feasting with your ealdormen and thegns in winter time; the fire is burning on the hearth in the middle of the hall and all inside is warm, while outside the wintry storms of rain and snow are raging; and a sparrow flies swiftly through the hall. It enters in at one door and quickly flies out through the other. For the few moments it is inside, the storm and wintry tempest cannot touch it, but after the briefest moment of calm, it flits from your sight, out of the wintry storm and into it again. So this life of man appears but for a moment; what follows or indeed what went before, we know not at all. If this new doctrine brings us more certain information, it seems right that we should accept it.[6]

As the council concluded, so Bede declares, the chief priest of the heathen gods embraced the new religion, and, with him, King Edwin himself became a Christian. The Church had won a notable triumph in a powerful kingdom.

The chagrin of the Christian party must have been great when, six years after his conversion, Edwin perished in battle (633). His adversary, the pagan King Penda of Mercia (c. 632–655), laid waste to Edwin's kingdom; Paulinus fled into exile; and Northumbria collapsed into chaos. But with the fall of Edwin and the Deiran royal house, the two heirs of the Bernician dynasty, long exiled in Scotland, now returned to claim their inheritance. These two princes, named Oswald and Oswy, brought with them the Irish-influenced Christianity they had learned at Iona. Oswald, the older of the two, won the Northumbrian throne by defeating the Mercians and Welsh in 634. At this crucial encounter, known appropriately as the battle of Heavenfield, Oswald set up a wooden cross to symbolize his devotion to the new faith.

Under the patronage of King Oswald (634–642) and his successor Oswy (642–670), Christianity established itself firmly in Northumbria. The Irish missionary St. Aidan founded a monastery on the "Holy Island" of Lindisfarne off the coast of northern Bernicia, which became a focal point of the hybrid Celtic and Anglo-Saxon culture for which Northumbria was to become famous. In the middle decades of the seventh century, missionaries from Ireland, Scotland, and Northumbria carried the gospel south of the Humber into Mercia and the other Anglo-Saxon kingdoms, bringing with them the fertile and diverse religious culture of the north.

---

[6]Bede, *Ecclesiastical* History, ed. McClure and Collins, p. 95. "Ealdormen" and "thegns" were ranks of nobility.

The Synod of Whitby (664) and the Origins of "Englishness"

In 664, King Oswy summoned an ecclesiastical council to meet in his presence at the abbey of Whitby, situated high atop a bluff overlooking the North Sea. Whitby was a "double monastery," comprising a house of monks and a house of nuns, both ruled by a powerful and remarkable abbess, St. Hild, a kinswoman of King Oswy. Present at the synod of Whitby were leading clergy from all over England, and the chief issue in question was the proper date for Easter. Oswy, who celebrated Easter according to the reckoning in use at Iona (as did St. Hild), was disturbed that his wife, who followed the custom in use at Canterbury and Rome, was still keeping the Lenten fast while he was enjoying the Easter feast.[7] He ordered the synod to agree on a single, proper date for Easter, the most solemn holy day in the Christian religious calendar.

The outcome of the synod was probably never in serious doubt, and may even have been prearranged. Oswy decided for the dating system used by Rome and Canterbury, and St. Hild immediately accepted this ruling for her own monastery at Whitby. Most of the other churches of Britain quickly followed suit, although Iona held out until 716 and certain Welsh churches did not change until the 760s.

That this synod was an important one cannot be doubted: Easter was a festival of profound significance, and the theological issues implicit in its celebration were weighty. Whitby was not, however, a turning point in relations between the "Roman" and the "Celtic" churches in England. That it has for long appeared to have been so to historians is largely due to the contemporary historian on whom we are primarily dependent for our knowledge of the event, the Venerable Bede (c. 673–735), whose *Ecclesiastical History of the English People* is one of the most influential works of history ever written. The theme of Bede's *History* is the gradual unification of the various peoples of Britain under the spiritual authority of the Roman Catholic Church. In Bede's hands, the chaotic warfare and the rise and fall of kings became a providential history, leading toward the divinely ordained unity of the English people (*gens Anglorum*) under papal authority. This is why Bede, for example, despite his admiration for the holiness of the abbots and monks of Lindisfarne and Iona, consistently underemphasizes their real role in the conversion of northern England to Christianity, instead portraying the conversion of England as arising directly and almost exclusively from Pope Gregory's decision to send Augustine to Canterbury.

For Bede, therefore, a key element in this divinely ordained process of conversion and unification was the acceptance by the Welsh, Irish, and Pictish churches in Britain of Roman direction in ecclesiastical matters

---

[7]Pious Christians were expected to abstain from meat and from sexual relations during the forty-day Lenten fast that precedes the Easter feast.

such as the dating of Easter. Although churches in these regions varied among themselves on such issues — as did churches elsewhere in the former territories of the Roman Empire — Bede portrayed the confrontation at Whitby as one between two unified but opposing religious traditions: the universal tradition of Rome on the one hand, and the local traditions of the Irish, Picts, and Welsh on the other. To emphasize this theme, when the principal "Roman" spokesman at Whitby, St. Wilfrid of Ripon, addresses the assembled "Celtic" clergy, Bede puts the following words into Wilfrid's mouth:

> For though your fathers were holy men, do you think that a handful of people in one corner of the remotest of islands is to be preferred to the universal Church of Christ which is spread throughout the world? And even if that Columba of yours — yes, and ours too, if he belonged to Christ — was a holy man of mighty works, is he to be preferred to the most blessed chief of the apostles, to whom the Lord said, "Thou art Peter and upon this rock I will build my Church and the gates of hell shall not prevail against it, and I will give unto thee the keys of the kingdom of heaven"?[8]

Bede then hammers the contrast home by reporting Oswy's observation that, because it is to Peter and not Columba that Christ gave the keys to Heaven, it is Peter's representative, the pope, whom he must follow on the date of Easter: "Otherwise, when I come to the gates of the kingdom of heaven, there may be no one to open them because the one who . . . holds the keys has turned his back on me."[9]

It is a mark of Bede's greatness as a historian that so many subsequent historians have followed his account by seeing in the debate at Whitby the climactic confrontation between "Roman" and "Celtic" Christianity in Britain. It is important to realize, however, that this interpretation of Whitby was Bede's own creation, carefully constructed to confirm Bede's view of the English people as a nation united by their allegiance to the papacy and to the traditions of Roman Catholic Christianity that the popes represented.

Even more influential than Bede's interpretation of Whitby, however, was his claim that the strife-ridden, politically fractured kingdoms of England nonetheless comprised a single people, the *gens Anglorum*. This would prove to be an idea of incalculable consequence for the history of England. Bede did not invent this idea by himself. It probably originated with Pope Gregory the Great, who thought that King Ethelbert of Kent was the undisputed ruler of a united English kingdom and who therefore granted Augustine, as Ethelbert's archbishop, authority over a *gens Anglorum* that did not, at the time, exist. But by grounding the authority of the archbishops of Canterbury upon the presumption that the English

---

[8]Bede, *Ecclesiastical History*, ed. McClure and Collins, pp. 158–159.

[9]Ibid., p. 159.

were a single people, Pope Gregory's misconception became a kind of self-fulfilling prophecy. Canterbury's authority over the English Church depended upon the claim that the English were a united people, while the reality of Canterbury's authority over the peoples of England encouraged the idea that they were in fact a single people. Bede's work declares this notion of "Englishness" in its title and powerfully reinforced it in the minds of his contemporaries and successors, including King Alfred (d. 899), under whom it would begin to become a political reality. At a time when England was divided into numerous separate kingdoms and loyalties were focused on one's kin or local lord, Bede took up the notion of a single English people and made that people the subject of his great *Ecclesiastical History of the English People.*[10]

Theodore and the Restructuring of the Anglo-Saxon Church

What Bede accomplished at the conceptual level was achieved at the level of ecclesiastical organization in the late seventh century through the efforts of Theodore of Tarsus, a distinguished Greek-speaking scholar from Asia Minor. Theodore had traveled to Rome and was there persuaded (no one else wanted to go) to journey on to England with a papal mandate to take up the vacant archbishopric of Canterbury. He arrived in England in 669 at the age of sixty-six, and immediately set about dividing the land into dioceses and selecting suitable bishops to rule over them. The challenges facing him were formidable. The English episcopate in the year of his arrival consisted of only three bishops: one, Wine, had purchased his position as bishop of London; the second, Chad, had been improperly consecrated as a bishop; and the third, Wilfrid, was one of the most aggressive, difficult, and self-aggrandizing men of the entire seventh century.

Of these three, Wilfrid is by far the most revealing figure.[11] Although Bede portrays him as the primary spokesman for the Roman side at Whitby, Wilfrid was anything but a team player. A Northumbrian nobleman who mirrored the values of his class in his life as a bishop, Wilfrid traveled in great style with a lordly retinue of warriors and clerics. He was exiled three times by kings who at first embraced him but soon came to fear him as a rival ruler to themselves, and he engaged throughout his life in what was in effect a feud with prominent members of the

---

[10]Patrick Wormald, "Bede, the Bretwaldas, and the Origins of the *Gens Anglorum,*" in *Ideal and Reality in Frankish and Anglo-Saxon Society: Studies Presented to J. M. Wallace-Hadrill,* ed. Patrick Wormald with Donald Bullough and Roger Collins (Oxford, 1983), pp. 99–129.

[11]On Wilfrid, see, in addition to Bede, Eddius Stephanus, "Life of St. Wilfrid," in *The Age of Bede,* tr. J. F. Webb and D. H. Farmer (New York, 1983).

Northumbrian nobility, both secular and ecclesiastical. In addition to his bishopric, he also controlled an enormous network of monasteries, ruled by his relatives and retainers. On his deathbed, he divided his possessions much as any secular warlord might have done, leaving treasures to his successors with which to purchase the friendship of those in power and funds to support the warriors in his retinue whom he had not previously provided with land. Many of his contemporaries, including Archbishop Theodore, regarded him as a menace. But to his friends and dependents, he was a powerful and saintly advocate for his churches. What was becoming clear, however, as the seventh century drew to a close, was that neither Archbishop Theodore nor the kings of Anglo-Saxon England could tolerate any longer the threat to their authority posed by independent-minded ecclesiastical warlords such as Wilfrid. Their day had passed, and in the eighth century there would be no more Wilfrids.

Theodore came to England to create a disciplined, well-organized, and hierarchical ecclesiastical structure. To a remarkable extent, he succeeded. In the course of his twenty-one-year archiepiscopacy, Theodore superimposed on the many Anglo-Saxon kingdoms a single, unified Church with clearly delineated territorial bishoprics and with ultimate administrative authority centered at Canterbury. At the synod of Hertford (672), he ordered each bishop to confine his activities to the people of his own diocese. He also prohibited monks and clergy from wandering about without the permission of their superiors. Even more importantly, he worked to create new bishops and to dismember some of the enormous dioceses that had come into existence during the course of the seventh century. Not surprisingly, he and his successor, Archbishop Berhtwald, encountered opposition. Among the most vociferous opponents — and targets — of this new policy of reducing the size of bishoprics was Wilfrid himself. But despite the resistance, Theodore of Tarsus succeeded in bringing the English Church into line with the political principles of the Roman papacy and, indirectly, the Roman Empire. He gave the English Church a degree of territorial organization and administrative centralization that contrasted sharply with the instability of the contemporary Anglo-Saxon kingdoms. Elsewhere in western Europe, the political unity of the Roman Empire underlay the spiritual unity of the Roman Church. In England, however, the unity that Theodore imposed on the Church prefigured the political unity of England itself.

Renaissance and Renewal

Theodore was a celebrated scholar who knew both Latin and Greek. He was accompanied on his journey to England by another scholar of eminence, a North African churchman named Hadrian. Together they made Canterbury a distinguished intellectual center. Theodore established a school that provided instruction in Greek and Latin letters and in the principles of Roman law. The Roman legal tradition was well preserved in Theodore's Byzantine homeland, and he introduced it into England along with his native Greek tongue. Through their wide experience and broad cultural heritage, Theodore and Hadrian brought to seventh-century Canterbury the rich intellectual legacy of the Mediterranean world.[12]

Canterbury's distinction as an intellectual center did not long survive Archbishop Theodore. It was not at Canterbury but in Northumbria that Anglo-Saxon ecclesiastical culture reached its apogee. There, at the northernmost edge of Christendom, the stimulating encounter between Celtic, Germanic, and Latin culture produced an intellectual and cultural achievement of the highest order. In Northumbria during the later seventh and early eighth centuries, Anglo-Saxon culture — and perhaps the whole of Christian culture in the early Middle Ages — reached its zenith.

One of the great patrons of this renaissance was Benedict Biscop (628–690), a Northumbrian nobleman who assumed the name "Benedict" because of his deep admiration for St. Benedict of Nursia. A man of vigor and piety and a devoted monk, Benedict Biscop made several trips to Italy and southern Gaul. During one of these trips, he accompanied Archibishop Theodore and Hadrian on their journey from Rome to England. In southern Europe, Benedict experienced the ordered life of Benedictine monasteries and collected armloads of books and precious works of art, which he brought back to his native Northumbria. He founded two neighboring Northumbrian monasteries of the strict Benedictine Rule — Wearmouth (674) and Jarrow (681) — which he filled with his books and other treasures. These two houses, which stand to this day and are open to visitors, became the center of Roman-Benedictine culture in Northumbria, while the older establishment at Lindisfarne remained the center of Irish culture.

Both cultures contributed to the renaissance in Northumbria. The impressive artistic achievements of the age were at once Irish and Anglo-Saxon in inspiration. The magnificently illuminated Lindisfarne Gospels (c. 700) display a complex, curvilinear style reminiscent of Celtic art, although the illuminator himself was probably an Anglo-Saxon whose designs reflect the traditions of both Irish and Saxon metalwork. Mediterranean influences are evident also in the portraits contained in the book. Another likely product of the interchange between Irish, Anglo-Saxon, and Mediterranean traditions in Northumbria is the Book of Kells, which, despite its name, was probably begun at Iona and taken later by monks fleeing the Vikings to the Irish monastery of Kells. Widely regarded as a masterpiece of the illuminator's art, the Book of Kells is famous for the intricacy of its design and must have employed several different artists. Curiously, given the skill and attention lavished on the

---

[12]On Canterbury, see Nicholas Brooks, *The Early History of the Church of Canterbury: Christ Church from 597 to 1066* (Leicester, 1984).

Illuminated Page from the Lindisfarne Gospels (c. 700)   Produced by an Anglo-Saxon artist, the manuscript illustrates the complex fusion of Irish, Anglo-Saxon, and Mediterranean influences that lay behind the Northumbrian renaissance. There are strong parallels between the decorative patterns in such illuminated manuscripts and in contemporary metalwork. *(Reproduced by courtesy of the Trustees of The British Museum)*

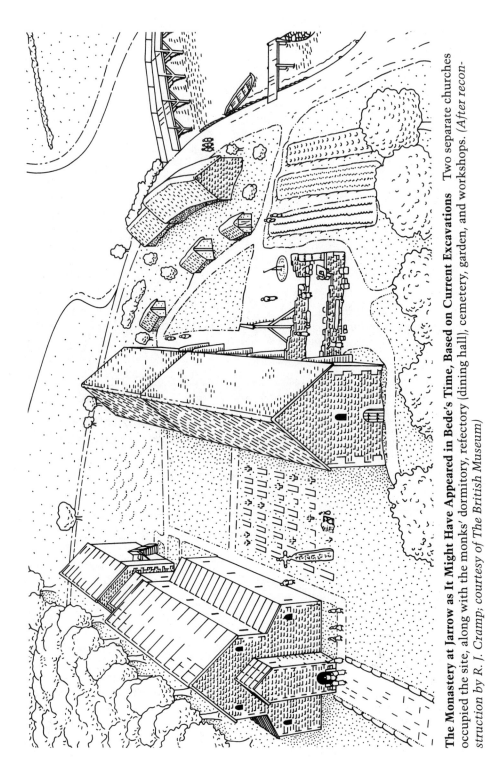

The Monastery at Jarrow as It Might Have Appeared in Bede's Time, Based on Current Excavations Two separate churches occupied the site, along with the monks' dormitory, refectory (dining hall), cemetery, garden, and workshops. *(After reconstruction by R. J. Cramp; courtesy of The British Museum)*

illustrations, the biblical text itself contains a number of errors. One scholar has suggested that because the copyist knew the book was to be used primarily for display, he chose not to pay much attention to the quality of his text.

The achievements of the Northumbrian renaissance extended to many fields: art, architecture, poetry, paleography, and manuscript illumination. But the supreme achievement of the age was the scholarship of the Venerable Bede. In the writings of Bede, particularly his *Ecclesiastical History of the English People*, the intellectual tradition of western Europe attained a level unequaled since the fall of Rome.

Bede was a product of the Benedictine tradition. He spent his life under the Benedictine Rule at Jarrow, where he was an exemplary monk. He was also a superb scholar whose investigations profited enormously from the fine library that Benedict Biscop had installed in the monastery. Bede regarded his theological writings as his most important work, but his fame in later centuries has rested primarily on his *History*. It was a pioneer effort, unprecedented in scope, and at the same time a work of remarkable maturity. Bede possessed an acute critical sense that caused him to use his historical sources with scrupulous care, evaluating their reliability and often quoting them in full. He was also the first major historian to use the Christian era as the chronological foundation for his work — to date events not in terms of kings' reigns or the old Roman calendar of indictions, but with reference to the year of Christ's birth. Bede did not originate this dating system — that honor belongs to a sixth-century monk named Dionysius Exiguus — but it was Bede's work that popularized this new and specifically Christian dating system. It is to Bede's sense of chronology and historical development, therefore, that we owe the division of history into the two eras B.C. ("Before Christ") and A.D. (*Anno Domini*, "in the year of the Lord") that western, Christian historians have utilized ever since.

Vernacular Literature

It was during Bede's time that the first literary fruits of the intersection of native and Latin culture began to appear. Anglo-Saxon England is unique among early medieval Germanic societies for its rich tradition of vernacular poetry and prose. The dates of this verse are hotly contested. Two heroic battle poems, *The Battle of Brunanburh* and *The Battle of Maldon*, must have been written after the battles they commemorate (in 937 and 991 respectively), but for the rest of Anglo-Saxon literature there is little firm evidence by which to date it. The dates proposed for the composition of the great epic poem *Beowulf*, for example, range from the seventh century up to the eleventh. It is Bede himself, however, who tells us of the first Anglo-Saxon author whose name we know: an illiterate shepherd named Caedmon, who through the special grace of God was

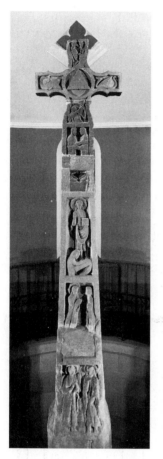

The Ruthwell Cross, Southern Scotland (Early Eighth Century)   On its face, this famous cross depicts Christ with Mary Magdalene and Christ healing a blind man; on its sides, surrounding carvings of birds in vines, are passages from *The Dream of the Rood*, carved in runes. The cross now stands 17 feet high. Although broken apart in the Reformation, it has since been reconstructed. The crossing piece is modern. *(Royal Commission on the Ancient and Historical Monuments of Scotland)*

suddenly given the gift of composing Christian hymns in the style of Anglo-Saxon songs.

If the compositional dates of this material are uncertain, however, its genius and abundant diversity cannot be questioned. Both secular and religious themes are well represented. The weariness of a bitter exile, the longing of the elderly for glories long past, the sadness of an absent love — all find expression in poems like *The Wanderer, The Seafarer, The Ruin,* and *The Wife's Lament*. The poet Deor mourns his displacement from his lord's favor by a rival; the sorrowful Hildeburh laments the deaths of her son and her brother on opposing sides of the battle at Finnsburg. Helena, mother of Constantine, sails to Palestine to find the True Cross in *Elene*; St. Andrew undertakes a holy voyage with God himself at the helm. One of the most lyrical of all early English poems is *The Dream of the Rood,* a poem in which the cross on which Jesus died speaks movingly of the glorious agony of the crucifixion and resurrection. Some Anglo-Saxon poems are based on Latin originals or reflect elements of continental tradition; some show evidence of acquaintance with classical authors such as Eusebius. But many are works of original genius, reflecting an extraordinary and creative fusion between Anglo-Saxon and continental Christian culture.

There are also word games and riddles, some of which were surely conceived of as humorous. Delicacy forbids the quotation of some of these riddles — modern people are not the only ones to take pleasure in the occasional sexual double-entendre! But the following is a printable example of the genre as a whole:

> My house is not quiet, I am not loud;
> But for us God fashioned our fate together.
> I am the swifter, at times the stronger,
> My house more enduring, longer to last.
> At times I rest; my dwelling still runs;
> Within it I lodge as long as I live.
> Should we two be severed, my death is sure.[13]

Those who guessed "fish" were right!

And then there is *Beowulf* itself, one of the finest pieces of sustained vernacular literature to survive from western Europe in the early Middle Ages. *Beowulf* is named for its hero, a great Geatish warrior who goes to the aid of the Danish king Hrothgar. Beowulf delivers Hrothgar and his people from the attacks of a fierce monster named Grendel and then from Grendel's revenge-seeking mother. Eventually, Beowulf returns home and becomes king of the Geats, but after many years of successful kingship he seeks out battle with yet another monster, a dragon guarding a great treasure hidden in a barrow. Although Beowulf wins the battle and captures the treasure, the dragon wounds him so severely that Beowulf dies. The poem ends with the cremation of Beowulf's body and the burial of his ashes beneath a large mound, along with the treasure Beowulf had died to win. As they mourn his death, the Geats also realize that, with their king gone, their days of peace as a people are now at an end. In its stirring evocation of heroic values and its sophisticated musings on kingship and fate, *Beowulf* encapsulates the best aspects of the reconciliation of native and Christian culture. It retains its power to move even a modern audience.

Missions to the Continent

During the eighth century, the dynamic Christian culture of England also made its impact on the continent of Europe, as Anglo-Saxon missionaries[14]

---

[13]From *An Anthology of Old English Poetry*, by Charles W. Kennedy. Copyright © 1960 by Oxford University Press, Inc. *Used by permission of Oxford University Press, Inc.*

[14]On these Anglo-Saxon missionary campaigns, see Fletcher, *The Barbarian Conversion* (as in note 5 above), and the classic work by Wilhelm Levison, *England and the Continent in the Eighth Century* (Oxford, 1946). There are useful translated sources in *The Anglo-Saxon Missionaries in Germany*, ed. C. H. Talbot (London, 1954).

and scholars reinvigorated the Frankish Church and spread Latin civilization and the Christian gospel among the pagan Germanic peoples east of the Rhine.

The most famous of these Anglo-Saxon missionaries was the West Saxon monk, St. Boniface (675?–754). Working under the general direction of the papacy and supplied with books and assistants by his supporters in Wessex, Boniface represented three of the most dynamic forces of his day: the papacy, the Benedictine order, and the ecclesiastical culture of Anglo-Saxon England. During the 740s, Boniface devoted himself to the regeneration of the Frankish Church, reforming monasteries and reconstructing Frankish diocesan organization on the disciplined pattern that Theodore of Tarsus had established in England. It was Boniface who, in 751, anointed Pepin, the first of the Carolingian kings of France, and it was the reformed Frankish Church Boniface helped to create that nurtured the impressive cultural achievements of Charlemagne's reign a generation later. Other English monks, most notably the great Northumbrian scholar Alcuin, went on to play a decisive role in the revival of Latin learning known as the Carolingian renaissance.

St. Boniface also committed himself to the immense undertaking of Christianizing the peoples of Germany. The task was far too great for a single person or a single generation to accomplish, but Boniface made a promising beginning. Among the several Benedictine houses that he founded in Germany was the monastery of Fulda, which, like Wearmouth and Jarrow in Northumbria, became a major intellectual and evangelical center. Boniface devoted himself particularly to the conversion of the Saxons, Hessians, and Frisians, peoples with whom the Saxons of England felt a special affinity, and whose language was sufficiently similar to Boniface's own West Saxon dialect to be mutually comprehensible. This may not have been an unqualified advantage, for it was at the hands of the Frisians that the aged Boniface died a martyr's death in 754.

Many of Boniface's supporters in England were nuns, who supplied him not only with financial and spiritual support, but also with copies of books. Boniface also brought religious women with him from Anglo-Saxon England to Germany to assist in the work of conversion, including his own cousin, St. Leoba, whose extraordinary knowledge of the Bible, combined with her robust common sense and personal sanctity, made her an influential advisor to the bishops and monks whom Boniface helped to establish in Germany.[15]

In assessing the impact of Christianization upon Anglo-Saxon England, the importance of these religious women should not pass unremarked.[16] Especially for aristocratic and royal women, Christian monasti-

---

[15]"Life of St. Leoba," in *Anglo-Saxon Missionaries*, ed. Talbot, pp. 203–226.

[16]The insights of Karl Leyser, *Rule and Conflict in an Early Medieval Kingdom: Ottonian Saxony* (Bloomington, 1979), pp. 63–73, are an indispensible starting point for thinking about these issues in Anglo-Saxon England also.

cism opened up an entirely new avenue through which they could exercise authority and power within their societies. An extraordinary number of such women founded and ruled convents during the seventh century. Many, including St. Hild's convent at Whitby, were in fact "double monasteries," in which a female abbess — usually a member of one of the kingdom's royal families — ruled over a house of religious women and a separate, linked house of religious men. As abbesses, these royal women produced no potential heirs to the throne. From the point of view of their male relatives, this was one of the great advantages of having them become nuns. But such abbesses also controlled large amounts of property and substantial financial and military resources, which they could make available (or, with risk, deny) to the male heads of their dynasties. As holy women, removed from the daily conflicts around the court, they were also well placed to exercise influence over the succession to the throne of their respective kingdoms. By the eighth century, the great days of the royal abbesses were passing, as the Church came more tightly under the control of kings and bishops. But as Boniface's career demonstrates, nuns continued to play a very important role in the life of the English Church up until the Viking invasions of the ninth century.

Northumbrian missionaries also participated in the work of evangelism on the Continent. St. Wilfrid, for example, had been active in missionary work across the Channel long before Boniface undertook his mission. St. Willibrord, another Northumbrian, had been archbishop in Frisia for twenty-four years before Boniface arrived there in 719. But even more influential than Northumbrian missionaries were the traditions of Northumbrian learning established by Benedict Biscop and Bede. The cathedral school at York, headed by Bede's pupil, Archbishop Egbert (732–766), had possibly the finest library in eighth-century northern Europe. This school, and the tradition of learning it represented, was carried on by Egbert's successor at York, Archbishop Elbert (766–780), and also by Egbert's student, Alcuin, whom Charlemagne brought from Northumbria to Francia to head his own court school in 782. From there, this tradition of Northumbrian scholarship would be carried throughout the Carolingian world.

At the end of the eighth century, however, this tradition of learning in Northumbria came to a sudden end. Viking raiders sacked Lindisfarne in 793, Jarrow in 794, and Iona in 802. Sixty years later, another Viking army destroyed the great cathedral library at York. But before its demise in the north, the ecclesiastical culture of Northumbria had spread its creative influence broadly among the Franks and Germans, and from the court of Charlemagne it would spread across all of Europe.

Kingship and Power in Early Anglo-Saxon England

In a famous passage, the late-first-century C.E. Roman historian Tacitus reports that the Germans of his day maintained a sharp distinction between kings and warlords. Kingship, says Tacitus, descended within specific royal dynasties, but its essential features were sacral and symbolic. Kings were the embodiment of their peoples; if they ruled properly, the rains would come, the crops would grow, and their people would prosper. If the rains did not come, or other natural disasters struck, these were signs of improper kingship, and kings might be deposed or even killed. Leadership in war was reserved for a separate class of men, not kings at all, and only tenuously bound to them. Tribes generally had several warlords, a fact that for Tacitus helped to explain the notorious fractiousness of the German people. Fiercely independent but incapable of uniting among themselves, the Germans seemed to him dangerous but manageable enemies, who could generally be bought off by the corrupting influence of Roman bribes and luxuries.

It is not at all clear how far to rely on Tacitus in describing even the Germans of his own day. Much of what he writes in his *Germania* is too obviously intended as a moralizing sermon to his Roman readers for it to inspire trust as reliable reportage about the Germans. There are scraps of evidence to suggest, however, that when the Anglo-Saxons first conquered Britain in the fifth and sixth centuries, they were led by warlords who were not descended from anciently established royal lines; and that when more stable Anglo-Saxon kingdoms began to be established, at least some of these peoples imported royal dynasties to rule over them. In other cases, successful warlords were able to establish their royal and sacral credentials by the very fact of their victories: for what surer sign of the gods' approval could there be than success in war? What matters, for our purposes, is not the origins of Anglo-Saxon kingship, but the fact that, in the sixth and even the seventh centuries, kingship was still a relatively new and rapidly evolving institution among the peoples of Anglo-Saxon England.[17]

This may help to explain the extraordinary fluidity of political power in this world. Bede recounts, for example, that there were seven kings whose power had extended over the greater part of the island of Britain: Aelle of Sussex (late fifth century?); Caewlin of Wessex (d. 591/2); Ethelbert of Kent (d. 616); Redwald of East Anglia (d. 627); Edwin of Northumbria (d. 633); Oswald of Northumbria (d. 642); and Oswy of Northumbria (d. 671). In the late ninth century, the West Saxon *Anglo-Saxon Chronicle* would copy this list, calling these kings *bretwaldas* ("rulers of Britain") or *brytenwaldas* ("wide rulers," roughly akin to "emperors") and adding an eighth name, Egbert of Wessex (802–839), to the list.[18] What strikes one immediately about Bede's list, however, is the speed

---

[17]J. M. Wallace-Hadrill, *Early Germanic Kingship in England and on the Continent* (Oxford, 1971).

[18]Eric John, *Orbis Britanniae and Other Studies* (Leicester, 1966), pp. 7–8; and Wormald, "Bede, the Bretwaldas" (as in note 10 above).

with which political dominance passed from king to king and from king-dom to kingdom. One observes the same rapid ebb and flow of power within the history of individual kingdoms. Rarely did kingship pass un-challenged from a father to a son; more often, it oscillated between com-peting dynasties, with the heirs of the losing dynasty fleeing into exile until the death of the victor provided them the opportunity to return. Nor was any monopoly on the title "king" exercised by the rulers of the largest kingdoms of sixth- and seventh-century England, the so-called "Heptarchy" of East Anglia, Essex, Kent, Mercia, Northumbria, Sussex, and Wessex. Below these kings there were other kings, ruling smaller ter-ritories or peoples, and below them yet more kings, and more kings be-low that. Like early medieval Ireland, early Anglo-Saxon England was a land in which there were hierarchies of kingliness. But in England, un-like Ireland, there was no firm dividing line between men who had a claim to be a king of some kind, and all other men who had no such claim to royal status. In England, therefore, men who were regarded as kings by the residents of their own tiny kingdoms (some as small as fifteen or twenty square miles) might not be recognized as kings by greater rulers.

One of the other striking features about royal power in sixth- and sev-enth-century England is the very wide geographical expanse over which it could be exercised. Bede claims that Edwin exercised dominion not only over all the kings of England (except for Kent), but also over the kings of Wales. Oswy, Bede claims, had all this plus dominion over the kings of the Scots and Picts too. Kings often fought battles far from the centers of their authority: Northumbrian kings raided in Wessex, and West Saxon kings raided in Northumbria. It is not easy to conceive how such far-flung campaigns could have been aimed at conquest, if we understand conquest to mean the incorporation of the geographical territory of one kingdom into that of another. One further feature of kingship in this pe-riod is how easily it seems to have been divisible. Bede tells of kings who split their kingdoms, but more interestingly, he also tells of kings who ruled together over a single kingdom. How could such arrangements work? What did they mean?

The larger kingdoms of the sixth and seventh centuries were not really territorial entities with boundaries (hence our reluctance in this book to speak of the "Heptarchy," except in quotation marks), but rather spheres of influence, within which a king's importance was relatively more intense. Royal rule was not so much the ability to command and legislate over a territory, but rather, first and foremost, control over trib-ute-rendering centers in the countryside. Kingship in early Anglo-Saxon England was a form of lordship. Like other forms of lordship, successful kingship depended on a king's ability to cement the loyalty of his mili-tary following through the giving of gifts: horses, weapons, jewelry, and land. Some of these treasures — like the gold and garnet belt buckles of Sutton Hoo, or the pattern-welded swords described in *Beowulf* — could be manufactured. That is one reason why it was so important for kings to control craftsmen. But much of it simply had to be taken from others who already possessed it and were not inclined to give it up. That is why raiding and plundering were such essential aspects of kingship in these centuries.

Raiding had another purpose, however: to secure control over the structures of agricultural lordship in the countryside. Across much of England, peasant landholders were organized into coordinated agricultural and economic units, which owed assigned rents and work services to a common, central place. The terms used for many of these assigned dues and services are Celtic, not Anglo-Saxon, suggesting that the origins of this system may lie in the Roman (or perhaps even the pre-Roman) period. We know about this system only because elements of it survived to be recorded in the great eleventh-century land register known as *Domesday Book*. What *Domesday Book* reveals, however, is that with striking regularity the central places where rents and services were paid were (or had once been) royal vills.

If we think, therefore, about royal rule in the sixth and seventh centuries as consisting of control over these central places, it becomes easier to understand the hierarchies of kingliness that characterized sixth- and seventh-century political society. A very small king might control only a few such tribute-rendering vills; a larger king might control more; and a yet larger king, yet more. The position of an overking could be acknowledged by allowing him a portion of the rents taken by an underking from his vills, or else by the direct payment to him of tribute, in the form of produce, cattle, honey, slaves, or silver. Imagining such a world, we can also understand better how kingdoms could be ruled jointly by two or more kings, because what was being divided was not sovereignty over a territory, but control over a collection of tribute-rendering centers. It also becomes possible to understand how the kings of this period could hope to rule over so much more of the island of Britain than did subsequent kings of England.

There are interesting parallels here with the Church. Through most of the seventh century, the bishops of Anglo-Saxon England were identified with the peoples over whom they ruled and with the kings who supported them in their missionary efforts. Kings, in turn, spoke freely of "so and so, my bishop." Wilfrid was, as usual, an extreme example of this pattern. At various times, he was bishop of the Northumbrians, bishop of the West Saxons, bishop of the South Saxons, and abbot/ruler of an extensive monastic empire in Northumbria and Mercia. Starting with Archbishop Theodore, however, the English bishops became increasingly territorialized. Diocesan boundaries were established, and bishops forbidden to exercise their authority outside their own dioceses. Anglo-Saxon kingship would follow the same path. During the eighth and ninth centuries, it too would become increasingly territorialized, and more and more like the kind of kingship we are accustomed to imagining. These developments were pioneered in Mercia, but it was in Wessex that they came to their fullest development.

Toward Political Consolidation: Mercia

During the seventh and eighth centuries, royal power was gradually consolidated into a handful of kingdoms. The smaller kingdoms of earlier years were more and more thoroughly subordinated to the larger ones until, by the later seventh century, three kingdoms — Northumbria, Mercia, and Wessex — overshadowed the others. To speak very generally, Northumbria was the leading Anglo-Saxon kingdom in the seventh century, Mercia in the eighth, and Wessex in the ninth and tenth.

The epoch of Northumbrian hegemony is celebrated in the pages of Bede's *History*, and the great days of Wessex are recorded in the writings of King Alfred the Great's court and in the *Anglo-Saxon Chronicle*. Mercia left to posterity no impressive scholarly works and no history of its age of greatness. The power of Mercia's eighth-century kings cannot be denied, but local patriotism prevented both the Northumbrian Bede and the later West Saxon authors of the *Anglo-Saxon Chronicle* from portraying the achievements of the rival Mercian kingdom sympathetically. We must therefore use these sources with caution and beware of underestimating the sophistication of the Mercian kings or the creativity of Mercian culture.

Mercia's political and military power was impressive indeed. Even Northumbria in its greatest days lived under an almost constant Mercian threat. Mercia's powerful pagan monarch, Penda, challenged Northumbrian hegemony more than once in the seventh century, defeating and killing King Edwin in 633 and King Oswald in 642 before being killed himself in battle against King Oswy in 655. During much of his reign, Penda exerted an authority over the kingdoms south of the Humber exceeding that of all earlier southern kings. By the end of his reign, he had absorbed a number of smaller neighboring subkingdoms and had asserted his supremacy over both Wessex and East Anglia. Although never a Christian himself, Penda fought frequently in alliance with the Christian kings of Wales and took steps to ensure that his sons would grow up as Christians.

Penda's son Wulfhere (658–674) continued his father's drive for control of southern England. Establishing dominion over Essex and London, he intimidated Wessex and secured control over Kent and Sussex. At his death, he was endeavoring to subdue Northumbria. Had he succeeded, he would have enjoyed virtually uncontested authority over all of England.

The growth of Mercian power stalled for a half-century after Wulfhere's death owing to the resurgence of Wessex, particularly during the reign of its able king Ine (688–726). For a time, Sussex, Essex, and Kent passed from Mercian into West Saxon control. It was obvious by now that these smaller kingdoms were too weak to maintain their independence. The only remaining question was which of the two neighboring "superpowers," Mercia or Wessex, would dominate them. During most of the eighth century, Mercia not only asserted its dominion over these states but usually managed to dominate Wessex as well.

ENGLAND IN THE EIGHTH AND NINTH CENTURIES

+   Assemblies of most southern bishops under Mercian kings
  Locations unverified:
  Acleah 805
  Clofesho 794, 798, 803, 824, 825

▲   Wics and places where tolls are known to have been taken

✩   Battles affecting Mercian supremacy

✦   Viking attacks before 865

▪▪▪▪   Line of Offa's Dyke

KENT   Kingdoms or sub-kingdoms

PICTS

DALRIADA

STRATHCLYDE

R. Tweed

Lindisfarne 793

NORTHUMBRIA

Tyne   Tynemouth 800
Jarrow 794

York

Humber

LINDSEY

R. Mersey

POWYS   Dee

MERCIA   Trent

Repton

Wrekin 855
Tamworth 799
+   + Croft 836   • Witham

Severn

▲ Droitwich   Northampton •   Ouse

Wye

HWICCE   ESSEX

Hereford   EAST ANGLIA

Ipswich

Burford 752   Brentford Chelsea 781 785–86–88–89–93, 801, 816

Kempsford 802   Bensington 779   Sheppey 835, 855
Wantage   London 842, 851   Thanet 851, 853, 864
Wroughton 825   Sarre
   Rochester 842   Fordwich
Thames   Otford 776   Canterbury 851

Cheddar   KENT 851

Carhampton 836, 848   Parrett 845   Winchester 860   Romney March 841   Sandwich 845
WESSEX   Hamwith 840, 842   SUSSEX
Dorchester •

Portland 786–802   Isle of Wight
Trewhiddle

Scale of Miles
0   25   50

James Campbell, ed., *The Anglo-Saxons.* Copyright © 1982.

Mercian supremacy in the eighth century resulted from the intelligent exploitation of its strategic position and considerable resources by two adroit, long-lived kings: Ethelbald (716–757) and Offa (757–796). Under their leadership, Mercia dominated the midlands, exacting allegiance and probably tribute from the kingdoms to the south and east. Ethelbald described himself in a charter as "king of all Britain," and the royal boast was not far from the truth.

The reality of Mercian power comes to light in a contemporary document known as the Tribal Hidage — a comprehensive assessment schedule for tribute payments claimed by the seventh- or eighth-century Mercian kings from a large number of kingdoms in southern and central England, including Wessex. In the early days of the Anglo-Saxon settlements, the term *hide* meant a unit of land sufficient to support the household of a single warrior. By the time of the Tribal Hidage, however, and certainly by the time of Bede (d. 735), the hide had already become an abstract unit of land assessment. In centuries to come, royal governments would exact taxes and military service from their subjects on the basis of the number of hides of land that each subject held. The fact that the Mercian monarchy produced a document enumerating the hidage assessments of most of the Anglo-Saxon peoples south of the Humber testifies to an administrative system of unprecedented scale — both predatory and sophisticated.

The reigns of Ethelbald and Offa witnessed not only an unparalleled degree of political power but also of commercial activity. King Offa's minters produced millions of high quality silver pennies, the weight and fineness of which was closely aligned with the contemporary coinage of Charlemagne. The importance of trade between Offa's kingdom and the empire of Charlemagne is further demonstrated by a remarkable exchange of letters between these two monarchs. In it, Charlemagne addresses Offa in these words:

> You have written to us about merchants, and by our mandate we allow that they shall have protection and support in our kingdom, lawfully, according to the ancient custom of trading. And if in any place they are afflicted by wrongful oppression, they may appeal to us or to our judges and we will then order true justice to be done. Similarly our men, if they suffer any injustice in your dominion, are to appeal to the judgement of your equity, lest any disturbance should arise anywhere between our men.[19]

It is noteworthy that English merchants were sufficiently active on the Continent at this time to require a formal arrangement between the two rulers. Perhaps even more significant is the fact that Offa should take such a broad view of his royal responsibilities as to intervene on behalf of English traders abroad. In Offa's hands, Anglo-Saxon kingship was assuming new and larger dimensions.

Many details of Offa's reign are hidden by a lack of historical evidence. He has rightly been termed the most obscure great monarch of Anglo-Saxon England. As one historian wrote, "We can be sure that Offa was a crucial figure in the development of Anglo-Saxon institutions, without being able to find out exactly what he did."[20] Alcuin wrote to

---

[19]*English Historical Documents, Volume I*, ed. Dorothy Whitelock, 2nd ed. (London, 1979), no. 197, p. 848.

[20]John, *Orbis Britanniae*, p. 35.

Offa from the Continent, praising him for being "intent on education, that the light of wisdom, which is now extinguished in many places, may shine in your kingdom,"[21] but we lack the details of Offa's educational program. A century after Offa's death, King Alfred of Wessex spoke respectfully of his laws, but the laws themselves have perished.[22] No contemporary history of his reign survives nor is there any celebration of his deeds. But we do know that Offa considerably widened the limits of the Mercian kingdom and the scope of Mercian royal authority. He advanced his power westward at Welsh expense by sealing off Wales with an immense earthen embankment up to twenty-five feet in height known as Offa's Dyke. The earthwork stretched nearly 150 miles — longer than Hadrian's Wall and the Antonine Wall combined — and was paralleled on the Welsh side by a ditch six feet deep. Recent excavations suggest that at least parts of the earthwork were topped by a stone wall. The resources necessary to construct Offa's Dyke were immense: tens of thousands of workers must have labored for years upon the project. One scholar aptly described it as "the largest archaeological monument in Britain" and "the most impressive monument of this type ever constructed by a known European king."[23]

Offa's Dyke was not, however, the only major monument erected during the Mercian hegemony. Excavations conducted between 1973 and 1986 at Repton, the site of a major Mercian religious center, unearthed what seems to be a great eighth-century stone mausoleum for the Mercian kings and high nobility — later taken over by the Vikings for mass burials. And in the center of the modern city of Northampton (in old Mercia), archaeologists have excavated the foundations of a vast timber hall of the eighth century, almost identical in scale to King Edwin's hall at Yeavering in Northumbria. Even more striking, the foundations of a second hall have been discovered on the same site, a massive structure of the late eighth or early ninth century — late in Offa's reign, perhaps — built entirely of stone. It would appear to be the first stone hall in Britain since Roman times; it measures some 123 feet long, 25 feet longer than the royal hall at Yeavering. Its vast dimensions and its stone construction make it an appropriate symbol of the Mercian monarchy at the height of its power.

In his quest for Mercian hegemony, Offa attempted also to reshape the hierarchical pattern that Archbishop Theodore of Tarsus had earlier imposed on the English Church. Under Theodore, the archbishopric of

---

[21]*English Historical Documents, Volume 1*, ed. Whitelock, no. 195, p. 846.

[22]Unless, as has been recently argued, Offa's laws are to be identified with the decrees sent to England by Pope Hadrian I in 786: see Patrick Wormald, "In Search of King Offa's 'Law-Code,'" in *Peoples and Places in Northern Europe, 500–1600*, ed. I. Wood and N. Lund (Woodbridge, 1991), pp. 25–45.

[23]Patrick Wormald, in *The Anglo-Saxons*, ed. James Campbell (Oxford, 1982), pp. 120, 101.

Canterbury had stood unchallenged at the apex of the hierarchy, but in 735 the pope established a second archbishopric at York in Northumbria, less venerable than Canterbury but nevertheless a potential rival. King Offa demanded a separate archbishopric for Mercia, and accordingly, in 787, a new archbishopric emerged at Lichfield. Shortly after Offa's death, however, the Lichfield archbishopric faded into oblivion, and thereafter the English Church was dominated by its two remaining archbishoprics of Canterbury and York.

The Church was active during Offa's reign. A papal legation came to England in 786 — the first since Augustine's time — and Offa himself contributed to poor relief in Rome. General councils of the English Church continued to meet in Offa's realm, and, at a lower level, country parishes were beginning to take shape. The development of an effective parish system, which would be the task of centuries, was of immense importance to both Church and society in the early Middle Ages. The Church had emerged from the highly urbanized Roman Empire with a diocesan organization based on the city. With the disintegration of Roman imperial society, the cities declined, but several centuries elapsed before the Church in western Europe adjusted its organization to the needs of the rural society in which it now worked. Peasants and small freeholders often were obliged to go many months without seeing a priest or attending Mass. Ultimately, the answer to this problem was the country parish, administered by a priest who was supported by the enforced tithes of his parishioners. Not until the twelfth century, however, did the parish system reach full development in England. In Offa's England, pastoral care in the countryside was more often carried on from large, usually monastic churches known as "minsters." These minsters were frequently located in or near royal vills, and from them priests and deacons fanned out into the countryside to attend to their spiritual flocks.[24]

In both ecclesiastical and secular affairs, Offa's regime marked a crucial stage in the development of Anglo-Saxon kingship. By the closing decade of his reign, he was issuing royal charters granting or confirming lands and privileges across much of England south of the Humber. The royal dynasties of Sussex, Essex, East Anglia, and Kent had succumbed to the expanding power of Mercia. The Mercian monarchy was transforming the vague overlordship exercised by earlier Anglo-Saxon kings into a direct control over its subject kingdoms. With the Northumbrian monarchy beset by civil war and Mercian authority extending across almost all of southern England, Offa's England attained a degree of political cohesion such as the Anglo-Saxons had never before experienced.

---

[24]*Pastoral Care Before the Parish*, ed. John Blair and Richard Sharpe (Leicester, 1992); John Blair, "Debate: Ecclesiastical Organization and Pastoral Care in Anglo-Saxon England," *Early Medieval Europe* 4 (1995): 193–212, provides references to the recent literature.

Toward Political Consolidation: Wessex

Notwithstanding their impressive achievements, the eighth-century Mercian kings fell short of giving England political unity. After Offa's death in 796, the Mercian crown passed to his able successor, Cenwulf (796–821), whose influence on Wessex and Northumbria diminished but who continued to dominate Kent and East Anglia and to advance against the Welsh. Cenwulf's brother Ceolwulf (821–823) extended the pressure on Wales, but thereafter the Mercian monarchy suffered from short-lived or inept kings and bitter dynastic rivalries. Despite their enormous power, the eighth-century Mercian kings never succeeded in establishing a single royal dynasty. Only Offa was succeeded by his son, and this son, Egfrith, died five months after his father, to be succeeded by a man (Cenwulf) who was at best a very distant cousin, and may have been no relative at all.[25] Conflict over the Mercian throne intensified during the ninth century, as two and sometimes three competing families fought for the throne. Viking invasions from the 850s onwards only exacerbated the chaos by providing the competing royal claimants with new allies in their struggles for the throne.[26]

It was the gifted King Egbert of Wessex (802–839) who won for his kingdom the hegemony that Mercia had so long enjoyed. At the battle of Ellendon in 825, he routed the Mercian army and gained control over the lesser kingdoms of southern England — Kent, Sussex, and Essex. Shortly afterward, he won the submission of East Anglia and, very grudgingly, Northumbria. For a brief time, he ruled even in Mercia itself. Egbert's power was impressive, although less so than Offa's. But unlike the Mercian kings, Egbert was able to solve the succession issue. His success was sufficient to establish his family as the sole legitimate kings of Wessex and to allow him to hand on his throne to his son Aethelwulf. Aethelwulf had four sons, who succeeded each other in turn. The last of these sons, King Alfred, then established his own descendants as the legitimate royal line by excluding the children of his elder brothers from the throne. Alfred thus managed to leave the throne to his own son Edward, who left it to his son Athelstan, and so on, more or less, throughout the rest of the tenth century. Egbert's reign was thus the beginning of a long epoch from which the West Saxon monarchy, tempered by the fires of a terrifying Viking invasion, would emerge as the rulers of a single, united English kingdom.

The Viking Age and the Birth of the English Monarchy

The era of Mercian ascendancy corresponded approximately to the period in which Charlemagne and his predecessors expanded the power of the

---

[25]Patrick Wormald, in *The Anglo-Saxons*, ed. Campbell, pp. 115, 138.

[26]On the Vikings, see *The Oxford Illustrated History of the Vikings*, ed. Peter Sawyer (Oxford, 1997); and Peter Sawyer, *Kings and Vikings: Scandinavia and Europe AD 700–1100* (London, 1982).

Frankish kingdom to such an extent that it embraced virtually all of continental western Christendom. We have already noted the important intellectual developments at Charlemagne's court and the role played by the Northumbrian Alcuin in the Carolingian renaissance. The hegemony of Wessex, on the other hand, coincided with the decline of the Carolingian Empire and the coming of the Viking Age.

Traveling from their Scandinavian homeland in long ships, the Vikings pillaged and conquered far and wide across northern Europe and the Atlantic. They subjected the Franks and Germans to fierce harassment, established a powerful dynasty in Russia, raided Islamic Spain, founded the principal cities of Ireland, settled Iceland, and even established a settlement on the coast of North America. Although the reasons for the Viking irruption are a matter of scholarly dispute, certain contributing factors suggest themselves. A steady rise in population, combined with political consolidation in Scandinavia, may have prompted adventurers (and exiled troublemakers) to seek their fortunes and satisfy their land hunger abroad. Innovations in Viking shipbuilding also added significantly to the mobility of these warriors. Even Charlemagne may have contributed to the future debacle. By conquering the Frisians, a maritime people who lived along the northern shores of Europe east of the Rhine, Charlemagne pushed his borders to the edges of the Scandinavian world and brought the Vikings into even closer contact with the Carolingian world. The revival of trade Charlemagne sponsored — and particularly the silver trade that flowed north from the Muslim empire of the Abbasids through Russia into the Baltic and the Rhineland — also brought Scandinavian traders and merchants into the center of northern European economic life. When that silver trade dried up during the ninth century, as a result of disorder in both the Abbasid and the Carolingian empires, the Vikings turned from trading to raiding on a massive scale.[27]

Trading and raiding were mutually reinforcing Viking activities. Frequently, Vikings traded in one place what they captured by raiding in another. One suspects, indeed, that small Viking raiding parties often waited to make a decision between raiding and trading until they had had a chance to inspect the local defenses. In the late 780s or 790s, for example, three Viking ships put into the English port of Dorchester, on the southwest coast of Wessex. The king's reeve rode down to meet them, presuming they were traders, and intending to collect tolls from them. The reeve guessed wrong. The Vikings slew him and sacked the town. Had the reeve met these visitors with a small army at his back, however, perhaps this Viking party would have revealed themselves to be traders after all.

The Viking invasions of the ninth and tenth centuries were thus driven not only by internal Scandinavian conditions. They were also a

---

[27]Richard Hodges and David Whitehouse, *Mohammed, Charlemagne, and the Origins of Europe: Archaeology and the Pirenne Thesis* (London, 1983).

The Gokstad Viking Ship   This remarkable ship was unearthed in 1880 from a burial site near Oslo, where it is now in the University Museum. Built of overlapping oak planks, its keel measures sixty feet; its overall length exceeds seventy-six feet. It would have been powered by both oars and a sail. Modern replicas of such Viking ships have demonstrated their extraordinary seaworthiness again and again. A replica of this ship, built in 1893, crossed the Atlantic from Norway in twenty-eight days. *(The Viking Ship Museum, Oslo, Norway/ The Bridgeman Art Library)*

response to the endemic disorder and the resulting military weakness of contemporary France, England, and Ireland by a group of people thoroughly knowledgeable about their world and prepared to take advantage of the opportunities it offered.

Organized into small groups of ships' crews, with some thirty to sixty warriors per ship, the Vikings had the immense advantage of mobility and surprise over their more numerous, sedentary victims. At first confining themselves to plundering expeditions, they later turned to conquest and settlement. Norwegian Vikings attacked Ireland, established several major cities, and founded a kingdom at Dublin that would last for several generations. A closely related group of Norse set up a sister kingdom in northern England, centered upon the old Roman city of York, known to the Vikings as Jorvik. Another Viking band established a permanent settlement in northern France at the mouth of the River Seine. Its ruler, a Viking chieftain named Rollo, adopted Christianity and received official recognition by the Frankish king, Charles the Simple, around 911. This settlement on the Seine evolved and expanded in later years into a powerful duchy known as Normandy (the land of the Northmen, or "Normans"), which gradually assimilated French culture,

To Greenland
and North America

THE NINTH-CENTURY VIKING WORLD

Scale of Miles
0   200   400

ICELAND

874

Faeroes
800

Shetlands
700

ATLANTIC
OCEAN

VIKINGS

NORTH
SEA

Novgorod
820

Volga R.

DANELAW

866–878

Dublin
839

841–884

Hamburg

Oder R.

Vistula R.

Kiev
882 *Dnieper R.*

WESSEX

Elbe R.

NORMANDY

Rouen

Seine R. Paris

Aachen

Rhine R.

Tours

Loire R.

847–865

843–882

896–911

Bordeaux

Santiago

Danube R.

907 941

866   BLACK SEA

Marseilles   Nice

Fraxinetum

Barcelona

Rome

Constantinople

Tagus R.

Lisbon
844

Valencia

Balearics

Sardinia

Seville 844

859–861

Sicily

MEDITERRANEAN SEA

From Mortimar Chambers, Raymond Grew, David Herlihy, Theodore K. Rabb, and Isser Woloch, *The Western Experience*, 6th ed., © 1995 The McGraw-Hill Companies. *Reprinted by permission of The McGraw-Hill Companies.*

French institutions, and the French language. The establishment of the Norman duchy went unmarked in English annals at the time, but Normandy would play a crucial role in England's later history.[28]

Midway through the ninth century, Viking attacks on England began to change from plundering expeditions to campaigns of conquest. In 850, a large group of Danish Vikings spent the winter on the Isle of Thanet (off the north coast of Kent, near the mouth of the Thames) rather than returning home at the close of the raiding season. In 865 a Danish host numbering in the thousands, known as the "Great Army," transformed the character of the Viking wars. A series of bloody and highly successful campaigns won them virtually all of England outside Wessex. Apart from an isolated section of northern Northumbria, the kingdoms and subkingdoms that had survived the eras of Northumbrian, Mercian and West Saxon hegemony all perished. By the end of the ninth century, only the West Saxon monarchy survived.

---

[28]The standard work on Viking-age Normandy is David Bates, *Normandy Before 1066* (London, 1982).

In the wake of these conquests, Danish settlers arrived in such numbers as to change permanently the social and institutional complexion of large areas of England. These areas of Danish settlement and occupation, later known as the Danelaw, included (1) Yorkshire (southern Northumbria), where the most intensive immigration occurred; (2) East Anglia; and (3) a large tract of central and eastern Mercia that came to be known as the Five Boroughs, after its five chief centers of settlement — Lincoln, Stamford, Nottingham, Leicester, and Derby. Nor were the Five Boroughs isolated examples of the Viking connection with towns. Vikings were also responsible for establishing the boroughs of Ireland, including Waterford, Wexford, Dublin, Limerick, and Cork. In England, Norwich may also have been a Viking foundation. Elsewhere in East Anglia, Vikings were probably responsible for introducing the manufacture of Ipswich ware, the highest quality pottery produced in Britain since the fourth century. Recent archaeological excavations at Coppergate in York have revealed the outlines of the Viking city of Jorvik. Like many Viking towns, Jorvik proves to have been a manufacturing center as well as a trading port, producing metalwork, leatherwork, and a variety of other small crafts.[29]

Alfred the Great

In 870, Viking efforts to conquer Wessex began in earnest. That these efforts were ultimately dashed is, to a remarkable degree, the achievement of a single man, King Egbert's grandson, Alfred the Great (871–899).[30] Alfred was a monarch of many talents — a warrior, an administrator, a diplomat, a devotee of Christian learning, and a singularly persuasive leader. On one of the excellent silver pennies coined by Alfred's mints, he is styled *rex Anglorum*, "king of the English," suggesting that Alfred and his contemporaries were aware of the political transformation to which his reign contributed so decisively: the evolution of the West Saxon monarchy into the English monarchy. Indeed, the legend on the coin obviously constituted a piece of royal propaganda contributing toward that evolution.

Alfred's accession came at a desperate moment in Anglo-Saxon history. In 872, he was obliged to purchase a truce from the Danes in order to gain time to put his defenses in order. During this brief intermission, he took the initial steps toward a thorough reorganization of the West

[29]Helen Clarke and Bjorn Ambrosiani, *Towns in the Viking Age* (New York, 1991), is a good survey.

[30]The best introduction to Alfred's reign is provided by *Alfred the Great: Asser's Life of King Alfred and Other Contemporary Sources*, ed. and tr. Simon Keynes and Michael Lapidge (New York, 1983). An excellent recent biography is Richard Abels, *Alfred the Great: War, Kingship and Culture in Anglo-Saxon England* (London, 1998). More controversial is Alfred Smyth, *King Alfred the Great* (Oxford, 1995), whose dismissal of Asser's *Life of Alfred* as a later forgery has not persuaded most historians.

Saxon military forces, a process that he continued throughout his reign. His military reforms consisted of three major innovations. First, he divided his army — his *fyrd*, as it was called in Old English — into two halves, each serving for six months per year. Thus, when half of Alfred's fighting men were at home tending their lands and crops, the other half were under arms, ensuring that at no time would Wessex be defenseless. This reform strained West Saxon resources to the limit by dramatically increasing the customary term of military conscription, and it was abandoned once the Viking threat waned. But in Alfred's time it provided the sizeable and ever-alert force necessary to resist large, mobile Danish armies.[31]

Second, recognizing that the Vikings must be challenged on the seas, Alfred established a fleet of sixty-oared ships. The *Anglo-Saxon Chronicle* reports that Alfred built numerous ships, both large and swift, "neither on the Frisian nor the Danish pattern, but as it seemed to him that they could be most useful."[32] Faster, higher, and much longer than those of the Danes, these new ships reflect the creative intellect that Alfred applied to the problems of war.

Alfred's third and most significant military reform was the establishment throughout Wessex of a system of large walled and fortified settlements known as *burghs* (boroughs). Asser wrote of "the cities and towns he restored and the others he constructed where none had been before."[33] A remarkable early-tenth-century document known as the Burghal Hidage — probably adapted from an Alfredian original — discloses a network of thirty large burghs scattered across the kingdom in such a way that virtually nobody in Wessex was more than a day's walk (twenty miles) from a burgh. The Burghal Hidage assigns responsibility for the maintenance and defense of each burgh to the occupants of a stipulated amount of surrounding countryside, reckoned in terms of hides of land. (We have already encountered the hide as the assessment unit of the Mercian Tribal Hidage: see p. 67.) Thus the Burghal Hidage assigns 2,400 hides to Winchester, 1,500 to Cricklade, etc., to a grand total of some 27,000 hides. An intriguing appendix to the document explains, "If every hide is represented by one man, then every pole [5.5 yards] of wall can be manned by four men. And so for the maintenance of 20 poles of wall 80 hides are required, and for a furlong [220 yards] 160 hides are required by the same reckoning. . . ."[34] The document thus records a carefully articulated, kingdomwide burghal defense system involving a force totaling no

---

[31]On Alfred's military reforms, see Richard Abels, *Lordship and Military Obligation in Anglo-Saxon England* (Berkeley, 1988).

[32]*English Historical Documents, Volume I*, ed. Whitelock, no. 1, p. 206, *sub anno* 896.

[33]*Alfred the Great*, ed. Keynes and Lapidge, tr. C. W. Hollister, p. 101.

[34]Ibid., pp. 193–194.

fewer than 27,000 men — a sizeable number for a relatively small ninth-century kingdom.

The Burghal Hidage provides a virtually unique opportunity to correlate written and archaeological measurements. And the dimensions of the surviving ramparts of Alfred's burghs that have been measured thus far match very closely the corresponding formulae in the Burghal Hidage. The 2,400 hides assigned by the Burghal Hidage to Winchester, for example, would provide for the manning of 9,900 feet of ramparts, which is within 1 percent of the circumference of the actual town wall (9,954 feet). Archaeological investigations have also shown that Alfred's burghs tended to be laid out on a standard plan. Whether in the case of old Roman walled towns like Winchester, or reoccupied Iron Age or Roman fortifications like Portchester, or newly founded burghs like Wallingford and Shaftesbury, they had approximately square or rectangular walls, a single main street (or "High Street") with parallel back streets and other streets running at right angles, intersecting with a street that ran around the inside of the wall. The similarity of these burgh layouts — combined with evidence from Anglo-Saxon charters establishing town markets, laws requiring that all trade take place in towns, and the subsequent use of burghs as the sites of mints — suggests that their purpose, even from the beginning, was commercial no less than military. Alfred's burghs not only served as a formidable barrier to Danish incursions into Wessex and, later, as forward bases in the reconquest of the Danelaw; they also provided a powerful stimulus to West Saxon commerce and, through rents and market tolls, a bonanza to the West Saxon royal treasury. The term *burgh* had originally meant "fortress," but in Alfred's age and thereafter, its meaning was changing to "town." (In American colonial times, for example, Pittsburgh was both a fortress and a commercial center.)

Alfred's military reforms were far-reaching, but he needed time to carry them out. And for Alfred, time was all too short. In 876, a Danish chieftain named Guthrum led a host against Wessex. Again in early 878, during the dead of winter, Guthrum led his army across the land, while another Viking army attacked Wessex from the northwest, threatening to trap Alfred in a pincers movement. Fleeing into the marsh country of Somerset, Alfred found refuge at a royal estate on the Isle of Athelney. For the moment, almost all of England was at the mercy of the Danes.

Athelney was England's Valley Forge. Alfred held out with a small group of followers throughout the winter, and in the spring of 878 he was able to rally the Wessex fyrd. (The Danish army was much too small to occupy Wessex completely or to prevent Alfred from summoning his army.) The armies of Alfred and Guthrum met in pitched battle at Edington, and Alfred won a decisive victory. As a consequence, Guthrum agreed to Alfred's demands that he accept Christianity and abandon Wessex forever. Guthrum was one of the first important Vikings to become a Christian. His baptism in 878, with Alfred as his godfather, foreshadowed the ultimate Christianization of the entire Viking world and its incorporation into the mainstream of western European civilization.

In this age of warfare, skillful military leadership was essential to a king's survival. And Alfred, the ablest of the Anglo-Saxon kings, was a military commander of the first order. In the years after 878, he continued to advance the frontiers of his kingdom. In 883, he occupied London, formerly a Mercian stronghold, but recently under Danish control. The pinnacle of Alfred's military successes came, however, in 886, when he ceremonially reincorporated London into the English realm, received the submission of all the English people not then under Danish control, and entered into a new treaty with Guthrum that defined the boundary between West Saxon and Danish authority as running northwestward from London along the old Roman road known as Watling Street. This new boundary placed a considerable portion of Mercia under direct West Saxon lordship. To rule the rest of Mercia, Alfred now recognized an *ealdorman* (but really a subking) named Ethelred, who had been one of the competing claimants to the Mercian throne. Alfred granted Ethelred control over the city of London. But Alfred also took steps to ensure Ethelred's future allegiance by marrying him to Alfred's daughter Ethelfleda, who thereafter ruled Mercia jointly with her husband, and came to be known as the "Lady of the Mercians."[35]

The struggle with the Danes dragged on to the close of Alfred's reign and well beyond. But by Alfred's death in 899, the crisis had passed. He had made southwestern England secure, seized London, and established an effective policy of military organization and fortification. The authority of the West Saxon monarchy over non-Danish England was supreme.

Alfred's dynasty, like those of the Northumbrians and Mercians, built royal palaces on a lavish scale. Excavations at Cheddar in Somerset have disclosed traces of a long timber hall, apparently dating from Alfred's time, along with smaller domestic buildings in an architectural complex partially encompassed by a light fence and a drainage ditch. Later on, in the tenth century, a new timber hall was built on the same site at a right angle to the old one, and a chapel stood at its side. As in the case of Yeavering, it is by no means certain that Cheddar was the primary residence of the royal dynasty. The kings of Wessex, like other monarchs of the early Middle Ages, were constantly moving with their courts from one royal vill, hall, or hunting lodge to the next. Their ceaseless traveling was an essential aspect of their power as kings.

The creative intelligence that Alfred applied to military tactics and organization was equally effective in law and administration. Several of Alfred's predecessors had issued law codes or dooms. Ethelbert of Kent had been the first to do so, and he was followed by other monarchs such as Alfred's own distant ancestor, Ine of Wessex (688–726). But Alfred, perhaps following the example of the Carolingian kings of France, seems to

---

[35]On the significance of the events of 886, see Sarah Foot, "The Making of *Angelcynn*: English Identity Before the Norman Conquest," *Transactions of the Royal Historical Society,* Sixth Series 6 (1996): 25–49, esp. 26–28.

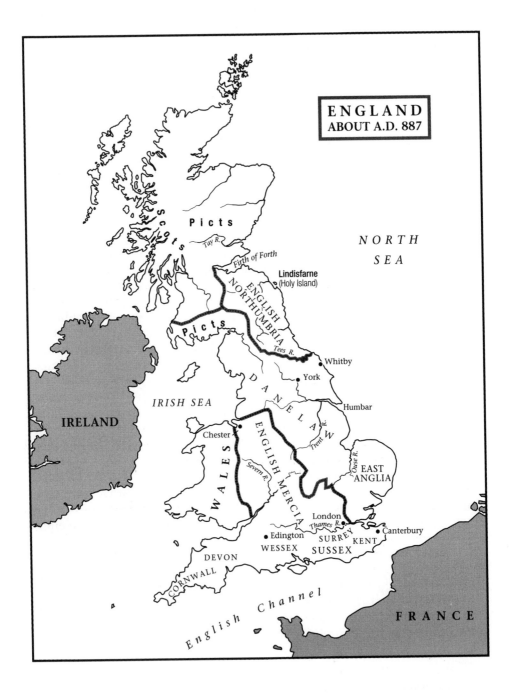

ENGLAND
ABOUT A.D. 887

NORTH
SEA

Picts

Tay R.

Firth of Forth

Lindisfarne
(Holy Island)

ENGLISH
NORTHUMBRIA

Picts

Tees R.

Whitby

York

D
A
N
E
L
A
W

Humbar

IRISH SEA

Trent R.

Ouse R.

IRELAND

Chester

W
A
L
E
S

ENGLISH MERCIA

Severn R.

EAST
ANGLIA

London
Thames R.

SURREY
KENT

Canterbury

Edington

WESSEX

SUSSEX

DEVON

CORNWALL

English Channel

FRANCE

have interpreted his lawmaking authority more broadly than his predecessors had. Although declaring himself hesitant to create new laws, he exercised considerable latitude in his selection or rejection of old ones, thereby placing his own imprint on the legal structure of his day. In the preface to his dooms, Alfred expressed himself in these words:

> Then I, King Alfred, collected these [laws] together and ordered that many of them which our forefathers observed should be written down, namely, those that I liked; and, with the advice of my *Witan* [councilors], I rejected many of those that I did not like and ordered that they be observed differently. I have not presumed to set in writing much of my own, because it was unknown to me what might please those who shall come after us. So I have collected here the laws which seemed to me the most just, whether from the time of Ine, my kinsman, or of Offa, king of the Mercians, or of Ethelbert, the first of the English to receive baptism; I have thrown out the rest. Then I, Alfred, king of the West Saxons, showed these to all my *Witan* who declared that they were all pleased to observe them.[36]

This passage reveals the king at work, surrounded by his advisers, respectful as always of past custom, yet injecting into his traditional royal role a strong element of creative judgment.

Alfred was not only a talented warrior and statesman but a scholar as well. Like Charlemagne a century earlier, Alfred was a patron of learning who drew learned men to his court from far and wide — the Welshman Asser, a Frankish scholar from Rheims, several Mercians (including one with the intriguing name of Werwulf), and a number of others. And Alfred himself made a far greater personal contribution to scholarship than Charlemagne had ever done. The contributions of Alfred's scholarly circle paralleled those of Charlemagne's in several ways. The renaissance of Charlemagne's era had been less an outburst of creative genius than a salvage operation designed to recover and preserve a classical-Christian heritage that was in danger of vanishing in the west. Charlemagne's scholars were not original philosophers but gifted schoolmasters who reformed the script, purged the Bible of scribal errors, established schools, copied manuscripts, and struggled to extend literacy and to guarantee correct liturgical practice in the Frankish Church.[37] These were humble efforts, but they were desperately needed. The Anglo-Saxon renaissance of Alfred's time was almost certainly inspired by Charlemagne's example.

By the late ninth century, the intellectual flowering of Bede's Northumbria had long passed. The widespread Viking destruction of monasteries and episcopal centers threatened the survival of classical Christian culture in England. Latin, the linguistic vehicle of classical

---

[36]*English Historical Documents I*, no. 33, pp. 408–409, slightly revised for readability.

[37]This description pertains specifically to the scholars of Charlemagne's court. It is not intended to demean the achievements of ninth-century Carolingian scholars like Eriugena, Hincmar, and Gottschalk.

Roman culture, was becoming virtually unknown in England. Priests could no longer understand the Latin Mass, much less study the works of Bede and the Church Fathers. And the Anglo-Saxon language, which everyone used, had only a perilously slender literary tradition behind it. Alfred himself described the decline of Latin in these words:

> Learning had declined so thoroughly in England that there were very few men on this side of the Humber who could understand their divine services in English, or even translate a single letter from Latin into English: and I suppose that there were not many beyond the Humber either. There were so few of them that I cannot recollect a single one south of the Thames when I succeeded to the kingdom.[38]

The king may have been exaggerating, but probably not by much.

Alfred was determined to revive ecclesiastical culture in his land, and he did what he could to create a literate priesthood. The scholars whom he gathered around him developed a notable school at his court. He established a few monastic schools as well, but a general monastic revival was out of the question in those turbulent times. Alfred founded a nunnery at Shaftesbury with a strict Benedictine Rule and an abbey at the isle of Athelney in which he established monks from the Continent who were dedicated to monastic reform. But his most far-reaching contribution to learning rose from his conviction that lay aristocrats should be educated — that his administrators and military commanders should have some knowledge of the civilized heritage of Christendom. Such men were too preoccupied with the political and military hazards of their time to learn Latin, but Alfred hoped that they might be taught to read their native Anglo-Saxon, or at least to have works in Anglo-Saxon read aloud to them. Accordingly, he and his court scholars undertook to translate into the vernacular some of the important Latin masterpieces of the past — Boethius's *Consolation of Philosophy*, Bede's *Ecclesiastical History of the English People*, and Pope Gregory's *Pastoral Care*. Alfred himself translated the *Pastoral Care*, and sent a copy of it to every bishopric in England in the hope that his bishops might be instructed by Gregory's wisdom and common sense. It is tempting to wonder whether the Alfred Jewel (see illustration, p. 81) might have been part of an *aestel* — a pointer for reading — which Alfred is known to have sent out with each of these copies of the *Pastoral Care*.

When participating in the work of translation, Alfred sometimes added comments of his own to the original texts. In his translation of Boethius, for example, Alfred injected the revealing observation: "In those days one never heard of ships armed for war"; and in the preface to the *Pastoral Care* he spoke nostalgically of the time "before everything was ravaged and burned, when England's churches overflowed with treas-

---

[38]*Alfred the Great*, ed. Keynes and Lapidge, p. 125: from the preface to Alfred's translation of Pope Gregory the Great's *Pastoral Care*.

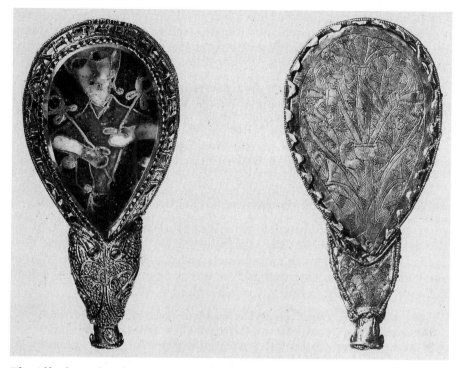

The Alfred Jewel   This remarkable piece, probably a depiction of King Alfred, dates from the late ninth century. The Old English inscription around the edge of the frame reads, in translation, "Alfred had me made." Its unique combination of massive rock crystal with cloisonné enamel and superb gold work is probably of Carolingian inspiration. *(University of Oxford, Ashmolean Museum, Department of Western Art)*

ures and books." Passages such as these forcefully demonstrate the enormous disadvantages against which Alfred worked.

Associated with Alfred's reign is another literary monument in the English vernacular, the *Anglo-Saxon Chronicle*.[39] This important historical project, which Alfred may possibly have instigated directly, was clearly inspired by the general surge of vernacular writing with which the king was associated. Its earliest compilers appear to have had some connections with Alfred's court circle. Around 892, an unknown West Saxon chronicler wrote a year-by-year account of English history and its Roman and British background, running from the birth of Christ to 891. The account was based on earlier sources, most of which are now lost.

---

[39]The *Anglo-Saxon Chronicle* is available in several modern English translations. The standard one remains *The Anglo-Saxon Chronicle*, ed. and tr. Dorothy Whitelock, David Douglas, and Susie Tucker (New Brunswick, N.J., 1961), published separately and also included in *English Historical Documents, Volumes I and II*. Citations here are from the *EHD* version.

The identification and reconstruction of these forerunners have occupied several generations of scholars, and many aspects of the problem remain obscure. In general, the early entries are characterized by extreme verbal economy:

> 634: In this year Bishop Birinus preached baptism to the West Saxons.
> 635: In this year King Cynegils [of Wessex] was baptized by Bishop Birinus in Dorchester, and Oswald [king of Northumbria] stood sponsor for him.
> 636: In this year Cwichelm, [king of Wessex] was baptized in Dorchester, and he died that same year. And Bishop Felix preached the faith of Christ to the East Angles.
> 639: In this year Birinus baptized Cuthred [king of Wessex] at Dorchester and also received him as his godson.[40]

Copies of the 892 chronicle were sent to a number of important ecclesiastical centers of the time, and in several instances these centers expanded the early entries to include facts and traditions available in other portions of England. One manuscript was sent to Northumbria, where the entry for 634, for example, was elaborated as follows:

> 634: In this year Osric, whom Paulinus had baptized, succeeded to the kingdom of the Deirans. He was the son of Elfric, Edwin's paternal uncle. And Ethelfrith's son Eanfrith succeeded to Bernicia. And also Birinus first preached baptism to the West Saxons under King Cynegils. This Birinus came there by the advice of Pope Honorius, and he was bishop there until the end of his life. And also in this year Oswald succeeded to the kingdom of the Northumbrians, and he reigned for nine years.[41]

At several ecclesiastical centers the 892 chronicle was continued thereafter on a year-by-year basis. In subsequent years copies continued to be exchanged and taken from one monastery to another, with the result that the *Anglo-Saxon Chronicle* is a very complex document indeed. Strictly speaking, it is not a single chronicle but a series of related chronicles. Altogether, seven distinct manuscripts survive, representing four more-or-less separate accounts. Of these, three end in the later eleventh century — between 1066 and 1079 — while the fourth continues to the accession of King Henry II in 1154.

The various versions of the *Anglo-Saxon Chronicle*, written by many different chroniclers in several religious houses over a number of generations, are exceedingly uneven. At times they fail to rise above the level of what one great English historian deplored as "our jejune annals"; at other times they provide fairly comprehensive accounts of the events of their day, sometimes even attempting a degree of historical interpretation. Like modern journalists, the chroniclers tended to pass over periods of peace and cultural creativity with a few bare allusions to royal deaths

---

[40]Ibid., p. 162.

[41]Ibid.

and accessions but waxed eloquent in times of upheaval and disaster. So little is made of the fruitful reigns of Alfred's successors, and so much is made of the second Danish invasions and the Norman Conquest, that readers of the chronicle are apt to be misled into regarding the Anglo-Saxon era as one vast, sterile bore relieved by occasional cataclysms. But whatever its shortcomings, the *Anglo-Saxon Chronicle* is unique in the European vernacular literature of its day and provides the modern student with an invaluable if sometimes aggravating narrative of later Anglo-Saxon history. It is appropriate that from the reign that marks the genesis of the English monarchy should come this remarkable national history in the Old English tongue.

In many respects, then, Alfred's reign is the watershed in the history of Anglo-Saxon England. It represents the turning point in the Danish invasions and in the gradual consolidation, both political and territorial, of the English monarchies. Alfred once modestly described himself as one who works in a great forest collecting branches with which others can build. He was alluding to his efforts toward intellectual revival, but the metaphor is equally appropriate to his military, administrative, and political achievements. As architect of the medieval English monarchy, he gathered the wood and also provided a preliminary blueprint that would guide his successors in constructing a durable political edifice.

CHAPTER 3

Late-Anglo-Saxon England

During the first three-quarters of the tenth century, King Alfred's able successors vastly extended his work of reconquest and political consolidation. At Alfred's death in 899, Wessex passed to his son Edward (899–924), whom later historians called Edward the Elder to distinguish him from subsequent monarchs of the same name. In his initial years, Edward the Elder was confronted with a serious bid for the throne by an ambitious first cousin who allied with the Danes but who, fortunately for Edward, died in battle in 903. Afterwards, Edward and his sister Ethelfleda, Lady of the Mercians, pursued an aggressive military policy against the Danelaw, strengthening Alfred's burghs and founding a number of new ones in the midlands to consolidate their conquests. By 918, all of the Danish settlers south of the Humber had submitted to Edward the Elder's rule, and the death of Ethelfleda that year resulted in the permanent unification of Wessex and Mercia under Alfred's dynasty. Edward the Elder now bore two titles: king of the West Saxons and king of the Mercians. The union was not without tensions. One of Edward's first acts as king of Mercia was to imprison his niece, Ethelfleda's daughter, so that she did not become a center around which Mercian resistance might be organized. But the union held, and in the years to come, West Saxons and Mercians would fight together against the Viking leaders of the north.

Edward's achievements were extended by his son Athelstan (924–939), a skillful military leader and a statesman of European significance. Athelstan had grown up at Ethelfleda's court in Mercia; as a result, he enjoyed personal connections with the interlinked nobility of Mercia and Northumbria, connections that his father had lacked. His reign was principally devoted to extending and consolidating West Saxon control over these northern kingdoms. In 937, he won his greatest military victory when he and his brother Edmund, leading a combined army from both Wessex and Mercia, annihilated an invading force of Norse Vikings from Ireland at the battle of Brunanburh. This victory secured Athelstan's control over Yorkshire and reinforced his hegemony over Wales. When Athelstan died in 939, nearly all of England was under his control. His successors would consolidate these conquests, put down revolts, and repulse further Viking invasions until, by 954, England stood united under the West Saxon dynasty of kings. The West Saxon kings had now begun to present themselves to their subjects not as the kings of Wessex, Mercia, and Northumbria, but as simply "kings (or sometimes emperors) of the Anglo-Saxons." By the end of the tenth century, Abbot Aelfric of Eynsham "could write of England, and use the word to mean substantially what it has meant ever since."[1] A united English kingdom had been born.

The Consequences of Political Unification

Yet *united* is perhaps too strong to describe England, even when the tenth century ended. Although the kingdom was now ruled by a single royal dynasty, deep regional divisions remained between Wessex, Mercia, Northumbria, East Anglia, and the southwest. The West Saxon kings were newcomers to northern and eastern England. In many respects, they were foreigners. For much of the period from 875 to 950, northern England's closest political links were to the Viking rulers of Dublin in Ireland, rather than to the West Saxon rulers and their capital at Winchester. Prior to the Viking invasions, of course, Northumbria (itself divided between Deira and Bernicia), East Anglia, and Mercia had been independent kingdoms. To their credit, the tenth-century West Saxon kings showed a consistent sensitivity to these regional divisions. Until 918, Edward the Elder was careful to rule Mercia through his sister Ethelfleda, whose husband Ethelred was a member of the old Mercian royal house. Edward also ensured that his son, Athelstan, would be raised in Mercia and so have connections with the nobility of the midlands and the southern Danelaw. Northumbria, however, remained a land apart, and Northumbrian separatism would continue as a potent force until the end of the eleventh century.

Linguistically also, the regional dialects of Wessex, Mercia, Yorkshire, and East Anglia differed significantly from one another, as they would continue to do throughout the Middle Ages. West Saxon emerged during the tenth century as the "standard" form of English for governmental (and increasingly for literary) purposes, but this written language was probably quite different from the language most people in England spoke. Beyond these regional differences between the English lay deeper divisions between English, Scandinavians, and Welsh resulting from the invasions and conquests of the previous five centuries. The Danish settlers of Yorkshire, East Anglia, and the Five Boroughs (Leicester, Lincoln, Nottingham, Stamford, and Derby) and the Norwegian settlers of the northwest would remain linguistically and culturally distinguishable from each other and from their English neighbors until at least the eleventh century. In Wales and the southwest, British languages (Welsh

[1]Eric John, "The Age of Edgar," in *The Anglo-Saxons*, ed. James Campbell (Oxford, 1982), p. 160. On this period, see also Pauline Stafford, *Unification and Conquest: A Political and Social History of England in the Tenth and Eleventh Centuries* (London, 1989); Eric John, *Reassessing Anglo-Saxon England* (Manchester, 1996); and the standard work of Sir Frank Stenton, *Anglo-Saxon England*, 3rd ed. (Oxford, 1971).

and Cornish) continued to be widely spoken throughout the Middle Ages and beyond.

Divisions remained, but the political unification of England achieved by 954 was substantial and would prove to be lasting. The reconquest of northern and eastern England from the Vikings made possible a generation of peace, prosperity, and reform in both Church and state. The pinnacle of these accomplishments came during the reign of King Edgar (959–975), known sometimes as "the Peaceable." In the words of the *Anglo-Saxon Chronicle,*

> His reign was marked by greatly improved conditions, and God granted that he lived his days in peace; he did his duty, and labored zealously in performing it; he exalted God's praise far and wide, and loved God's law; he improved the security of his people more than all the kings before him within human memory.[2]

Edgar's supremacy within the island of Britain was acknowledged in 973 when, after his long-delayed coronation, he traveled to Chester to receive the submission (expressed, in one tradition, by being ceremonially rowed upon the river Dee) of six (or perhaps eight; the sources differ) Welsh and Scottish kings. Edgar's supremacy was the product of military strength as well as statesmanship. A well-organized English fleet maintained constant coastal patrols to guard against renewed Viking assaults, and Edgar is reported to have led armies as far afield as Ireland.[3] But he was also confident enough in the security of his kingdom and the loyalty of its inhabitants to allow his Danish subjects in eastern England the right to live by their own distinctive customs and laws, without fear that this concession might encourage regional separatism.

The Monastic Reform Movement

Edgar's reign also witnessed an impressive movement of monastic reform[4] that paralleled and drew inspiration from contemporary reform movements unfolding on the Continent. Throughout western Europe, monasteries had suffered severely from the civil wars and foreign invasions of the ninth century. In England, however, the damage had been particularly severe. Viking raiders in England concentrated their attacks upon monastic foundations, which tended to be both wealthy and poorly defended. But in the chaos of the ninth and early tenth centuries, monastic houses suffered as much from the depredations of their neighbors as they did from the Vikings. The economic and commercial importance of mon-

---

[2]*English Historical Documents, Volume I,* ed. Dorothy Whitelock, 2nd ed. (London, 1979), no. 1, p. 225, slightly revised for readability.

[3]On Edgar's fleet and his contacts with Ireland, see John, *Reassessing,* pp. 95, 107, 109.

[4]*St. Dunstan: His Life, Times and Cult,* ed. Nigel Ramsay, Margaret Sparks, and Tim Tatton-Brown (Woodbridge, 1992); John, *Reassessing,* pp. 99–123.

asteries, together with their extensive landed wealth, made them tempting targets for local lords, bishops, and kings. In peacetime, such lords were often patrons and protectors of monks, but in times of trouble, even patrons could become oppressors, extracting favors in return for their protection. The result was a degradation of religious standards, as patrons sought to control monastic houses' resources by controlling the selection of their abbots. Kings bore a special responsibility to protect the religious houses of their kingdoms and might sometimes intervene to protect a monastic house from its local rivals, but even kings were not immune from the temptation to fleece Christ's flock while pretending to protect it.

These problems affected monastic houses all over western Europe, but they were particularly acute in England. By 950, Viking raids, local disorder, and economic devastation had crippled the monasteries of southern England, while eliminating almost every monastic house in the northern two-thirds of the country. To restore and reform the monastic life of the kingdom was a daunting task. A great deal of monastic property had passed into the hands of lay families, sometimes by extortion and usurpation, but often when the monastery itself had been abandoned. Monastic buildings lay in ruins or were occupied by secular clerics — clerics who were not monks and so had not taken perpetual vows of chastity, poverty, and obedience to an abbot. Some monasteries even had laymen serving as abbots. Even where monastic life had survived, traditions of proper worship had been forgotten or altered through ignorance and isolation.

The condition of the nonmonastic church was no better. It may even have been worse. Throughout northern and eastern England, bishoprics had been abandoned and parish churches had ceased to exist during the chaos of the Viking invasions. Even in southern England, priests were rare, and pastoral care almost nonexistent across much of the country. Edward the Elder took some preliminary steps to deal with the chaos in the West Saxon church, by increasing the number of bishops in the kingdom from two to five, but Edgar was the first West Saxon king to attempt a thoroughgoing restoration of the structures of Christian life throughout the country.

Edgar's efforts to reform the English monasteries were modeled on earlier reform efforts in the Rhineland, where lay lords, and especially kings, had played an important role in the work of reform. An alternative tradition, associated with the Burgundian monastery of Cluny, took a more radical view and saw the proper goal of religious reform as being to eliminate the control of laymen, including kings, over monastic life altogether. The Cluniac monks were famous for the elaborate and highly liturgical style of their worship, and their example did have some influence in England, particularly through Fleury, a Cluniac house on the banks of the Loire with which several English monastic reformers had close associations. Edgar and his successors were unwilling, however, to allow any English monastery to become formally a member of the

Dunstan Prostrates Himself at Christ's Feet
A contemporary, tenth-century drawing, perhaps by St. Dunstan himself. *(North Wind Picture Archives)*

Cluniac congregation of monasteries. Instead, they claimed the protection of all English monasteries as a uniquely royal privilege, and set about the work of reform as an obligation incumbent upon a Christian king.

The most celebrated champion of monastic reform in King Edgar's England was St. Dunstan, a member of the royal family who became abbot of Glastonbury and, in 960, archbishop of Canterbury. Dunstan was already a well-known figure around the royal court, who during the brief reign of Edgar's brother Eadwig (955–959) had spent time in exile at a reformed monastery in Ghent. Edgar brought Dunstan back to England, and he quickly became the directing figure of the reform effort at Edgar's court.

Other key reformers included St. Aethelwold, abbot of Abingdon and bishop of Winchester, and St. Oswald, abbot of Ramsey and bishop of Worcester, who in 972 became archbishop of York also. Holding two bishoprics simultaneously would have scandalized twelfth-century church reformers, but in tenth-century England it made good sense, not only because it allowed Oswald to use the more secure revenues from Glastonbury and Worcester to restore the devastated archbishopric of York, but also because it acted as a powerful check on northern separatism. As Edgar well knew, only a generation earlier an archbishop of

York had joined with the Vikings in a war against the conquering West Saxon kings. This was not an experience he wished to repeat.

St. Aethelwold was the most radical of the reformers, and it was under his direction that King Edgar expelled the secular clerics from Winchester, the West Saxon capital, and replaced them with Benedictine monks. From Abingdon, Aethelwold founded reformed monasteries throughout the southern and eastern Danelaw. He also wrote the *Regularis Concordia*, which established a standard rule for English monastic life. St. Dunstan, meanwhile, maintained the reformers' cause at the royal court and presided over the entire English Church as archbishop of Canterbury, while Oswald oversaw the reform efforts in the north and west. All three of these men were monks as well as bishops, and the tradition they established, of associating monasteries with cathedrals and of appointing abbots to be bishops, would continue to distinguish the ecclesiastical life of England until the Reformation.

Under King Edgar's sponsorship, old monasteries and nunneries were reformed and reorganized; new houses were established, and ruined abbeys were restored. In all these reformed houses, the traditional Benedictine duties of individual poverty, chastity, obedience, and communal living were strictly enforced, and local aristocrats were replaced as monastic patrons and protectors by the king himself or, in the case of nunneries, by the queen. Although individual Benedictine monks were forbidden to possess property, Benedictine abbeys could rightfully acquire considerable corporate wealth, and most of them did. The landed endowment of a great Benedictine house — deriving from the accumulation of pious lay donations — could rival the landed wealth of a family in the upper aristocracy. Thus, whoever exercised authority over England's monasteries commanded immense power and riches.

In the course of the tenth century, a great deal of monastic land passed into the control of the West Saxon monarchy: first, during the process of reconquest when kings took direct possession of estates formerly belonging to destroyed or abandoned abbeys; second, during the monastic reform movement when aristocratic control of many of the remaining abbeys gave way to royal control. The monarchy was particularly generous in founding and refounding abbeys in formerly Danish lands; the effect was to establish across the southern and eastern Danelaw a network of royalist religious communities loyal to the West Saxon dynasty. The reform movement thus had the further effect of enhancing royal power and extending the influence of the West Saxon royal house throughout Mercia and East Anglia. To Northumbria, however, the tenth-century monastic reform movement did not extend. The reestablishment of Northumbrian monastic life would not take place until the twelfth century.

Piety, no less than political calculation, prompted King Edgar to cooperate so fully with the monastic reformers. Edgar shared the standard presumptions of his age in believing that it was his duty as a Christian king to protect and reform the religious life of his kingdom. Unlike the other kings of tenth-century Europe, however (including even the Ottonian kings of Germany, with whom Edgar had close contacts and many similarities), Edgar was powerful enough to carry through his reform ambitions on an unprecedented scale. But we should not underestimate the difficulties he faced or the disruptions his reform efforts caused. Edgar restored a great deal of property to monastic houses throughout southern England, but much of this property first had to be taken back from the local noble families who had acquired it. The resulting animosities are easy to imagine. Moreover, by establishing in the countryside wealthy and highly privileged new monasteries under direct royal sponsorship, Edgar not only diminished the jurisdictional authority of his own local royal officials, he also turned many formerly free peasants into serfs (unfree dependents) on these newly restored monastic estates. The king's insistence that all his subjects pay tithes (a tenth of their produce or income, paid to the church as a spiritual offering) was another source of grievance, guaranteeing that even peasants not resident on monastic estates would pay a price for their king's reforming efforts.

Resistance to these reform measures would seriously weaken Edgar's sons when they succeeded him as king, opening the way for a new round of Viking invasions and ultimately for the accession of a Danish king, Cnut (1016–1035), to the English throne. But before turning to the disasters that followed upon Edgar's death, we need first to understand the sources of his strength. On what foundations did Edgar's extraordinary power rest?

The Administrative Strength of the Late-Anglo-Saxon State

First and foremost, Edgar's authority rested on the widespread acceptance by his subjects of the West Saxon dynasty's own view of the sacred and God-given nature of its rule. Alfred and his successors drew consciously on the models of Christian kingship established by the ninth-century Carolingian kings of France and the tenth-century kings of Saxony — models that emphasized the king's role as the representative of Christ on earth. At their coronations, for example, all these monarchs were anointed with the same holy oil as was used in the ordination of priests and bishops, making them in some sense priestly figures. Edgar, however, extended these associations between earthly and heavenly kingship further than had any of his Anglo-Saxon predecessors. He delayed his coronation (and so his anointing) until he was twenty-nine, the same age at which Jesus began his own public ministry. Edgar also employed at his coronation a new liturgy that emphasized explicitly the king's position as *Christus Domini*, the Lord's anointed one.[5] Edgar's successors (and

---

[5]John, "The Age of Edgar," in *The Anglo-Saxons*, ed. Campbell, p. 188; John, *Reassessing*, pp. 124–138, esp. 135–136.

perhaps Edgar himself: the custom seems to begin in the tenth century) also displayed their Christocentric style of kingship in liturgically elaborate crown-wearing ceremonies marking the principal feasts of the Christian year. The king's great men, secular and ecclesiastical, were expected to attend these ceremonies. After 1066, and perhaps earlier, crown-wearings were accompanied by the assembled clergy singing to the king the *Laudes Regiae* ("Royal Praises"): "Christ conquers; Christ reigns as king; Christ rules as emperor."[6] The confusion (if we wish to call it that) the *Laudes* created between Christ and a consecrated earthly king was deliberate; for, as an anonymous late-eleventh-century English author explained:

> The power of the king is the power of God. This power . . . is God's by nature, and the king's by grace. Hence the king too is God and Christ, but by grace; and whatsoever he does, he does not simply as a man, but as one who has become God and Christ by grace.[7]

More prosaically, however, Edgar's strength depended upon the most extensive and effective system of local administration existing anywhere in Europe. Here, too, we can see the influence of Carolingian models on the West Saxon monarchs, but by the late tenth century, the administrative system of the English state far surpassed anything the Carolingians had achieved. This administrative system enabled the tenth-century Anglo-Saxon kings to preserve and extend throughout their kingdom a notion of public power, exercised in the king's name by appointed local officials through public courts, at a time when such notions were collapsing everywhere else in Europe. By so doing, Alfred and his successors laid the administrative and political foundations upon which the subsequent legal and political history of England would be built.

The kingdom of Wessex in Alfred's day was already subdivided into large administrative regions called *shires* (or counties, as these units were sometimes called after the Norman Conquest). As the West Saxon kings expanded their authority into Mercia and the Danelaw, they organized these districts into shires on the West Saxon model also. Some of the new tenth-century shires corresponded to old kingdoms or subtribal districts — Norfolk, Suffolk, Kent, Sussex, and Essex, for example. Others were new creations, centered on the important towns after which they were named: Bedfordshire, Northamptonshire, Cambridgeshire, Worcestershire, and others. Four of the five formerly Danish boroughs — Lincoln, Leicester, Derby, and Nottingham — became the nuclei of new shires, with Stamford, the fifth borough, being incorporated into Lincolnshire. The process of "shiring" the Danelaw progressed rapidly, and by Athelstan's reign it was virtually complete. Farther north, it progressed

---

[6]In Latin, *Christus vincit; Christus regnat; Christus imperat.*

[7]Translation of the "Anglo-Norman Anonymous" by Ernst Kantorowicz, *The King's Two Bodies: A Study in Medieval Political Theology* (Princeton, 1957), p. 48.

THE SHIRES OF ENGLAND AND WALES

Scale of Miles

0   25   50

SCOTLAND

NORTH SEA

NORTHUMBERLAND

CUMBERLAND   DURHAM

WESTMORELAND

Isle of Man

IRISH SEA

YORKSHIRE

LANCASHIRE

ENGLAND

CHESHIRE   DERBY   LINCOLN

CAERNARVON   DENBIGH   FLINT   NOTTINGHAM

MERIONETH   STAFFORD   RUTLAND   NORFOLK

MONTGOMERY   SHROPSHIRE   LEICESTER   HUNTINGDON

CARDIGAN   RADNOR   WORCESTER   WARWICK   NORTHAMPTON   CAMBRIDGE   SUFFOLK

BRECKNOCK   HEREFORD   BEDFORD

PEMBROKE   CARMARTHEN   GLOUCESTER   OXFORD   BUCKINGHAM   HERTFORD   ESSEX

GLAMORGAN   MONMOUTH   MIDDLESEX   LONDON

WALES   BERKSHIRE

WILTSHIRE   SURREY   KENT

SOMERSET   HAMPSHIRE   SUSSEX

DEVON   DORSET

Isle of Wight

CORNWALL

ENGLISH CHANNEL

Clayton Roberts and David Roberts, *A History of England*, 3rd edition. Copyright © 1991. *Reprinted by permission of Prentice-Hall, Inc., Upper Saddle River, NJ.*

more slowly, but by 1016, the shires of England were largely in place. With only minor modifications, the shire boundaries would remain unchanged until 1974, when they were redrawn by a tidy-minded English Parliament.

The shires of Alfred's time were governed by officials, drawn from the upper nobility, known as *ealdormen*. In earlier centuries, ealdormen had often been local kings, inferior in power but not in status to the kings who claimed to be their overlords. By Alfred's reign, however, the ealdormen of Wessex had been decisively subordinated to the West Saxon kings; and although ealdormen continued to be drawn from among the great noble families, it was this model of the ealdorman as an appointed royal official that Edward the Elder and Athelstan extended into Mercia and the Danelaw. Ealdormen exercised a general responsibility for the governance of their shire, but they had a particular responsibility for defense. When the warriors of the shire were summoned to join the royal *fyrd* (army), the ealdorman led them. In an emergency, an ealdorman might summon the shire's forces himself. Ealdormen also presided in the king's name over the shire court, a twice-yearly meeting of the important freemen of the shire, where judicial cases were decided and royal directives were read out. Ealdormen also supervised the crown's financial resources within the shire and probably played a role in collecting and accounting for the king's shire revenues. In return, they were entitled to retain a portion of these revenues (often a third) for themselves.

At once royal officials and local nobles, ealdormen might easily have become so powerful in their shires as to put at risk the king's ability to control them, as had happened with the counts of the ninth-century Carolingian Empire. Athelstan's decision to appoint ealdormen with authority over several shires simultaneously increased this risk and raised the further possibility that England might break apart again into regions, especially when he appointed a single ealdorman to each of the three ancient kingdoms of Mercia, Northumbria, and East Anglia. Wessex he divided between two and sometimes three ealdormen; not until Cnut would any king allow a single ealdorman to rule over all Wessex. The dangers of concentrating so much power into the hands of such a small body of aristocrats are obvious and can be clearly traced in the fractured histories of tenth- and eleventh-century France and Germany. But in acknowledging the dangers of this policy in Anglo-Saxon England, we must also acknowledge its success. Tenth-century England did not dissolve into its ancient, constituent parts. It emerged instead as the most highly centralized and administratively sophisticated monarchy in Europe, an achievement for which the ealdormen of England deserve some credit. To be effective, medieval administration had to be local. The ealdormen answered to this requirement.

So too did the shire reeves or sheriffs. As ealdormen began to exercise authority over several shires at once, administrative and military command of individual shires passed increasingly to the shire reeves. Shire reeves were not drawn from the ranks of the nobility; like the reeves who supervised the king's estates, some shire reeves may even have been unfree. Nor did sheriffs owe their authority to the regional ealdormen, although in practice sheriffs and ealdormen must often have cooperated. Sheriffs, however, were appointed directly by the king and were dependent for their power and position upon the king. As such, they acted as an important check upon any ealdorman aspiring to an unwarranted degree of independence.

The late-Anglo-Saxon shire was divided into smaller territorial units called hundreds — or, in parts of the north, *wapentakes*. Like the shires, the hundreds originated in Wessex and spread northward with the expansion of the West Saxon monarchy. The boundaries of some tenth-century hundreds corresponded closely with the "small shires" ruled by petty kings within Wessex or Mercia in the seventh and eighth centuries. It is not known how old these small shires were. They may date back to the invasion period of the fifth and sixth centuries, when a host of minor notables carved out tiny kingdoms for themselves that were ultimately swallowed up within the "super kingdoms" of Wessex, Mercia, and East Anglia. But they could be much older than that: possibly Roman, and perhaps even pre-Roman in origin. Despite the uncertainties, the potential antiquity of these hundred boundaries is a reminder of the extent to which the tenth-century West Saxon kings built their administration upon pre-existing structures of authority and power in the countryside whose roots date back a very long way indeed.

In tenth-century England, the hundred was simultaneously a territorial district and a jurisdictional entity centering on a hundred court. Similar in purpose and organization to the shire court and presided over by a royal reeve, the hundred court met more frequently (normally every three or four weeks) than did the shire court and played a more intimate role in the affairs of the average free subject. Like the shire, the hundred also functioned as a community of freemen, who might be called upon by the crown to raise a military force or pursue escaping criminals. But the hundred was also a unit of fiscal and military assessment comprising 100 (or sometimes 120, a so-called long hundred) hides. Centuries before, the hide had been regarded as the amount of land necessary to support a free warrior and his family. By the tenth century, however, the hide had become a more or less standardized unit of value upon which the Anglo-Saxon monarchy based taxation, the construction of fortifications and bridges, and the levying of troops for war.

Within each hundred, every estate or village was assigned to pay a portion of the hundred's total hidage assessment. In practice, these local assessments were often erratic and unfair. Two estates of equal size and value might be assessed at radically different levels if one were owned by a royal crony. And villages, or even whole hundreds, might find their hidage assessments raised or reduced through bribery, good fortune, or disaster. But for all the inconsistencies of hidage assessments, the system was also flexible, effective, and readily adaptable to new requirements. Hidage reassessments were carried through frequently in tenth- and eleventh-century England, on a surprisingly large scale. Taxation rates based on the hide were also adjustable. And since the crown knew how many hides there were in England, by setting the taxation rate at, for example, 2 shillings per hide it could know precisely how much money a tax ought to produce.

Hidage assessments were also used to spread the burdens of military service. A single hide had once been thought sufficient to support the family of a single warrior, but by the tenth century that equation had for long been unrealistic.[8] By Edgar's reign at the latest, it took five hides to support a single warrior, and England had been effectively divided into five-hide units for this purpose. Naval forces could be mustered on the same principle of proportion. When King Ethelred, in the early eleventh century, sought to raise a navy to ward off the Danes, he created special administrative units known as "shipsokes" of three hundred hides each and demanded a ship from every shipsoke.[9] Remarkably, the ships arrived — but bad weather and poor seamanship sent the new fleet quickly to the bottom of Sandwich harbor.

Law and Justice

The tenth-century Anglo-Saxon kingdom was the product of successful wars. The most remarkable accomplishment of its kings, however, was not the wars they won, but the domestic peace they maintained. In his coronation oath of 973, King Edgar made three promises:

> first, that God's Church and all the Christian people of my realm shall enjoy true peace; second, that I shall forbid robbery and wrongful deeds to all ranks of men; third, that I shall command justice and mercy in all judgments, so that the gracious and merciful God who lives and reigns may grant us all His mercy.[10]

Edgar's emphasis on peace and justice is an accurate reflection of the preoccupations of his dynasty.[11] Anglo-Saxon England had no police force and no professional lawyers or judges. It did, however, have a network of shire and hundred courts headed by royal officials who were responsible for maintaining peace and doing justice within their territories. Crimes such as robbery, rape, counterfeiting, and murder were regarded as offenses against the king's own peace, and might therefore be prosecuted directly by royal officials. But the vast majority of crimes would be brought to court for judgment only through the self-help efforts of the victim and his or her family. Private enforcement (sometimes termed "feud") was in this respect an essential element in the Anglo-Saxon legal system, not because it provided a way for families to exact unregulated vengeance upon their enemies — kings strove hard to prevent this — but because it was only through such means that adversaries could be forced into court to have their cases adjudicated. The West Saxon kings tried

---

[8]Thomas Charles-Edwards, "Kinship, Status, and the Origins of the Hide," *Past and Present* 56 (1972): 3–33.

[9]On shipsokes, see John, *Reassessing*, pp. 106–107.

[10]From *English Coronation Records*, ed. Leopold G. Wickham Legg (Westminster, 1901), p. 15.

[11]Patrick Wormald, *The Making of English Law, King Alfred to the Twelfth Century, Volume I: Legislation and Its Limits* (Oxford, 1999).

hard to regulate and control feud through legislation because the self-help actions meant to force an adversary into court — seizing his cattle, for example, or breaking down his fences — could easily degenerate into further violence and even war. But no one contemplated eliminating altogether the role feud played in the legal process. There simply were no viable alternatives to it.

Violence was a fact of life in tenth-century England, as it was everywhere in medieval Europe. Kings strove not to eliminate violence, but to control it and regulate it within accepted legal channels. On the Continent, royal efforts to regulate violence met with little success. The tenth century saw a surge of private castle building and the attendant collapse of the Carolingian system of private courts. Partly as cause and partly as consequence, private warfare on the Continent was endemic, as were the mundane extortions perpetrated by the powerful upon the weak. Late-Anglo-Saxon England, by contrast, was a land without private fortifications and without privileged areas of judicial immunity. No castles or fortified towers dotted the landscape; Anglo-Saxon towns were without walls, and the king's judicial authority was considered to apply everywhere and equally throughout the country. The peace kept by the Anglo-Saxon kings was far from perfect, but it was remarkable for its day.

The kings of tenth- and eleventh-century England were extraordinarily active legislators on a wide variety of subjects. It has sometimes been suggested by historians that in the early Middle Ages law was "found, not made": that is, law was customary and unchanging, the timeless possession of a folk community, and so could not be altered by active and assertive monarchs. Nothing could be further from the truth, at least in late-Anglo-Saxon England. It is true that Anglo-Saxon England had no single, authoritative legal code defining all aspects of the country's legal system. But neither did any other western European country before the end of the eighteenth century. Anglo-Saxon England did, however, have a tradition of royally sponsored written law codes, dating back to at least the year 600, which culminated with King Alfred's compilation and revision of the West Saxon and Mercian laws. Alfred's successors issued no codes so comprehensive as Alfred's, but they regularly issued detailed provisions concerning the detection and punishment of crime, court procedure, inheritance, the buying and selling of goods, and a host of other issues. Taken as a whole, these administrative and legal provisions represent the largest surviving body of vernacular written law enacted by kings anywhere in tenth- and eleventh-century Europe. In their scope and scale, they are comparable only with the capitularies of the eighth- and ninth-century Carolingian Empire.[12]

---

[12]The largest body of vernacular law to survive from the early Middle Ages comes from Ireland, but the Irish laws were put into writing between the seventh and the ninth centuries, and were not regarded as having been issued or authorized by kings, as were the continental and Anglo-Saxon law codes and capitularies.

Important legal changes were frequently announced as the joint decision of the king and his *Witan*, or council. The membership of this council varied according to the nature of the business to be discussed. Meetings of large councils, attended by both secular and ecclesiastical magnates, were long-established features of Anglo-Saxon political life. King Edwin had summoned such an assembly to consider whether his kingdom should convert to Christianity; King Alfred had presented his laws to a *Witan* before he pronounced them; and King Athelstan had summoned such a council before embarking on his military campaigns in Yorkshire. A *Witan* was not a representative assembly in the sense that a modern parliament is. No one was elected to attend, and no special powers were delegated to those whom the king summoned. But we should not underestimate the practical political importance of these occasional assemblies to the exercise of effective kingship. No medieval king could succeed if the majority of his most important subjects refused to support him. The need for consent and consultation was a practical requirement in Anglo-Saxon England, not a legal one. But even though no Anglo-Saxon king was legally bound to follow his *Witan*'s advice, monarchs were rarely so foolish as to flout it. In an age lacking precise definitions of constitutional relationships, the deeply ingrained expectation that the king should govern in consultation with his great men, implicit in almost every important royal document of the period, made the *Witan* one of Anglo-Saxon England's fundamental political institutions.

Finance, Coinage, Towns, and Taxation

The expanding monarchy of late-Anglo-Saxon England drew on an increasing variety of financial resources. The king's own estates, known collectively as the royal demesne, provided much of the crown's regular annual income, at first directly in grain, meat, honey, wool, and hides, then later in cash as the Anglo-Saxon economy became increasingly monetarized. Towns too belonged to the royal demesne, providing another ready source of cash through customs duties, fines, and other charges. The monarchy delegated responsibility for the fiscal exploitation of its demesne estates and towns to royal reeves, who paid a fixed annual amount (known as a "farm") from the districts they supervised. Each shire was also assigned a fixed farm, payable by the shire reeve. With only minor adjustments, sheriffs continued to account for these shire farms until 1832.

The wealth of late-Anglo-Saxon England rested in part on the productivity of its agriculture. But the country also boasted rich deposits of silver, tin, and lead in the southwest and the north — deposits that had been worked as governmental monopolies in Roman times and that remained under the control of the Anglo-Saxon kings. The valuable saltworks at Droitwich in Worcestershire were another royal resource that dated back to the Roman period. But perhaps the most valuable of all the country's resources, at least from the standpoint of foreign trade, was wool. Huge quantities of silver passed into England during the late tenth and eleventh centuries from a triangular trade connecting the Rhineland, the Low Countries, and England. Silver from the Harz Mountains of Saxony traveled from the Rhineland to the Low Countries in exchange for wool cloth, and then passed from the Low Countries to England in exchange for raw wool. Some of this silver was in turn exported from England to Spain and the Mediterranean in return for silks, spices, and gold. Between 991 and 1051, some of it went also to Scandinavia in trade, plunder, or as protection money against Viking attacks. But a great deal of the silver that entered England simply remained in the kingdom, either as silver plate — the Normans were astonished by the quantities of silver bowls, platters, cups, and other containers they looted from England after 1066 — or as silver pennies, which circulated in the millions by the late tenth century and made England the most highly monetarized economy in Europe.

Silver coins had been struck in England since the end of the seventh century, but in 973 King Edgar ordered the minting of reformed, standardized silver pennies that would circulate everywhere (and exclusively — no other coins were permitted) throughout the kingdom. Bearing Edgar's name and portrait, this new coinage was at once a stimulus to the economy and a subtle instrument of royal propaganda. Thereafter, the monarchy maintained tight control over its currency. Every few years, it commanded that all coins be returned to its mints for redemption, whereupon a new coin type would be struck to supersede the previous issue. Such periodic recoinages ensured that the weight of the silver pennies in circulation remained constant. Silver is a soft metal, and silver pennies were light and thin. As a result, coins might easily lose a portion of their proper weight either through deliberate mutilation (called "coin-clipping," in which a fingernail-shaped sliver of silver would be trimmed from the outer edge of a coin) or simply through the wear and tear resulting from circulation. Recoining the money thus guaranteed the high standard of the English coinage, because the crown controlled the weight and fineness of each new issue.[13] Recoining also provided the king with a steady income from minting fees, but the beneficial effects of this policy on the economy, especially on international trade, were probably uppermost in Edgar's mind in initiating this new minting policy.

To make possible such a massive reminting effort, Edgar established a network of royal mints throughout the kingdom. From 973 on, almost everyone in England lived within twenty miles of a royal mint. Because no foreign coins were permitted to circulate within the kingdom, merchants bringing silver coins into England were required to have their coins reminted before they could use them to purchase goods. Mints, therefore, were generally established at markets, and markets were usu-

---

[13]"Fineness" refers to the percentage of silver versus alloyed metals in each coin.

MINTS IN LATE ANGLO-SAXON ENGLAND

●	Undetermined
▲	New mints of Edgar
○	New mints of Edward the Martyr
■	New mints of Aethelred II to 999
□	New mints of Aethelred II from 1000
⋯⋯	Shire boundaries

Scale of Miles

0   25   50

James Campbell, ed., *The Anglo-Saxons.* Copyright © 1982.

ally held in towns. Where a mint was established outside a market, a market and a town would usually develop around it. By establishing this network of mints, Edgar thus ensured that almost everyone in his kingdom would now live within twenty miles of a market also. This made it enormously easier than it had been for people, and especially for peasants, to buy and sell their goods for money, thus providing another important stimulus to economic growth.

Edgar's minting policy not only stimulated the economy; it also spurred the growth of towns in late-Anglo-Saxon England. The towns of England were not large by modern standards. In 1066, when Domesday Book gives some basis upon which to estimate urban populations, only London (which is not recorded at all in Domesday Book) is likely to have had a population of more than 15,000 people, and only five (York, Norwich, Winchester, Bristol, and Thetford) had a population between 5,000 and 10,000. If, however, we define as a town any settlement with more than 500 or so people residing in it and where the principal economic activities were not agricultural, then at least 10 percent of the entire population of England was living in towns in 1066. These figures should give pause. If they are valid (and to the best of our current knowledge, they are), England in 1066 was the most urbanized kingdom in Europe.

Anglo-Saxon towns were centers of exchange both for merchants and for the population of the surrounding countryside. Towns were where butchers, bakers (it was only a wealthy village that would have had its own communal oven), and other food processors were ordinarily found, and where peasants brought their own surplus produce for sale. Fish, especially herring, was another crucially important staple of the medieval diet that was commercially distributed from towns. Ale would have been brewed locally — it spoiled quickly and traveled poorly — until the fifteenth century, when the introduction of hops into England made possible the emergence of large-scale breweries centered in towns. But beef, mutton, pork, and goose bones have been excavated in large numbers from Anglo-Saxon London, suggesting that the urban population was by no means solely dependent upon grain products for its supply of protein.

Town were centers for the distribution and consumption of foodstuffs, but they were also important manufacturing centers, producing pottery, cloth, leather, and metalwork in enormous quantities. In Thetford, one excavated Anglo-Saxon street was found to be four feet deep in the residues from ironworking. In another, there was a comparable depth of pottery shards. By and large, these items were manufactured for local (or at least domestic) consumption rather than for foreign trade. It may well be, therefore, as James Campbell has suggested, that "the production of consumer goods for a countryside in which coin circulated freely was a major reason for the extent to which late Anglo-Saxon England was urbanized. Such developments may have done more to transform the economy in the last Anglo-Saxon generations than any which took place for some centuries afterwards."[14]

Revenues from the growing towns of late-Anglo-Saxon England were an important element in the crown's demesne revenues. Besides these revenues, however, the late-Anglo-Saxon kings also collected a kingdomwide land tax. These taxes were used to pay protection money to buy off Danish attacks. They could also be used to hire Viking raiders into the king's service, as King Ethelred is said to have done in 1012. Like military service, Danegeld (as these taxes are usually known) was levied on the basis of hidage assessments, frequently at a rate of two shillings (24 silver pennies) per hide, and was imposed on all land in England. Land taxes to hire or bribe Vikings were well known to the Carolingian Franks also, but nowhere except in Anglo-Saxon England was there a land tax at once so comprehensive and so long-lived. Although Edward the Confessor abolished it in 1051, William the Conqueror revived it. It did not fully die out until the end of the twelfth century, when it was replaced by a tax on wealth.

---

[14]James Campbell, "Norwich and Winchester," in *The Anglo-Saxons* (1982), p. 175.

The Danegeld, with its associated system of hidage assessment, illustrates vividly the administrative sophistication of the late Old English state. To a considerable extent, such sophistication was possible because the agents of the Anglo-Saxon state were literate in English. The crown's insistence that its officials be literate dates back to King Alfred, who ordered that all his nobles should learn to read at least English, and preferably Latin also. Some did. At least one tenth-century nobleman, a man named Aethelweard, wrote a version of the *Anglo-Saxon Chronicle* in Latin and sent it to his cousin, a nun in Saxony. But the working language of late-Anglo-Saxon administration was English, not Latin. The writing office of the late-Anglo-Saxon kings (known as the *chancery*, from *chancel*, the space in a church reserved for officiating clergy) produced charters in both Latin and English. Its unique contribution, however, was the invention of a short English document known as a *writ* — a direct, even brusque statement of a royal command to a subject, usually bearing an imprint on wax of the king's Great Seal to prove its authenticity.

> King Cnut sends friendly greetings to Bishop Eadsige and Abbot Alfstand and Aethelric and all my thegns in Kent. And I inform you that my will is that Archbishop Aethelnoth shall discharge the obligations on his landed property belonging to his episcopal see now at the same rate as he did before Aethelric was reeve and after he was reeve up to the present day. And I will not permit that any wrong be done the [arch]bishop whoever may be reeve.

> King Edward sends friendly greetings to Bishop Stigand and Earl Harold and all my thegns in East Anglia. And I inform you that I have granted to [the abbey of] St. Edmund, my kinsman, the land at Pakenham as fully and as completely as Osgot possessed it.[15]

The idea of a brief, written, authenticated command may seem obvious enough, but in late-Anglo-Saxon England it was a new and powerful means of projecting throughout the kingdom the increasing power of a highly centralized, but still distinctly West Saxon monarchy.

Changes on the Land

It is easy to imagine the Anglo-Saxon peasantry — who constituted, by any count, the vast majority of the English population — as if they were an undifferentiated group of impoverished equals, surviving in an unchanging world through a timeless cycle of sowing, harvesting, and general hardship. This was, after all, very much the view taken of them by their literate contemporaries. Abbot Aelfric of Eynsham, for example, writing in the late tenth century, ascribed the following words to a fictional peasant of his times:

---

[15]Florence Harmer, *Anglo-Saxon Writs* (Manchester, 1952), pp. 184, 158.

I work hard. I go out at daybreak, driving the oxen to the field, and then I yoke them to the plow. Be the winter ever so stark, I dare not linger at home for fear of my lord; but having yoked my oxen, and fastened plow-share and coulter, every day I must plow a full acre or more. I have a boy, driving the oxen with an iron goad, who is hoarse with cold and shout-ing. Mighty hard work it is, for I am not free.[16]

Aelfric's words describe an important social reality. By 1066, across most of southern and western England, the majority of Anglo-Saxon agricul-tural workers lived in some form of bondage to a lord. Slaves did exist, perhaps accounting for as much as 10 percent of the total population, and a slave trade, illegal but active, continued between Ireland, Scotland, and the western shores of England and Wales until the end of the eleventh century. But the vast majority of Anglo-Saxon bondsmen and bonds-women, even in the south and west, were not slaves, but rather serfs (or villeins, as they are sometimes called). Serfs were bound to the soil and forbidden to flee it, but unlike slaves they were protected (at least in the-ory) from being bought and sold apart from the land they cultivated. And since there were no private lordly courts in Anglo-Saxon England, their legal cases probably came before the local hundred courts and so fell un-der the jurisdiction of the king's officials, just as did the cases of their free peasant neighbors. Slaves, by contrast, had no right to bring cases before the courts at all.

Serfdom was most common in Wessex and Mercia. It was especially prevalent on ecclesiastical estates. In East Anglia and the Danelaw, by contrast, free proprietors probably constituted the majority of the peas-ant population during the tenth and eleventh centuries. *Ceorls*, as the more prosperous members of the free peasantry are sometimes known, bore arms in the fyrd, took part in the hundred and shire court assem-blies, and sometimes owned slaves themselves. From the ninth century on, however, changes in agricultural patterns began to reduce the num-bers of free peasants. Lords now began to organize peasants, both free and serf, into larger villages of the typical late-medieval and early-modern type, with houses set close together along one or two roads, fronting on a green or a common well, and surrounded by large fields farmed in com-mon by the villagers. These changes did not affect all areas of England equally. Large villages with common fields were much more common in the grain-growing regions of central and southern England, for example, than they were in the hill country of the north and the extreme south-west. But while one would not want to underestimate the role of inde-pendent peasant initiative in the development of villages and common fields, lordly compulsion probably played the most important role in forcing such a fundamental and wide-ranging change in settlement pat-terns. Peasants residing in villages and farming common fields were much more easily controlled and exploited by lords than were individual

---

[16]*Aelfric's Colloquy*, ed. G. N. Garmonsway (London, 1939), lines 23–35.

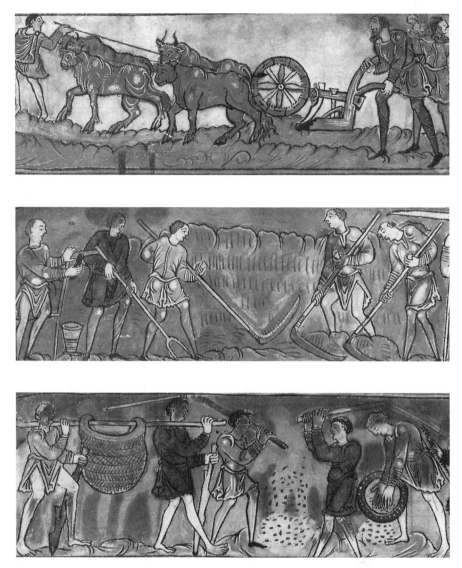

From an Early-Eleventh-Century Anglo-Saxon Manuscript *Top:* Peasants plowing with a heavy wheeled plow and four-ox team. *Center:* Cutting grain with scythes. *Bottom:* Threshing grain with flails and winnowing the grain and chaff. *(Reproduced with permission of The British Library)*

peasant proprietors scattered across the landscape in separately enclosed houses. The usual result of these changes in settlement patterns was therefore a marked reduction in peasant freedom.

There were compensations to village life, of course. Aside from the pleasures of intensified social contact with neighbors, villages also made it possible to construct and support common institutions such as mills, ovens, and parish churches. Lords generally derived a profit from these, but they were beneficial to the villagers also. The common fields surrounding the village were usually divided into long, narrow strips, which were apportioned among individual village households. Since the common fields constituted a single agrarian unit, however, a village council was usually required to make decisions on such matters as crop rotation, boundary disputes, and the apportionment of agricultural obligations such as plowing or seeding. Here, too, a lord (or his estate official) might play a dominant role in organizing the agricultural work of the village. But the village council exercised real power nonetheless over the daily life of the village community.

Between the ninth and the twelfth centuries, the village gradually became the fundamental agrarian unit of medieval England. Alongside the village, however, there often existed another, more artificial unit — the estate belonging to a *thegn* (local aristocrat), churchman, or higher noble, known later as a *manor*. Sometimes, a single village constituted a single manor. But frequently a manor comprised several villages and outlying farms, while sometimes a single village might be divided between several manors. The village and the manor differed in that the village was a social and demographic entity, whereas the manor was a unit of lordship and of agricultural exploitation.

As the Anglo-Saxon era drew to a close, manorial lords exercised an increasing degree of control over the peasants on their manors. Lords often controlled the village water mill and charged peasants for its use. Tithes from the local parish church might also find their way into the lord's pocket. Lords collected a variety of payments from their peasants, including rents, inheritance duties, and many other exactions. Most lords also had their own strips of demesne lands, interspersed among their peasants' strips in the village fields, on which serfs were obliged to labor for a certain number of days per week, depending on local custom and the season of the year. Free peasants too might owe such labor services, although often these were of a more "honorable" kind: driving a cart, for example, instead of ploughing or harvesting a field. Lords, however, did not do such farm work themselves. Like lords in every age, they lived from the taxes and labor of their peasants.[17]

Social Mobility

Like other early medieval peoples, Anglo-Saxon authors took a keen interest in the structure of their society. Their descriptions tended to be rather static, however, and it is doubtful whether we will get very far by following closely the Anglo-Saxons' own vision of their society as organized into "ceorls and earls," "villeins and thegns," or into the three "or-

---

[17]On peasant labor services, see the important article by Paul Harvey, "*Rectitudines Singularum Personarum* and *Gerefa*," *English Historical Review* 108 (1993): 1–22.

ders" of those who prayed, worked, and fought. But however we might describe the structure of late-Anglo-Saxon society, it is clear that a great deal of social mobility existed within it. Free peasants or serfs might become slaves by incurring debts they could not pay or as a penalty for crimes they had committed. But free peasants could also rise into the ranks of the thegns, particularly through commerce. Close connections existed in late-Anglo-Saxon England between merchants and nobles and between nobles and towns. A late-tenth-century tract claims, for example, that if a merchant went three times across the sea in his own vessel, he would henceforward be accorded the legal status of a thegn. There were also close associations between merchants, minters, moneychangers, and moneylenders. It was not uncommon, indeed, for a single man to engage in all four pursuits. There were also close connections between merchants, moneylenders, minters, and the crown. The advantages to the crown of such connections are obvious, not least in the ease with which kings could raise loans when they needed them. But these connections benefited the merchants also. It was probably this alliance between the crown and the kingdom's merchants, minters, and moneylenders, for example, that prevented Jews (who were actively involved in these activities on the Continent) from settling in Anglo-Saxon England until after the Norman Conquest. These close associations between nobility, trade, and the crown made Anglo-Saxon England a world more closely comparable to the emerging towns of northern Italy and the Low Countries than it was to the countryside of central France or even Normandy.[18]

Late-Anglo-Saxon Art

In the arts, too, late-Anglo-Saxon England demonstrated the signs of a maturing and urbanizing civilization. No Anglo-Saxon cathedrals survive — most of them were torn down and replaced in the generation or two after the Norman Conquest — but descriptions by contemporary writers, confirmed by modern excavations, attest to the existence of spacious, well-designed cathedrals in episcopal centers such as Canterbury and Winchester. Excavations at Canterbury, for example, have revealed that the Anglo-Saxon cathedral was as large as the present, late-twelfth-century building. Enormous, non-episcopal churches, such as the one surviving at Brixworth in Northamptonshire, demonstrate how very important church building was to the economy of Anglo-Saxon England. So too does the fact that eleventh-century Norwich contained within it almost fifty parish churches. The last great church of pre-Conquest England, Westminster Abbey, was built in the Norman Romanesque manner under the personal supervision of King Edward the Confessor (1042–

---

[18]Robin Fleming, "Rural Elites and Urban Communities in late-Saxon England," *Past and Present* 141 (1993): 95–108.

The Abbey Church at Jumièges Built between 1037 and 1067, the church remains, even in its ruined state, a fine example of Norman Romanesque architecture. *(Lee Snider)*

1066). Although totally rebuilt by Henry III in the thirteenth century (again in the style of contemporary France), we can imagine its original appearance by looking at the majestic ruins of the Norman abbey of Jumièges, built at about the same time and in much the same style. Vast and massive, its great round arches and heavy columns convey a feeling of solidity and permanence, much as would the Anglo-Norman cathedral at Durham, constructed about a generation later.

In the countryside also, a large number of parish churches have survived that date wholly or in part from Anglo-Saxon times. Although influenced to a degree by the styles of Carolingian France and the Rhineland, these churches show in their proportions and in the rhythm of their textured surfaces a strong native originality. The Anglo-Saxons also had a particular fondness for adding strongly built square towers to their churches. These towers often look like defensive fortifications, and they have sometimes been mistaken for such. But in fact, these towers — such as St. Michael's Tower at Oxford, illustrated on the following page — were stylish rather than military constructions. Their main practical purpose was to hold bells.

Tower, St. Michael's, Oxford   The rough rubble surface and double-splayed, double-arched windows are characteristic of Anglo-Saxon architecture. *(Edwin Smith)*

The tenth-century English monastic reform movement produced an important body of original religious literature, written in the Anglo-Saxon language and intended for lay as well as ecclesiastical readers. A number of these manuscripts are illuminated in decorative styles that show the influence of both continental and earlier Northumbrian traditions. Tenth-century Winchester, for example, was the center of a highly original style of manuscript illumination that drew from Carolingian models and yet was thoroughly distinctive in its fluid outlines of human and animal figures, its fluttering draperies, and its soft pastel colors. In the eleventh century, the Winchester style developed a degree of emotional intensity unparalleled in Europe, but which had a lasting influence on continental styles of manuscript illumination. The poignant crucifixion scene from the Gospel Book of Countess Judith (Winchester, c. 1050–1065) discloses a profound change in the mood of medieval piety — from the awesome to the human, from Christ in majesty to Christ in suffering. Perhaps better than any other contemporary work of art, it shows the level of technical skill and emotional depth attained in the closing years of the Anglo-Saxon era.

**Late-Anglo-Saxon
Crucifixion Scene**
From the Gospel Book of
Countess Judith, M. 709,
f. lv. *(The Pierpont Morgan
Library)*

The Reign of Ethelred "the Unready" (978–1016) and the New Invasions

A century after Alfred turned the Danish tide at the battle of Edington, disaster struck England. Few at the time could have foreseen the catastrophe, for in the year 978 England seemed as prosperous and secure as it had been during the previous generation. But in 978 a child-heir, Ethelred "the Unready," rose to the throne following the murder of his older half-brother, King Edward "the Martyr," apparently by men of Ethelred's own household.[19] Ethelred himself was blameless for his brother's murder — he was only ten or eleven years old at the time — but the assassination

---

[19]"The Unready" is actually a mistranslation of Ethelred's nickname. The Old English term is *Unraed*, which means "no council" or "bad council," while *Ethelred* itself means "noble council." Thus, *"Ethelred Unraed"* makes a fine pun in Old English but a very obscure one in modern English. Some scholars have tried to compromise, with "Ethelred the Redeless," which has the disadvantage of being absolutely meaningless except to scholars trained in Old or Middle English. We will stick with "the Unready," which catches the original punning spirit and makes sense — even though not precisely the original sense.

produced a kingdomwide shock that did not subside quickly. We know little about the unfortunate Edward "the Martyr," except that he was singularly ill-tempered. But a cult developed around his memory and his tomb, and Ethelred's reputation was darkened accordingly.

To add to Ethelred's problems, a split had developed within the Anglo-Saxon aristocracy over the monastic reform movement. Some favored continuing the initiatives of Archbishop Dunstan and King Edgar. Others urged the young king to oppose them. Many important men, including several bishops, had lost wealth and influence as a result of the flood of land grants and privileges that the royally reformed monasteries had received from King Edgar. Ethelred's accession was their first opportunity to reverse their losses. The child-king thus inherited an aristocratic power struggle and a tainted reputation — neither of his own making.

Ethelred has been portrayed, from the eleventh century to the twentieth, as a bumbler predestined to fail. The twelfth-century historian William of Malmesbury reported the rumor that Ethelred's troubles began early:

> His worthlessness had already been foretold by Archbishop Dunstan, warned by a filthy token of it: when as a baby he was being plunged in the font at his christening with the bishops standing round him, he interrupted the sacrament by opening his bowels, at which Dunstan was much concerned — "By God and His Mother," he said, "he will be a wastrel when he is a man."[20]

A century before, the *Anglo-Saxon Chronicle* had criticized the efforts of Ethelred's regime to repel the Danes:

> And when the Danes were in the east, the English army was kept in the west; and when the Danes were in the south, our army was in the north. Then all the councillors were summoned to the king, and it was then to be decided how this country should be defended. But even if anything was decided, it did not last even a month. Finally there was no leader who would collect an army, but each fled as best he could, and in the end no shire would even help the next.[21]

Despite such contemporary testimony, recent studies have demonstrated that Ethelred was the victim of nearly hopeless circumstances.[22] As a child he rose to a royal title clouded by his brother's murder. His aristrocracy was badly split between supporters of monastic reform (who

---

[20]William of Malmesbury, *Gesta Regum Anglorum: The History of the English Kings, Volume I*, ed. and tr. R. A. B. Mynors, R. M. Thomson, and M. Winterbottom (Oxford, 1998), p. 269.

[21]*English Historical Documents I*, no. 1, p. 243.

[22]See Eric John, "War and Society in the Tenth Century: The Maldon Campaign," *Transactions of the Royal Historical Society*, 5th Series 27 (1977): 173–195; Simon Keynes, *The Diplomas of King Ethelred the Unready: 978–1016* (Cambridge, 1980); and *Ethelred the Unready*, ed. David Hill, *British Archaeological Reports*, British Series 59 (1978).

tended to be East Anglian) and opponents of monastic reform (who tended to be Mercian). At the same time, he also faced a renewed series of highly organized Viking attacks of unprecedented size and duration, which revived the old hostilities between English and Danish settlers within England itself. Despite such obstacles, however, his government held out against the Viking attacks for thirty years, fighting off some, fending off others with Danegeld payments, while hiring yet others into its own military service. Meanwhile, Ethelred threaded his way between the friends and enemies of monastic reform, attracting to his court powerful aristocrats from both parties (as his charter attestations disclose). He issued law codes on a larger and more ambitious scale than any of his predecessors. He maintained close control of the coinage, presided over great councils, and issued charters and writs through a smoothly functioning royal chancery. In the end, some of his Anglo-Danish nobles betrayed him, and the Vikings defeated him. Ethelred made mistakes, but he was also unlucky. Had the battle of Maldon gone differently in 991, as it could well have done — the nearly contemporary *Song of Maldon* breaks off in the middle, with the battle still undecided; it is only from other sources that we learn it ended with a crushing Danish victory — Ethelred's reign might be remembered very differently by its historians.[23]

The Viking raids with which Ethelred had to cope were more than mere private-enterprise raiding parties. To an increasing degree, they were directed and organized by the kings of Norway and Denmark themselves. But despite English disunity and superior Viking military organization, the Anglo-Saxons held their own against the attacks until 991, when a Viking army under Olaf Tryggvason, king of Norway, annihilated the East-Anglian fyrd under Ealdorman Byrhtnoth at the Battle of Maldon. Later that year, King Ethelred won a respite by paying protection money to the Viking forces. But in 994 the Danes returned, this time led by King Swein of Denmark, son of Harold Bluetooth.[24] Once again, Ethelred paid protection money, as he did again, in ever-increasing sums, in 1002, 1007, and 1012. This tactic bought peace for a time, but it also made vividly clear the extent of England's wealth and of its military weakness.

In 1009 King Swein threw all his resources into a campaign of conquest. Three years later, the Danes made peace in exchange for an immense Danegeld of £48,000. But the peace thus purchased lasted less than a year. In 1013, Swein led a renewed attack on England, convinced that any kingdom rich enough to pay such huge bribes would be worth

---

[23]*The Battle of Maldon, AD 991*, ed. D. Scragg (Oxford, 1991), is the most extensive analysis.

[24]Harold Bluetooth was the first king of Denmark to convert to Christianity. Like him, many other characters from Viking history and sagas bore memorable nicknames: Eric Bloodaxe, Halfdan the Generous-with-money-but-stingy-with-food, Ragnar Hairy-Breeches, Ivar the Boneless, etc. An Icelandic musician was called Einar Jingle-Scale; a Norwegian poet, Eyvind the Plagiarist.

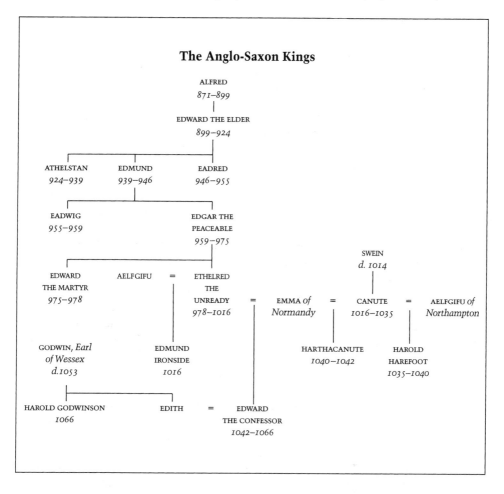

The Anglo-Saxon Kings

ALFRED
871–899

EDWARD THE ELDER
899–924

ATHELSTAN
924–939

EDMUND
939–946

EADRED
946–955

EADWIG
955–959

EDGAR THE
PEACEABLE
959–975

SWEIN
d. 1014

EDWARD
THE MARTYR
975–978

AELFGIFU   =   ETHELRED
THE
UNREADY
978–1016   =   EMMA *of*
Normandy   =   CANUTE
1016–1035   =   AELFGIFU *of*
Northampton

GODWIN, *Earl*
of Wessex
d.1053

EDMUND
IRONSIDE
1016

HARTHACANUTE
1040–1042

HAROLD
HAREFOOT
1035–1040

HAROLD GODWINSON
1066

EDITH   =   EDWARD
THE CONFESSOR
1042–1066

even more if conquered. Only now did Ethelred's kingdom unravel ir-
reparably. Defections among Ethelred's supporters were numerous, even
in the heartland of Wessex, while the Danelaw gave Swein its firm support. Ethelred fled to Normandy, the homeland of his wife Emma, and
most of the English accepted Swein as their new king.

Swein, however, enjoyed his triumph only briefly. He died in 1014,
leaving England to his son Cnut. The English magnates thereupon invited Ethelred to return as king, "if he would govern them more justly
than he did before."[25] In 1016, however, Ethelred died, worn out by his
troubles. His son, a skillful warrior named Edmund "Ironside," fought on
for a season, successfully defending London and inflicting heavy casualties on Cnut's army in a costly defeat at the battle of Assandun (either
Ashdon or Ashingdon, both in Essex). But when Edmund died in the

---

[25]*Anglo-Saxon Chronicle,* in *English Historical Documents I,* no. 1, p. 246.

autumn of 1016, the *Witan* concurred in Cnut's accession to the throne of Alfred the Great. Edmund's young children were taken off to Hungary; his two half-brothers Edward and Alfred, the sons of King Ethelred and Queen Emma, remained at the Norman court where they had lived since 1013. Queen Emma made the best of the new situation by marrying Cnut. Cnut, however, did nothing to divorce his existing wife, a Mercian noblewoman named Aelfgifu of Northampton.[26] The competing claims of Cnut's sons Harthacnut (with Emma), Swein, and Harold Harefoot (with Aelfgifu) would embroil England after his death, and contribute to the collapse of Cnut's brief-lived Anglo-Scandinavian empire. In 1016, however, Cnut's marriage to Emma enabled him to preserve, at least temporarily, Ethelred's alliance with Normandy and to assert symbolically the continuity of his own reign with that of his Anglo-Saxon predecessors. On these terms at least, the marriage must be judged a success.

The Reign of Cnut (1016–1035)

Cnut[27] consolidated his triumph by ordering a bloody purge of the English aristocracy and by levying an enormous geld to pay off his troops. But in these as in other respects, his policies were distinguished from those of Ethelred chiefly by their greater success. Cnut's legislation (at least as it survives to us) largely repeated the provisions of his predecessors. He maintained the assessment, coinage, and taxation systems essentially unchanged, although he did alter the weight of the English coinage to bring it into a closer exchange relationship with his Danish currency. By and large, he seems to have maintained good relations with the English bishops. He was a generous patron of monastic houses and promoted the cults of several English saints, including that of St. Edward the Martyr, King Ethelred's murdered brother. Cnut's own Christianity was recent but fervent. As king, he developed a reputation for extravagant displays of Christian piety, the most famous of which — his futile command to the tide to stop and the lesson in royal humility he drew for his followers — is still referred to today.[28]

Cnut's initial purge of the English aristocracy, following as it did upon the heavy casualties among this group at the Battle of Assandun,

---

[26]Despite the official disapproval of the Church, polygyny — having more than one wife — was common among the Christian rulers of the early Middle Ages. Monogamy, even serial monogamy, with its corresponding disapproval of children born to unmarried parents, did not become the standard marital practice of European kings until the twelfth century.

[27]On Cnut, see M. K. Lawson, *Cnut: The Danes in England in the Early Eleventh Century* (London, 1993); and Robin Fleming, *Kings and Lords in Conquest England* (Cambridge, 1991).

[28]The story is told by the twelfth-century historian Henry of Huntingdon in his *Historia Anglorum*, ed. Diana Greenway (Oxford, 1996), pp. 367–368. It may have some basis in fact, as Lawson, *Cnut*, pp. 133–134, has observed.

allowed him to promote his supporters to the top ranks of English society with only minimal disruption to the existing structures of aristocratic power in the kingdom. The two Scandinavian military leaders who had done most to put Cnut on the English throne became the new ealdormen (or earls, as these officials would hereafter be called, a term deriving from the Old Norse *Jarl*) of Northumbria and East Anglia. The Mercian earldom went to an Englishman, Leofric. Leofric's father had been one of King Ethelred's ealdorman, but Leofric had supported Cnut. Leofric's wife, Godgifu, was the Lady Godiva of legend, not the first, but certainly the most famous, of tax resisters.

Initially, Cnut held Wessex himself, but within ten years of his accession he constituted it as a fourth earldom and awarded it to Godwine, a West Saxon nobleman whose father had allied himself with the Danes after a brief career as an unaffiliated plunderer of the countryside. The power of these great earls would prove to be a crippling handicap to Cnut's successors, who found themselves unable to rule England except in alliance with them, and who then compounded the difficulties by permitting these offices to become heritable within families. Godwine's family benefited the most from this new policy. By 1065, Godwine's sons would control not only the earldom of Wessex, but the earldoms of East Anglia and Northumbria as well.

Cnut himself, however, must have considered that the benefits of these powerful earldoms outweighed their risks. He was, in the first place, much more than merely the king of England. Soon after his English coronation, he also became king of Denmark, succeeding his brother Swein. In 1028, he became king of Norway also. This meant he would have to spend much of his time outside England and would need to rely on others to rule it in his name. But possession of this Scandinavian empire also meant that Cnut had a power base outside England from which he could draw money and troops to suppress any English rebellions that might arise in his absence. Cnut may also have calculated, correctly, that it would take at least a generation for these new earls to establish the kinds of connections with the local nobility of their new provinces that would be necessary to make them truly dangerous. Finally, we must also remember that when his reign began Cnut had relatively few supporters in England upon whom he could rely. He was, after all, a conqueror and usurper in a foreign land. His willingness to entrust so much of his authority to a few great men reflects not only confidence in his own strength, but an absence of viable alternatives.

Had it survived, Cnut's Scandinavian Empire might have redrawn the cultural and political map of northern Europe; England might well have become a Scandinavian rather than a west European country. But Cnut's empire begun to crumble even before his own death in 1035. In 1034, Aelfgifu of Northampton and her son Swein were expelled from Norway in a revolt led by Magnus, the son of St. Olaf, thus bringing to an end Cnut's control over that kingdom. Swein died in Denmark soon thereafter. Harthacnut, Cnut's son by Emma, was already established as king of Denmark, but was not so securely in control of that kingdom as to be able to leave it to pursue his father's English throne. When Cnut died, therefore, in November 1035, Harold Harefoot, the younger son of Aelfgifu, was the only one of Cnut's sons who came to England to claim the throne. There seems little doubt but that Cnut had expected Harthacnut to succeed him in England; this may, indeed, have been a provision in the prenuptial agreement between Cnut and Queen Emma. In any event, Emma and Godwine held out for Harthacnut. Harold and Aelfgifu, however, had strong support from the earls of Northumbria and Mercia, and with Harthacnut unable to leave Denmark support for Harthacnut's cause began to dry up even in Wessex. Emma and Godwine, casting about for an alternative candidate, then invited Edward and Alfred, Emma's sons by Ethelred, to return from Normandy to claim the throne. Edward wisely declined the offer. Alfred took the bait, but in the time it took him to gather supporters and cross the Channel, Godwine decided to throw in his lot with Harold. When Godwine met Alfred and his party, he escorted them to Guildford, ostensibly to meet Queen Emma. But at Guildford, Harold's men fell upon the drunken party by prearrangement, slaughtering Alfred's followers and blinding Alfred, who died from his injuries a few days later. Queen Emma now went into exile, and Harold Harefoot became king of England, with the support of all three of the dominant earls.

Harthacnut, meanwhile, had made a treaty with Magnus of Norway, in which each recognized the other as his heir should he die without issue. This helped to resolve the continuing hostilities between Denmark and Norway. By the end of 1038, Harthacnut was at last free to make an attempt on England. But he continued to wait, perhaps knowing that his half-brother Harold was unwell. In 1040, Harold died, and Harthacnut ascended the English throne unopposed. Harthacnut immediately took steps to identify himself with the "legitimate" line of the West Saxon dynasty. He put Godwine on trial for his involvement in Alfred's murder.[29] He brought Queen Emma back from her exile in Flanders. And Harthacnut also summoned his surviving half-brother Edward from Normandy, establishing him as a member of his household and recognizing him as the heir to the English throne. In 1041, there was probably more fraternal piety then real policy behind Harthacnut's relationship with Edward. Harthacnut was still in his early twenties, and it cannot have seemed likely that Edward would ever in fact sit on the English throne. But a year later, in 1042, Harthacnut suddenly dropped dead in the middle of a wedding feast. The Londoners immediately acclaimed Edward, and the great men of England followed suit. Only Queen Emma seems to have opposed Edward, preferring the claims of King Magnus of Norway, faithful to the

---

[29]Godwine responded that he had been acting under orders of his lord, King Harold; the other earls backed him up in this "Nuremberg defense," and Godwine escaped by paying Harthacnut an enormous fine in compensation for his half-brother's death.

end in her preference for the sons of her second marriage over those of her first marriage.

The Reign of Edward the Confessor (1042–1066)

The new King Edward[30] had lived as an exile in Normandy from his twelfth until his thirty-sixth year of age. When he came to the English throne, he brought little knowledge of the country and no established party of supporters with him. He was indeed, in many respects, more Norman than English. He spoke French by preference and installed Norman favorites in his court and kingdom. These appointments alienated many Englishmen, and have sometimes been seen as evidence of Edward's limited political talent. One must ask, however, what alternatives Edward had. Unlike Cnut, Edward had no power base outside England upon which he could draw. In 1042, Denmark and Norway were again at war with each other, and the king of Norway, Magnus, had his own claims to the English throne as a result of his treaty with Harthacnut. Only in 1047, when Magnus died, did the threat of a Norwegian invasion of England lessen. Normandy, where Edward did have friends, was in an equally disturbed state, ruled by an illegitimate child-duke whose own domestic difficulties made it quite impossible for him to lend any effective support abroad.

Within England, meanwhile, power lay increasingly in the hands of the three great earls: Leofric of Mercia, Siward of Northumbria, and Godwine of Wessex. They were Cnut's creations and had served him loyally, but in the years since Cnut's death they had begun to assert an increasing autonomy. Godwine was now the most powerful of the three, and because he controlled the territory within which the great bulk of the royal demesne lands lay, he held something like a stranglehold on the monarchy. By 1051, indeed, Godwine and his sons held more land than the king himself. Swein, Godwine's eldest son, was earl of Berkshire, Oxford, Gloucester, Hereford, and Somerset; Harold, his second son, held an enlarged East Anglian earldom that included Essex, Cambridgeshire, and Huntingdonshire, in addition to Norfolk and Suffolk. The family's influence extended also into the royal household, for in 1045 Godwine had arranged the marriage of his daughter Edith to the previously unmarried King Edward.

In late-Anglo-Saxon England, however, royal power meant much more than merely control over land or the king's bedchamber. As we have seen, the crown commanded substantial revenues from justice, customs duties, land taxes, and the coinage. Political power within the kingdom was equally complex. The three great earls were the dominant

---

[30]On Edward's reign, the best guides are Frank Barlow, *Edward the Confessor* (Berkeley, 1970), and the chapters by Eric John in *The Anglo-Saxons*, ed. Campbell.

figures, but neither they nor the king could rule effectively without the support of a much larger group of local aristocrats, the thegns. The thegnage was hardly a united body, but they shared a common interest in protecting the kingdom from renewed Viking attacks and from the ravages of a civil war. In the right circumstances, these were sentiments that might attach the thegns of Wessex directly to their king, and so allow him to throw off the controlling yoke of the Godwine family.

In 1051, Edward seized his opportunity. Duke William the Bastard was by now in firm control of the duchy of Normandy, while Edward had succeeded in installing a number of Normans in powerful positions within England, including, most recently, Robert of Jumièges, whom Edward had appointed to be the new archbishop of Canterbury, against the opposition of Earl Godwine. Edward was still childless, however, and after six years of marriage, it must have seemed increasingly likely that he would remain so.[31] In 1051, Edward therefore promised the succession to Duke William of Normandy. The earls of Mercia and Northumbria must have supported this arrangement as the one likeliest to ensure that the Norwegians would not return to English soil, and even Godwine seems initially to have gone along with it. But as it became clear that this was but the first in a series of moves designed to check the power of the Godwines, the family rebelled. They quickly discovered, however, that not only the earls of Mercia and Northumbria, but also the thegns of Wessex were already in Edward's camp. Godwine and three of his sons fled to Flanders. His sons Harold and Leofwine fled to Ireland, whereupon Edward sent Edith, his wife but Godwine's daughter, to a convent. For the moment, it appeared that Edward had won a bloodless victory. Duke William now came to England to meet with King Edward, and Edward continued to appoint Normans to positions of influence in England.

In 1052, however, the tables turned. Godwine and his sons returned from Flanders with a fleet of mercenaries. Harold joined them off the southwest coast with another fleet gathered from Ireland, and the Godwines began recruiting additional naval support from the southern coastal towns. As they had the year before, the thegns of Wessex showed themselves unwilling to risk a war, but since this time it was Godwine who was the aggressor, their desire for peace now made them allies instead of enemies to the Godwine family. Edward's own fleet was disorganized; unwisely, he had abandoned the heregeld the previous year, and he may therefore have lacked the resources to outfit a proper navy. Edward's fleet found itself outnumbered. The earls of Northumbria and Mercia changed sides, and by the end of 1052, Godwine and his family had recovered their positions. Along with a number of the king's other Norman appointees, Robert of Jumièges fled the country and was re-

---

[31]Stories of Edward's alleged celibacy only began to circulate after his death, in connection with the claims made for his sanctity. His title, "the Confessor," is a title bestowed by the Church upon individuals whose lives exhibit special signs of holiness. Eric John, *Reassessing*, pp. 166–167, however, believes Edward was a celibate.

placed as archbishop by a creature of the Godwines named Stigand — a vainglorious popinjay of a man who presided over the English Church with a singular lack of distinction.

After 1052, King Edward became more and more of a figurehead. Real power over southern England was exercised by Earl Godwine and, after Godwine's death in 1053, by his eldest surviving son Harold, who succeeded him as earl of Wessex. The succession issue, meanwhile, remained on the shelf. In 1056, Edward the *Aetheling*,[32] the Hungarian-raised son of Edmund Ironside, returned to England, perhaps at King Edward's invitation, presumably to play the same role that King Edward himself had played in 1041–1042. But Edward the Aetheling died almost immediately after his arrival, before he even reached the royal court. Thereafter, if the succession was spoken of at all, no record of the discussions has come down to us. Everyone seems to have been biding time, waiting for the old king to die.

Harold emerges from the writings of his age as a more attractive, less crassly ambitious figure than his father. Between 1053 and Edward's death in 1066, king and earl seem to have worked together on reasonably good terms. Harold behaved with proper deference toward Edward, did most of the necessary frontier campaigning in Wales, and left the monarch to his favorite pastimes — hunting, churchgoing, and directing the construction of the great Romanesque abbey at Westminster. Harold proved himself a leader of political talent and exceptional generalship, and in the years of his power the kingdom flourished.

By the standards of the day, England on the eve of the Norman Conquest was prosperous and well governed, even though good governance had become dangerously dependent on the friendly relations between a submissive king and his over-mighty earl. The military organization was efficient; towns and commerce were growing; and money circulated on a scale unmatched elsewhere in Europe. Despite differences in language and custom between one region and another, Anglo-Saxon England had achieved by 1066 a genuine sense of national unity, which contrasted sharply with the political chaos and endemic private warfare that plagued most of France. A vivid illustration of this sense of a common national identity occurs in a passage from the *Anglo-Saxon Chronicle* under the year 1052. On Earl Godwine's return from exile, both he and King Edward had large military forces behind them, and for a time open battle seemed unavoidable. But as the chronicler explains, the chief military leaders on both sides, still deeply apprehensive of the Viking threat, decided against a test of arms: "It was hateful to them that they should fight against men of their own race, because very few worthy men on either side were not Englishmen."[33] As this passage makes clear, Bede's

---

[32]*Aetheling* is an Anglo-Saxon term for a close male relative of the king with a possible claim to the throne. The closest modern English equivalent is "prince."

[33]*Anglo-Saxon Chronicle, sub anno* 1052, tr. C. Warren Hollister.

vision of the English as a single people was by now widely shared by the laity also.

The Reign of Harold II and the Norman Conquest (1066)

King Edward the Confessor died in January 1066, an old man, still childless. His death was a lengthy and lingering affair. Earl Harold, who had attended the deathbed, claimed that the old king had designated him as his heir. This claim was backed up by Archbishop Stigand of Canterbury, a longtime ally of the Godwine family, who was also at the king's bedside, but Queen Edith, who must also have been present, would later dismiss it as a fabrication. How important a role this claim played in Harold's selection by the *Witan* as the new king, we cannot say, but the choice was made within a day of the old king's death, suggesting that Harold's accession must already have been widely expected, whatever King Edward may have said in his final hours. So speedily was Harold crowned that the coronation and Edward's funeral wound up being held on the same day.

Part of the explanation for the *Witan*'s haste in selecting Harold lay in the recurrent English fear of another invasion from Norway. Harold Hardrada, an illustrious Norse warrior whose military exploits had won him fame from Byzantium to Scandinavia, had become king of Norway in 1047. As such, he also had a claim to the throne of England, arising out of the treaty made between Harthacnut and King Magnus of Norway in 1038 to recognize each as the heir of the other should either die childless, as Harthacnut had done. In 1042, King Magnus had been too preoccupied by his war with Denmark to enforce his claim on England. In 1066, however, Harold Hardrada was known to be preparing an invasion force, while awaiting news of King Edward's death.

The third claimant to the English throne was, of course, Duke William of Normandy, whom Edward had named as his heir in 1051. By 1066, this might seem to have been old news. The 1056 recall of Edward the Aetheling certainly suggests that King Edward was no longer committed to the idea that William of Normandy would succeed him. But William also claimed priority over Harold Godwineson on the basis of a peculiar episode that had occurred in 1064 or 1065. Norman sources recount that Harold, visiting the Continent, fell into the hands of a vassal of the duke of Normandy who handed him over to Duke William. William treated Harold as an honored (although likely unwilling) guest. Eventually, in a solemn public oath, Harold acknowledged William's right to the English throne, accepted him as his lord, and accompanied him on a military campaign to Brittany, after which he returned home to England. No English sources report these events, and we cannot be certain that they ever took place. The Norman sources, however, tell a consistent story in asserting that they did take place, and the story they told convinced not only William's followers of the righteousness of his cause, but also the pope in Rome, who in 1066 granted William a papal banner to carry with him when he invaded England. The story of Harold's oath did more, however, than provide an additional element to Duke William's legal claim to the English throne. It also allowed William and his supporters to paint Harold as a perjuror who had betrayed his lord. By associating Harold in this way with Judas, Norman propagandists could identify Duke William implicitly with Christ. In a world that saw legitimate kings as inherently Christlike figures, these were powerful associations that damaged Harold's reputation and undermined support for his cause abroad.

Beyond the threats posed by Harold Hardrada and William of Normandy, Harold Godwineson had two additional liabilities. By 1066, the reformed papacy begun by Pope Leo IX was beginning to assert its authority over the bishops of the western European church. As the guardian of proper canonical processes in the selection and deposition of bishops, the papacy had refused to accept the deposition of Robert of Jumièges as archbishop of Canterbury and the elevation of Stigand. Stigand, moreover, had further offended Rome by continuing as bishop of Winchester even after becoming archbishop of Canterbury. Harold's association with Stigand confirmed the papacy's hostility toward him, and the Norman allegation that Harold had allowed himself to be crowned by Stigand, though almost certainly false, cast further doubt upon the validity of Harold's own coronation. Duke William, by contrast, had a Europeanwide reputation as a church reformer and a patron of monks. In the eyes of the papacy, therefore, Duke William's cause was almost a kind of holy war.

Harold Godwineson's other liability was his brother Tostig, the recently exiled earl of Northumbria. In thrusting Tostig into the Northumbrian earldom, the Godwine family probably overreached itself. But Tostig made a difficult situation much worse by the violent incompetence of his rule. In 1065, an uprising by the Northumbrian aristocracy overthrew him, and Tostig fled to his wife's homeland of Flanders. The Northumbrians chose as their new earl a magnate named Morcar, brother of Earl Edwin of Mercia and unrelated to the Godwine family. Harold now threw his support behind Morcar and made no effort to reinstate his troublesome brother. By so doing, Harold earned the gratitude of both Edwin and Morcar, who repaid the favor a few months later by supporting Harold's bid for the English throne. But Harold's refusal to assist him enraged Tostig, who from his base in Flanders now nursed his resentment and planned his revenge. In the months following his coronation, Harold established his position securely at home. But he had more than his share of dangerous enemies abroad.

Normandy on the eve of the battle of Hastings was a well-organized principality whose duke controlled his vassals to a degree unmatched elsewhere in France. But the high degree of ducal control that Normandy enjoyed in 1066 was to a considerable extent Duke William's own achievement. Winning a pivotal victory over his rebellious barons in 1047, he spent the years thereafter founding and enriching grateful abbeys, working to eliminate private warfare, and reshaping the Norman nobility into a cohesive group of ducal kinsmen and supporters. Normandy remained, however, a land of private castles and of mounted knights whose military obligations to their duke were not yet strictly defined. And although it had by now shed much of its Viking past in becoming a well-integrated part of the northern French economic and cultural world, the duchy remained economically poorer and less administratively sophisticated than England.[34]

Had Edward the Confessor died ten years earlier, it is doubtful whether William of Normandy would have been able to launch an invasion effort. His powerful neighbors — the counts of Anjou and Flanders, and the Capetian king of France — would almost certainly have united to prevent such an enormous increase in Norman power as would result from a successful conquest of England. But the count of Anjou and the king of France had both died in 1060, leaving their territories to child-heirs, and William had neutralized the traditional alliance between the Godwine family and Flanders by his own marriage to Matilda, the daughter of the count of Flanders. Harold's refusal to support Tostig in Northumbria was another lucky stroke for William. Tostig was married to the sister of the count of Flanders, and Harold's betrayal of Tostig (or so at least it must have appeared in Flanders) threw the count of Flanders into William's camp. Diplomatically, therefore, the way was clear for William to launch his invasion.

In 1066, therefore, William was in a position to make good his claim to the English throne. Good fortune provided the opportunity, and William had the courage, imagination, and greed to grasp it. The barons of Normandy agreed to the daring enterprise at a council early in 1066, and William set about augmenting his Norman force with volunteers from all over Europe. Adventurous knights flocked to his banner from Brittany, Maine, Flanders, Aquitaine, central France, and even southern Italy, drawn by William's formidable military reputation, by the generous wages that he promised, and by the lure of treasure and estates to be acquired in England. But despite the support of his duchy, the size of his army, and the moral backing of the papacy, William's projected invasion was an audacious gamble nonetheless. England was far larger and wealthier than Normandy and was capable of mustering, on short notice, much larger armies than William could transport across the Channel; and it was ruled by a warrior-king of ability and resolution.[35] Gamblers might have bet on William in 1066, but the house would have bet on Harold.

---

[34]On Normandy, see David Bates, *Normandy Before 1066* (London, 1982); David C. Douglas, *William the Conqueror: The Norman Impact upon England* (Berkeley, 1964); and for a very different view, Eleanor Searle, *Predatory Kinship and the Creation of Norman Power, 840–1066* (Berkeley, 1988).

[35]For the most recent attempt to estimate the size of the respective forces, see M. K. Lawson, "Observations upon a Scene in the Bayeux Tapestry, the Battle of Hastings, and the Military System of the Late Anglo-Saxon State," *The Medieval State: Essays Presented to James Campbell*, ed. J. R. Maddicott and D. M. Palliser (London, 2000), pp. 73–91.

The Bayeux Tapestry (Late Eleventh Century)   *Top:* The appearance of Halley's Comet alarms King Harold and his followers, whose fear of a Norman landing is depicted by the ships on the lower border. *Bottom:* A scene from the battle of Hastings, showing English foot soldiers repulsing Norman knights. *(Giraudon/ Art Resource, NY)*

Harold also faced a daunting military challenge, however. Two invading armies were gathering against him, one in Norway, the other in Normandy. The Norwegians would land in the north; the Normans would presumably land in the south. But there was also Tostig, gathering his own force in Flanders, who might land almost anywhere. Harold could predict neither the place, the time, nor the source of the first attack on his kingdom. As a result, he had to keep almost the entire kingdom on military alert while he waited to see which of his enemies would strike first.

As it happened, the intitial assault came from Tostig. In May 1066, Tostig and his mercenaries began harrying the coasts of southern and eastern England by sea. But Tostig's force was relatively small, and his men were turned back by local contingents of the fyrd. He retired to Scotland and entered into an alliance with Harold Hardrada, merging his forces with those of the Norse king.

By July, Duke William's forces were assembled on the Norman coast ready for the invasion, but the persistence of contrary winds prevented their crossing the Channel for three months. William's success during these months in keeping his force of perhaps 14,000 men and 3,000 horses together, without the army either dissolving or succumbing to disease, was one of the great logistical accomplishments of the Middle Ages.[36]

---

[36]Bernard Bachrach, "Some Observations on the Military Administration of the Norman Conquest," *Anglo-Norman Studies* 8 (1985): 1–25.

King Harold, meanwhile, had assembled the fyrd in southern England to await William's arrival and had stationed a large fleet off the Channel shore. But week after week, the winds kept the Norman fleet in port, and the English watched their coasts in vain. In mid-September, Harold was finally forced to dismiss his army and fleet. Fyrd service may have been limited by custom to two months. But in any event, by the middle of September his soldiers were restive, provisions were running low, and farmers were anxious to return home for the harvest. The contrary winds had served William after all, for Harold now had only his professional military retainers, known as the housecarls, to guard the coastline.

Immediately after disbanding his army, Harold received news that Harold Hardrada had landed in Yorkshire. Hardrada's army consisted of three hundred shiploads of Norse warriors, in addition to Tostig and his following. The combined force moved quickly toward the northern city of York. On September 20, 1066, Hardrada's host encountered the northern fyrd led by the two earls, Edwin and Morcar, at Fulford Gate, two miles south of York. The battle of Fulford raged for the better part of a day. In the end, after heavy casualties on both sides, the northern fyrd broke before the invaders. Receiving the submission of York, Harold Hardrada then withdrew to the strategic crossroads at Stamford Bridge, seven miles east of York, to await hostages from the conquered city.

Harold Godwineson reassembled his army as best he could and dashed northward. Five days after Fulford, on September 25, his army surprised the Norwegian host at Stamford Bridge and crushed it after a long and savage battle. Tostig and Harold Hardrada both perished, and the battered survivors of the three-hundred-ship host returned to Norway in only twenty-four vessels. Stamford Bridge was one of the greatest military triumphs in Anglo-Saxon history. The English had removed a Scandinavian threat of twenty years' standing, and the mightiest Viking warrior of the age lay in his grave.

Two days after the battle of Stamford Bridge, the Channel winds shifted at last, and the Norman invasion began. At nine in the morning on Thursday, September 28, the Norman fleet entered Pevensey Bay in Sussex, and William's army disembarked at leisure on an undefended shore. The Normans immediately occupied the important port of Hastings and proceeded to build a fortification there to protect their avenue of escape should the war turn against them. Some modern historians, with the advantage of hindsight, have assumed that the Norman victory at Hastings was inevitable. But this was not how it appeared to Duke William. At the time, William did not even know which Harold, Godwineson or Hardrada, he might have to fight.

On news of the Norman landing, King Harold acted with remarkable speed. Within thirteen days he settled affairs in Yorkshire, pulled together his tired and decimated army, and marched 240 miles from York to Hastings, gathering additional soldiers as he went. From a strictly military standpoint, Harold's haste was probably an error. There was no real need for it, since William was too cautious to proceed far from the Sussex shore until he had done battle with the English. Perhaps Harold had grown overconfident after his tremendous victory at Stamford Bridge, or perhaps he hoped to surprise William as he had surprised Hardrada. He may also have been anxious to prevent a long, drawn-out campaign of Norman plundering across the West Saxon countryside. Whatever his reasons, Harold chose to engage William with an exhausted army well below its full strength. On Friday, October 13, William's scouts sighted King Harold's army, and on the following day there occurred the most decisive military engagement in English history.

The Battle of Hastings was fought on Saturday, October 14, from morning until dusk. For the English it was their third major battle in less than four weeks. The northern troops of Earls Edwin and Morcar had been too badly mauled by the Norsemen at Fulford Gate to join Harold on his southward march, and there had been insufficient time even for the full complement of the southern fyrd to arrive on the battlefield. Harold's forces therefore consisted of his highly trained professional housecarls, armed with double-headed battle-axes, the London militia, and such additional forces as he had been able to gather on his march south. Many of his soldiers must have ridden to the battlefield — it is difficult otherwise to understand how they could have moved so far, so fast — but in the battle itself Harold's army would depend upon traditional Anglo-Saxon infantry tactics to turn back William's cavalry.

Harold did, however, have the advantage of choosing the battleground. He took up a strong defensive position on the crest of a low hill, placing the forward line of his troops shoulder to shoulder to form a shield wall against the Norman cavalry and archers. Behind them stood the housecarls in the center and the shire levies on the flanks. These tactics very nearly succeeded: in no sense was Hastings a clear triumph for the "new" military technology of cavalry over the "old" technology of infantry. The shield wall turned back repeated Norman cavalry charges, so often, indeed, that at one point the Normans fled in panic until Duke William rallied them to counterattack and slaughter the English forces (most likely the nonprofessional shire levies) who unwisely broke ranks to pursue them. Eventually, however, King Harold fell victim to an arrow fired on a high arc and falling at random behind the English line. With the king's death and the coming of dusk, the shield wall broke at last. The English army, now leaderless, fled into the Sussex woods, leaving behind them, dead on the battlefield, their king, his brothers, and a significant portion of the aristocracy of southern England.

Resistance to William's army did not end at Hastings. In London, a council of magnates sought a successor to Harold Godwineson to carry on the fight. But with its king dead on the battlefield, along with every single male member of his family; with the English aristocracy decimated by the casualties at Fulford, Stamford Bridge, and Hastings; and with the unfortified cities and towns of England now at the mercy of the victorious Norman army, it became quickly clear that further military resistance was futile. London held out until December. William, unwilling to risk a direct assault on the city, instead began a pillaging campaign around it, cutting a 25-mile-wide swath of devastation around the city until London capitulated. On Christmas Day 1066, William the Conqueror was crowned king of England in Westminster Abbey, having made good his claim to be the legitimate successor of King Edward the Confessor.

It remained only for William to consolidate his conquest and establish firm rule over an already highly centralized kingdom. There is, of course, an irony here. A less thoroughly centralized kingdom, less administratively sophisticated, and less dependent upon a single crowned king, would have been a far more difficult country to conquer and hold. By 1066, however, England was already a unified kingdom whose people shared a common national identity. William of Normandy was in this sense the heir, not only of King Edward, but of all the kings of Anglo-Saxon England since Alfred. It was upon the foundations laid in the Anglo-Saxon period that medieval England would be built. Without these foundations, the Norman achievement would have been impossible.

PART TWO

THE GROWTH
OF THE REALM

1066 to 1216

CORONATION OF WILLIAM THE CONQUEROR ON CHRISTMAS DAY, 1066
A rather fanciful fifteenth-century depiction.
(The Granger Collection)

CHAPTER 4

The Impact of the
Norman Conquest

William the Conqueror was a gifted warrior and leader: tenacious in the pursuit of his goals, cruel or magnanimous as it suited his purposes, phenomenally energetic. A monk of the next generation described him in these words:

> He was of a proper height, immensely stout, with a ferocious expression and a high bald forehead; his arms extremely strong, so that . . . no one [was] able to draw his bow, which he himself, while spurring his horse to a gallop, could bend with taut bowstring. He had great dignity both seated and standing, although his prominent corpulence gave him an unshapely and unkingly figure. He enjoyed good health, for he was never laid up with any dangerous illness except at the end of his life; and he was . . . devoted to hunting in the forest.[1]

Having won his audacious gamble at Hastings, William moved purposefully but cautiously to complete his conquest. London was the key to England, not least because it was from London that the surviving Anglo-Saxon leaders — Earls Edwin and Morcar, Edgar the Aetheling, and Archbishops Ealdred of York and Stigand of Canterbury — were attempting to reorganize the remaining English forces. Before William risked an assault on the city itself, however, he took steps to secure his escape routes. From Hastings, he went first into Kent, where he captured the port of Dover and erected a castle. After seizing the ancient Kentish capital of Canterbury, William then turned west to secure control over Winchester, the administrative center of the West Saxon kingdom and the site of the royal treasury. Only now did he turn toward London. Finding London Bridge too well defended to allow him to cross the Thames and attack the city directly, he led his army westward again, devastating the countryside as he went, until he reached the town of Wallingford in

---

[1]William of Malmesbury, *Gesta Regum Anglorum: The History of the English Kings, Volume I*, ed. and tr. R. A. B. Mynors, R. M. Thomson, and M. Winterbottom (Oxford, 1998), p. 509. The most complete biography is David C. Douglas, *William the Conqueror* (Berkeley, 1964), which also provides an excellent account of pre-Conquest Normandy. The most recent biography, also excellent, is David Bates, *William the Conqueror* (London, 1989).

Berkshire. Here Archbishop Stigand met him and surrendered. Crossing the Thames, William then advanced eastward toward London along the north side of the river as his forces continued to loot the rural areas from which London drew its food supplies. The London-based resistance now collapsed. The English leaders, accompanied by a delegation of London citizens, met William at Berkhamstead, about twenty-five miles west of London, to offer their personal submissions and the surrender of the city. But William's army did not stop. It continued to plunder all the way from Berkhamstead to London. Only when William entered London itself did the pillaging come to an end.

On Christmas Day 1066, Duke William was crowned king of the English in the new Westminster Abbey, with all the pomp and ceremony that traditionally accompanied Anglo-Saxon coronations. All those present, both Norman and English, promised their allegiance to the new king. William, for his part, undertook to abide by the laws in effect during Edward the Confessor's reign and to rule in the tradition of the West Saxon kings. Normans and English alike acclaimed William so loudly that the Norman soldiers on guard outside the abbey, fearing a riot, began to set fire to some nearby houses, to clear room for their cavalry should a battle erupt. The incident illustrates vividly how little the Normans knew of their new country, and the insecurity they felt within it.

The Conquest Consolidated

To an extent, William abided by his promises to rule as King Edward had done, but it soon became clear that he would need more than words to pacify his new kingdom. In the first few years following the Conquest, William maintained a number of Englishmen in prominent positions. Although he replaced Morcar as earl of Northumbria, he retained Morcar's brother Edwin as earl of Mercia. Waltheof, the son of Siward the former earl of Northumbria, resided at William's court, and eventually became earl of Huntingdon. Edgar the Aetheling, the last surviving male member of the West Saxon royal house, was another resident of William's court. In 1068, however, these relationships began to break down. Edwin and Morcar rebelled; Edgar the Aetheling fled to the king of Scotland; and King William was compelled to campaign in the north, where he built a series of powerful castles. Edwin and Morcar were forgiven and received back into favor, but the peace did not last.

In 1069, an even more serious revolt erupted in Yorkshire, once again involving Edwin and Morcar, but aiming now to place Edgar the Aetheling upon the English throne. The rebellion, clearly well-coordinated, spread quickly to Mercia and the southwest and received further support from both the king of Scotland and a large Danish fleet that appeared off the English coast. But the rebels were unable to capture the new Norman castles, and their disunity of purpose — Edgar the Aetheling and the king of Denmark both had claims to be king of a united England, while the northern rebels were more a Northumbrian separatist movement than they were the champions of West Saxon legitimism — proved their undoing. William's armies devastated the north, waging systematic war against the civilian population. Contemporary chroniclers report hundreds of rotting corpses in the Yorkshire countryside and thousands of refugees driven out by the Normans to starve in the depth of the Yorkshire winter. But when the Danish forces withdrew, following negotiations between William and King Swein, the military threat of the northern rebellion collapsed.

By the spring of 1070, the northern revolt was over. Around Ely, however, guerrilla operations under the leadership of a Lincolnshire thegn named Hereward ("Hereward the Wake," as he is often known) would continue for another year, giving rise to a romantic tradition that would attract both English and Norman readers in later generations. Edwin and Morcar joined Hereward, but the rebels were no match for the Normans. Edwin fled to Scotland, but was murdered by his own men before he arrived there. Morcar was captured and spent the rest of his life in a Norman prison; while the feckless Edgar returned to the Scottish court, where his sister Margaret was now the Scottish queen. Hereward himself, however, disappears from the pages of history. Like others of the defeated Anglo-Saxons, he may even have left the country, perhaps to serve with the Varangian guard in Byzantium.

This was not the last of the rebellions against King William's rule. In 1075, Waltheof, now the earl of Northumberland, joined with several of William's most important Norman supporters in yet another rebellion against the king. Once again, a Danish fleet appeared to support the rebels, but this time the rebellion was crushed before the Danes arrived. The chief Norman rebels were exiled; as an Englishman, Waltheof was beheaded, the penalty for treason under English law.

Waltheof's execution marked a turning point in the Norman occupation of England. In 1075, King William was able, for the first time, to draw upon significant English military support to suppress a rebellion against him. Revolts would continue, but after 1075 they would lack the nationalist element that had made the rebellions of William's first decade so dangerous. After Waltheof's death, only Edgar the Aetheling remained as a potential center for English opposition to the Normans. But Edgar was a spent force. He had made his peace with King William in 1074 and took no part in Waltheof's rebellion. By this time, however, William had come to distrust all Englishmen in positions of authority. Edgar was kept under close supervision at William's court, until finally, in 1086, he joined a Norman expedition to southern Italy. Waltheof was the last English noble to hold an earldom in England. Indeed, by 1086, when William surveyed his new kingdom, only four Englishmen held land directly from the king, and of these none were significant figures. The great men of pre-Conquest England had been completely dispossessed. Even the abbeys and bishoprics of England passed, almost without exception, into the hands of Norman prelates. Never again in its history would England experience such a revolutionary change in its power structure.

Controlling England was not William's only challenge during these bitter years. King Philip of France had by now come of age, and although he could do little to reverse the Norman conquest of England, he did all he could to undermine William's efforts to control the strategically important territories bordering the duchy of Normandy. In 1076, William suffered an important defeat at Dol, in Brittany; in 1077, he lost to King Philip the border region between Normandy and France known as the Vexin. Thereafter, William was on the defensive in both areas. Anjou, now under the forceful rule of a new count, was another potential enemy, which had claims to Maine, the crucial province bordering Normandy's southern flank; while Flanders, an ally of Normandy in 1066, was by 1071 also under the rule of a new count who regarded the Normans with hostility. William's enemies were also able to capitalize on the dissatisfaction of William's eldest son, Robert Curthose ("short boots"), who resented the fact that although he was a grown man and the acknowledged heir to Normandy, he had few resources and little authority apart from what his father permitted him (which wasn't much). Defending Normandy was no less of a problem for William than was defending England; in some ways, indeed, it may have been even more difficult. After 1072, William visited England only four times, for a total of about forty months. He spent the other 130 months of his reign defending his position in Normandy.

That William, despite these difficulties, succeeded in subduing England resulted from several interrelated factors. First, the English lacked a plausible candidate to put upon the English throne, around whom opposition to William might have gathered. Legitimate kingship was a potent ideological force in eleventh-century England. But after Hastings, there were very few candidates other than William of Normandy who could lay claim to the throne with even a pretense of legitimacy. In 1066, Edgar the Aetheling was still a teenager; and when he grew up, he impressed no one with his ability or his judgment. Neither Earl Edwin nor Earl Morcar had the support of Wessex; and the only other candidate, King Swein of Denmark, was regarded by the English as an even greater threat than William. Indeed, the chief argument for the traditional eleventh-century alliance between England and Normandy (of which William's kingship was the culmination) was precisely the fact that this alliance helped to keep the Vikings out of England. William was hated, but outside the north, English hatred of the Danes was even greater.

Like Cnut, William also benefited from his ability to draw resources from abroad to sustain his position in England. Normandy was a poorer country than was England; in the long run, the conquest of England did more to strengthen the Norman dukes' grip over their duchy than their control of Normandy did to strengthen their grip over England. But in the first few years after 1066, William's secure possession of Normandy was a critical factor underlying his English success. Many of the Norman

aristocrats who conquered England with Duke William were his kinsmen, and those who were not the Duke's relatives were mostly new men,
who had risen to power in the previous generation through their service
to the ducal family. These connections began to fray as sons succeeded
their fathers, and the chains of loyalty and kinship binding William to his
Norman followers began to lengthen. But in the first few years after the
Conquest, William could count on the support of a group of Norman
warriors and aristocrats who now held lands both in England and in

A "Motte and Bailey" Castle   This model, based on archaeological excavations of the early post-Conquest castle of Abinger, Surrey, and on evidence from the Bayeux Tapestry, shows the typical wooden tower encircled by a palisade atop an artificial mound surrounded by a moat. Such castles, new to England, were at once simple to build and difficult to storm, and the Normans consolidated their occupation of England by building hundreds of them. *(Courtesy of The British Museum)*

Normandy and who owed their prosperity on both sides of the English Channel to Duke William.

Normandy also provided William with a ready market wherein his English plunder could be turned into cash — and cash, in the eleventh century, could be converted speedily into troops and castles. Everywhere they went in England, William and his followers built castles; we have commented already on the crucial role these fortifications played in foiling the 1069–1071 rebellion. In a land that had previously lacked defensive fortifications aside from a few walled towns, the impact of these new Norman castles was revolutionary. Most of the castles built immediately after the Conquest were crude by later standards, consisting of nothing more than an earthen mound encircled by a moat and surmounted by a square wooden tower within a palisade. Such "motte and bailey" castles could be erected in a matter of days, as William demonstrated in 1066. Although relatively primitive, they were nonetheless difficult to capture by assault.

In the countryside, "motte and bailey" castles remained the norm until the middle decades of the twelfth century. In the cities, however, William and his sons more often built stone castles of monumental proportions, with great square keeps surrounded by heavy stone walls, such as the Conqueror's Tower of London, and the somewhat later castles at Porchester and Castle Hedingham. Large or small, stone or wood, castles

Porchester Castle   A great stone keep of the early twelfth century (center) stands at a corner of a larger defensive work built by the Romans some 800 years earlier to protect the "Saxon Shore." *(C. M. Dixon)*

functioned both as bastions of Norman power and as stark symbols of Norman authority in the conquered realm.

Castles were not the only architectural evidence of the changes wrought in England by the Norman Conquest. Under the Conqueror and his sons, countless churches rose in the Norman Romanesque style, which had already been introduced into England in Edward the Confessor's Westminster Abbey. After 1066, almost every English cathedral was

Castle Hedingham, Essex   A great baronial castle built in the 1140s by the de Vere earls of Oxford. *(A. F. Kersting)*

Chancel Arch, Tickencote Church, Rutland   The arch exemplifies the exuberant decoration of late-Norman Romanesque architecture. *(The Ancient Art & Architecture Collection)*

rebuilt in the new fashion, along with a great many village and abbey churches. In the early post-Conquest days, the style was heavy and stark, but by the opening years of the twelfth century it was growing more decorative. Stonemasons carved complex geometrical designs around portals and arches. Interiors were often painted in bright colors and decorated with frescoes, some of which survive to this day. As architects grew in skill and daring, wooden roofs gave way to stone vaulting, greatly lessening the risk that fire would destroy such expensive buildings. Much of this Norman construction still stands and can be seen in parish churches such as Iffley and Tickencote, and in cathedral and abbey churches such as Norwich, Durham, Tewkesbury, and Battle. The thick walls and columns, round-arched arcades, square, solid towers, and dominating proportions of these churches evoke a feeling of strength and permanence unique in English architecture, bearing witness even now to the Normans' vision of their own power.

Yet in architecture, as in so many other areas, major changes would surely have come to England even if Harold had won at Hastings. The Romanesque style was spreading across western Europe in the later eleventh century, although not always with the massive proportions favored by the Normans. Recent excavations at Winchester and Canter-

Durham Cathedral Showing the Transept (foreground) and Nave   This dramatic example of Norman Romanesque architecture was built largely between the 1090s and 1130s. *(Scala, Art Resource, NY)*

bury have demonstrated that some late-Anglo-Saxon cathedrals were approximately as large as their Norman successors. And Anglo-Saxon England was already a land filled with parish churches ranging in size from the very small to the very large. The Norman Conquest occurred at the beginning of a notable epoch of European expansion — economic, political, military, religious, cultural, and intellectual — a creative surge that has been termed "the renaissance of the twelfth century." In actuality, this "renaissance" affected the entire period between the mid-eleventh century and the late thirteenth — the era conventionally called the High Middle Ages. France was the core of this remarkable cultural development — the source of Gothic architecture, the site of the great University of Paris, the home of many of medieval Europe's most distinguished scholars and writers, and the birthplace of the Crusades and related military adventures that expanded the frontiers of western Christendom. Many historians have suggested that because the culture of the High Middle Ages was preeminently French, the conquest of England by a French duchy left England much more susceptible to the creative trends of the era. This is an attractive theory, but it should not be pressed too far. England had had strong ties with the Continent for more than a thousand years. With or without the Norman connection, England would have been deeply influenced by the culture of high-medieval Europe.

The Norman Church

This fact must be kept in mind when turning to the problem of Norman influence on the English Church.[2] William came to England with the blessings of the papacy on his head and holy relics around his neck. By 1066, however, the papacy that blessed William's invasion was a very different organization from what it had been a generation before. By appointing a series of popes drawn from the reformed monasteries of the Rhineland and by staffing the papal court with like-minded clerical reformers, the emperor Henry III of Germany (1039–1056) freed the papacy from the local Roman political factions whose influence had so degraded it during the previous century and a half. The newly reformed papacy thereupon began a concerted attempt to raise the bishops and priests of the entire church to the high spiritual standards expected of monks in a reformed monastery. Clerical marriage ("concubinage") and the buying and selling of church offices ("simony") were now strictly prohibited, while the right of clerics to elect their own bishops and abbots without lay interference was powerfully reasserted. Efforts were also begun to bring the bishops and abbots of the western Church into conformity with papally defined norms with governing liturgy and canon law.

The papacy considered the Anglo-Saxon Church to be out of step with these new expectations for clerical life. Most obviously, the reformed papacy objected strenuously to King Harold's archbishop, the usurper Stigand, who had become archbishop of Canterbury after the forced exile of Robert of Jumièges. In 1070, William had him deposed. Stigand's successor was a skillful ecclesiastical statesman named Lanfranc — a noted scholar, abbot of the newly founded Norman ducal abbey of St. Stephen's in Caen, and one of William's most trusted advisers. Lanfranc had also been the teacher, years before, of the reigning pope, Alexander II (1061–1073), who had given the papal blessing to the Norman Conquest.

Under Archbishop Lanfranc, the English Church began a thoroughgoing reform in keeping with the recent policies of the papal court and with the reform currents emerging out of Cluny and the Rhineland. Lanfranc summoned a series of kingdomwide synods that banned simony and prohibited the marriage of clergymen — a practice long disapproved of in the

---

[2]The standard accounts are Frank Barlow, *The English Church, 1066–1154* (London, 1979), and Martin Brett, *The English Church under Henry I* (Oxford, 1975).

western Church but widespread nevertheless. Existing monasteries were reformed, new monasteries founded, and more stringent rules of living imposed upon the English cathedral clergy — all in keeping with the rising expectations for holiness held by eleventh-century monastic reformers. Lanfranc also cooperated in transferring several English bishops out of the small towns from which they had traditionally ruled their dioceses into the major cities of the kingdom. Such transfers necessitated a great deal of new building, and in the generation following the Conquest massive stone cathedrals and bishops' palaces arose right smack in the middle of Norwich, Lincoln, Exeter, and Gloucester, disrupting street patterns in ways still clearly visible on modern roadmaps. Frequently, these new cathedrals were built next to the new royal castles. Together, they dominated the urban landscape and skyscape, bearing powerful witness to the ecclesiastical and political unity of the new Norman regime.

King William had already established his reputation as a supporter of ecclesiastical reform efforts in Normandy. He furthered these efforts in England by issuing an ordinance clarifying the jurisdictional authority of bishops over spiritual matters that might arise in the royal courts. Although William's ordinance is sometimes said to have separated secular from ecclesiastical courts, in fact bishops probably continued to sit together with the local sheriff as judges in the shire courts, as they had done since at least the tenth century. But a stricter effort was now made to ensure that when cases involving religious obligations or offenses were brought to court, the bishop (or one of his officials, usually an archdeacon) would judge such cases rather than the sheriff. There is no question, however, that William's ordinance reflected the efforts of the papal reform movement to distinguish more clearly the spiritual from the earthly realm and that it contributed in the following century to the emergence in England of a highly organized system of ecclesiastical courts institutionally separate from the royal courts of shire and hundred.

Nevertheless, despite the undoubted impact of the Norman Conquest, one should not overemphasize the change that papal reform ideals brought to the post-Conquest English Church. William had no intention of surrendering the traditional rights of the English kings to appoint and install bishops and abbots in their offices; to try Church officials for secular crimes in royal courts; and to expel bishops and abbots for political disloyalty to his regime. Nor did he intend to reduce in any respect the exalted, even sacred, position Anglo-Saxon churchmen had traditionally ascribed to their kings as the earthly representatives of Christ in their kingdom. In some ways, indeed, William further emphasized the sacrality of his kingship by regularizing the traditional Anglo-Saxon practice of crown-wearings at the principal feasts in the Christian year and by introducing the "Royal Praises" into the liturgy celebrated on these occasions. It is well to remember also that the English king about whom the Anglo-Norman Anonymous wrote in such extraordinarily elevated terms was either William the Conqueror or one of his sons.[3] William's kingship derived from his Anglo-Saxon predecessors. It was a religious as well as a political inheritance. He had fought hard to win it, and he would not surrender any part of it.

Times, however, were changing. The new pope Gregory VII (1073–1084) and his advisers held more radical views than did William and Archbishop Lanfranc about the requirements of Church reform. Gregory was no less committed to ending simony and clerical marriage within the Church than his reforming predecessors had been. But in contrast to previous reform popes, Gregory came to believe that he could not succeed in rooting out simony and concubinage until he had first ended the control kings and other laymen wielded over the appointment of bishops and abbots. Spirit, he argued, is greater than matter, and the spiritual authority of the Church ought to take precedence over all other worldly authority. Emperors should not appoint popes, as they had often done prior to 1059, and kings should not appoint bishops. Instead, the cathedral clergy should be allowed to elect a suitable candidate freely, without lay influence. In 1075, therefore, Gregory issued a formal ban on the claims of laymen, including kings, to dress ("invest," hence "investiture") bishops and abbots with the symbols of their spiritual office, including the pastoral ring and staff. Symbols and rituals had profound meaning in the Middle Ages, as they have in most societies. In forbidding lay investiture, Gregory VII was deliberately striking at the vital principle of lay (and especially royal) control over the clergy.

The gulf between papal and secular opinion on this crucial matter provoked a protracted and sometimes violent struggle. In theory, Gregory's ban on lay investiture applied equally throughout the Church. But in practice, because Gregory's chief opponent in the investiture controversy was Henry IV, king of Germany and prospective Holy Roman emperor, the fiery pope was in no position to press the issue in England or Normandy. He could not fight all Europe at once. William the Conqueror had no intention of loosening his grip on the Anglo-Norman Church, but he received deferential treatment as a friend of the papacy and a sincere opponent of ecclesiastical corruption. Wisely, Pope Gregory never pressed King William on these issues, and the issue of lay investiture therefore did not explode in England until a generation later. During the Conqueror's reign, it remained dormant.

Nevertheless, certain tensions did arise in relations between the papacy and England. Gregory assumed that the preeminent spiritual position he claimed for the papacy carried with it broad secular powers. He persuaded a number of important Christian princes to acknowledge that they were papal vassals — that the pope was their "overlord." Indeed, he demanded the allegiance (fealty) of the Conqueror himself, along with a

---

[3]See Chapter 3, p. 91 above.

request for the resumption of a papal tax known as Peter's Pence. William replied politely but firmly:

> Your legate Hubert, Most Holy Father, coming to me on your behalf, has admonished me to profess allegiance to you and your successors, and to think better regarding the money which my predecessors were wont to send to the Church of Rome. I have consented to the one but not to the other. I have not consented to pay fealty, nor will I now, because I never promised it, nor do I find that my predecessors paid it to your predecessors.[4]

With this assertion, the issue was abruptly closed. The reform of the English Church would proceed, but under strict royal supervision and authority.

The Problem of Feudalism

For more than 150 years, scholars have been debating whether or not the Norman Conquest introduced feudalism into England.[5] During the nineteenth century, many scholars inclined toward the view that feudalism developed gradually in eleventh- and twelfth-century England and that the Norman Conquest merely hastened a development that was already well underway. During much of the twentieth century an opposite view prevailed: feudalism was introduced by the Normans quite suddenly; pre-Conquest England was fundamentally nonfeudal, and without Norman intervention it would probably have remained so. The debate has been further confused by the fact that historians have been unable to agree on what feudalism actually was, or even if it existed at all. Recently there have been influential suggestions that historians of the Middle Ages could (and should) do without the term altogether.[6] The greatest of all historians of medieval England, F. W. Maitland, perhaps put it best when he concluded, only half in jest, that feudalism was introduced into

---

[4]*English Historical Documents, Volume II*, ed. David C. Douglas and George W. Greenaway 2nd ed. (London, 1981), p. 693.

[5]The classic account of the Norman Conquest as "feudal revolution" is Sir Frank Stenton, *The First Century of English Feudalism, 1066–1166*, 2nd ed. (Oxford, 1961), ably supported by R. Allen Brown, *Origins of English Feudalism* (London, 1973). For the debate up to the 1960s, see *The Impact of the Norman Conquest*, ed. C. Warren Hollister (New York, 1969). More recent work can be traced in two contending articles with the same title, "The Introduction of Knight Service into England," John Gillingham, *Anglo-Norman Studies* 4 (1982): 53–64, and Sir James Holt, *Anglo-Norman Studies* 6 (1984): 89–106; and in the work of Susan Reynolds in the following note. The most recent summary is Marjorie Chibnall, *The Debate on the Norman Conquest* (Manchester, 1999).

[6]Susan Reynolds, *Fiefs and Vassals: The Medieval Evidence Reinterpreted* (Oxford, 1994); Elizabeth A. R. Brown, "The Tyranny of a Construct: Feudalism and Historians of Medieval Europe," *American Historical Review* 79 (1974): 1063–1088.

England by Sir Henry Spelman, a seventeenth-century legal historian in whose works the term first appeared in English-language scholarship.

Feudalism is conventionally understood as referring to a network of personal and territorial relationships between members of the medieval warrior aristocracy. Although rooted distantly in the ancient ideals of loyalty between the members of a war band and their lord, feudalism in its developed form, during the twelfth and thirteenth centuries, involved a relationship between two warriors — a lord and a *vassal* who held land from that lord in return for services of various sorts, most notably, military service as a mounted knight. The lord granted a parcel of land to his vassal and undertook to protect the vassal's interests. The vassal, in return, performed a ceremony of homage and took an oath of fealty to his lord, through which he guaranteed his service and allegiance. The estate granted by a lord to his vassal was known as a fief or *feudum*, from which the word *feudal* is derived. Feudalism, in this sense, is usually said to have begun in northern France during the ninth and tenth centuries as a way of supporting heavily armored knights with their expensive military equipment of horses, arms, and armor, and to have spread elsewhere in Europe during the course of the eleventh century.

The difficulty for historians in dealing with feudalism prior to the twelfth century (when lawyers began to "systematize" it) is that these "feudal" relationships between lords and vassals were in no way regularized or predictable. Many of the knights who served in a lord's military household held no land from their lord at all, while some of the men who held land from a lord might not serve him in war. Some knights who held land from a lord did homage for it, but most did not. Some vassals owed strictly defined knight service quotas to their lord, but others did not. There was also much regional variation. In many areas of eleventh-century Europe, feudal relationships are not detectable, while in other areas feudal relationships coexisted with entirely different arrangements. Much of the land in eleventh-century Europe was probably held unconditionally, owing service to no one. It was not "feudal" at all. And even where we do find lords granting fiefs in return for service, political power frequently rested on public sovereign authority (rooted in the old Carolingian Empire) rather than on private lordship over vassals. And nearly everywhere, loyalty rested as often upon kinship or wages as it did upon homage and land tenure.

In traversing this minefield, it may be best, therefore, to begin by describing what we know about the structures of English lordship and aristocratic landholding prior to 1066 and then to consider the changes the Norman Conquest brought to these earlier patterns, before trying to weigh up the problem of feudalism in eleventh-century England. The focus upon lordship and landholding will of course address two of the essential elements in traditional definitions of feudalism. But we will also need to compare the ways in which military service was recruited and enforced before and after the Conquest, because some historians have argued that feudalism was at heart a military system. We will not, however, discuss here the impact of the Normans upon the English peasantry. That subject will arise when we consider the impact of the Norman Conquest upon the English economy and society.

Anglo-Saxon England was already a hierarchical society, dominated by a landowning aristocracy of nobles and thegns whose wealth rested upon their ability to exploit the labor of a dependent peasantry. The eleventh-century English economy was highly monetized, and many aristocrats profited from their connections with towns and trade, but their wealth was overwhelmingly agricultural. The Anglo-Saxon aristocracy was bound together by kinship (both with each other and with the royal family) and by lordship. Amongst the aristocracy, however, these ties of lordship were personal rather than tenurial. Less powerful men often found it advantageous to commend themselves into the protection and service of more powerful men. Predictably, Earl Harold of Wessex was a particularly frequent patron, who attracted clients throughout southern England. In return for his protection and lordship, these clients would accompany Harold when he traveled through their region, support him in his quarrels, and perhaps make gifts to him on solemn occasions. But very few of Harold's clients held any land from him. Loyalty and landholding were to this extent disassociated from each other.[7]

This pattern seems to have been a general one throughout the upper ranks of Anglo-Saxon society. Only rarely did aristocratic clients actually hold land from their lord in return for their service. The English aristocracy held most of its lands free of any obligations to anyone except the king. Like all landholders, an aristocrat owed the king the standard public obligations to pay taxes, obey the laws, perform military service when summoned, and act faithfully toward the king and kingdom. Anglo-Saxon aristocrats who failed to perform these duties could expect to lose their property. Frequently, they were also sent into exile. There was nothing about these obligations, however, that was distinctively aristocratic. With only minor differences, these same obligations were owed to the king by all freemen, and were reinforced by oaths of fidelity (or fealty — the two words are the same) periodically required from all freemen throughout the kingdom.[8]

Nor did jurisdictional rights attach to the lands held by Anglo-Saxon lords prior to 1066. All courts in England belonged to the king, and although lords must often in practice have exercised some de facto judicial authority over their slaves and serfs, jurisdiction over crime was a royal

---

[7]Robin Fleming, *Kings and Lords in Conquest England* (Cambridge, 1991), is the best account of Harold's pattern of lordship.

[8]Nobles and thegns were expected to serve personally in the fyrd when summoned; by the eleventh century, freemen generally served on a proportional basis (one soldier from every five hides, as in Berkshire; or twenty soldiers for an entire town, as at Oxford). Aristocrats, on the other hand, would not have owed the public works obligations (the construction of bridges and fortifications, for example) that were expected of lesser men.

monopoly, irrespective of the status of the criminal. Nor did Anglo-Saxon landholders hold any property over which the king's judicial authority did not extend — what later generations would call a *liberty* or an *immunity*.[9] By continental standards, therefore, the legal rights of Anglo-Saxon lords were severely limited. They could not judge criminals, except when serving as royal justices; they possessed no immunities or special legal privileges; they could not coin their own money; and they held no rights over towns or abbeys, because these too were regarded as royal monopolies.

The Normans came from a very different world. In 1066, Anglo-Saxon England was still a fully functioning, Carolingian-style monarchy in which landholding and lordship were rooted in concepts of public power and public obligation. In Normandy, however, Carolingian-style kingship had largely collapsed in the disorder of the tenth century, as it had done throughout northern France. A few Carolingian-style public courts survived in eleventh-century Normandy, but for the most part rights of justice were shared between the duke and his aristocratic followers, each of whom administered his own court wherein he judged his own followers and dependents. The Norman duke coined his own money, but he could not exclude the money of other lords from circulating within his duchy. Patronage over abbeys and towns was another privilege shared between the duke and his great men.

As in England, what held Norman aristocratic society together during the eleventh century were ties of kinship and lordship. William's family connections to the most important noble families in his duchy were an important element in his success. In Normandy, however, aristocratic lordship had a much more directly tenurial aspect to it than it did in England. Relationships of protection and service were common in Normandy, and not all the men who served a lord would have held land from him. Many of the soldiers who surrounded a Norman lord served him for wages alone or simply in return for food and shelter. But much more often than in England, relationships of protection and service between aristocrats in Normandy were cemented by grants of land from lords to their followers. Such grants created ties of tenurial as well as personal dependence.

Norman knights who received grants of land from their lord (whether that lord was the duke or simply another aristocrat) would be expected to serve that lord militarily when summoned to do so, to ride with him when the lord passed through their territory, and to attend him on solemn occasions. If he served his lord faithfully, a vassal could expect to pass his fief on to his heirs. Should a vassal fail to fulfill his duties to his lord, his lord would probably try to revoke his fief. In practice, however, a lord's ability to revoke a fief he had granted would depend not only upon

---

[9]The only exception to this claim, the immunity claimed in Oswaldslow by the bishop of Worcester, is now believed to have been based on a post-1066 forgery of a pre-1066 charter.

his own military strength, but also upon the willingness of the lord's other knightly followers to join him in taking punitive action against a fellow vassal. Lordly power in a society as fractured as eleventh-century Normandy necessarily rested upon a bedrock of consent between lords and their men. Ducal authority was no exception to this rule. William might claim the mantle of a Carolingian-style ruler by asserting his right to the obedience and loyalty of all freemen. But in practice, most of the freemen of Normandy held no land from him, and without such ties of landholding, loyalty and obligations of service in Normandy were often tenuous. Private warfare in Normandy was common, and private castles abounded. Of necessity, Duke William spent much of his reign suppressing such threats to his rule.

Monasteries in Normandy also found themselves caught up in these webs of obligation and service, but prior to 1066 the levels of military service owed by knightly vassals or monasteries to the Norman dukes were not defined with any precision. This fact is one of the chief arguments against interpretations of feudalism that would see it as fundamentally a way of raising troops for war. In practice, Norman lords recruited the majority of their warriors in other ways, as William himself did in gathering the army that fought with him at Hastings. Only a small part of any Norman army would have consisted of landholding vassals fighting alongside the lord from whom they held the bulk of their land.

After 1066, however, the situation changed both in England and Normandy. In England, William claimed the kingdom as the designated heir of King Edward the Confessor, but William was also, quite clearly, the conqueror of the kingdom. All those aristocratic Englishmen who fell in battle against King William automatically forfeited their lands as punishment for having resisted their lawful king. But there are signs that William decided, early in his reign, that this principle should be generalized, so that no English aristocrats, male or female, could retain their lands unless they had King William's permission to do so. By this measure, William staked a claim to be the rightful possessor of all the land in England, by whomever it was held.

Operating on this principle, and angered by repeated English rebellions, he seized huge numbers of English-owned estates. Some of these lands he added to the royal demesne — the territory controlled directly by the crown. The remainder he granted to trusted Norman followers in return for military and other services. Through these confiscations and redistributions, the lands of several thousand Anglo-Saxon thegns were gradually consolidated into the hands of about 180 great Anglo-Norman barons, all of whom held their lands directly from King William. The result was that in England, by 1086, all the land in the kingdom could thus be regarded as a fief of some kind, held from the crown in return for service. In no other European country did feudalism in this sense take such firm hold. But this was entirely a consequence of the Conquest itself. It did not derive from any feudal "model" William had brought with him from Normandy.

Most of these vast baronial landholdings consisted of widely scattered estates rather than compact territorial blocks. Only on the borders with Wales and Scotland did William allow large, territorially contiguous blocks of land to be held by a single lord. Such scattering of baronial estates diminished local particularism, and was long thought to have been a deliberate piece of royal policy. More likely, however, the scattering was accidental, arising from the facts that (1) pre-Conquest estates themselves tended to be scattered (although to a lesser degree than in William's time), and (2) William distributed lands in piecemeal fashion as the estates of one rebellious Anglo-Saxon lord after another fell successively into his hands.

This ethic of conquest applied also to William's Norman followers. All the land they held in England they received by King William's gift, either directly — through a grant — or indirectly — through violence, chicanery, or extortion directed at their English (and occasionally Norman) neighbors and sanctioned (or at least not prohibited) by the crown. In return for their direct grants of land, William and his sons claimed the right to specify the levels of military service each tenant-in-chief (as those who held land directly from the king were known) would owe the king in return for the lands he held. But William himself did not always act on this claim. Some bishops and abbots were assigned specific knight service quotas during the first few years after the Conquest. For most lay tenants-in-chief, however, the process by which their knight service quotas were fixed was much more gradual and may not have been fully complete until the reign of King Henry I (1100–1135). In Normandy, the imposition of defined knight service quotas proceeded equally slowly. But here too there is evidence of gradually increasing specificity in the years after 1066, reflecting the enormous increase in ducal power the conquest of England brought to William and his sons.

Lords could find the knights they owed the king in a variety of ways. They could retain a force of knights in their households, in return for food, clothing, and shelter; they could hire mercenaries; or they could grant out land to their own knightly followers in return for military service. Many lords pursued all three strategies. By 1100, however, most had given away a substantial portion of their lands to their own knightly tenants in return for fixed quotas of knight service.

The Conquest also brought a regularization of other obligations owed by fiefholders. A knightly tenant might be obliged to contribute to his lord a monetary payment, known as an *aid*, on certain special occasions, such as the marriage of the lord's eldest daughter or the knighting of his eldest son. Tenants were also expected to contribute toward their lord's ransom should he be captured by an enemy. Lords, in turn, might claim the right to control the marriage of a tenant's widow or heiress (on the grounds that if she married the lord's enemy, a portion of the lord's own land would thus wind up in the hands of his enemy); to act as guardian of a tenant's heir, and to occupy his land until the heir reached the age of majority; to collect a payment, known as a *relief*, when the heir succeeded to his father's landholding; and to reclaim the landholding should a tenant die without close heirs. All these rights gradually became customary between aristocratic lords and their knightly tenants in post-Conquest England. In a general way, these rights had originated in Normandy and been transferred to England, but the highly specific and well-defined customs with respect to aids, reliefs, and inheritances that we find in twelfth-century Normandy developed mostly in the post-Conquest period and probably emerged first in England. In theory, these customary rights and payments were owed to all lords who granted lands to vassals in return for knight service. But in practice, the lord who was most effective in collecting and enforcing them was the king.

If we wish to use the term "feudalism" to describe this new system of aristocratic landholding and service, we may of course do so. But if we do choose to adopt this term, we must immediately note its anomalies. In continental Europe, feudalism — understood as a system in which knights hold land from lords in return for military and other services — developed during the tenth and eleventh centuries as a way to perform basic political tasks in societies where central authority had collapsed. As a result, the "feudal systems" of eleventh-century northern Europe were completely unsystematic. In England, by contrast, feudalism developed out of the circumstances of the Conquest, in which a powerful king successfully claimed to be the ultimate lord over every acre of land in the country. William was able to enforce this claim partly because of his military strength, but principally because he inherited a functioning, Carolingian-style administration in England that made it possible for him to define, record, and enforce the services he demanded from his aristocratic tenants. Nowhere else in Europe did feudalism of the sort we find in post-Conquest England exist.

Feudalism in Norman England, being the product of a single will, was thus far more orderly and thoroughgoing than its French counterparts. Above all, it was rigorously subordinated to the interests of the ruler, who was at once sovereign king and chief lord within his kingdom. The sweeping authority of this lord-king — *dominus rex* — was the product of a skillful melding of Norman and Anglo-Saxon traditions. William preserved the Danegeld, and he exploited it thoroughly as a unique and highly lucrative source of royal revenue. He also preserved the Old English fyrd, sometimes utilizing it to assist him in suppressing rebellions by his own Norman lords. William permitted his most important vassals to build castles, as they had been accustomed to do in Normandy. But recognizing that these fortresses were potential centers of insurrection as well as strong points in England's defensive system, he allowed his vassals to build them only by royal license and required that they surrender their castles to him when military necessity demanded. Like his Anglo-Saxon predecessors, he also prohibited private war. He further tempered the centrifugal forces of feudalism by calling on the Old English custom of universal allegiance to the crown. In England, even knightly tenants who held no land from the king were expected to owe their primary loyalty to him and not to the lord from whom they directly held their property. In 1086, William made this claim explicit when he summoned the most important landholders of England, tenants-in-chief and sub-tenants alike, to a great assembly at Salisbury to receive their oaths of allegiance. In so doing, he was following a venerable English tradition. The knights of Norman England, like the soldiers of the Old English fyrd, were expected to be loyal to the king alone.

The Administrative Contributions of William the Conqueror

With a royal demesne twice the size of Edward the Confessor's, with Danegeld revenues flowing in regularly, and with the backing of a Norman aristocracy tied to him by bonds of kinship and landholding, William ruled England with unprecedented authority. But this authority was far from absolute. Rather, it was hedged about by a variety of restrictions, some customary — such as the expectation that a freeman should be dealt with honorably and that a son should be permitted to inherit his father's property — and some institutional. Among the latter, the roles of councillors and consultative gatherings were particularly important. Like so many other aspects of their administration, the royal council of the Norman kings — the *curia regis* — represented a blending of two parallel institutions: the ducal court of Normandy and the Anglo-Saxon *Witan*. The *Anglo-Saxon Chronicle* describes William's councillors as his *Witan*; like the Old English *Witan*, the Anglo-Norman *curia regis* could be either the small and more or less permanent council of household officials and intimate friends, or a larger and more formal council augmented by the presence of great magnates and prelates. The councils of England and Normandy were similar in composition. Even in England, William's large, formal councils, attended by the greater tenants-in-chief, were predominantly Norman in personnel.

While on their numerous visits to Normandy, the Norman kings left the administration of England in the hands of some trusted subordinate empowered to act in the king's name. William the Conqueror delegated his authority to different people at different times — to his wife Matilda, to a trustworthy household official, or to a powerful churchman such as Archbishop Lanfranc. In subsequent reigns, this viceregal authority came to be assigned permanently to a particular individual who, in the later twelfth century, bore the title of "Justiciar." But the Conqueror, with his boundless energy, preferred to rule for himself or to delegate authority on an ad hoc basis. No one person shared William's authority for any significant time. But as with Cnut, William's frequent absences from England — after 1072 he spent fewer than four years altogether in England — may have done more to spur administrative development than his constant presence would have done, precisely because his absences required William to delegate so much authority to his administrators.

The vigor of English royal government under William the Conqueror, unmatched elsewhere in western Christendom, is illustrated vividly in his greatest administrative achievement: the Domesday survey. As the *Anglo-Saxon Chronicle* describes it,

> The king had important deliberations and deep discussions with his council about this country, how it was peopled and with what sort of men. Then he sent his men all over England into every shire and had them determine how many hundreds of hides there were in each shire, and how much land and cattle the king himself had in the country, and what annual dues he ought to have from each shire. He also had recorded how much land belonged to his archbishops, his bishops, his abbots, and his earls, and — though I relate it at too great length — what and how much everybody had who was a landholder in England, in land or cattle, and how much money it was worth. So very thoroughly did he have it investigated that there was not a single hide or virgate [a quarter of a hide] of land, or even (it is shameful to record but it did not seem shameful to him to do) one ox or one cow or one pig which was omitted from his record; and all these records were afterwards brought to him.[10]

The Domesday survey, later consolidated into two large volumes known as Domesday Book, would have challenged any modern government. For its age it was altogether unique. Although by no means free of errors and omissions,[11] it is nevertheless an utterly extraordinary and immensely valuable historical source. Nothing comparable to it survives from any eleventh-century European country — or indeed, from any twelfth- or thirteenth-century European country either.[12] The labor of compiling it was immense. Circuits of royal administrators toured the countryside, gathering information from as many as 7,000 jurors representing the local shire and hundred courts. Although farm animals were for the most part omitted from the final record (they still appear in Little Domesday: see footnote 11), the king's officials undertook to list every manor, the name of the person who held it in 1066 and in 1086, from whom it was held, its assessment in hides, its value in 1066 and in 1086, and the number and social status of its tenants. And all this was accomplished in less than a year. The project was planned during the 1085

---

[10]*Anglo-Saxon Chronicle, sub anno* 1085, tr. C. Warren Hollister.

[11]London and several other towns are left out of Domesday Book. The north of England is covered only very spottily, and much of it does not appear at all. The second volume of the survey, known as "Little Domesday," covering Norfolk, Suffolk, and Essex, was never purged of its detailed accounts of farm animals as was done in the first volume, the "Great Domesday." Scholars have suggested that the scribes ran out of time and elected therefore to present the second volume in its unexpurgated form to the king, in order to meet the August 1 deadline.

[12]The Hundred Roll inquiries launched by Edward I in 1279 may have been even more extensive than the Domesday survey, but only a few of the returns to these inquiries now survive.

Christmas court at Gloucester; by August 1, 1086 it was completed and presented to the king.

We know a great deal about Domesday Book. We do not know, however, the purpose or purposes for which it was compiled. It is clearly based upon a number of pre-existing, Anglo-Saxon records of assessments for geld; and this has suggested to many historians that Domesday's primary purpose was to compile a record of the entire kingdom's hidage assessments, perhaps in preparation for a thoroughgoing reassessment. Other historians — noting that the survey is organized not by shires and hundreds (as one would expect of a geld record), but rather by tenants-in-chief within each shire — have suggested that Domesday was intended to inform the king about the new structures of landholding that had emerged in his kingdom since 1066, so that when a tenant-in-chief's property fell to the king, the king would know where his estates were located and how much they were worth. The trouble with this hypothesis, however, is that Domesday includes a great deal of information — including the information on geld assessments and the accounts of shire and borough customs — that are irrelevant to a mere register of "who holds what land, and from whom."

The most sweeping explanation of Domesday's purposes comes from Professor J. C. Holt.[13] Noting that the presentation of Domesday Book to the king coincided with the Salisbury Oath — when William the Conqueror demanded an oath of direct allegiance from all the landholding tenants of England — Holt has suggested that these two events were related and that they were planned together at the 1085 Christmas court. Domesday, Holt has argued, was intended to survey the new patterns of landholding that had emerged in England in the two decades after the Conquest. In so doing, it would inform the king about the potential wealth of his kingdom and its existing tax assessment system. The survey would also tell him the value of all the estates that might, through death or forfeiture, fall into the king's hands, for which the royal sheriffs might be required to account. But the reason William's great men went along with the Domesday survey and with the Salisbury Oath was because in return for the homage and fealty they swore to him at Salisbury, William guaranteed their clear title to all the property Domesday Book recorded them as holding. After twenty years of conquest, expropriation, forfeiture, and exchange, many Normans had no clear legal title to the lands they currently possessed. Domesday Book provided this title and thus set a seal of permanence on their acquisitions. Thereafter, William's followers would not need to appeal to the charters and writs of their Anglo-Saxon predecessors to defend their rights to their property. They

---

[13]J. C. Holt, "1086," in *Domesday Studies*, ed. J. C. Holt (Woodbridge, 1987), pp. 41–64. See also Robin Fleming, *Domesday Book and the Law: Society and Legal Custom in Early Medieval England* (Cambridge, 1998).

would need to appeal only to the record of Domesday itself. From Domesday, however, there would be no appeal: and hence its title, which means "judgment day."

The Impact of the Norman Conquest upon English Society and the English Economy

The effect of the Norman Conquest on England has long been one of the most hotly contested issues in English medieval scholarship. No one doubts that it transformed aristocratic society, for it brought to power a French-speaking nobility accustomed to knightly cavalry warfare, castle building, and a chivalrous doctrine of brotherhood in arms, different in many respects from the aristocracy of Anglo-Saxon times. But the new aristocracy, powerful though it was, constituted only a tiny fraction of the population. What of the rest?

English towns were growing in size and economic importance before the Conquest and continued to expand afterwards. On the whole, the dynastic and aristocratic revolution brought about by the Conquest left urban life intact, despite the initial destruction the Conquest caused in a number of English cities. When Norman merchants and artisans emigrated to England after 1066, they generally moved into the new "French" quarters that quickly grew up in many English towns. But town life and town law remained predominantly English, despite the presence of new Norman residents. Some towns suffered severely from the Conquest. York's population was probably cut in half, from perhaps 10,000 in 1066 to around 4,000 or 5,000 by 1086, a consequence both of the Norman ravaging of the north and of the declining levels of commerce with Scandinavia. Trade with the Continent, however, intensified, and while York shrank, Southampton, London, and the other southeastern ports probably grew. Altogether, the percentage of the English population living in towns probably remained around 10 percent — a higher concentration of urban-dwellers than existed anywhere else in eleventh-century Europe.

William dealt warily with the English towns. When Exeter revolted in 1068, he negotiated an agreement with the city rather than launching a frontal assault upon it. Normandy was not so urbanized a land as England, but William understood clearly the importance of towns and merchants to his own power and prestige as a ruler. Rouen was already a major city, whose merchants included an important Jewish community. These merchants helped to fund the Norman Conquest, and after 1066 William was careful to promote their interests. Norman merchants had enjoyed special trading privileges in London since at least the reign of King Ethelred, but it was the Conqueror who for the first time encouraged Jews from Rouen to settle in London. No Jews had lived in England since Roman times. Under the Anglo-Saxon kings, they were probably deliberately excluded from the country.

Peasant life, too, went on much as before. In the long run, the Norman Conquest tended to make the peasantry more uniform than in Anglo-Saxon times, lessening the privileges of free status, but also ending the practice of slavery. Both these processes, however, were already underway before the Conquest occurred and probably owe more to European-wide patterns of economic and social development than to the specific impact of the Norman Conquest upon England. Slavery, for example, had disappeared from France and Germany by the year 1000 and was probably declining in eleventh-century England also, although slaves still numbered around 10 percent of the English population when the Normans arrived. The Conquest accelerated the decline of slavery in England, not least because King William himself took steps to stop the slave trade that still operated between the western coasts of England and Ireland. The Church also disapproved of enslaving fellow Christians, and with the reduction in Viking raids, the supply of slaves was drying up. By the early twelfth century, slavery in England was gone. Those men and women who had once been slaves were amalgamated into the much larger class of serfs: men and women who were bound to the soil they farmed and forbidden to leave it without their lord's permission, but who could not (in most cases) be sold apart from that land.

The Normans were not champions of peasant freedom, however. They also continued, and probably accelerated, the process whereby formerly free Anglo-Saxon peasants were reduced in status to serfs bound to the lands of their manorial lords. The Normans were notably rapacious landlords, particularly in the first generation after the Conquest, when they were not yet certain that their Conquest would last. The manorial valuations recorded in Domesday Book are frequently much higher in 1086 than they had been in 1066, reflecting the more intense exploitation of agricultural resources and peasant labor by the new Norman lords. Some free peasants survived, of course, especially in the north and east; but after 1066, Norman law in England presumed that the normative status of an English peasant was servility.

The Norman Conquest may also have reduced the legal standing of Anglo-Saxon women, and particularly aristocratic women, with respect to landholding. Prior to 1066, England had developed a landholding system in which it was possible for both men and women to leave some kinds of landed property by will to individuals who would not otherwise have been entitled to inherit it. For both sexes, such testamentary freedoms were severely restricted by the system of feudal tenures introduced by the Conquest. Under Norman law, daughters inherited land from their families only if they had no brothers. After 1066, a mother could never have denied her son's rights in her land and moveable property, leaving everything instead to one of her female relatives, as we know at least one Anglo-Saxon mother did. As independent landowners, Anglo-Saxon widows and heiresses were therefore particularly desirable marriage partners for Norman lords seeking to consolidate or to expand their landholdings after 1066.

We need to be careful, however, not to overemphasize the change the Conquest represented, even for aristocratic women. Although 350 women appear as landholders in Domesday Book under Edward the Confessor, only about 5 percent of the land recorded there was held by women. Half of this land was held by only three women, all of them members of the Godwine family. Like the Godwine women, several of the other important female landholders in 1066 also probably held their land not so much as independent figures, but as representatives of the noble families to which they belonged. Land-ownership by women did not always lead to greater independence for landholding women. As Pauline Stafford has remarked, "The more land a woman holds the more likely she is to be controlled and manipulated by male relatives or lords." Anglo-Saxon women may, in some cases, have been able to control their own property within marriage more fully than was possible for their Norman sisters. But Anglo-Saxon noblewomen had no more control over their choice of marriage partners than did the aristocratic women of post-Conquest England. Aristocratic marriages in both eras were fundamentally arrangements about property and power. Norman custom may have been more assertive in assigning primacy to male property rights over female property rights, but against this, we must note also that by 1130, the Norman kings had guaranteed by law the inheritance rights of daughters if a family had no sons. The actual differences in the degree of control women could exercise over their property may thus have been smaller than the contrast in laws might suggest. For non-aristocratic women, we have too little evidence to make useful comparisons. We must suspect, however, that the contrast between their pre- and post-Conquest positions would have been even smaller than it was for aristocratic women.[14]

The End of the Reign

The last few years of the Conqueror's reign brought renewed threats to William's control over both England and Normandy. In 1085, the new Danish king (who bore the significant name Cnut) was preparing to launch an invasion of England in alliance with Count Robert of Flanders, whose daughter King Cnut had married. This threat evaporated only in late 1086, when Cnut was unexpectedly assassinated by one of his own men. King Philip of France was another enemy, whose possession of the Vexin, the border region between Normandy and France, put William's control over Rouen in perpetual jeopardy. To meet these threats, William brought a sizeable force of mercenaries into England during 1085, and

---

[14]For further discussion, see Pauline Stafford, "Women and the Norman Conquest," *Transactions of the Royal Historical Society of England*, 6th ser. 4 (1994): 221–249; Julia Crick, "Women, Posthumous Benefaction, and Family Strategy in Pre-Conquest England," *Journal of British Studies* 38:4 (1999): 399–422.

levied a huge Danegeld on the kingdom, the largest of his reign. Disease, famine, and bad weather during the following two years made the suffering even worse.

It was in the midst of these difficult circumstances that the Domesday survey and the Salisbury Oath were carried out. When "all the landholding men of any account throughout England" came before the king at Salisbury, "and they all bowed to him and became his men, and swore oaths of fealty to him that they would be faithful to him against all other men," William may already have been looking toward the military campaign he would launch against King Philip in the following year. This is uncertain. What is certain, however, is that from at least 1086 on, tenants who held land in England would acknowledge that their military service obligations extended not only to campaigns fought in England, but also to those fought in Normandy. This remarkable concession may be yet another consequence of the arrangements sealed at Salisbury as a consequence of the Domesday survey.[15]

The Conqueror died in 1087 of wounds suffered on his campaign against King Philip of France. The injured duke was brought to Rouen, the chief city of Normandy, where he settled his affairs, made his last confession, and died. As the Conqueror's eldest son, Robert Curthose might appear to have been the obvious heir to both England and Normandy. But Curthose had rebelled frequently against his father and was again in rebellion when his father died. By 1087, it was probably also clear to the old king that his eldest son lacked the qualities necessary to hold the Anglo-Norman realm together. William therefore decided to leave only Normandy, the land he himself had inherited, to Robert, to whom the Norman barons had already done homage and fealty some years before. England, however, the land William had acquired, he could leave by custom to one of his younger sons. He chose to give it to his second son, William Rufus ("the Red"). To his youngest son, Henry — the future King Henry I — the Conqueror granted a treasure of £5,000 (the equivalent of several million dollars today). With this sum, Henry purchased a substantial portion of Normandy from the perpetually impoverished Robert and began to make trouble between his two brothers. The struggles between these three brothers over the next two decades would ultimately lead to the reunification of England and Normandy, but not before their machinations had brought destruction and ruin to baronial families on both sides of the English Channel.

Of William the Conqueror's ability there can be no question, but judgments of his character have varied widely. He enforced justice and kept the peace. He was evidently faithful to his wife, a virtue all the more admirable for being so rare among the rulers of his age. But he was also avaricious and could be savagely cruel. A modern biographer describes

---

[15]Holt, "1086," pp. 62–64.

him as "admirable; unlovable; dominant; distinct."[16] One encounters a similar ambivalence in the judgment of a well-placed contemporary observer — an anonymous Anglo-Saxon monk who had once lived at William's court:

> This King William of whom we speak was a very wise man, and very powerful and . . . stronger than any king before him. He was gentle to those good men who loved God, but stern beyond all measure to those who resisted his will. . . . And he was such a stern and violent man that no one dared go against him. Earls who resisted him he placed in chains, bishops he deprived of their sees, abbots of their abbacies, and thegns he imprisoned. . . . Among other things we must not forget the good order he kept in the land, so that an honest man could traverse his kingdom unharmed with his bosom fell of gold. No one dared kill another, however much he had wronged him, and if any man raped a woman he immediately had his genitals chopped off. He ruled over England and by his cunning it was so investigated that there was not one hide of land in England that he did not know who owned it, and what it was worth, and then set it down in his record. . . . Certainly in his time people had much oppression and very many injuries:
>
> > He had castles built
> > And poor men hard oppressed.
> > The king was very stark
> > And took from his subjects many a mark
> > Of gold and more hundreds of pounds of silver,
> > That he took by weight and with great injustice
> > From his people — with little need for such a deed.
> > Into avarice did he fall,
> > And loved greediness above all . . .
> > Alas! Woe, that any man should go so proud,
> > And exalt himself and reckon himself above all men!
> > May almighty God show mercy on his soul,
> > And grant unto him forgiveness for his sins.

These things we have written about him, both good and bad, that good men may imitate his good points and entirely avoid the bad, and travel along the road that leads us to the kingdom of heaven.[17]

---

[16]Douglas, *William the Conqueror*, p. 376.

[17]*Anglo-Saxon Chronicle, sub anno* 1087, translation modified by C. Warren Hollister on the basis of *English Historical Documents, Volume II*, no. 1, pp. 170–171.

CHAPTER 5

Norman England: William II, Henry I, and Stephen

As the Conqueror lay dying at Rouen, William Rufus left for England with his father's blessing. Through the good offices of Archbishop Lanfranc, he received the customary approval of a council of magnates, and the aged archbishop crowned him in Westminster Abbey on September 26, 1087.[1]

The Reign of William Rufus (1087–1100)

William Rufus was an even greater puzzle than his father. The monk William of Malmesbury describes him as

> squarely built, ruddy in coloring, with rather yellow hair . . . , eyes of no one color but spangled with bright specks; of great strength, although of no great height, and inclined to be pot-bellied.[2]

Elsewhere, Malmesbury remarks,

> When he was in public and in large assemblies, he wore a haughty look and darted his threatening eyes on those around him, and with pretended severity and fierce voice he would assail those who conversed with him. From fear of poverty and of the treachery of others, presumably, he was excessively devoted to money and to cruelty. In private, when he was

---

[1] For the period from Edward the Confessor to Richard I, see the selection of sources in English translation in *English Historical Documents, Volume II*, ed. David C. Douglas and George W. Greenaway, 2nd ed. (London, 1981). The best of several fine medieval historians is William of Malmesbury, *Gesta Regum Anglorum: The History of the English Kings*, ed. and tr. R. A. B. Mynors, R. M. Thomson, and M. Winterbottom (2 vols., Oxford, 1998). On William Rufus, see Frank Barlow, *William Rufus* (Berkeley, 1983); and C. Warren Hollister, *Monarchy, Magnates, and Institutions in the Anglo-Norman World* (London and Ronceverte, 1986), pp. 97–115, and "William Rufus, Henry I, and the Anglo-Norman Church," *Peritia: The Journal of the Medieval Academy of Ireland* 6–7 (1987–1988): 119–140.

[2] *Gesta Regum, Volume I*, p. 567.

dining with his intimate companions, he gave himself over to joking and mirth.[3]

To illustrate Rufus's extravagance, Malmesbury tells of how he raged at a chamberlain for buying him a pair of boots worth only three shillings:

> "You son of a whore! Since when has the king worn such cheap boots? Go and bring me a pair worth a silver mark." The chamberlain went, and bringing the king a much cheaper pair than before, told him falsely that they cost as much as he had commanded. "Yes, indeed," said the king, "these are much more suitable to the royal majesty!"[4]

Rufus was said to have "feared God too little, and man not at all."[5] He scorned religion (except at such times as he expected imminent death), and he exploited the Church ruthlessly, demanding that prelates render him large gifts of money to retain the royal favor. Not surprisingly, Rufus earned a terrible press among the monastic chroniclers. They described his itinerant court as a traveling den of iniquity: the courtiers looted food, drink, and property from the people of the countryside through which they journeyed, molested local wives and daughters, pillaged and later sold the goods of villagers, got drunk on stolen liquor, and, when they could drink no more, washed their horses with what was left or poured it onto the ground. Rufus's courtiers dressed in the height of fashion, with

> long flowing hair, luxurious garments, shoes with curved and pointed tips. . . . Softness of body rivaling the weaker sex, a mincing gait, effeminate gestures and a liberal display of the person as they went along, such was the ideal fashion of the younger men. Spineless, unmanned, they were reluctant to remain as Nature had intended they should be; they were a menace to the virtue of others and promiscuous with their own. Troops of effeminate men and gangs of wastrels followed the court.[6]

On the other hand, even Rufus's enemies conceded that he was an excellent soldier and was as loyal to his trustworthy vassals and his knightly followers as he had earlier been to his father. Although remorseless in his financial exploitation of the English Church and people, he was generous to his military companions and prodigal in the wages and bounties that he gave to his numerous mercenary knights.

Rufus ruled with a rod of iron. By inspiring fear in his subjects and maintaining the devotion of his household knights, he managed generally to keep peace in his land. The *Anglo-Saxon Chronicle* may perhaps have exaggerated when it branded Rufus as "hated by almost all his people and odious to God," but other writers of the period were scarcely

---

[3]Ibid., pp. 554–557, translation by C. Warren Hollister.

[4]Ibid., pp. 556–559, translation by C. Warren Hollister.

[5]Ibid., p. 555.

[6]Ibid., pp. 558–561, slightly revised by Robert C. Stacey.

Contemporary Seal from a Charter of William Rufus Showing the King as a Mounted Knight   *(C. M. Dixon)*

more sympathetic. William of Malmesbury described him as a man much pitied by churchmen for losing a soul they couldn't save, beloved by the mercenary soldiers for his innumerable gifts, but unlamented by the people because he caused the plundering of their property.

Rufus's reign had scarcely begun when, in 1088, many of his barons rebelled in favor of Duke Robert Curthose of Normandy, a much more amiable man than his royal brother. Through armed force, the rebels sought to reunite the Anglo-Norman state under Robert's relaxed, dull-witted rule. But Rufus kept the loyalty of the Church, some of the barons, and most of the English freeholders. In view of the above appraisals of his character, it may well be wondered why the Church and the English stood by him. They did so for two reasons. First, the reign was young, and Rufus had yet to make his abhorrent impression. He won the English with lavish promises of just taxes and good government, which he did not keep. Second, the Church and the English consistently favored strong government, however harsh, over the prospect of baronial anarchy, which usually involved a good deal of aristocratic bullying and land grabbing. Consequently, the English fyrd, the military tenants of the bishoprics and monasteries, and the remaining loyal barons rallied to Rufus and enabled him to put down the rebellion. In 1095, he suppressed another baronial insurrection in similar fashion (although Rufus barely escaped an ambush), and for the final five years of his reign he ruled in peace.

As the Anglo-Saxon chronicler observed, Rufus, even more than his father, claimed ultimate control of all the English lands — "he claimed to be the heir of every man, cleric or lay." Accordingly, he denied the security of a normal succession to laymen and churchmen alike. A baronial heir could succeed to his father's estates only after paying, as a relief, whatever sum struck the king's fancy — and Rufus's reliefs were notoriously high. He exploited the feudal privilege of vetoing the marriage of a vassal's widow or female heir by literally selling her in marriage to the highest bidder. He abused the right of wardship by taking possession of the estates of minor heirs and milking them dry before the heirs came of age. He behaved in the same way toward church lands, keeping abbacies and bishoprics unfilled for scandalously long periods after the deaths of their former incumbents, in the meantime diverting their revenues into the royal treasury and selling off their capital resources (plows, timber, cattle, etc.).

Indeed, Rufus did not hesitate to deal in this manner even with the archbishopric of Canterbury. At Lanfranc's death in 1089, the king seized the vast Canterbury lands, plundered them pitilessly, and left the archbishopric empty for four years. It might well have remained vacant still longer, but in 1093 Rufus suffered a near-fatal illness. Fearing death, he yielded to the pressures of his lay and ecclesiastical subjects — pressures that had been mounting ever since Lanfranc's death — and appointed to the archbishopric of Canterbury the saintly and scholarly Anselm, a distinguished Italian churchman who had spent many years in Normandy as prior and then abbot of the great monastery of Bec.[7]

It is ironic that such an irreligious king should appoint such a holy and remarkably gifted churchman to the archbishopric. St. Anselm was not only a man of profound piety; he was also the foremost theologian of his age and perhaps the greatest philosopher in western Christendom since St. Augustine of Hippo, whom he admired. St. Anselm's philosophical and theological works constitute the initial achievement in the intellectual awakening of the High Middle Ages. He stood at the onset of a philosophical flowering that culminated in the thirteenth century in the works of such men as St. Bonaventure and St. Thomas Aquinas.

Notwithstanding his philosophical achievements, St. Anselm traveled a rocky road as an ecclesiastical statesman. A man of deep integrity, he was prepared to cooperate, at least in part, with the revolutionary drive toward papal supremacy and ecclesiastical independence that Pope Gregory VII had pioneered. Anselm was in his early sixties at the time of his appointment to Canterbury, and he claimed to have accepted the archbishopric reluctantly, likening himself to a weak old sheep being yoked to an untamed bull (William Rufus). But as archbishop, Anselm was far from sheepish in his defense of the prerogatives of Canterbury, and he soon clashed with Rufus on a multitude of issues. Anselm wished to go to Rome to receive the *pallium* — the sash that symbolized his spiritual authority — from the reform pope, Urban II (Gregory VII's second

---

[7]Sir Richard Southern, *Saint Anselm: A Portrait in a Landscape* (Cambridge, 1990), is the best biography.

successor). Rufus refused to let Anselm out of the kingdom and for a time refused to recognize the claims of Pope Urban over those of an antipope supported by the Holy Roman emperor. Most trying of all to Anselm, Rufus forbade him to hold kingdomwide ecclesiastical councils, which had previously provided the chief means by which the archbishops of Canterbury ruled and passed legislation for the English Church. At length, late in 1097, these and other difficulties forced Anselm to abandon England for exile in Italy and France, and Rufus resumed control of the Canterbury revenues. Anselm eventually returned to England, at the beginning of the next reign, but for the time being the Norman monarchy had rid itself of its troublesome saint.

Rufus's financial exactions were carried out by a loyal subordinate and thoroughly roguish churchman, Ranulf Flambard, whom the king had made first a royal chaplain and later bishop of Durham. Flambard performed an array of executive and legal tasks. He served briefly as the king's regent in England when Rufus traveled overseas. His primary function, however, was the raising of revenues for the king, and he set about that mission with such malicious ingenuity that he was soon roundly hated. On one occasion, he summoned the English fyrd to Hastings for service overseas, collected ten shillings from every soldier, and sent them directly home.

Rufus was a man of limitless ambition who needed every penny that Flambard could collect. Once secure in his kingdom, he undertook to conquer Normandy, but his plots and campaigns against Duke Robert Curthose met with only partial success. He brought portions of Normandy under his control through warfare and bribes, but he could not win it all. In 1096, however, Duke Robert was seized with crusading fervor in response to Pope Urban II's appeal to the nobility of western Christendom to drive the Muslims from the Holy Land. Having determined to participate in this First Crusade, Duke Robert was hindered by a lack of money to support a worthy knightly retinue on the long journey. Accordingly, in 1096 the two brothers struck a bargain: Robert Curthose pawned Normandy to Rufus for three years in return for 10,000 silver marks, which the king obtained by levying a double Danegeld on his kingdom. Robert could go crusading in style, and William Rufus had Normandy at last. By all indications, he never intended to return it.

Rufus quickly transformed Robert's anarchic, carefree duchy into a centralized, firmly ruled state on the English pattern. He defended Normandy's frontiers and endeavored to expand them. Shortly before his death, he arranged to receive Aquitaine in pawn from its crusade-bound duke, the troubadour-prince William IX. One contemporary writer suggested that Rufus even aspired to the throne of France.

But these schemes all went unfulfilled. On August 2, 1100, Rufus was killed by an arrow while hunting in the New Forest — a vast royal hunting preserve in southern England that the Conqueror had established by evicting a number of peasants and imposing severe restrictions on those who remained. The New Forest had become a symbol of the

Conqueror's "tyranny," and contemporaries thought it fitting that his son and successor should die there.

The Reign of Henry I (1100–1135)

Rufus was in his early forties when he was killed, and his abrupt death provoked a crisis in the royal succession. Because he had never married and left no children, the kingdom might well have passed to his elder brother, Robert Curthose. But the luckless Robert was only now traveling homeward from the Crusade, whereas the Conqueror's youngest son, Henry, was on the scene. Henry had been a member of Rufus's final hunting party, and some historians have suggested that Rufus may have been murdered at Henry's instigation. But there is no hint of fratricide in any of the surviving sources, and although suspicions linger, Rufus's death probably was an accident, albeit a well-timed one for Henry.[8]

At Rufus's death, Henry moved swiftly and surely. He galloped to nearby Winchester, seized the royal treasury, won the approval of a hastily assembled royal council, and then dashed to London where he was crowned at Westminster Abbey on August 5, a mere three days after the shooting. In preparation for Robert's return, Henry did everything in his power to win the support of his subjects. He sought to appease the barons and the Church by issuing an elaborate coronation charter, known in later years as the "Charter of Liberties," in which he agreed to discontinue the predatory practices of William Rufus. Among other things, Henry promised to

> neither sell nor put at farm nor, on the death of an archbishop, bishop, or abbot, take anything from a church's demesne or from its vassals during the interval before a successor is installed. . . . If any of my barons or earls or other tenants shall die, his heir shall not redeem his land as he did in my brother's time, but shall henceforth redeem it by a just and lawful relief. . . . And if the wife of one of my tenants survives her husband . . . I will not give her in marriage unless she herself consents.[9]

Henry did not keep all of these campaign promises. It has been estimated that they would have cost him £4,000 or £5,000 a year — perhaps a quarter of the total royal revenue under Rufus — and Henry was no less parsimonious than his predecessors. The coronation charter was neither a prelude to constitutional monarchy nor an open act of royal generosity, but one of several gambits that Henry employed to gain needed support in the oncoming crisis.

---

[8]The question is re-examined in C. Warren Hollister, "The Strange Death of William Rufus," *Speculum* 48 (1973): 637–653, reprinted in *Monarchy, Magnates, and Institutions*, pp. 59–75.

[9]*English Historical Documents*, Volume II, no. 19, p. 433, translation by C. W. Hollister.

To win Anglo-Saxon and Scottish backing, the new king married a Scottish princess named Matilda, who was a direct descendant of the Old English royal family — a great-granddaughter of Ethelred the Unready's son, Edmund Ironside. Henry I courted popular opinion still further by imprisoning the detested Ranulf Flambard in the Tower of London. But early in 1101, Flambard managed a daring escape, climbing down a rope that had been smuggled into his cell inside a wine keg (and skinning his hands in the process). Slipping out of London, sore hands and all, he hastened across the Channel to Normandy, guided by his mother (who was reputed to be a witch), and joined Robert Curthose, who had by now resumed his rule of Normandy and was eager to wrest England from his younger brother. Henry I, alarmed by the growing threat, sent letters into every shire confirming his coronation oath and requesting that all his free subjects swear to defend England against all men — especially against Robert of Normandy.

In late July 1101, Robert Curthose led a large force across the Channel to Portsmouth, where he was joined by many Anglo-Norman barons who longed for the reunion of the two lands and the more lighthearted rule of the Norman duke. Meanwhile, Henry had assembled a sizeable army of his own, consisting chiefly of episcopal contingents, common

Queen Matilda, Wife of Henry I From the Golden Book of St. Albans. *(Reproduced with permission of The British Library)*

knights, and a large force of native Englishmen (rather like Rufus's army of 1088; see p. 156). Although some barons joined King Henry's army, the loyalty of many of them was suspect. Henry seems to have placed great confidence in the English, and we are told that he took pains to instruct them personally in the techniques of fighting mounted knights. One contemporary writer asserts that Henry's army would have promptly driven Robert's forces out of the country, but as it happened the two sides settled the issue by negotiation. "The more discreet on each side" — evidently the barons — arranged a truce. Henry was happy to avoid the uncertainty of a pitched battle, while Curthose lacked the funds to support a sustained military campaign. The duke recognized Henry's royal title in return for an annuity of £2,000 (which Henry discontinued two years later), and returned to Normandy.

With the settlement of 1101, the great crisis of the reign had passed, and Henry's throne was secure. In 1102, he put down one further rebellion, centering on the earldom of Shrewsbury on the Welsh frontier, and thereafter he ruled England unchallenged until his death in 1135. Indeed, the lands that he confiscated in the wake of the uprisings of 1101 and 1102 served as an invaluable source of royal revenue and patronage in the years ahead. Having secured England, Henry turned to the conquest of Normandy. Paving his way with bribes to Norman barons and neighboring princes, he campaigned in Normandy in 1104 and 1105. On September 28, 1106, his army met Duke Robert's in open battle near the Norman castle of Tinchebray and won an overwhelming victory. Among Henry I's many captives was Robert Curthose himself, who languished in comfortable imprisonment for the next twenty-eight years until his death in 1134.

Contemporaries noted that the battle of Tinchebray occurred forty years to the day after William the Conqueror's landing at Pevensey Beach. By this "English conquest of Normandy," Henry became master of the duchy and reunited the Anglo-Norman state that the Conqueror had forged. Thenceforth, Henry spent a good part of his time in Normandy. Occasionally, he had to defend the duchy against invasions by the king of France and the counts of Anjou and Flanders, usually accompanied by Norman baronial rebellions. But for the most part, Normandy remained at peace under his firm rule. William of Malmesbury credits Henry with establishing such peace in Normandy as had never been known before, even under the rule of his imperious father, William the Conqueror.

By the time of Henry's victory at Tinchebray, another, related crisis of his early years was nearing resolution. At the beginning of his reign, Henry, in keeping with his conciliatory policy, had invited the exiled archbishop Anselm to return to England. But Henry and Anselm were at odds from the first. The king willingly conceded all the issues that had divided Anselm and Rufus, but Anselm was forced by papal policy to raise new issues. Henry expected Anselm to render him the customary feudal homage for the Canterbury estates (which owed him sixty knights), but the archbishop, who had earlier done homage to Rufus, now felt conscience-bound to obey a recent papal decree — promulgated at a Roman ecclesiastical council in 1099 that Anselm had personally attended — forbidding churchmen to render homage to laymen. Anselm also regarded himself as morally bound to uphold another decree of the Roman council of 1099 prohibiting the ritual of lay investiture. This practice had been condemned previously by Pope Gregory VII, as we have seen. But Anselm — who had tolerated investiture by William Rufus — could no longer condone a custom that had been formally forbidden by a great papal council in which he himself had participated.

Henry I, for his part, was just as determined not to relinquish an important royal ritual that his predecessors had traditionally performed — a symbolic expression of the king's status and prestige. The positions of both men were reasonable and neither would relent. At length, in 1103, Anselm returned to exile, and Henry confiscated the Canterbury revenues. But the two men continued to negotiate by letters and messengers throughout the archbishop's exile. The issue reached a crisis in 1105 when Anselm, with skillful timing, threatened Henry with excommunication just in the midst of the king's Norman campaign against Curthose. The threat forced the king to compromise, and after lengthy negotiations, Henry, Anselm, and the pope ratified an agreement in 1106 — shortly before Henry's decisive victory at Tinchebray. Determined to get on with his war against Curthose, Henry agreed to relinquish lay investiture. The pope, for his part, reluctantly permitted Henry to continue receiving homage from his ecclesiastical tenants-in-chief. (Anselm himself, however, never rendered homage to Henry I.) Although the English Church was never again quite so completely under the royal thumb, the king's authority remained substantial, and Henry usually succeeded in controlling ecclesiastical appointments. He had agreed to allow his clergy the privilege of free canonical elections, but free elections and strict royal management were by no means incompatible, as is demonstrated by a royal writ from King Henry II to the monks at Winchester in the later twelfth century: "I order you to hold a free election, but nevertheless I forbid you to elect anyone except Richard, my clerk, the archdeacon of Poitiers."

Henry I was a very different sort of king from William Rufus. Quieter and more calculating, he was less given to explosions of anger — or of mirth. He was less reckless, less emotional, and considerably more intelligent. William of Malmesbury describes Henry in these words:

> In person he was more than short and less than tall, with black hair retreating from his forehead, a glance serene and kindly, a muscular chest and thickset limbs. In season, he was full of fun, and once he had decided to be sociable, a mass of business did not damp his spirits. As a fighter he was of less repute than some, and embodied that saying of [the ancient Roman general] Scipio Africanus, "My mother bore me for command, not combat." As a result, being in political wisdom second to none among the kings of our day, and I would almost say, easily first among all

his predecessors in England, he preferred to do battle in the council-chamber rather than the field, and won his victories without bloodshed if he could, and with very little if he could not. . . . At table he was not particular, eating to stay his appetite rather than plying his stomach with a succession of delicacies, and never drinking except to quench his thirst; the least intemperance, whether in his own servants or in general, met with severe rebuke. His sleep was heavy, and broken by frequent snores. He was a ready speaker, but owed more to chance than art, not hasty, but deliberate.[10]

Henry was, in short, altogether less flamboyant than Rufus. In one respect, however, he stands out among all kings of English history. To the best of our knowledge, he holds the record for illegitimate royal offspring, having sired at least twenty-two bastards by a throng of mistresses. For this exploit, Henry has been severely reprimanded by a number of nineteenth- and twentieth-century historians, but the monastic writers of Henry's own time, thankful for his peace and strong government, did not hold his bastards against him. Indeed, William of Malmesbury sprang to Henry's support with this ingenious defense:

All his life he was completely free from fleshly lusts, indulging in the embraces of the female sex (as I have heard from those who know) from love of begetting children and not to gratify his passions; for he thought it beneath his dignity to yield to amorous delights unless the royal seed could fulfill its natural purpose; employing his bodily functions as their master, not obeying his lust as its slave.[11]

Another contemporary monk, Orderic Vitalis, describes Henry simply as "the glorious father of his country."

Despite Henry's reconciliation with Anselm, his reign was not, on the whole, a great age of Christian reform. In view of his personal life, he could hardly have been a dedicated proponent of clerical celibacy. He did agree to the official prohibition of clerical marriage but enforced it only halfheartedly. On more than one occasion, he simply assessed fines against married clergy as a trick to increase royal revenues. Henry's most powerful and trusted administrator, Roger bishop of Salisbury, made no secret of his mistress; and Roger's nephew Nigel, bishop of Ely, had a wife and son. Among Henry I's other bishops known to have had either wives, concubines, or children (or all of the above) are the bishops of Worcester, Lincoln, Chester, London, and two successive bishops of Durham, the second of whom served for a decade as Henry's chancellor.

If the reign of Henry I is not noted for ecclesiastical reform, it contributed significantly to royal administration. Henry was known as the "Lion of Justice," and he did indeed rule firmly and, on the whole, justly. To defend the Anglo-Norman state, however, he needed a flow of revenue

---

[10]*Gesta Regum, Volume I,* pp. 744–747.

[11]Ibid., pp. 744–745, translation revised by C. Warren Hollister.

for building castles along the borders of his dominions, bribing barons and neighboring feudal princes, and hiring mercenaries to curb rebellions and protect the frontiers. Henry and his ministers exploited the wealth of England to the full, although with more discretion and less gusto than had been customary in Rufus's reign. Henry's severity is a recurring theme in the *Anglo-Saxon Chronicle:*

> 1104: . . . It is not easy to describe the miseries this land was suffering at the time because of various and different injustices and taxes that never ceased or diminished. . . .
> 1110: . . . This was a very severe year in this land because of the taxes that the king collected for the marriage of his daughter.
> 1116: . . . This land and people were also this year often severely oppressed by the taxes which the king collected both in and out of the boroughs.
> 1118: . . . England paid dearly . . . because of the various taxes that never ceased during the course of all this year.
> 1124: . . . It was a very troublous year; the man who had any property was deprived of it by harsh taxes and harsh judgments at court; the man who had none died of hunger.[12]

The customary laws of Henry's time were harsh by modern democratic standards, and on occasion Henry could enforce them without pity. In 1125, having discovered that his minters were debasing the coinage, the king ordered Roger of Salisbury to subject many of them to the traditional punishments of having their genitals and right hands chopped off — thereby effectively ending their careers. Yet according to the *Anglo-Saxon Chronicle,* "it was done very justly, because they had ruined all the country with their great false dealing." And on Henry's death the chronicler remarked, "He was a good man, and people were in great awe of him. No one dared injure another in his time."[13] In short, despite his severity — or because of it — he enforced justice and kept the peace.

Justice could be lucrative to an English monarch. Judicial fines added to the royal revenue, and by extending the scope of the king's justice, Henry increased the flow of money into his treasury. But more importantly, effective royal enforcement strengthened the king's authority over his realm and contributed to the general peace by discouraging crime and encouraging the amicable settlement of private disputes.

Henry's reign witnessed a dramatic growth in the royal judicial system and the royal administration. Although local justices were appointed in each shire to assist the sheriffs in judicial business, the most impor-

---

[12]Apart from 1110, when Henry I required an immense sum for his daughter Matilda's marriage settlement, these years of exceptional taxation are also, by no coincidence, years of major military campaigning in Normandy. Henry's three major Norman wars occurred in 1104–1106, 1116–1119, and 1123–1124.

[13]*English Historical Documents, Volume II,* no. 1, p. 209: *Anglo-Saxon Chronicle, sub anno* 1135.

tant legal cases were judged by the king and his great men at the royal court. Since it was often difficult for litigants to reach the court (which was always on the move), the practice developed of sending royal justices to various parts of England to hear pleas. These itinerant justices, or "justices in eyre," acted in the king's name. By hearing important cases in the shires, they enormously widened the scope of the king's justice, often diverting cases from the baronial courts or adjudicating pleas that otherwise might not have been heard at all. The presence of one or more of Henry's itinerant justices transformed the shire court temporarily into a royal court, and ordinary country people thus came face to face with the judicial authority of the royal curia. During the reign of Henry I, the judicial tours grew ever more systematic until, by the reign's end, they had developed into a comprehensive, regularized procedure.

Henry's chief instrument of command over the considerable areas that he ruled was the royal writ. We have already traced the origin of the writ to Anglo-Saxon times in Chapter 3. In its Anglo-Norman form, it was a brief royal command or statement, written in Latin on a strip of parchment, witnessed and authenticated by the attachment of the royal seal. Ordinarily, a writ would be addressed to the local sheriff or justiciar, or to the baronial or ecclesiastical lord of an area, or to all the king's officials and faithful men of a particular shire or group of shires, for example:

> Henry king of the English to Hugh of Bocland and Robert of Ferrers and William sheriff of Oxford and Nicholas of Stafford, greeting. I order that you justly and immediately cause all fugitives of the abbey of Abingdon to return there with all their goods, wherever they are, so that I may hear no further complaint on the matter for lack of right; and in particular, restore to Abingdon the man who is on the land of Robert of Ferrers, and with all his goods. Witness: Robert fitz Richard. [issued] At Wallingford.[14]

Some 1,500 royal acts, including many writs, have come down from Henry I's reign (compared with fewer than 300 surviving acts from William the Conqueror's), and it is certain that those that have survived constitute only a small fraction of the original total pouring out of Henry's chancery. They address an immense variety of judicial and administrative matters: grants or confirmations of lands and privileges, orders of restitution, commands to act in some way or to cease acting in some way, exemptions from certain taxes, or freedom from tolls. Taken together, they convey a powerful impression of the scope and authority of royal government under Henry I. England had never before been so thoroughly administered. There were some who complained, with justice, about the abuses of royal officials. But for most of his subjects,

---

[14]*Regesta Regum Anglo-Normannorum, Volume II, Regesta Henrici Primi, 1100–1135*, ed. Charles Johnson and H. A. Cronne (Oxford, 1956), no. 726 [1105?], translation by C. Warren Hollister.

Henry's administration provided a welcome contrast to the civil tumult and local thuggery that characterized most of Europe in the early twelfth century.[15]

When Henry traveled to Normandy, he left a regent in England to hear important legal cases, issue writs, and head the administration. Dur-

---

[15]On the administrative history of Henry I's reign, see C. Warren Hollister, "The Rise of Administrative Kingship: Henry I," *American Historical Review* 83 (1978): 867–891, reprinted in *Monarchy, Magnates, and Institutions,* pp. 223–245; and Judith Green, *The Government of England under Henry I* (Cambridge, 1986).

Henry I's Bad Dreams Henry I was reported, on good authority, to have had three nightmares in a single night in 1130, anticipating Scrooge by more than seven centuries. In the first panel (from a mid-twelfth-century manuscript), angry peasants threaten the king with their tools; in the second panel, knights approach him with drawn swords; in the third, churchmen attack him with the points of their staves. Such dreams were the psychological penalty for the building of a powerful, centralized monarchy with an advanced system of taxation. *(President and Fellows of Corpus Christi College, Oxford)*

ing the first half of the reign, his English regent was usually his wife, Queen Matilda, assisted by such seasoned administrators as Roger bishop of Salisbury. After Matilda's death in 1118, Roger of Salisbury acted as regent in Henry's absence — as a kind of English viceroy. Roger was one of medieval England's most gifted administrators, and even when Henry was in England, he supervised the royal administration. Although Roger had no official administrative title, similar viceroy-administrators of later reigns were called "justiciars." Bishop Roger's main responsibilities lay in the area of royal finances, and it was probably he, more than anyone else, who forged the powerful instrument of fiscal accounting known as the "exchequer."

In later generations, the exchequer became an important department of state. Yet in the beginning, under Henry I, it was not a department at all but a twice-yearly audit of the royal income from the shires. All the sheriffs of England traveled to the treasury at Winchester to report their revenues to a panel of auditors. Some of these auditors were officials from the Winchester treasury; others were trusted barons and churchmen from the king's court. The audit was usually presided over by Queen Matilda or, after her death in 1118, by Roger of Salisbury.

The term *exchequer* derives from the table around which the auditors worked. On the table lay a checkered cloth (British: "chequered cloth") resembling a checkerboard, divided into columns representing various denominations of money. The auditors placed markers on these columns to represent the accounts of sheriffs who reported in. The method of accounting was based on the principle of the abacus and the decimal system of arithmetic, which had recently been introduced from the Islamic world. The exchequer accounts were recorded on long rolls of parchment known as "pipe rolls," now precious historical sources. Unfortunately, only one of Henry I's pipe rolls has survived, but we have a continuous set of these annual records from 1156 on. The single surviving pipe roll of Henry I, for the year 1129–1130, constitutes the earliest extant fiscal account of a major principality in the history of western Europe.

The exchequer served as an important control over the activities of the king's sheriffs. In the early Norman period, these royal agents were by no means faceless professionals. Only a person of wealth and stature could protect the royal interests in the turbulent countryside of post-Conquest England. Indeed, many sheriffs seem to have grown too powerful for the king's liking. Often, they abused their positions to enrich themselves and their families and sought to make their positions hereditary. The exchequer audits restrained them to a degree, but Henry I took further measures to ensure his control over his local officials. He deposed old sheriffs and appointed new ones from among his own trusted subordinates. The new sheriffs were often men from families of the lesser landholding class. Having risen in the royal service, and hoping to rise still further, they attached their hopes — and their unswerving loyalty — to the crown. Not uncommonly, such a man might become sheriff of several counties at once, thus extending his own power while simplifying royal governance.

Henry I's reign marks the coming of age of Anglo-Norman royal administration, which some historians have seen as the seed bed of the modern state.[16] The functions of the royal household officials were expanding in importance and specialization. The exchequer provided Henry with the first modern accounting office known to the medieval west. And the tightly controlled sheriffs and itinerant justices forged the essential links between the royal administration and the countryside. Northern Europe had known no comparable bureaucratic system since Roman times, and no other northern monarch was as wealthy as Henry I. Henry had discovered that efficient administration brought larger rev-

---

[16]For a somewhat different view, see W. L. Warren, "The Myth of Norman Administrative Efficiency," *Transactions of the Royal Historical Society*, 5th series 34 (1984): 113–132.

enues, that strong government was good business, and, conversely, that a penniless king could not keep the peace.

Henry's regime contained many low-born administrators, and in enforcing public order he deprived his aristocrats of the freedom to fight one another. Still, Henry cannot be described as anti-aristocratic. The disasters of the reigns of such later kings as John, Henry III, and Edward II demonstrate that a medieval English monarch could not succeed without significant baronial support. And Henry proved himself adroit in winning the allegiance of a number of his subjects — nobles and upstarts alike — through a well-oiled system of royal patronage. For those who demonstrated their loyalty and won his favor, he provided tantalizing opportunities to advance their careers and fortunes in the royal service. Such men gained an inside advantage in acquiring forfeited lands, wealthy wives, lucrative wardships, Danegeld exemptions, administrative offices, and the various other spoils at the crown's disposal. In this way, great baronial families flourished if they were loyal to the king, while a number of lesser aristocrats rose to high positions and men of still lower station ascended into the prosperous middle levels of the aristocracy. To be sure, these royal favorites had to pay the king for every privilege he gave them — in Henry's government nothing was cheap — and they seldom rose to high position overnight. Nevertheless, they fully realized that they owed their success to the king's favor and that similar service in the future would bring further rewards. Through his astute use of patronage, Henry created a royalist core in the aristocracy. Royal patronage would be a central and enduring element in English politics and society for many centuries thereafter. Under Henry I, it made its first appearance as a fully articulated system.

Henry's government was complex, sophisticated, and to a degree impersonal, yet it depended ultimately on the existence of a strong, fear-inspiring king. Accordingly, Henry devoted much attention to the problem of the royal succession. Although he had a gaggle of illegitimate offspring, he produced only two legitimate heirs: a daughter named Matilda (or Maud) and a younger son named William, whom he carefully groomed for the throne. It is the supreme tragedy of Henry's reign that William was killed on the eve of adulthood in 1120, when a vessel carrying the prince and a distinguished but intoxicated party of aristocratic fun-lovers from Normandy to England struck a rock and sank. This catastrophe, known to history as the wreck of the White Ship, threw the royal succession into chaos. Henry, whose first wife Matilda had recently died, promptly remarried, but the second marriage proved childless. Finally, in 1127, Henry secured oaths from his barons to accept his daughter Matilda as the royal heir.

Matilda had earlier married, at the age of eleven, the Holy Roman emperor Henry V, but by 1127 she was a childless widow. Having secured the pledges of his barons, Henry arranged a fateful marriage between Matilda and Count Geoffrey of Anjou. This was a bold stroke of policy, for it promised to end the long struggle between Normandy and Anjou for hegemony in northern France, but it also gave rise to myriad problems. For one, some Anglo-Norman barons chafed at the prospect of being ruled by a woman, particularly by a woman of Matilda's explosive temperament. The commanding, terrifying demeanor that had served Henry I so well as king would prove unacceptable in his daughter when she asserted her claim to her father's throne. Kingship and queenship both carried with them strongly marked and distinctly different expectations with respect to gender and behavior. As a result, Matilda was never able to establish a style of female rule that the Anglo-Norman baronage would accept.[17]

Her marriage to Geoffrey of Anjou compounded her difficulties. Anjou and Normandy were not traditional enemies, but they had been frequently at odds during Henry I's reign. The marriage between Matilda and Geoffrey was intended to patch up these quarrels, but not everyone was prepared to bury the animosities the recent conflicts had stirred up. Geoffrey himself was largely unknown in both England and Normandy, but to the extent that he was known, he seems to have been disliked. And he was no better liked by his new wife. Matilda was a widow of twenty-five, Geoffrey a boy of fifteen when they were married in 1128. Matilda may have considered the marriage demeaning. She was, after all, a dowager empress, and her new husband was a mere count. But whatever the explanation, their personalities clashed. After a year of marriage they separated, and Matilda returned to Normandy. At length, however, Geoffrey and Matilda made up, and in 1133 Matilda gave birth to a son, the future King Henry II.

For a brief time, Henry I relaxed, enjoying the pleasures of being a grandfather and the comfort of having obtained a male heir at last. But the peace was shattered in mid-1135 when Matilda and Geoffrey demanded that Henry I turn over to them several border castles between Normandy and Anjou that he had promised to Matilda as part of her dowry. When Henry refused to yield them, a small-scale war broke out along the southern approaches to Normandy. Hostilities were still smoldering in December 1135, when the old king, now in his late sixties, died of indigestion after a meal of lamprey eels. Because he was surrounded by his most loyal followers at the time and was at odds with Matilda, his death threw the succession into confusion. Henry's peace died with him, and Matilda's untimely quarrel with her father helped to cost her the English crown.

The reign of Henry I was long and significant. He had reunited the Anglo-Norman state, kept the peace in England, successfully defended his far-flung frontiers, and instituted notable administrative advances. A perceptive modern scholar speaks of the reign in these words: "Looking to the future, it is here, we feel, that the history of England begins — a

---

[17]Marjorie Chibnall, *The Empress Matilda: Queen Consort, Queen Mother, and Lady of the English* (Oxford, 1991), is an excellent study that makes this point clearly.

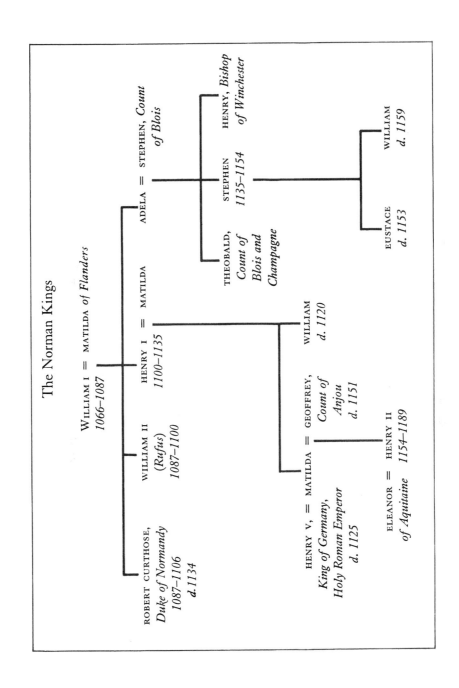

The Norman Kings

history which is neither that of the Norman conquerors, nor that of the Anglo-Saxons, but a new creation."[18]

The Reign of King Stephen (1135–1154)

When Henry I died, his grandson was a child of two whose ambitions did not yet extend to duchies and kingdoms. The English barons had sworn to accept Matilda and any son she might bear, but their enthusiasm was dimmed by the fact that they had been fighting on Henry's side against her in 1135 — and that her eldest son was as yet a child. Hence, the great English landholder Stephen of Blois, a son of the Conqueror's daughter and a nephew of Henry I, acting with much the same dispatch that Henry himself had demonstrated in 1100, was able to seize the throne, supported by the claims of the old king's death-bed attendants who swore that the dying king had designated Stephen as his successor.[19] Matilda had the better hereditary claim, but hereditary right was not everything in the making of an English monarch. Indeed, nearly a century had passed since an English king had been succeeded by his eldest offspring, and the claims of all the Norman kings thus far had been clouded.

Stephen had long been a loyal follower of Henry I, and Henry had showered him with lands and privileges. At Henry's death, only one other Anglo-Norman landholder could compete in wealth with Stephen — Robert, earl of Gloucester, King Henry's favorite illegitimate son. A century before, Earl Robert would likely have succeeded his father as king, just as his grandfather, William the Bastard, had become Duke of Normandy. But the Church's attitude toward legitimate matrimony had hardened in the intervening years, and illegitimate children were now barred from inheriting their parents' property, including of course their thrones. Earl Robert could play the role of king-maker; but he could not expect to become king himself.

Stephen was the most genial of the Norman kings and the least competent. Erratic and lacking in firmness, he was in many respects Henry I's opposite. To the great men of England, this may have been part of his appeal. After thirty-five years of Henry I's harsh rule, they initially welcomed the prospect of a lighter hand that would allow them more independence. But such lightness quickly turned into chaos. In the words of the *Anglo-Saxon Chronicle*, "He was a mild man, and gentle and good, and did no justice."[20]

---

[18]Sir Richard Southern, "The Place of Henry I in English History," *Proceedings of the British Academy*, 48 (1962): 128–129.

[19]On Stephen's reign, see H. A. Cronne, *The Reign of Stephen, 1135–1154: Anarchy in England* (London, 1970); R. H. C. Davis, *King Stephen*, 3rd ed. (London, 1990); *The Anarchy of King Stephen's Reign*, ed. Edmund King (Oxford, 1994); Keith J. Stringer, *The Reign of Stephen: Kingship, Warfare and Government in Twelfth-Century England* (London, 1993).

[20]*Anglo-Saxon Chronicle, sub anno* 1137, translation by C. Warren Hollister.

Great Seal of Stephen   One side shows the king enthroned as king of the English and, verso, mounted on horseback as duke of the Normans. *(Mansell/Time)*

During the first two years of his reign, he squandered Henry I's treasury on bribes and wages for mercenaries, but managed, more or less, to keep the peace. By 1138, however, Count Geoffrey of Anjou had attacked Normandy in force, Earl Robert of Gloucester had rebelled in support of his half-sister Matilda's claim to the throne of England, and David king of Scots (Matilda's uncle) had invaded England on her behalf. Stephen's expedition to defend Normandy dissolved in confusion. He never returned to the duchy, which fell to Count Geoffrey in the early 1140s. In 1139, Matilda herself arrived in England to press her claims to the throne, adopting as her headquarters Earl Robert's castle at Gloucester. In 1141, it looked briefly as if the civil war might end, when King Stephen himself was captured by Matilda's forces. But Stephen's queen (also named Matilda) rallied his supporters, gathered a new army, and promptly captured Earl Robert of Gloucester. The two prisoners were exchanged, and the war went on, with Stephen by and large controlling the eastern portion of the kingdom, and Matilda controlling the southwest.

The next decade witnessed a seesaw battle between Stephen and Matilda, accompanied by a great deal of private baronial warfare. The most destructive period came between 1141 and 1146. Trade, both international and domestic, was severely disrupted; private baronial coinages began to emerge; and many productive estates were ravaged and destroyed. In 1135, the great men of England had probably looked forward to a less-exacting style of kingship. By the 1140s, however, it was rapidly becoming clear to them how much they stood to lose as a result of Stephen's weak kingship. They had prospered during the previous reign under the firm rule of a monarch friendly to their interests, but now, with Stephen and Matilda battling on equal terms, the civil war threatened to go on forever. In some areas, barons began to make private truces between themselves, in an attempt to bring the destruction to an end. But such arrangements could not bring peace to the entire country. If prosperity was to be restored to such a highly integrated kingdom, it would come only through a renewal of the powerful kingship of King Henry I.

The turbulence of these years was by no means universal — it was limited to particular areas and particular times — but it terrified the kingdom nonetheless and left a deep impression on contemporaries. The twelfth-century historian Henry of Huntingdon, commenting on the horrors of Stephen's reign, remarked that "whatever King Henry had done, whether in the manner of a tyrant or that of a true king, appeared most excellent in comparison."[21] As an astute British historian recently described it, the reign of Stephen was "a true and terrible Anarchy."[22]

The most vivid descriptions of the civil war occur in the *Anglo-Saxon Chronicle*. Although the chronicler's picture of general and total chaos is doubtless exaggerated, his specific impressions ring true:

> Every powerful man built his castles and held them against the king, and they filled the country full of castles. They oppressed the wretched people of the country severely with castle building. When the castles were built they filled them with devils and wicked men. Then both by night and day they took those people that they thought had any goods — men and women — and put them in prison and tortured them with indescribable torture to extort gold and silver from them — for no martyrs were ever so tortured as they were. They were hung by the thumbs or by the head, and armor was hung on their feet. Knotted ropes were put around their heads and twisted until they penetrated to the brains. They put them in prisons where there were adders and snakes and toads, and killed them in that way. . . . Many thousands they killed by starvation. I have neither the ability nor the power to tell all the horrors and all the torments that they inflicted on the wretched people of this land. And all this lasted the whole nineteen years while Stephen was king, and it was always going from bad to worse. They levied taxes on the villages at intervals, and called it "protection money." When the wretched people had no more to give, they robbed and burned the villages, so that you could easily go a whole day's journey and find nobody occupying a village, nor land tilled. . . . Some lived by begging, who had once been rich, and many others fled the country. . . . Wherever cultivation was done, the ground produced no grain, because the land was all ruined by such doings. And they said openly that Christ and his saints slept.[23]

At length the dynastic struggle settled into an uneasy truce. Robert of Gloucester's death in 1147 deprived Matilda of her ablest champion,

---

[21]*English Historical Documents, Volume II*, no. 10, p. 331.

[22]David Crouch, *The Beaumont Twins: The Roots and Branches of Power in the Twelfth Century* (Cambridge, 1986), p. 138.

[23]*Anglo-Saxon Chronicle*, *sub anno* 1137, translation by C. W. Hollister.

and in 1148 she retired to the Continent. But in the meantime her husband, Count Geoffrey, had conquered Normandy, creating a new source of instability for barons who previously had held lands in both England and Normandy. With the two contending parties separated by the English Channel, the conflict diminished — but only for a time.

By 1153, Henry I's grandson, Henry of Anjou (or Henry Plantagenet, after the broom plant — *plante genêt* — that served as his paternal family's emblem) was ready to undertake a decisive struggle to make good his inherited claims to the throne of England. This ambitious young man of nineteen was already the foremost prince in France. He had been the de facto duke of Normandy since 1149. In 1151, when his father suddenly died, he also became count of Anjou and ruler of the satellite provinces of Maine and the Touraine (see map, p. 131). In 1152, Henry Plantagenet also acquired the extensive duchy of Aquitaine in southern France by marrying its heiress, Eleanor.[24] Eleanor's marriage to King Louis VII of France had been annulled by the papacy only weeks before, ostensibly because they were too closely related to each other, but in fact because in fourteen years of marriage Louis had succeeded in fathering only two daughters with Eleanor, and he desperately needed a male heir. Henry and Eleanor had met for the first time in Paris in the summer of 1151, when negotiations for the annulment of her marriage to Louis were already underway. We will never know if their attachment was "love at first sight" or a carefully crafted political alliance. Perhaps it was both. Eleanor was eleven years older than Henry, but she would bear him five sons and three daughters before the marriage broke down into hostility and ultimately civil war. But in addition to heirs, the marriage also secured for Henry control over the vital southern borders of Anjou, as well as dominion over Aquitaine itself, a sprawling, poorly organized duchy of immense potential wealth that stretched from the Mediterranean Sea to the Pyrenees. From the standpoint of the age, we must therefore account the marriage between Henry and Eleanor a success, despite the problems to which it eventually gave rise.

Henry came to England in 1153 as a man of great substance and significant resources. As duke of Normandy, he was in a position to court the English barons by promising them the restoration of their Norman lands or by threatening their confiscation. But most of all, Henry was the rising star, who alone offered the prospect of bringing the anarchy to an

---

[24]Eleanor of Aquitaine is one of the legendary figures of the Middle Ages, but her legend does not make it easy to assess her real historical importance. The best study of Eleanor's place in both history and literature is D. D. R. Owen, *Eleanor of Aquitaine: Queen and Legend* (Oxford, 1993). W. L. Warren, *Henry II* (Berkeley, 1973), is the most critical and deflating account of Eleanor's involvement in the politics of Henry II's court. Amy Kelley, *Eleanor of Aquitaine and the Four Kings* (Cambridge, Mass., 1950; paperback ed., 1959), is colorful but unreliable, especially on the subject of Eleanor's "Courts of Love." On Henry's marriage to Eleanor, see also Chibnall, *The Empress Matilda*, pp. 155–156, whose views are followed here.

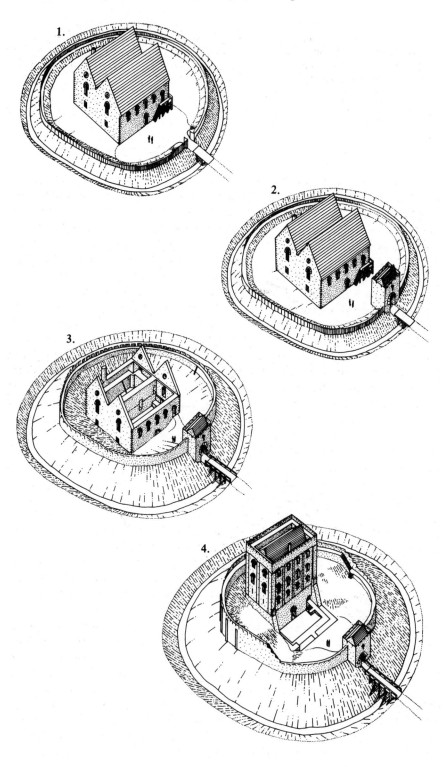

end. The pope's refusal to accept the claims of King Stephen's son Eustace to succeed to his father's throne underlined the point even further. Sooner or later, Henry would become king. Now was the time to make some arrangement with him.

Henry's 1153 campaign in England was largely bloodless. With the reappearance of able and determined leadership, Stephen's baronial supporters declined to fight for him against Henry and instead negotiated a series of truces to keep the two adversaries apart. Many now shifted to what they clearly recognized as the winning side. With declining support, advancing years, and sinking spirits, Stephen submitted to a compromise that deprived his own sons of the right to succeed him and assured Henry the throne. The agreement, known as the Treaty of Winchester (1153), stipulated that Stephen would rule England unmolested until his death, but that Henry Plantagenet would be his heir. Baronial partisans on both sides were guaranteed their lands and were promised immunity from punishment. England returned at last to a state of peace. Nine months after the Treaty of Winchester, King Stephen died, and Henry Plantagenet acceded unopposed to the English throne as King Henry II. With his coronation, the Norman era of English history came to an end, and the Angevin (from Anjou) era began.

Historians once regarded the troubled reign of Stephen as an epoch of feudal anarchy, a reaction against the strong government of Henry I, and an age when greedy barons exploited a good but pliable king. Recent research has modified this view somewhat, without altering its essentials. Stephen was not so openhearted or simple-minded as scholars have sometimes pictured him. He was a cheerful man, by and large, but he was also sly and treacherous. In particular, he had an irritating habit of arresting his barons and administrators by surprise and without good cause. His arrest of Henry I's great administrator Roger of Salisbury in 1139 damaged the royal administrative machinery and disrupted Stephen's

Castle Acre, Norfolk, a Great Private Fortified Residence of the Warenne Earls of Surrey   Reconstructions based on archaeological excavations show four successive phases of construction from the late eleventh century to about the mid-twelfth: (1) A two-story stone country house, lightly fortified by an encircling ditch and a palisaded mound. (2) The wooden palisade was replaced by a stone wall with a fortified gate, but the central building remained essentially a house rather than a castle. (3) The country house was then remodeled internally for conversion to a strongly fortified castle tower, while the surrounding embankment was heightened and surmounted by a high stone wall. (4) Half of the former house was converted into a well-defended castle tower, the other half was demolished, and the encircling fortifications were greatly strengthened. Phases 3 and 4 appear to date from King Stephen's reign and bear witness to the growth of civil unrest and the increasing militarization of the countryside. *(After R. Warmington; courtesy of The British Museum)* links with his sheriffs, thereby depriving him of vital intelligence information in the civil war that followed. His peremptory arrests of two of England's most powerful magnates — Geoffrey de Mandeville, earl of Essex, and Ranulf, earl of Chester — prompted both of them, once released, to revolt against their king. His refusal to accept the belated homage of Baldwin de Redvers, earl of Devon, cost him the support of another critically important figure, this time in the southwest.

The list of Stephen's mistakes is endless, but the most important lesson of his reign was learned not by the king but by his barons, who discovered just how much they needed the rule of a strong, supportive king to resolve quarrels that might otherwise end in destructive private wars. As the twelfth century progressed, the holdings of magnates great and small became increasingly subject to dispute, with disappointed families reviving old claims and rival heirs contending for the same estates. During the closing decades of Henry I's reign, outright royal confiscations of baronial lands were rare, and the royal court adjudicated most conflicting claims. In Stephen's reign, however, civil strife deprived the aristocracy of a single authoritative tribunal and a firm royal protector. Barons tended to assert every possible claim to every scrap of disputable land and to grab what they could. Disputes multiplied as Stephen and Matilda granted different persons the same estates and offices. Often, two contending claimants to a particular fief would choose opposite sides in the civil war, and a shift of loyalty by one baron could prompt a countershift by his rival.

The Treaty of Winchester and the subsequent accession of Henry II marked a return to secure inheritances and the peaceful adjudication of disputes. Indeed, the victory of the hereditary principle is nowhere more evident than in Henry's own succession to the throne. He succeeded in part through the approval of the royal council, in part by the designation of his predecessor — but above all, and unlike the Norman kings, he succeeded by hereditary right as the eldest grandson of Henry I. It was not, of course, a model instance of hereditary succession: Henry II succeeded Stephen, not Henry I. The difficulty was resolved first by having Stephen "adopt" Henry II, and later by declaring Stephen a usurper and his reign a "nonevent." But for all that, hereditary right based on primogeniture has governed the succession of English monarchs, with very few exceptions, from that day to this.

CHAPTER 6

"The Devil's Brood": Henry II, Richard, and John

Henry II reigned for thirty-five years (1154–1189), almost exactly as long as his grandfather, Henry I. The two reigns are similar in other respects as well, for Henry II undertook quite deliberately to revive Henry I's policies and to rule in his imperious tradition. Yet the new king was a vibrant personality in his own right. He has been aptly described as "a man of intense, mercurial temperament who could shift in a moment from sunshine to thunder."[1] His contemporaries regarded him as a fear-inspiring, peacekeeping monarch — impulsive, explosive, always on the move, and overwhelming in personality. One writer of the time described him thus:

> A man of reddish, freckled complexion, with a large, round head, grey eyes that glowed fiercely and grew bloodshot in anger, a fiery counte-nance and a harsh, cracked voice. His neck was poked forward slightly from his shoulders, his chest was broad and square, his arms strong and powerful. His body was stocky, with a pronounced tendency toward fat-ness, due to nature rather than self-indulgence — which he tempered with exercise.[2]

Henry was almost perversely energetic. At the end of a hard day he would refuse to sit down, before or after dinner. His courtiers, so as not to risk offending him, had to stand as well. As one of them complained, the king would "wear out the whole court by continually standing."[3]

The scholar Peter of Blois, who spent some time at Henry's court, described it as a scene of chaotic confusion. Henry I had planned his

---

[1]Christopher Brooke, in *The World of John of Salisbury*, ed. Michael Wilks (Oxford, 1984), p. 17. The best study of Henry II and his reign remains W. L. Warren, *Henry II* (Berkeley, 1973).

[2]Gerald of Wales, *Expugnatio Hibernica: The Conquest of Ireland*, ed. and tr. A. B. Scott and F. X. Martin (Dublin, 1978), pp. 126–127, translation by C. Warren Hollister.

[3]Ibid., p. 127.

Tomb Effigy of Henry II at Fontevrault Abbey in Anjou   The carving shows an idealized likeness of the king in his youth. *(Copyright ARS NY/SPADEM 1994)*

itineraries carefully, but Henry II's movements through the countryside seemed to depend only on the royal whim. "If the king promises to spend the whole day somewhere," Peter of Blois grumbled, "you can be sure that he will leave the place bright and early, and upset everyone's plans in his haste." Then everybody will be "rushing madly about, urging on the packhorses, hitching the teams to their wagons, everyone in total confusion — a perfect portrait of hell. . . . And I believe our plight added to the king's pleasure." The harassed scholar eventually elected to resign from the royal entourage. "I shall dedicate the remainder of my days," he concluded, "to study and peace."[4]

But Peter of Blois's portrayal of directionless royal effort is misleading. Henry knew where he was going, even if his followers did not. And it is significant that a scholar of Peter of Blois's talents should belong to the royal household at all. Henry II was the best-educated English king since Alfred. He delighted in associating with scholars and patronizing their works. As Peter of Blois himself said of Henry:

> Whenever he can get breathing space in the midst of his business cares, he occupies himself with private readings or endeavors to work out some difficult intellectual problem with his learned clerics. . . . With the king

---

[4]Peter of Blois, Letter 14, in *Patrologia Latina*, ed. J. P. Migne, vol. 207, pp. 48–49.

of England it is school every day, constant conversation among the best of scholars, and discussion of problems.[5]

Military and Financial Reforms Under Henry II

Henry II began his reign by endeavoring to revive in all its fullness the royal authority exercised by his grandfather. He set about immediately to reverse the process of political disintegration that England had experienced under Stephen. He ordered the destruction of the unlicensed castles that barons had built during the anarchy and was stingy in granting permission to erect new castles or refortify existing ones. He also worked energetically to reconstruct the powerful government of Henry I and to expand it. Three areas of royal government received Henry II's particular attention: military organization, financial administration, and above all, the administration of justice.

Henry II's military reforms are well illustrated by two important documents from his reign: the *Cartae Baronum* (Barons' Charters) of 1166 and the Assize of Arms of 1181. The first is a series of written statements from all the tenants-in-chief of the realm, lay and ecclesiastical, in response to a royal inquest relating to knights' service. The inquest required the tenants-in-chief to tell the king (1) how many knights they had enfeoffed (bestowed a fief upon) before Henry I's death in 1135; (2) how many they had enfeoffed between 1135 and 1166; and (3) to what degree — if any — the enfeoffments fell short of the knightly military quota each tenant-in-chief owed to the crown. Each knightly tenant was also to be identified by name.

The *Cartae Baronum* constituted the first general survey of knight service since the establishment of the quotas under William the Conqueror. Henry II was doubtless interested in discovering the extent of his feudal military resources, but he also seems to have had two further, very specific reasons for the inquest. First, he wished to identify all the knightly subvassals of England so that he might secure their formal oaths of allegiance, much as William the Conqueror had done at Salisbury in 1086 (see p. 148). Second, on the basis of the data supplied by the *Cartae Baronum*, he attempted to obtain additional scutage and aids from those vassals whose enfeoffments exceeded their royal quotas.

This effort to increase the knight service quotas upon which his tenants-in-chief paid aids and scutages reflects an important shift in the way Henry II and his sons financed their government. Although Henry I had continued to collect geld — the traditional Anglo-Saxon land tax, based on hidage assessment — throughout his reign, under Stephen the

---

[5]*Materials for the History of Thomas Becket, Archbishop of Canterbury*, ed. J. C. Robertson, 7 vol., Rolls Series (London, 1885), vol. 7, pp. 570ff.

nationwide system for assessing and collecting geld collapsed. Henry II tried to revive the land tax early in his reign, but after 1162 he abandoned this attempt in favor of taxes assessed upon the knight service quotas owed by his tenants-in-chief: scutages, which he charged whenever a tenant-in-chief was exempted from bringing his full knight service quota to a military campaign; and aids, which were in theory voluntary, but were owed by custom on such occasions as the knighting of the king's eldest son and the marriage of his eldest daughter.[6] Henry I had collected scutages and aids also. But under Henry II and his sons, taxes assessed on knights' fees became a more regular and important feature of crown financial policy than ever before.

This shift from land taxes to taxes based on knights' fees had important implications for Angevin government. Geld was an obligation owed by every landowner in the kingdom directly to the crown. There was no tradition by which anyone had to be consulted before the king could levy a geld — much less that the king's great men had a right to consent to it in advance. Scutages and aids, by contrast, were owed to the king only by his tenants-in-chief; and although in practice these tenants-in-chief probably passed a substantial portion of these taxes down onto their own knightly tenants, it was still the case that the "tax-paying public" for aids and scutages was both narrower and more politically powerful than had been the case under the old system of gelds. Crown finance under the Angevins thus rested much more directly upon the backs of the most powerful men in the kingdom than had been the case under Henry I.

There was also a clear tradition that although scutages and aids might be customary, they nonetheless required some degree of prior consultation and consent on the part of the king's great men before they could be levied. This too raised important political complications. In some ways, the new Angevin system was more efficient, because the most powerful men in the kingdom were also the richest men in the kingdom. But it was also much more dependent than the Anglo-Norman system had been upon the willingness of the Angevin aristocracy (both tenants-in-chief and their knightly followers) to support the king and his policies. Where such political support was lacking, Angevin government quickly ran into problems.

During the 1160s, Henry II abandoned the Anglo-Saxon geld system and the hidage assessment system that went with it. But he had no intention of relinquishing the traditional Anglo-Saxon royal claim to the military service of every freeman in England. With the hidage assessment system gone, however, some new basis had to be found upon which these military service requirements could be assessed. Henry's 1181 Assize of Arms marks the first of a series of attempts, which would continue

---

[6]Henry also developed a new tax upon his own royal demesne estates and towns, known as tallage.

throughout the thirteenth century, to reorganize English military obligations on the basis of wealth.

The Assize of Arms divided the freemen of England into four categories, with specific requirements of military equipment and service assigned to each. Anyone who held a knight's fee was required to own a shirt of chain mail, a helmet, a shield, and a lance. Every nonknightly freeman whose goods and rents were worth sixteen marks or more[7] was also expected to have the equipment of a knight. The Assize thus implicitly redefined the knight's fee as a measure of wealth equivalent to sixteen marks. Every freeman with goods and rents worth between ten and sixteen marks was required to have a coat of light chain mail, an iron headpiece, and a lance. Freemen with goods and rents worth less than ten marks per year were to have quilted coats, iron headpieces, and lances. And all freemen were to swear fidelity to Henry II and bear their arms in his service alone.

The equation made by the Assize of Arms between a knight's fee and an estate of some specified monetary value constitutes the start of a long process by which the feudal knight service quotas were incorporated into a standardized national system of military assessment. The Assize thus paved the way for the efforts of thirteenth-century kings to force all men with estates of a certain annual value (usually twenty pounds) to become knights. But the Assize never lost its fundamental military purpose. Thirteenth-century reissues of the Assize altered the categories of nonknightly military service from three to five, incorporated the nonfree peasantry into the military system, and provided for new military classes such as archers and light horsemen. But the notion of a universal male military obligation was never lost. In the fourteenth century, the ability of English kings to summon and recruit non-noble archers and foot soldiers would be a decisive element in the military victories of the Hundred Years' War with France.

Henry II and the Common Law[8]

In the 1153 Treaty of Winchester that recognized him as the heir to the English throne, Henry II had promised to restore to their inheritances all

---

[7]A mark was two-thirds of a pound. A pound contained 240 silver pennies. Sixteen marks would thus be the equivalent of £10 13s. 4d, or 2,560 silver pennies.

[8]The classic work on this subject is F. Pollock and F. W. Maitland, *The History of English Law before the time of Edward I*, 2 vols., 2nd ed. (Cambridge, 1898). A more recent introduction is John Hudson, *The Formation of the English Common Law: Law and Society in England from the Norman Conquest to Magna Carta* (London, 1996). The discussion of Henry II's legal reforms that follows is much indebted to Paul Brand, "Multis Vigiliis Excogitatam et Inventam: Henry II and the Creation of the English Common Law," *Haskins Society Journal* 2 (1990): 197–222, reprinted in his book, *The Making of the Common Law* (London, 1992).

those persons who had lost them during King Stephen's reign.[9] When Henry became king in 1154, the effect of this promise was to channel a very large number of legal cases over landholding into the royal courts. These cases provided the king with an important means of controlling his great men in the first few years of his reign. No one expected the king's justice to be impartial — the whole point of being the king's friend was, after all, that the king should favor his friends' cases over their opponents' cases — but it was nonetheless important that the royal courts be seen to deal fairly and speedily with the mass of legal business that now confronted them.

Henry and his advisers adopted a variety of expedients to handle the legal cases that poured into his courts. When a case involved the greatest men of the realm, such as the trial of Archbishop Thomas Becket in 1164 at Northampton, Henry would summon a great council of magnates and prelates to hear and determine the case. These were not cases on which a king wanted to appear to be acting alone, without advice. Pleas involving lesser men were usually heard by the ill-defined group of administrative officers and royal intimates who accompanied the king on his endless travels. But clearly the king and his traveling companions could hear personally only a few of the cases that came before his courts. By the 1160s, therefore, the exchequer court (now most often resident at Westminster, though still occasionally to be found at Winchester) had begun to hear legal cases, even cases that did not involve the king's revenues. By the 1170s, a group of legal professionals had emerged around the exchequer court who specialized in hearing judicial cases. This group would evolve, during the 1190s, into the Court of Common Bench, a judicial tribunal entirely separate from the exchequer.

Henry also took steps to extend the reach of royal justice into the countryside. The public courts of shire and hundred continued to function, as they had done since Anglo-Saxon times. But beginning in 1176, Henry began a nationwide series of general eyres, in which teams of royal justices toured the countryside to hear judicial cases. Henry I had also sent royal justices "on eyre" through the countryside. But although Henry I's justices presided over the shire courts, they did not actually judge the cases that came before them. Judgment remained in the hands of the court's "suitors," the body of local landowners who had for centuries constituted the court and who rendered their judgments in accordance with the differing local customs of each shire and hundred. Under Henry II, however, the royal justices "on eyre" took over the shire court, turning the shire court into an extension of the king's own court and judging cases according to the common custom of the king's courts. The customs by which the king's justices rendered their decisions were

---

[9]For discussion, see J. C. Holt, "1153: The Treaty of Winchester," in *The Anarchy of King Stephen's Reign*, ed. Edmund King (Oxford, 1994), pp. 291–316.

recorded late in Henry II's reign in a famous law book ascribed (wrongly) to Henry's chief justice, Ranulf de Glanville. "Glanville's" treatise is practical and utilitarian rather than philosophical — by and large it is a manual explaining the nature and uses of the judicial writs for sale at the royal chancery. But the work is nevertheless a major intellectual landmark in the rise of a coherent body of written royal law, which its author did not hesitate to compare with the *Corpus Juris Civilis*, the great collection of Roman law compiled by the sixth-century emperor Justinian. With "Glanville's" famous *Treatise on the Laws and Customs of England*, the history of the English common law really begins.[10]

Notwithstanding the activities of the justices "on eyre" (known also as "justices itinerant"), much of the king's power in the counties depended on the loyalty and effectiveness of the royal sheriffs. During Stephen's reign, the office of sheriff had tended either to pass directly into the hands of great hereditary earls (the number of earls tripled under King Stephen) or else to fall under an earl's control. Henry II was determined to reassert his authority over the sheriffs and, above all, to prevent the supposedly royal office of sheriff from passing from father to son as an inheritable right.[11] In 1170, he ordered a thoroughgoing inquiry into the activities of all the sheriffs and then replaced most of them with men more directly dependent upon the king. The king's authority hinged on his ability to control his sheriffs, for it was they who collected royal demesne revenues and accounted for them at the exchequer. The sheriffs also presided over the shire court and carried out a variety of royal orders transmitted to them by sealed writs from the royal chancery. As the regional representatives of an increasingly literate administration, efficient sheriffs needed to be literate themselves. Government by the written word demanded local officials who could read. Henry II's growing authority in the countryside rested upon increasing levels of lay literacy in Latin, French, and English among nobles and non-nobles alike.

Yet even with active itinerant justices and effective, trustworthy sheriffs, Henry II still faced the formidable problem of maintaining local law and order without a police force. In his Assize of Clarendon of 1166, augmented by the Assize of Northampton of 1176, he ordered inquest juries of four men from every town and twelve men from every hundred to meet periodically to report the names of notorious local criminals to the sheriff or the itinerant justices. The accused criminals were then forced

---

[10]The best edition, with facing page Latin text and English translation, is *The Treatise on the Laws and Customs of England Commonly called Glanville*, ed. G. D. G. Hall, 2nd ed. (Oxford, 1993), with a new introduction by Michael Clanchy.

[11]On this point, see Michael Clanchy, *England and Its Rulers, 1066–1272*, 2nd ed. (Oxford, 1998), pp. 82–84; and also Julia Boorman, "The Sheriffs of Henry II and the Significance of 1170," in *Law and Government in Medieval England and Normandy: Essays in Honour of Sir James Holt*, ed. George Garnett and John Hudson (Cambridge, 1994), pp. 255–275.

to submit to trial by ordeal.[12] Those convicted by the ordeal were savagely punished; even those judged innocent by the ordeal, if they were of bad reputation, were to be exiled from the realm.

The juries established by the Assize of Clarendon differed fundamentally from the modern trial jury. In Henry II's system, the ordeal performed the task of the modern jury: deciding whether the accused is guilty or innocent. The juries required by the assize were closer in spirit to our grand juries: they were indictment juries, whose function was to supply information to the justices, who would determine whether there was a case for the accused to answer. Informational juries of this type were a common feature of both Anglo-Saxon and Carolingian governments, which used them not only to identify criminals but also to funnel information to the royal administration. Domesday Book, for example, was largely based on the information provided by such local juries. But no previous monarch had made such systematic use of juries as did Henry II. The Assizes of Clarendon and Northampton made juries an integral part of royal procedures in both criminal and civil cases. By so doing, these assizes marked a significant advance of royal jurisdiction into areas traditionally reserved for the courts of hundred and shire.

Henry II also extended royal jurisdiction into the vast, bewildering area of land disputes. We have already traced the growth of rival claims to land in Norman England and their explosive consequences during Stephen's reign. Although the Norman kings — particularly Henry I — had adjudicated landholding conflicts between their tenants-in-chief and had occasionally intervened in the land disputes of lesser tenants, disputes involving lesser tenants had normally fallen under the jurisdiction of private baronial courts or else to the public courts of shire and hundred. It was Henry II who, for the first time, systematically applied the particular customs of the king's own court to the adjudication of land disputes that did not involve the king's tenants-in-chief.

The most important of Henry II's new measures with respect to land law was the Assize of Novel Disseisin, first pronounced in 1166 as part of the Assize of Clarendon. *Novel disseisin* means "recent ejection." As its name implies, the measure was intended to provide a speedy legal remedy for anyone who had been wrongfully and recently dispossessed of an estate. Any free tenant could purchase from the king the writ that began

---

[12]In this case, the accused would be thrown, bound, into a body of water. Persons who sank were judged innocent because the water had accepted them. Persons who floated were judged guilty because the water had rejected them. Another common method of trial by ordeal involved holding a piece of red-hot iron in the hands. If, after three days, the wounds were healing cleanly, the accused was judged innocent. If the wounds became infected, the accused was declared guilty. Clearly, a great deal of local judgment was involved in determining whether a body floated or sank, or whether hands healed cleanly or not. This is probably one reason why Henry II is reported to have distrusted such verdicts. Trial by ordeal gradually came to an end after 1215, when the Fourth Lateran Council prohibited priests from participating in such trials by blessing the water or the iron.

a Novel Disseisin case; those who could not afford the 80 silver pennies the writ usually cost were sometimes granted it for free. The writ ordered the sheriff to assemble a jury of local knights and freemen and to ask them a simple question: had the claimant bringing the writ been ejected from his or her free tenement recently, unjustly, and without the judgment of a proper court? If the jury's answer was "Yes," then the claimant was restored to the property, and the person who had committed the ejection paid a fine to the king. If the answer was "No," then the claimant paid a fine to the king for bringing a false claim.

The effect of this measure was to transfer a great deal of the ordinary judicial business over landholding from the private baronial courts to the king's own courts, including of course the shire courts. Historians continue to debate whether Henry intended this result when he designed the measure. Some baronial courts probably welcomed the king's involvement, not least because it saved them the bother and expense of adjudicating such cases themselves. Other barons clearly felt that the measure was undermining the powers of their own courts. But in practice, there was little that baronial court holders could do to resist the encroachment of the king's courts upon their traditional rights of jurisdiction. By the early thirteenth century, many barons had ceased to hold regular court sessions at all.

Another of Henry's new measures, the writ of Mort d'Ancestor ("the death of an ancestor"), offered speedy help to persons claiming heritable property. Once again, the writ asked a few simple questions of a local jury: did the claimant's relative hold the land on the day he or she died? And was the claimant a closer heir to this relative than was the current occupant of the property? If the jury answered "Yes" to both questions, then the sheriff would eject the current occupant and put the claimant in possession of the property. The previous occupant could still claim a better "right" to the property than the "nearer heir" whom the writ of Mort d'Ancestor had favored. But to claim that right, the previous occupant would now have to bring a "writ of right" against the nearer heir, a much longer and more difficult procedure that took the case into a baronial rather than a royal court. Novel Disseisin and Mort d'Ancestor cases could usually be resolved within weeks or months. Cases brought under a writ of right could drag on for years and years, sometimes for generations.

One of the other problems with procedure under the writ of right was that if the case ever did come to a decision, it would be decided by trial by battle. The two litigants (or their champions) were required to fight a duel. The winner got the land; the loser, if he was not killed outright, might be executed for perjury, because he had sworn an oath that his case was true and that oath had now been shown to be false. Understandably, trial by battle was an unappealing prospect to most litigants. It also offended the increasingly "rationalistic" sensibilities of contemporary justices and jurists. Near the end of his reign, Henry II therefore instituted an alternative to trial by battle through the Grand Assize. This allowed

Trial by Battle as Depicted in a Mid-Thirteenth-Century Assize Roll *(North Wind Picture Archives)*

the defendant in a writ of right to decline trial by battle and choose instead to have his case transferred from a baronial court to the king's court, where a jury of twelve local knights would decide which litigant had the "greater right" to the land in question.

Henry II's legal reforms had the ultimate effect of making the royal courts the chief adjudicators of land quarrels of all kinds. Criminal law too was increasingly becoming a matter for the king's own courts. Long-standing regional peculiarities in legal custom were giving way to a uniform royal law, a common law shared by all the free subjects of England. The legal system would continue to evolve; the pace of change was at least as rapid between 1189 and 1236 as it had been between 1154 and 1189. And clearly Henry II's reforms owed much to the precedents already established by his grandfather, King Henry I. But it was Henry II and his advisers who gave shape to the new legal system and who created the institutional structures of justices and courts that would preserve and extend it. Historians continue to debate the point, but it seems to us that Henry II deserves his traditional reputation as the father of the English common law.

Henry II and the Church

High-medieval Europe witnessed a series of ecclesiastical reform movements and an intensification of piety at all levels of society. The struggles over lay investiture left the popes and bishops of the twelfth century more powerful than ever before. Standards of pastoral care and of personal character on the part of these high church officials were probably also higher than they had been since the late Roman period. Kings and nobles, however, retained a strong voice in ecclesiastical appointments, and the universal Church still suffered from unworthy, time-serving bishops and abbots. At the local level, the educational and moral standards of parish priests often left much to be desired. Still, the moral caliber of the clergy was clearly rising, as the papacy tightened its control over the Church through its wide-ranging legates and its increasingly effective administrative organization.

In England, as elsewhere in western Europe, the Church devoted more and more attention to such areas as church law, administration, and education. Monasteries and cathedrals became increasingly active in the education of the young, and centers of higher education such as Paris, Oxford, and, in the thirteenth century, Cambridge, emerged under ecclesiastical auspices. Canon law (as the law of the Church was known) was developing during the twelfth century into a vast, coherent body of knowledge; and in England, this law was being administered by an increasingly elaborate network of ecclesiastical courts separate from those of king and barons. In secular administration also, clerics played critical roles. Well-equipped by the excellence of their education, they ran the exchequers and chanceries, served as trusted royal counselors, wrote the histories of their times, and carried on the work of scholarship. Archbishops and kings might sometimes clash, but there could be no separation of Church and state.

The English Church participated fully in these new currents of religious life. At the same time, however, it had remained very tightly under the control of the Anglo-Norman kings. This control had loosened somewhat under King Stephen. But when Henry II became king, he attempted to reclaim the "traditional" rights that his grandfather, King Henry I, had exercised over the Church in England, without taking notice of the extent to which the ecclesiastical world had changed in the intervening years. As Henry extended the jurisdictional claims of his own royal courts, he ran directly into the expanded judicial authority the Church was now claiming for itself. During the first eight years of his reign, conflicts of this sort were largely held in check by the wise pliancy of Archbishop Theobald of Canterbury, a veteran of the anarchical years under King Stephen. In 1162, however, when Theobald died, Henry arranged to have his chancellor and good friend Thomas Becket elected to be the new archbishop of Canterbury. This decision would prove a tragic one for all concerned.[13]

The public career of Thomas Becket ran through two phases of about equal length. For eight years, from 1154 to 1162, he served as Henry II's chancellor and boon companion. In 1162 Henry appointed him archbishop of Canterbury, and for the following eight years, until his murder in 1170, he was Henry's implacable foe. Much has been written of the transformation in Becket's character from the roistering, worldly chancellor to the stern archbishop, yet the complexities of Becket's personality remain obscure. It is clear that he was an exceedingly talented man — the offspring

---

[13]The best biography is F. Barlow, *Thomas Becket* (London, 1986). More sympathetic to Becket is David Knowles, *Thomas Becket* (London, 1970). Warren, *Henry II*, pp. 399–555, is the best overall account of Henry II's relations with the Church.

of a London merchant family whose intelligence and charm propelled him up through the ecclesiastical hierarchy into the royal chancellorship, and finally into the supreme ecclesiastical office in Britain. His career was dazzling, and as he rose he devoted himself zealously to each of his successive positions. As chancellor, Becket served his king faithfully and skillfully; as archbishop he fought with equal ardor for the interests of the Church. The perfect chancellor, and one of England's most celebrated churchmen, he has been described as a mere actor who played each of his roles to the hilt. Yet this judgment is superficial. Becket in fact hoped to maintain a cooperative relationship with Henry II, but he also took his archiepiscopal responsibility very seriously. As archbishop he felt duty bound to uphold the rights of God's Church — all the more so because some churchmen had criticized him for being the first archbishop since the Norman Conquest who had not previously been a monk or regular canon. Deeply aware of this alleged shortcoming, Becket went to considerable lengths to demonstrate his piety — to his contemporaries and doubtless to God as well. He adopted the ascetic custom of wearing a hair shirt concealed under his religious habit. Although he desired Henry's continued friendship, he would not be Henry's tool. If the archbishop sometimes lacked a certain generosity of spirit, one must nevertheless recognize that he made his later years immensely more difficult for himself by his uncompromising dedication to what he took to be his solemn religious duty. We must grant him the honesty of his convictions.

Henry II, on the other hand, could not have anticipated Becket's change of heart. In appointing Becket to the archbishopric, the king must have supposed that he was installing a chum at the apex of the English Church. But Becket soon asserted his independence in a variety of ways. He declined Henry's request, for example, that he continue to serve as royal chancellor, and he began to treat Henry not as his master but as his political colleague and spiritual son. Henry was surprised and resentful, and hostility soon developed between the two.

Early in 1164 Henry brought the issue to a head by forcing Becket and the other English bishops to consent to a list of customs bearing on Church-state relations — a document known as the Constitutions of Clarendon. These customs were, of course, strongly pro-royal. Henry II maintained that they represented common practice in the days of Henry I, and with one or two possible exceptions they did. Yet for several reasons, reform clergy found them hard to accept. For one thing, although Henry I had often acted contrary to the spirit of ecclesiastical reform, he had never been so bold — or so foolish — as to commit his practices to writing. He may have ignored many of the privileges that ecclesiastical reformers claimed, but he never asked his clerics to give their written approval to his policies. Moreover, the English Church had achieved a considerable measure of independence during Stephen's reign, rising to a position much more in harmony with contemporary reform ideology. Some of the provisions in the Constitutions of Clarendon would therefore have struck reformers as distasteful backward steps. This was particularly true of the ban on appeals to Rome without royal permission (a policy that dated back to William the Conqueror) and of the provision establishing a degree of royal jurisdiction over "criminous clerics," who had previously been subject to church courts alone.

The proper treatment of clerics who committed crimes was the most bitterly disputed issue in the Henry-Becket controversy. Henry complained that such offenders often received absurdly light sentences from ecclesiastical tribunals. In the royal courts the penalty for murder was death or mutilation, but a cleric who murdered someone might simply be dismissed from the priesthood (defrocked) and released. The Constitutions of Clarendon provided that once a cleric was tried, convicted, and defrocked by an ecclesiastical court, the Church should no longer prevent his being brought to a royal court for further punishment: "If a cleric has confessed or been convicted, the Church shall protect him no further." Becket replied that no one ought to be put in double jeopardy.

The Becket dispute discloses two worlds in collision: the secular world of the royal bureaucracy and the spiritual world of the English and international Church. Two different governments — royal and ecclesiastical — met head-on. Similar disputes occurred off and on throughout high-medieval Europe and were, indeed, merely particular manifestations of a deeper conflict — a power struggle between the universal Church and the rising secular states. The battle between Henry II and Becket was one of its most dramatic episodes, and it might well have been avoided if both men had possessed cooler heads.

Shortly after subscribing to the Constitutions of Clarendon, Becket reversed himself and appealed to Pope Alexander III for support. Alexander equivocated: he could hardly repudiate Becket, yet his own conflict with the Holy Roman emperor, Frederick Barbarossa, left him reluctant to make further enemies among Europe's monarchs. Moreover, as a trained legal scholar, Alexander would have realized that Becket's position on clerical immunity was more radical than that of most canon lawyers.

By now Henry II had lost all patience with Becket and resolved to break his spirit. Toward the end of 1164 Henry ordered him to stand trial before the king's great council in Northampton. Becket was accused of various offenses allegedly committed during his service as chancellor. Claiming clerical immunity from royal jurisdiction, Becket fled the country to appeal his case to the pope. In so doing he was challenging one of the basic articles of Henry's Constitutions of Clarendon — the prohibition of unlicensed appeals to Rome.

A protracted struggle ensued between the fiery king and the exiled archbishop. For nearly six years the papacy managed to placate Becket while restraining him sufficiently to avoid a complete break between England and Rome. The crisis reached its climax in June 1170. Henry II, anxious to forestall another succession crisis after his death, took steps to have his eldest suviving son crowned. Since the archbishop of Canterbury was unavailable, Henry turned to Canterbury's ancient rival, the archbishop of York. When Becket heard that the archbishop of York had

Becket's Murder in Canterbury Cathedral, 1170 In the upper panel of this nearly contemporary manuscript illumination, the archbishop, while dining, is warned of the arrival of four hostile barons. In the lower panel, he is murdered while his monks hide in terror. *(Reproduced by courtesy of the Trustees of the British Museum)*

presided over a royal coronation, he was furious at the affront to the dignity of Canterbury. With papal backing, he threatened to lay England under the ban of interdict. Alarmed at this threat, which would have resulted in closing all of England's churches, Henry II worked out a temporary reconciliation with Becket that left all major issues unresolved but allowed the archbishop to return to England.

A truce that failed to resolve anything was perhaps worse than no truce at all. Just before returning to England, in the late autumn of 1170, Becket shocked Henry by excommunicating all the bishops who had participated in the coronation of the Young Henry. Henry II, livid with rage, is reported to have cried out to his court, "Will no one rid me of this turbulent priest?" And four of his barons, responding to their king's fury, journeyed to Canterbury with vengeance in their hearts. On the evening of December 29, 1170, they hacked Becket to pieces in Canterbury Cathedral before a group of terrified onlookers. Becket murmured, "I accept death for the name of Jesus and his Church." And he fell to the stone floor with his arms outstretched in prayer.

The deed had a powerful impact on public opinion in England and the Continent. Becket was hailed as a martyr, and his tomb at Canterbury became an immensely popular pilgrimage center. He was quickly canonized, and his body was reputed to be a source of miraculous cures. His stance on criminous clerics now won the assent of Europe's canon lawyers, and the papacy itself issued legislation protecting clerics from secular punishment.

To Henry, Becket's murder was a source of profound embarrassment. The king denied that the four barons had acted under his orders, and one can well believe that Henry would not have been so foolish as to undertake deliberately such a violent and self-defeating policy. Nevertheless, Henry did not escape all responsibility for the murder. He had been Becket's archenemy, and if the four killers were not acting on his command, they were at least responding to his anger. Bowing to the outrage of both Church and laity, the king did penance for his part in Becket's death. Walking barefoot through the streets of Canterbury, he submitted to a ceremonial whipping by the Canterbury monks. He was also compelled to repudiate the Constitutions of Clarendon, to permit appeals to Rome without specific royal license, and to refrain from subjecting clerics who committed crimes to capital punishment. On the surface of things, the martyred archbishop would seem to have won.

In reality, the expansion of royal justice at ecclesiastical expense suffered only a partial eclipse. Although Henry withdrew the Constitutions of Clarendon, most of their provisions remained effective in fact if not in law. Henry continued to place trustworthy royal servants in high ecclesiastical offices, and in the later years of his reign he kept tight control over the English Church without any dramatic violations of canon law or harsh conflicts with the papacy. His earlier policy of flamboyant aggression, symbolized by the Constitutions of Clarendon, gave way to a more effective policy of subtle backstairs maneuvering. Learning from the Becket affair, Henry II succeeded, in ecclesiastical affairs as elsewhere, in advancing his realm toward administrative and legal centralization.

The Angevin Empire

In discussing the development of England under Henry II, one must never overlook the fact that Henry's authority extended far beyond the island kingdom. He was the first of England's kings to possess greater wealth and power outside the kingdom than within it. He applied many of his English legal and administrative policies to his continental dominions as well — Normandy in particular. The Norman ducal court and exchequer came to parallel those of England. Henry issued a military ordinance for his French lands similar to the English Assize of Arms, and he undertook a feudal survey of Normandy in 1172 that echoed the *Cartae Baronum* of 1166. Nevertheless, one can separate England from the remainder of the Angevin Empire[14] without doing excessive violence to historical reality, for Henry's constellation of territories was in reality no empire at all. Each principality that he controlled had its own government and distinctive customs; the heterogeneous lands were linked solely by their allegiance to a single individual. There was no central "imperial" government, no unified body of imperial law, but rather myriad separate

---

[14]In addition to Warren, *Henry II*, see also John Gillingham, *The Angevin Empire* (London, 1984), reprinted in idem, *Richard Coeur de Lion: Kingship, Chivalry and War in the Twelfth Century* (London, 1994).

THE ANGEVIN EMPIRE

DOMINIONS OF HENRY II

Held from Henry II by vassals.

Ruled by Henry II directly as king.

Royal Domain of the King of France.

Held by Henry II as vassal of the King of France.

Held by vassals of the King of France

administrations of varying efficiency, held together by Henry's intelligence and energy. Still, from the military and diplomatic standpoint — if not from the standpoint of law and administration — the Angevin Empire must be regarded as a single entity. England was its most tightly administered district and a major source of its wealth, whereas the continental territories required most of Henry's military efforts.

Having inherited a huge conglomeration of territories, Henry aspired to still more. He campaigned — with only partial success — to extend his authority into the province of Toulouse in southern France. And he won a degree of control over eastern and central Ireland through the invasion and settlement of a few of his ambitious vassals and, later, through his direct intervention. In 1185 he went so far as to install his son John as lord of Ireland, recalling him later when he suffered a military disaster at Irish hands. But for Henry II, the Irish campaigns, so significant to later English history, were of mere secondary importance — little more than an afterthought. From the beginning of his reign to the end, he focused his military and political interests on France.

During the years of Henry II, the French monarchy was coming of age. Since 987 the crown had been in the hands of the Capetian family. This dynasty had managed to secure its hold on the French throne by producing male heirs at the proper time. But until the twelfth century it exercised direct authority only over the district around Paris and Orleans, known as the Ile de France, and even there the Capetians were plagued by a host of unruly minor barons. In theory, the great dukes and counts of France — even the duke of Normandy himself — were vassals of the French kings, but they tended to ignore their obligations to their feeble monarch unless it was in their interest to ally with him.

In the twelfth century, however, Capetian power was growing. King Louis VI (1108–1137) succeeded in taming the barons of the Ile de France, thereby providing the monarchy with a secure, if limited, territorial base. His successor, Louis VII (1137–1180), was a genial, pious man who extended the prestige of the monarchy by serving as a rallying point for the French nobility against the immense power of the Angevin Empire. More and more, the French nobles outside Henry II's dominions looked to Louis VII for leadership and submitted their disagreements to the court of this self-effacing, honest king.

To Louis VII, the growth of the Angevin Empire was an ominous development. From his modest possessions in the Ile de France, he faced a vast configuration of territories controlled by his nominal vassal, Henry II. England, Normandy, Maine, Anjou, Brittany, Touraine, and Aquitaine were now joined together in an empire that dwarfed the French royal domain. On the other hand, the Capetian monarchy had the advantage of formal overlordship over Henry II's French dominions, and the further advantage that these territories were heterogeneous — too extensive to defend easily and in some cases quite loosely governed. Aquitaine, in particular, had a long tradition of baronial independence, and outside the northern Aquitainian province of Poitou the ducal authority tended to be nominal.

Thus, the Angevin Empire had serious weaknesses that the French monarchy might exploit. But Louis VII took only halfhearted advantage of the overextended empire, primarily by fomenting revolt among Henry II's sons and his long-suffering wife, Eleanor of Aquitaine (King Louis' own former wife). Henry left himself open to such tactics. He alienated Eleanor of Aquitaine by his infidelities (Queen Eleanor absolutely loathed Henry's mistress, "the Fair Rosamund" Clifford), and he annoyed

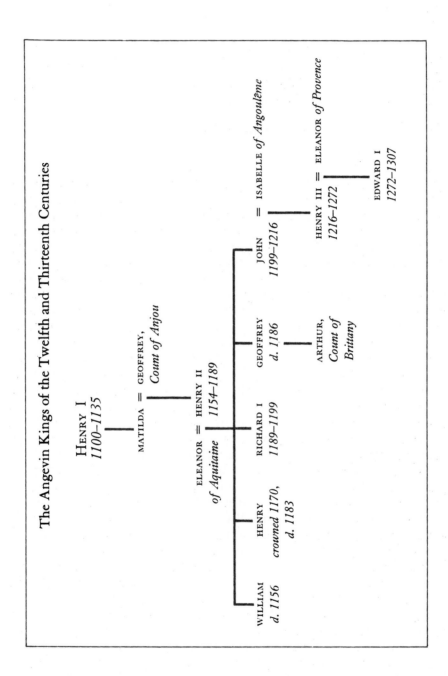

The Angevin Kings of the Twelfth and Thirteenth Centuries

HENRY I
1100–1135

MATILDA = GEOFFREY,
Count of Anjou

ELEANOR = HENRY II
of Aquitaine   1154–1189

WILLIAM
d. 1156

HENRY
crowned 1170,
d. 1183

RICHARD I
1189–1199

GEOFFREY
d. 1186

JOHN
1199–1216
= ISABELLE of Angoulême

ARTHUR,
Count of
Brittany

HENRY III =
1216–1272
ELEANOR of Provence

EDWARD I
1272–1307

his sons by giving them titular rule over various districts of his empire while reserving actual political authority for himself. Urged on by the French king, and resentful of their father's authoritarian policy, Henry II's three eldest sons, Henry, Richard, and Geoffrey, rebelled against him in 1173–1174, supported by their mother; indeed, because the three rebellious sons were, at the time, fourteen, fifteen, and barely eighteen years old, Eleanor was probably the primary architect of the revolt. A number of nobles in Henry II's continental possessions joined the rebels, but they won the backing of only a few English barons. In the end the rebellion collapsed, and Henry II sought to prevent future ones by consigning his wife to comfortable imprisonment in a castle and placating his sons with greater responsibility and authority. All this did little good. Young Henry and Geoffrey both died in the midst of plots or insurrections — Henry in 1183, and Geoffrey three years later. At Louis VII's death in 1180, the French crown passed to his shrewd and ruthless son, Philip II "Augustus" (1180–1223), who adopted a much more aggressive anti-Angevin policy than his father had pursued.

Consequently, Henry II's final years were troubled. The great king could keep the peace everywhere except within his own family, and Philip Augustus exploited the rebelliousness of Henry's offspring to the fullest. In the late 1180s both of Henry's surviving sons, Richard and John, conspired with Philip Augustus and rebelled against their aging father. On the eve of Henry's death in 1189, the hostile coalition forced him to make a humiliating submission. Tradition has it that Henry's dying sentence was one of bitter self-reproach: "Shame, shame on a conquered king."

But Henry II's defeat in 1189, although a personal tragedy, had little effect on French or English history. Despite Philip Augustus's involvement, the rebellion was fundamentally a family affair, and on Henry II's death the Angevin Empire passed intact to his eldest surviving son, Richard the Lion-Hearted. Philip Augustus's machinations had done him little good. But Philip was both patient and persevering, intent on the destruction of the Angevin Empire and prepared to devote his whole life to the task if necessary. Henry II had clung grimly to his continental lands. It remained to be seen whether his sons could do as well.

Richard the Lion-Hearted (1189–1199)

Richard the Lion-Hearted[15] was above all else a warrior. He was much admired by the military nobility for his skill at arms, his mastery of siege-craft, and his passion for battle. While crusading in the Holy Land, he conducted the siege of Acre with such enthusiasm that even when he

---

[15]John Gillingham, *Richard I* (New Haven, 1999) supersedes all previous biographies of Richard.

was ill he had his men carry him to the city walls on a litter so that he might fire his crossbow at the enemy.

Richard was also attuned to the new aristocratic style of courtly manners, witty talk, and chivalrous display that was becoming fashionable among the Anglo-French nobility. A troubadour at the court of Henry II had complained about its lack of style: "There was no banter, no laughter, no giving of presents." At Richard's court the mood was different, for the new king had spent his youth in Aquitaine — the homeland of the troubadours — and he wrote troubadour songs himself. There were those who criticized him for his outbursts of temper and his acts of cruelty; the contemporary writer Gerald of Wales described him as a person who "cared for no success unless it was reached by a path cut by his own sword and stained with his enemies' blood." But many of Richard's contemporaries respected him as a warrior and crusader, and in subsequent generations his reputation rose to heroic heights.

Richard has fared less well at the hands of modern historians. He made no personal contribution to English constitutional and legal development and, indeed, spent less than six months of his ten-year reign in England. (This statistic is enshrined in every textbook, and we have no intention of neglecting it here!) The nineteenth-century historian Sismondi dismissed him as "a bad son, a bad brother, a bad husband, and a bad king." But historians who condemn Richard in such uncompromising terms are judging him by anachronistic standards. Because we now know that the Angevin Empire was ephemeral and that the crusading movement ultimately failed, we are prone to discount Richard's activities in defending his French territories and in winning glory on the Third Crusade. Yet these are the very activities that earned him respect among his contemporaries and ensured the success of his reign. His military prowess and chivalric reputation retained for him the loyalty of his vassals and subjects, even when he himself was far away. Hence, he preserved the integrity of the Angevin Empire and was never seriously threatened by internal rebellion.

The Reign of Richard I

Immediately after his coronation in 1189, Richard began preparing for a crusade. Jerusalem, which had fallen to the Christian warriors of the First Crusade in 1099, had been retaken by the talented Muslim leader Saladin in 1187. Beginning in 1190, a multitude of European warriors set off on the Third Crusade with the goal of recapturing the Holy City. They were led by three monarchs: Emperor Frederick Barbarossa of Germany, King Philip Augustus of France, and King Richard I of England. Considering the magnitude of the effort and the distinction of its leaders, the Third Crusade must be regarded as a failure, but it was a failure that added much to Richard the Lion-Hearted's fame. Richard became the real leader of the movement. Frederick Barbarossa drowned while

Richard I Enthroned *(Ms. Royal 20.A.II Richard I Enthroned from Historia Major Matthew Paris, c. 1240. The British Library, London/Bridgeman Art Library, London)*

crossing a river on his way to the Holy Land; and Philip Augustus — whose dour temperament was unsuited for crusading — abandoned the venture after joining Richard in the capture of the important port of Acre. The longstanding French-Angevin conflict made the two monarchs natural rivals, and having quarreled with Richard, Philip returned to France to plot against him. Richard was left in command of the campaign against Saladin.

In this great Muslim chieftain Richard found an adversary as valiant as himself. While fighting one another the two warriors developed a strong mutual admiration. And when, after months of campaigning, Richard found it impossible to take Jerusalem, he entered into a treaty with Saladin that guaranteed the rights of Christian pilgrims in the Holy City. He then set out for home to take his revenge on Philip Augustus. On his return journey, he had the extreme bad luck to be captured by the duke of Austria and handed over to his enemy, Emperor Henry VI of Germany, Frederick Barbarossa's son and heir.

Europe was outraged that a crusading hero should receive such treatment, but Henry VI refused to give up his valuable hostage until England met his terms. In the end, the English submitted to ruthless taxation in order to raise the immense sum of one hundred thousand pounds — literally a king's ransom — and Richard was obliged to grant

Henry VI the overlordship of England, to hold his kingdom as a fief of the Holy Roman Empire as long as he lived. Only then was Richard set free.

On his return in 1194 Richard had several scores to settle. Philip Augustus had been doing what he could to subvert the Angevin Empire, which was held together by the loyalty of its barons to their chivalric, ill-treated lord, and by the heroic efforts of Richard I's mother, Eleanor of Aquitaine, who, at the news of his captivity, assumed a position of direct authority in England. King Philip had even sought to persuade Emperor Henry VI to keep Richard in perpetual custody. Accordingly, Richard spent the last half of his reign waging war against France; and it soon became clear that on the battlefield Philip Augustus was no match for him. Richard more than held his own. By 1198 he had recovered all the lands and castles lost during his captivity, and at his untimely death from a chance battle wound in 1199, he was threatening the French throne itself.

In England, during Richard's absence, the Anglo-Norman and Angevin tradition of family discord had asserted itself in the person of his younger brother, John. When Richard departed from England for the Crusade, he left the kingdom in the control of his chancellor, William Longchamp, bishop of Ely. Longchamp was an able but heavy-handed administrator whose low birth and pompous behavior made him widely unpopular. John attempted to place himself at the head of the movement against Longchamp, with the ultimate goal of wresting England from Richard's control. He succeeded in having Longchamp removed from office but failed to win the Angevin Empire for himself. Thereupon, he began to plot against his absent brother with the ever-willing Philip Augustus, but again without success. On Richard's return John was obliged to beg his mercy and forgiveness. Richard is recorded as replying in a generous but patronizing tone: "Think no more of it, John; you are only a child who has had evil counselors."

In the years after Longchamp's fall, the administration of England passed into the hands of a skillful royal official, Hubert Walter, who was raised in 1193 to the archbishopric of Canterbury. More an administrator than a pastor, Hubert Walter did not distinguish himself as a spiritual leader. But he provided Richard with something that Henry II had sought in vain: a trusted supporter at the head of the English Church. More than that, Hubert Walter, who dominated the English administration during the last half of Richard's reign and the first third of John's, presided over an era of immense significance in English administrative history. In addition to his exalted position as archbishop of Canterbury, he served as Richard's justiciar and as John's chancellor. In his time the royal administration functioned with unprecedented efficiency (the raising of the hundred-thousand-pound ransom provides merely one illustration of this), and royal records were maintained far more systematically than ever before.

Hubert Walter and his able administrative colleagues provided a degree of continuity between the reigns of Richard and John. The two brothers were so contrary in personality, however, that their reigns form two distinct epochs. Royal administration had made great progress in the twelfth century, but the quality of individual royal leadership remained of fundamental importance. And even more than the chivalrous Richard, John was to make his own distinctive impression on the development of the English state.

King John (1199–1216): **An Evaluation**

John's reign witnessed three great conflicts: with the French monarchy, with the papacy, and with the English barons. Each of these struggles ended in failure for John, and his failures were of momentous consequence for the making of England. They resulted in the disintegration of the Angevin Empire, the establishment of papal lordship over the English realm, and the issuing of Magna Carta.[16]

John himself is an elusive figure. In many respects he was Richard's opposite — unchivalrous, moody, suspicious, a mediocre general, but highly intelligent and deeply interested in the royal administration. He is at once repulsive and fascinating. Historians of the nineteenth century tended to regard him as a brilliant, unscrupulous villain. J. R. Green described him in these words:

> "Foul as it is, hell itself is defiled by the fouler presence of John." This terrible view of his contemporaries has passed into the sober judgment of history.... In his inner soul John was the worst outcome of the Angevins. He united into one mass of wickedness their insolence, their selfishness, their unbridled lust, their cruelty and tyranny, their shamelessness, their superstition, their cynical indifference to honor or truth.[17]

Since the time these words were written, historians have modified their appraisal of John. A French historian, writing in the 1930s when Freud was popular, ascribed John's difficulties to mental illness: "It is our opinion that John Lackland was subject to a mental disease well known today and described by modern psychiatrists as the periodical psychosis.... Among his Angevin ancestors were fools and madmen."[18] Modern psychology shares with medieval penance the happy quality of forgiving all sins; portraying John as a psychotic permits us to absolve him.

Subsequent historians have also attempted to rehabilitate John — in a variety of ways. Modern scholars tend to be skeptical of such concepts as the foulness of hell, corrupt inner souls, masses of wickedness, and

---

[16]King John has received much attention. Three scholarly accounts are highly recommended: Sidney Painter, *The Reign of King John* (Baltimore, 1949); W. L. Warren, *King John* (London, 1961; Berkeley, Calif., 1978); and Ralph V. Turner, *King John* (London, 1994).

[17]J. R. Green, *History of the English People*, I (special ed., Nations of the World Series, n.d.), p. 237. Green's *History* was first published in London in the years 1877–1880.

[18]Charles Petit-Dutaillis, *The Feudal Monarchy in France and England* (London, 1936), p. 215.

Tomb Effigy of King John in Worcester Cathedral, Carved Shortly After His Death   Beside him are depictions of two Anglo-Saxon bishops of Worcester, Oswald and Wulfstan, whom John regarded as patron saints. *(A. F. Kersting)*

even of Freud. Some have argued that John was considerably maligned by his contemporaries. Many of the most infamous atrocity stories relating to his reign, for example, come from the writings of two thirteenth-century historians from St. Albans Abbey — Roger Wendover and Matthew Paris — both of whom were strongly biased against him. Roger Wendover despised John, and Matthew Paris copied from Wendover and elaborated his tales. From the works of these men comes the story that John ordered his soldiers to seize Archdeacon Geoffrey of Norwich, bind him with chains, cast him into prison, and torture him to death by crushing him beneath a covering of lead. This grisly event is said to have occurred in 1209. Yet sixteen years later, in 1225, this same Archdeacon Geoffrey became bishop of Ely. It is known that there were several Geoffreys connected with Norwich and that Roger Wendover may have gotten them confused; but if so, we can accept the remainder of the anecdote only with grave reservations. Again, Matthew Paris reports that at the death of Archbishop Hubert Walter in 1205, John made the disrespectful statement: "Now for the first time I am king of England." The same historian relates that when John's talented justiciar, Geoffrey Fitz Peter, died in 1213, the monarch exclaimed: "By the feet of God now for the first time am I king and lord of England." Unless we wish to add redundancy to John's numerous sins, we must view both tales with skepticism.

Still, even though such stories may be exaggerated or even false, John was the sort of person about whom they could be believed. He was a repellent, unlovable man who probably murdered his nephew (Arthur of Brittany) in a drunken rage, who killed hostages, starved prisoners, and broke his word with exuberant abandon. Such behavior fell far short of the standards that twelfth- and thirteenth-century England demanded of its kings. John's behavior cost him the respect of his subjects and diminished his effectiveness as a political and military leader. The story is told of how St. Hugh, bishop of Lincoln, once tried to frighten John into changing his ways by showing him a carving of tormented souls in hell at the Angevin abbey of Fontevrault. But John turned to gaze instead at some carvings of proud kings, telling Bishop Hugh that he intended to pattern himself after them.

Richard had been successful in preserving his patrimony because his barons and lesser subjects trusted and respected him. John failed because he lost his barons' confidence. They did not demand a living saint as their monarch — many of John's predecessors had been ruthless and cruel — but they did expect consistency of policy and military prowess. And John was, above all, inconstant. He was capable of almost senseless lethargy, excessive caution, even panic. The barons, who were willing to forgive much in an able warrior-king, gave John the humiliating nickname "Softsword," and right or wrong the image had a fatal effect on John's leadership. His barons, regarding him as suspicious and untrustworthy, often refused to join his military expeditions or fight his battles. The more they did so, the more suspicious and untrustworthy John became. In the generations since the Norman Conquest, monarchy and nobility had often been at odds, but never before was the cleavage so sharp. As one historian observed: "John was the most incompetent and overrated of the Plantagenet kings."[19]

Nonetheless, John's reign was not without its triumphs. His military and diplomatic policies toward Wales and Scotland succeeded as seldom before. His vassals extended their authority over two-thirds of Ireland, and the native Irish kings of the remaining third recognized him as their overlord. He maintained the strong, well-organized navy his brother had built: by 1205 it numbered fifty-one oared galleys and could be expanded to several times that figure by commandeering merchant ships. He devoted much intelligent attention to the royal administration. He enforced the law strongly and — unless it was against his interest — justly. Indeed, his accession marks the beginning of a great new epoch in the administrative history of the realm. Three of medieval England's foremost administrators worked under him and evidently received his full support:

---

[19]Gillingham, *Richard Coeur de Lion*, pp. 155–180.

the chancellor-archbishop, Hubert Walter; the justiciar, Geoffrey Fitz Peter; and the treasurer, William of Ely. Royal records grew more abundant and exact. Now for the first time, royal charters and other correspondence issuing from the chancery were systematically copied and preserved.

Like his predecessors, John was keenly acquisitive. His tightening of royal law and administration brought a surge in tax revenues. But John carried many of the revenue-raising practices of his royal predecessors to extremes — demanding arbitrarily high reliefs, abusing royal authority over wardships and marriages — and adding to these abuses new fiscal expedients such as higher and more frequent scutage levies and more numerous taxes on rents and chattels. England was prosperous enough to afford such exploitation, and John needed money desperately. He had inherited an empty treasury from Richard, and a surge of inflation plagued his reign. Nevertheless, the overall effect of John's financial policies was to increase his unpopularity and to heighten his reputation as an arbitrary tyrant.

The Collapse of the Angevin Empire

When John acceded to the throne of England and assumed the leadership of the Angevin Empire, he faced a multitude of difficulties.[20] His reputation was already damaged, not so much by his earlier machinations against his crusading brother (filial and fraternal disloyalty were by no means unprecedented) as by their utter futility. He inherited from Richard an effective but expensive and demanding military policy in France. Moreover, he was confronted from the first with a rival to the throne in his nephew, Arthur of Brittany, son of his late brother Geoffrey and grandson of Henry II. Because John managed to win England and most of the continental territories, Arthur predictably received the full support of the persistently troublesome Philip Augustus of France.

Philip and Richard the Lion-Hearted had been at war when Richard died, and the hostilities continued into the early months of John's reign. In 1200 the two kings arranged a truce, but Philip continued to await his opportunity to shatter the Angevin inheritance. The opportunity came a mere three months later when John, on a tour of Aquitaine, suddenly and unexpectedly entered into marriage. The bride was Isabel, heiress of the important Aquitainian county of Angoulême, a girl in her early teens or possibly as young as twelve.

John's motives in choosing his young wife seem to have been a blend of passion and politics. Isabel was a beautiful young girl, and Angoulême

---

[20]The collapse of the Angevin Empire under John is treated masterfully and in great detail by Sir Maurice Powicke, *The Loss of Normandy, 1189–1204*, 2nd ed. (Manchester, 1961). See, more recently, J. C. Holt, *Magna Carta and Medieval Government* (London, 1985), pp. 23–65; John W. Baldwin, *The Government of Philip Augustus* (Berkeley, 1986); and Gillingham, *Richard Coeur de Lion*, pp. 66–86.

was one of the more disorderly principalities in turbulent Aquitaine. By establishing firm control over Angoulême, John could extend his authority in southern France considerably. But Isabel's hand was already promised to the neighboring lord of another important Aquitainian principality, Hugh the Brown of Lusignan. In making Isabel his wife, John forestalled a dangerous alliance between Lusignan and Angoulême. But as a political act it was hardly worth the trouble it caused, for John had gravely offended the Lusignan family. According to the custom of the day, he might have smoothed things over by granting Hugh the Brown certain territorial compensations, but the headstrong king chose to scorn the Lusignans and thereby earned their hatred. In the months that followed, John alienated other Aquitainian barons by seizing their lands and accusing them of treason. He was creating a dangerously hostile faction within his continental dominions.

In the spring of 1202 King Philip Augustus made his move. Taking advantage of an appeal by the Lusignans to his court, Philip summoned John to Paris to answer their complaints, and even demanded that John turn several of his castles over to him as security. As king of England John was subject to no one; but as duke of Aquitaine and Normandy, count of Anjou, and lord of numerous other continental principalities, he was the vassal of the king of France. As such he was bound by feudal custom to answer the summons to his lord's court. When he refused to do so (very sensibly), Philip formally deprived him of his French fiefs. Philip had contrived to place himself in the position of the good lord whose vassal had wronged and defied him. He sent his armies against Normandy with the full force of feudal law behind him.

The campaign went well for John at first. In a bold military stroke he succeeded in capturing Hugh the Brown, several of Hugh's Lusignan kinsmen, and Arthur of Brittany. But John nullified the victory with subsequent blunders. He released the Lusignans in return for a ransom and promises of loyalty that they did not keep, and he apparently murdered his nephew Arthur. Conclusive proof of the murder has never materialized, but rumors of it spread quickly, and John's reputation was darkened still further. Meanwhile, the king was abusing his barons, friend and foe alike, and increasing his unpopularity among his continental vassals.

Ultimately, John had to depend on the loyalty of these vassals to defend his continental inheritance, and his mistreatment of many of them proved a fatal error. In the course of the year 1203 one Norman castle after another fell to Philip Augustus, while John moved aimlessly around the duchy watching his patrimony crumble. In December 1203, with much of Normandy still under his control, he departed for England, apparently in panic, leaving his Norman loyalists in the lurch. By the middle of 1204 all Normandy lay in King Philip's hands. Meanwhile Maine, Anjou, and all of John's former continental territories north of Aquitaine fell to the French monarchy. All that remained were portions of distant Aquitaine, whose barons preferred a remote and ineffective lord like John to a powerful monarch near at hand. The Angevin Empire was defunct. John had sustained a monstrous military and political disaster.

England's French territories were not severed completely and would not be until the mid-sixteenth century. But from 1204 on, England was far more autonomous than before, and its monarchs tended to devote most of their attention to the island kingdom itself. Modern English historians, viewing the past through the distorting lens of hindsight, tend to regard this development as a Good Thing. To John, however, it was a profound humiliation that had to be avenged. Over the next decade he devoted his considerable political and diplomatic talents to weaving an alliance system designed to crush Philip Augustus and permit the reconquest of Normandy and Anjou.

The Struggle with the Papacy

In the meantime, John had become embroiled in a struggle with the papacy over the selection of a new archbishop of Canterbury to replace Hubert Walter (d. 1205). The archbishopric of Canterbury had been a storm center in the reigns of William Rufus, Henry I, and Henry II. Under John, as on these previous occasions, the conflict centered on ecclesiastical independence versus royal sovereignty over the English Church. As before, it became a trial of strength between the claims of the universal Church and the kingdom of England. But far more than before, the Church-state struggle in John's reign was a direct confrontation between monarchy and papacy.

The investiture controversy had been settled long before in compromise, but the question of lay control over the appointments of bishops and abbots remained unresolved. The kings of England subscribed overtly to the policy of free canonical elections but in fact controlled appointments to important offices in the English Church through subtle — or sometimes not so subtle — maneuvering. As long as they applied royal influence quietly and without serious opposition, all was well. But if the king acted clumsily and created a messy issue, the papacy could be expected to intervene on behalf of proper canonical practices. This was particularly true in the opening years of the thirteenth century, when the papal throne was occupied by Innocent III — a man of keen intelligence and resolution. Innocent III was the most powerful pope of the Middle Ages; it was John's misfortune to lock horns with him.

Hubert Walter had been a masterful royal administrator but a less than inspiring prelate. The monks of Canterbury, who enjoyed the traditional canonical privilege of electing their archbishop, were anxious to avoid having another royal agent on the Canterbury throne. John was just as anxious to install one of his own loyal subordinates. Working quickly to forestall the king, the Canterbury monks elected one of their own number and sent a delegation to Rome to have him confirmed. Infuriated at their insubordination, John forced the monks to retract their

St. Francis Gains the Sanction of Pope Innocent III in 1210　From a painting by Giotto about a century later. *(The Granger Collection)*

choice, elect his own man, and send another delegation to Rome to obtain confirmation of the new candidate. Thus the issue had been raised, and Innocent III was in a position to judge the dispute. He made good use of his opportunity by repudiating both nominees and persuading the Canterbury monks in Rome — by now a goodly number — to elect a churchman of his own choice. The new archbishop was a noted English scholar, Stephen Langton, who had been teaching on the Continent for some years.

John refused to accept an "outsider" and rejected Innocent's interference. Every archbishop of Canterbury in memory — even troublesome ones like Anselm and Becket — had been royal nominees, and John refused to abandon control of the Canterbury succession. Accordingly, he barred Stephen Langton from entering England. Innocent III, for his part, regarded Langton's election as strictly canonical and gave him full support. To break the impasse, Innocent laid England under interdict, suspending all church services and all sacraments except baptism and confession for the dying.

The interdict lasted seven years. John survived this awesome penalty remarkably well and even turned it to his financial advantage by confiscating ecclesiastical revenues. But in the end he had to submit. Innocent III was threatening to depose John, and Philip Augustus was contemplating an invasion of England. And John himself — whose grand design for the reconquest of Normandy and Anjou was nearing its climax — needed all the support he could obtain. Hence he made peace with the papacy in 1213, and in the following year Innocent lifted the interdict. Stephen Langton returned to England and received his archbishopric, and John agreed to restore at least a portion of the confiscated revenues.

Having surrendered, John sought to cut his losses by winning the full support of the pope. Of his own accord, he gave to Innocent III what William the Conqueror had long ago refused to Gregory VII: he made England a papal fief, undertook to become Innocent's vassal, and promised an annual tribute payment to the papacy (above and beyond the traditional Peter's Pence).[21] He took the further step of vowing to lead a crusade to the Holy Land. The crusade never materialized, for John always claimed more urgent business at home. But by his submission and his crusading vow, he succeeded in capturing the friendship of Rome. Consequently, historians have credited John with snatching victory from defeat. This interpretation seems doubtful, for Innocent's future support was of no great use to John, and Archbishop Stephen Langton turned out to be a man of independent spirit. Nevertheless, in 1214 John still had hopes of recovering Normandy and Anjou. With the papal struggle behind him, he prepared to move decisively against Philip Augustus.

During the interdict years, John had built a formidable coalition of French and German princes against the French monarchy. In 1214 the chief parties in the coalition were (1) Otto of Brunswick, John's nephew and a serious contestant for the disputed throne of the Holy Roman Empire; (2) the counts of Flanders and certain neighboring principalities; and (3) John himself. After several false starts, John set out for the county of Poitou in northern Aquitaine with as many English knights as he could persuade to accompany him. He intended his campaign to be part of a

---

[21]England continued to pay papal tribute off and on until the fourteenth century, repudiating it officially only in 1366. At the time of John's submission, a number of other kingdoms — Poland, Sicily, Denmark, Sweden, and Aragon — were also papal vassal states.

grand design: he was to attack Philip Augustus through Poitou while his German and Flemish allies invaded France from the northeast. The strategy was well conceived, but it ended disastrously. John subdued Poitou and incorporated numerous Poitevin knights into his army. But when his men encountered an army led by Philip Augustus's son, the future King Louis VIII, they refused to fight, claiming that they could not engage in armed conflict against their overlord. In rage and frustration, John withdrew from the campaign.

Philip Augustus himself led an army against John's German and Flemish allies and won an overwhelming victory over them near the Flemish village of Bouvines. Philip's triumph extinguished John's last hope of recovering the lost continental lands. It also marked a significant advance in the authority of the French monarchy, which surged ahead of Germany as the great power on the Continent. Thus the disintegration of the Angevin Empire in 1204 was confirmed by the decisive French victory at Bouvines in 1214. France was jubilant. Philip's subjects strewed flowers in the path of his triumphant army as it returned home, and the students of the University of Paris partied for two straight weeks.

Magna Carta (1215)

There were no flowers for John. Ten years of savage taxation had come to nothing, and he returned to England to face a sullen baronage. In the wake of Bouvines, the calamitous failure of John's foreign policy became clear to all. His prestige had never been lower, and many of his tax-ridden English barons were ready for rebellion. Early in 1215 the insurrection broke out, and by early summer it was obvious that the king could not contain it. His enemies demanded a written guarantee of good law and just governance based on the coronation charter of Henry I, which Henry II had confirmed at his own coronation in 1154. In June 1215, after protracted negotiations, John came to terms on the meadow of Runnymede and affixed his seal to Magna Carta.[22]

The Great Charter was a much fuller statement of rights and privileges than the charter of Henry I. It was the product of long bargaining between John, Stephen Langton, barons still loyal to John, and barons of various degrees of hostility toward him. Its sixty-three clauses embraced the full spectrum of baronial grievances, mapping the limits of royal authority more precisely than ever before. Despite the specific and practical nature of many of its provisions, collectively they reflected, at least by implication, the rudiments of a coherent political philosophy.

Historians have not always agreed on the implications of Magna Carta. It used to be regarded as the fountainhead of English liberty and the bulwark of constitutional monarchy. Some historians, reacting against this naive view, have described Magna Carta as a reactionary

---

[22]On the Great Charter, see J. C. Holt, *Magna Carta*, 2nd ed. (Cambridge, 1992).

document — an assertion of feudal privileges at the expense of the enlightened Angevin monarchy. In reality, the Great Charter was both feudal and constitutional. It looked backward and also pointed forward. It was a step in the transition from the ancient Germanic notion of sacred custom, and the feudal idea of mutual contractual rights and obligations, to the modern concept of limited monarchy and government under the law. In 1215, however, the dissident barons were looking neither backward nor forward; they were grappling with problems of the moment.

Their demand for a written confirmation of privileges had precedents not only in earlier English coronation charters but also in documents drafted elsewhere in Europe — by Emperor Frederick Barbarossa to the towns of Lombardy in 1183, by King Alphonso VIII of Leon to his barons in 1188. And similar charters were being forced out of European rulers throughout the thirteenth century — in Germany, Hungary, southern Italy, Sicily, and elsewhere. They were products of many of the same forces that underlay Magna Carta: military misfortune; the rising expenses of government; more effective administration, producing more inventive and ruthless means of collecting taxes; and a growing conception on the part of powerful subjects of their specific legal rights. But whereas other charters aimed at achieving autonomy for provinces or other local districts, Magna Carta was kingdomwide in scope and viewpoint. King John's foremost barons, perhaps because their ancestral holdings had in many cases been scattered widely across the land ever since the Norman Conquest, sought not to cripple the royal government but to influence it — to make it act in their interests and respect their customary rights.

Baronial rights and privileges were the chief items of business in Magna Carta, yet the barons were capable of a wider social vision. They incorporated into the charter the concept that the king was limited by tradition and custom in his relations with free Englishmen of every class — peasants and townspeople as well as knights and barons. And when the document referred to "Englishmen," it could sometimes include women as well. For example, "No widow shall be compelled to remarry so long as she wishes to live without a husband."

"To no one," John promised, "will we sell, deny, or delay rights of justice." "No free man may be arrested or imprisoned or deprived of his land or outlawed or exiled or in any way brought to ruin, nor shall we go against him or send others in pursuit of him, except by the legal judgment of his peers or by the law of the land." The exact nature of "the law of the land" remained vague, but the barons felt it important to assert that such a law existed, to be discovered in custom and traditional usages, and that the king was bound by it. The concept found more precise expression a generation later in the great legal treatise traditionally (and wrongly) ascribed to Henry de Bracton: "The king should be under God and the law." Political philosophers of the twelfth and thirteenth centuries were drawing sharp distinctions between the king who abided by the law and the "tyrant" who abused and ignored it. In Magna Carta these notions received practical expression.

John had said, "The law is in my mouth." Such a doctrine was clearly a threat to baronial rights and interests. The king whose will was law could, at least in theory, charge reliefs, levy scutages, and confiscate property as he pleased. Magna Carta forbade such practices in specific clauses: "Scutage and aid shall be levied in our kingdom only by the common counsel of our kingdom." "No one shall be required to render greater service from a knight's fee or from any other free holding than is in fact owed from it." It was with practical building blocks such as these that the structure of the English limited monarchy took shape. For implied in the numerous specific, pragmatic provisions of Magna Carta was the concept of an overarching body of customary law that circumscribed the power of the king.

There remained the problem of creating some kind of machinery to force the king to honor his concessions. Henry I had made many promises to his subjects in his coronation oath, but he forgot a number of them once the crisis of his accession had passed. A series of royal promises was obviously insufficient to control an ambitious king backed by the full power of the royal administration. The search for some institutional means of incorporating the nobility into royal government would occupy England for centuries to come. Subsequent generations found a tentative solution in Parliament. The barons of 1215 relied on the simpler sanction of a watchdog committee of twenty-five barons who were to act against the king, if he violated the charter, by summoning the English people "to distrain and distress him in every way possible." The committee was not long idle.

"In 1215," writes Sir James Holt, "Magna Carta was a failure. It was intended as a peace and it provoked war. It pretended to state customary law and it promoted disagreement and contention. It was legally valid for no more than three months, and even within that period its terms were never properly executed." Yet it survived the turbulence of John's final months, was reissued several times in the thirteenth century, and became a part of the common law. Largely ignored in the days of the Tudors, it was revived, reinterpreted, and passionately supported by the opponents of the seventeenth-century Stuart kings. It has never been entirely forgotten. In later centuries it came to be regarded as a document fundamental to the protection of individual liberty. This was far from the intention of its original drafters, but it is a tribute to the quality of their work. "It was adaptable. This was its greatest and most important characteristic."[23]

But for John, Magna Carta was merely an expedient to escape a temporary difficulty. He had no intention of honoring his promises; he quickly secured from his sympathetic papal overlord absolution from his oath to the barons, which was, he argued, obtained under duress and therefore invalid. Consequently, John's reign closed with a full-scale insurrection. The rebelling barons appealed for aid to King Philip Augustus,

---

[23]Holt, *Magna Carta*, pp. 1, 2.

and the French king sent an army to England led by his son, Prince Louis. John died in 1216 with the French in London and the country wracked by war.

The dissident barons were fighting not against the traditions of Angevin kingship but against a single man — a monarch who had earned their hostility by his duplicity and ruthlessness. This fact is dramatically demonstrated by the speed with which the baronial insurrection dissolved in the wake of John's death. In the words of an earlier historian, the French invasion "was doomed to fail when the kingdom ceased to be divided against itself; and the one insuperable obstacle to the healing of its divisions was removed in the person of John."[24]

---

[24]Kate Norgate, *John Lackland* (London, 1902), p. 286.

CHAPTER 7

Society, Economy, and Culture in High-Medieval England

In the two centuries following the Norman Conquest, the society, economy, and culture of England were transformed. Some of these changes — the introduction of castles; the emergence of baronial courts as competitors with the royal courts; the replacement of a native, English-speaking aristocracy with a French-speaking one; the economic reorientation of the country away from the North Sea toward western and southwestern France — were directly the result of the Conquest itself. But many of the most fundamental changes that took place during these two centuries would have occurred with or without the Normans and the Angevins. The growing population of the country — between Domesday Book and the end of the thirteenth century, the population of England doubled, from somewhere between two and three million people to around five million people — combined with the rapid growth of markets for the exchange of goods and services, produced a vastly more specialized, integrated, and efficient economic system than had existed when the Normans arrived. To support this growing population, new agricultural methods began to be widely employed in the countryside, and new lands were cleared for farming. As agriculture became more productive, it became possible for larger numbers of people to leave the land to pursue other occupations. Towns flourished, and a new educated elite began to emerge from the cathedral schools and universities of twelfth- and thirteenth-century Europe. Many, though not all, of these newly educated people entered the Church. Some became lawyers and administrators in the increasingly sophisticated legal systems that now governed both the Church and the kingdoms of western Europe. But others went directly into pastoral care, bringing with them a new interest in the psychology of sin, piety, and human identity as core elements in the Christian life.

All these changes were part of what historians have called "The Renaissance of the Twelfth Century." Together, they represent the most fundamental set of changes that occurred in western Europe between the end of the Roman Empire and the beginnings of the Industrial

Revolution. As is so often the case, historians cannot fully explain why so many profoundly important developments took place during this particular period. Once begun, these developments reinforced each other. But what started the process rolling remains unclear. The European climate was warming again, after several centuries during which colder weather had reduced the growing season for marginal crops. An improving climate, a growing population, and increasingly efficient agricultural techniques — including new crops, new systems of crop rotation, and the development of windmills for grinding grain into flour — all contributed to the growing prosperity of Europe. But despite the growth of local and regional markets, distribution of food supplies remained very unequal, even in a country as highly commercialized as high-medieval England. Drought, flooding, or famine in local areas could quickly bring the populace to the brink of starvation. There was more wealth, more widely distributed, than there had ever been before in medieval Europe, but poverty remained an ever-present and growing fact of life amidst the prosperity of the twelfth and thirteenth centuries. Food supplies barely kept pace with population growth. In England, two straight years of poor harvests between 1256 and 1258 sent thousands of starving people wandering the roads in search of food. Hundreds, and probably thousands, died — so many that in some areas the anonymous dead had to be buried in mass graves. Across northern Europe, in the terrible years of the Great Famine between 1315 and 1322, 10 to 15 percent of the entire European population may have died of starvation and disease.[1] Europe's economy was developing rapidly during the High Middle Ages, but supplying adequate food to its people remained its biggest single challenge.

The economic transformation of the High Middle Ages was accompanied by far-reaching changes in political and social organization and in mental attitudes. The growth of literacy slowly reshaped the contours of European life, nowhere more clearly than in England. Although the majority of the English people, even in 1300, still could not read, a much wider cross-section of English society now depended on written records — deeds, letters, wills, government surveys — to define their rights, property, and status than at any time since the Roman period. The growth in literacy was not steady — the shift from English to Latin as the language of administration after 1066 probably meant that Anglo-Norman England had lower levels of practical literacy than did late-Anglo-Saxon England — but by 1300 the written word affected the lives of virtually everyone in England. By the end of the thirteenth century, English freeholders and even some serfs were having their property transactions recorded in writing. Written records of agricultural production were even more common. A farmer who could not read the simple num-

---

[1]William C. Jordan, *The Great Famine: Northern Europe in the Early Fourteenth Century* (Princeton, 1996), is now the standard account.

**Reconstruction of a Fourteenth-Century Windmill Excavated in Buckingham-
shire** The upper structure in this reconstruction is based on contemporary
manuscript illuminations. *(Courtesy of The British Museum)*

bers of a manorial account would find himself defenseless against the
widespread corruption of manorial officials.

Production and preservation of government documents in England
also increased spectacularly during these centuries. About fifteen royal
acts per year have survived from the reign of William Rufus. The figure
rises to about forty-one per year from Henry I's reign and 115 per year
from Henry II's. These figures reflect only documents that have survived.
The actual production of Henry I's chancery has been estimated, very
roughly, at 4,500 acts per year, and the figures for William Rufus and
Henry II should doubtless be revised upward by a comparable proportion.
But however it is measured, the volume of paperwork issuing from the
chancery rose constantly and swiftly across the High Middle Ages.[2] By

---

[2]Paper was not regularly used for English administrative documents until the sixteenth
century. In the Middle Ages, English documents were written on thin sheets of sheepskin
known as parchment.

the thirteenth century, the English government was recording the amount of wax that the chancery was using to seal royal letters. The records disclose that in the years between Henry III's coming of age and his death (1226–1272) the use of sealing wax increased tenfold, suggesting a parallel increase in the number of letters themselves.[3]

Financial records too were becoming more and more widespread and systematic. In the recording and accounting of financial transactions, England established a clear and early lead over the remainder of high-medieval Europe. Annual written accounts of royal revenues commenced in England around 1110, in France around 1190. Comparable fiscal accounting systems also emerged in Flanders and Catalonia, but only toward the end of the twelfth century. Even in Normandy, the fiscal and administrative system lagged considerably behind that in England. It was probably not until the 1130s that Normandy had an exchequer accounting system comparable to that of England, and not until the 1170s that the system became a permanent part of Norman administrative life.[4]

These new records bear witness to the growth of increasingly effective and complex royal administrative systems, first in the Anglo-Norman state and later throughout western Christendom. As a result of these developments, skills such as reading, writing, and mathematical calculation were becoming vital to the functioning of secular and ecclesiastical governments, urban businesses, and even agricultural enterprises. Possessors of these skills, the reasoners and reckoners, shifted into positions of control throughout society, changing its attitudes and its character. Schools sprang up everywhere, and the age of the university dawned.

The growing complexity of high-medieval society opened an array of new possibilities for social mobility. Clever social nobodies could rise to power in royal and ecclesiastical administrations. Devout Christians could now choose from an increasing number of new religious orders. And to restless serfs and poor freeholders, the burgeoning towns of western Europe beckoned. Most sons and daughters continued to follow in their parents' footsteps, but the more daring and ambitious found opportunities to break from the family pattern. The result was greater social mobility and, for many, increased anxiety. Career choices were no longer as narrowly predetermined as before, but it could be a traumatic experience to move from a village community of one or two hundred familiar faces into a town with thousands of strangers. Some historians have seen as a consequence of such mobility an increased awareness of self and a growth of introspection. In high-medieval Europe, more people were collecting and preserving their personal letters. Autobiographies began to appear for the first time since St. Augustine of Hippo wrote his *Confes-*

---

[3]On literacy and the production of documents in England, see Michael Clanchy, *From Memory to Written Record: England 1066–1307,* 2nd ed. (Oxford, 1993).

[4]Judith A. Green, "Unity and Disunity in the Anglo-Norman State," *Historical Research* 62 (1989): 115–134.

sions at the end of the fourth century C.E. The fact that these letter collections and autobiographies tended to emerge from monastic, non-urban settings suggests that the new ideas and attitudes were spreading throughout medieval European society.

One of the best-known autobiographers of twelfth-century France, Peter Abelard, also pioneered in the development of a new, rational attitude toward humanity and the universe. The seeds of such an attitude had existed in the Jewish and Christian doctrine that the material world was created by God yet separate from God (and thus natural rather than supernatural). Nevertheless, early-medieval people viewed the world as a theater of miracles: a storm or fire was a divine punishment for sin, a military victory was a mark of God's favor. But in the view of Abelard and many who followed him, God's creation was a natural order that could function by its own rules, without incessant divine intervention. Miracles were possible, of course, but they were rare. Similar attitudes were circulating in England before and after Abelard's time. The collapse of the central tower of Winchester Cathedral in 1107 was attributed by many to the fact that the blaspheming King William Rufus lay entombed beneath it, but the gifted historian William of Malmesbury (Abelard's contemporary) had his doubts: "The structure might well have fallen because of faulty construction even if the king had never been buried there."[5]

The spread of such attitudes encouraged a growing skepticism toward the judicial ordeal — the appeal to God for a "miracle on demand" to determine the guilt or innocence of someone accused of a crime. We have seen how Henry II used the ordeal in his Assizes of Clarendon and Northampton but stipulated that persons of notoriously bad reputations be banished anyway, even if they passed the ordeal. Earlier, in the 1140s, the English theologian Robert Pullen had expressed his firm belief that ordeals ought to be abolished from God's Church. Later in the twelfth century the ordeal came under increasingly severe attack in university circles, until in 1215 a great Church council known as the Fourth Lateran Council, chaired by Pope Innocent III, prohibited clergy from participating in it, thereby dooming the procedure to gradual extinction. The judgment of God gave way to the testimony of witnesses, the verdicts of juries, and the decisions of judges. The twelfth century also saw the introduction in Church courts of a novel procedure that in time evolved into a major characteristic of European jurisprudence: the cross-examination of witnesses.

These deeply significant shifts in attitude toward self and the world, and the fundamental economic and social changes that accompanied them, have sometimes been described as Europe's "coming of age." Such

---

[5] *Gesta Regum Anglorum: The History of the English Kings, Volume I*, ed. and trans. R. A. B. Mynors, R. M. Thomson, and M. Winterbottom (Oxford, 1998), pp. 574 575. This translation is by C. Warren Hollister.

metaphors are misleading. Neither countries nor cultures are living creatures that pass through the stages of human life from childhood to adolescence to maturity and then old age. But the changes of the High Middle Ages were, nevertheless, essential preconditions for modern Western civilization. Behind the seventeenth-century scientific revolution lay the high-medieval idea of a universe functioning by natural rules and open to rational investigation. Behind the fifteenth-century invention of moveable-type printing lay the high-medieval shift toward the large-scale production of standardized written documents and books, including, of course, the Bible. Behind the nineteenth-century Industrial Revolution lay the intensified commerce and technological developments of the twelfth and thirteenth centuries. The origins of the modern, Western world lie in the High Middle Ages. These were the centuries that witnessed "the making of Europe."[6]

Towns and Commerce in High-Medieval England

The revival of town life in England dates back at least to the time of King Alfred and his West Saxon successors. As commerce increased during the tenth and eleventh centuries, existing towns expanded and new ones emerged as centers of trade and production. After a brief period of disruption following the Norman Conquest, urban growth in England resumed during the twelfth and thirteenth centuries, probably reaching a peak around 1300, when the percentage of the English population living in towns may have been as high as 20 percent.[7] Existing towns expanded, and new towns multiplied across the countryside. As money began to circulate more rapidly, towns emerged as centers for the distribution of goods locally, regionally, and internationally. England's ports, already active in international trade before 1066, expanded into new markets as the focus of their trade shifted away from Scandinavia and the Rhineland toward Normandy, southwestern France, and Spain. Flanders remained the largest single market for English wool, as it had been in the late-Anglo-Saxon period. But in addition to Flemish woolen cloth, merchants now also brought wine from central and southern France; silks and spices from the Mediterranean world; iron, gold, and olive oil from Spain.

With the development and increasing integration of these local, regional, and international commercial networks, regions could now begin

---

[6]The phrase is Robert Bartlett's: *The Making of Europe: Conquest, Colonization and Cultural Change, 950–1350* (Princeton, 1993).

[7]R. H. Britnell, *The Commercialisation of English Society, 1000–1500*, 2nd ed. (Manchester, 1996), pp. 49, 87, 115, 170; Christopher Dyer, "How Urbanized Was Medieval England?" in *Peasants and Townsmen in Medieval Europe: Studia in Honorem Adriaan Verhulst* (Ghent, 1995), pp. 172–180; and for a broader view, David M. Palliser, "Towns and the English State, 1066–1500," in *The Medieval State: Essays Presented to James Campbell*, ed. J. R. Maddicott and D. M. Palliser (London, 2000), pp. 127–145.

to specialize more effectively in the agrarian and manufactured products for which they were best suited. Trade in foodstuffs — grains, meats, and fruits — along with a growing diversification of domestic crops, also brought improvements in diet. The English people were now consuming more iron-rich and protein-rich foods — peas and beans, cheese and eggs, meat and especially fish — and were living longer and healthier lives as a result. The marked increase in iron in their diet contributed particularly to a longer life expectancy for women, whose iron requirements much exceed those of men, particularly during their reproductive years. As a result, for the first time in the history of western Europe, women began to outnumber men in the general population.

In England, new towns were founded in unprecedented numbers between 1150 and 1250. Staffordshire, for example, had only three royally licensed boroughs at the time of the Domesday survey of 1086, but by 1300 it had twenty-two. The boroughs of Devonshire increased from five in 1086 to eighteen in 1238. And many other towns grew up without ever achieving the status of a royal borough. Existing towns were also growing in size during these years, adding new "French" quarters for the Norman immigrants, raising houses and buildings on previously undeveloped urban land, and, in some instances, physically relocating the towns themselves from cramped to more commodious sites nearby. Salisbury is perhaps the best example of this last phenomenon, moving from its restricted hilltop location within an ancient ring-fort (Old Sarum) down to the neighboring plain where the thirteenth-century cathedral still stands.

With town growth and commercial prosperity came a general improvement in the standards of urban construction. By the late twelfth century, wealthy merchants were often living in impressive stone houses with roofs of slate or tile. Such houses have been excavated in towns as widely separated as Southampton and Norwich, Lincoln and Canterbury. The shift from wood to stone occurred not only in urban domestic architecture but also in the building of churches, castles, and manor houses. For rich merchants, large stone houses with tiled roofs provided not only comfort and protection against fire, but increased security for the coin and silver plate they customarily stored there — not to mention, of course, the welcome opportunity to display their success before the eyes of their urban neighbors.

Towns such as Bristol, Newcastle, Northampton, and, above all, London were becoming major commercial centers. The monarchy, recognizing their importance, granted them charters providing valuable privileges, such as the right to elect their own town officials, to try their citizens in their own courts, and to trade free of taxes and tolls with other cities. Kings did not grant such privileges out of sheer goodheartedness. Townspeople had to buy their charters of liberties, usually at a stiff price, and they would continue to pay the crown a yearly lump-sum "farm" out of their revenues. But town dwellers regarded their charters as well worth the price. The new urban privileges freed the burghers from the obligations and tenurial complexities of manorialism and feudalism: "A burgher can give or sell his land as he pleases and go where he wishes, freely and undisturbed."[8]

Most urban manufacturers worked for themselves in their own shops, producing their own goods and selling them directly to the public. Young artisans learned their trade as apprentices in the shops of master craftsmen. After a specified period, sometimes as long as seven years, the apprenticeship ended, at which time — with good luck and the right connections — the apprentice might become a master. But most young artisans had to work for some years beyond their apprenticeships as day laborers — "journeymen" (French: *journée*, "day") — improving their skills and saving their money until they could establish shops of their own. Toward the end of the Middle Ages, as prosperity waned and urban society became more rigid, it became increasingly common for artisans to spend their entire lives as wage earners, never becoming masters.

Throughout the High Middle Ages and beyond, women took an active part in town life. Because the master craftsman's shop was also his home, the modern distinction between home and workplace, between public and private spheres of activity, did not exist in urban society, any more than it did in aristocrats' castles or peasants' cottages. This blurring (from a modern standpoint) of domestic and business life worked to women's advantage: a master's wife and daughters could learn his skills just as his apprentices would, by observing and practicing in the household workshop. Indeed, master craftsmen and their wives normally shared authority over apprentices, not only because apprentices generally lived within the household (which was the wife's sphere of responsibility), but also because the wife would be well acquainted with her husband's craft. If a master craftsman died, his widow sometimes carried on the business. Even while married, women sometimes owned and operated their own businesses, distinct from those of their husbands. It was even more common for young, unmarried women in towns to support themselves by wage labor or domestic service while saving money for the future. Town records show women collecting taxes, exchanging and lending money, and engaging on their own in a wide variety of craft and merchant enterprises.

All this commercial activity required supplies of capital. As we have seen, Anglo-Saxon England was already a highly monetized and enormously wealthy country. Not surprisingly, it was also a land in which moneylending was already common. The moneylenders of late-Anglo-Saxon and Anglo-Norman England were often the same men (almost invariably English) who struck the king's money at his mints. Frequently, these men were merchants as well; and because no foreign coin was per-

---

[8]From the customs of Newcastle-upon-Tyne under Henry I, *English Historical Documents, Volume II*, ed. David C. Douglas and George W. Greenway, 2nd ed. (London, 1981), no. 298, pp. 1040–1041.

mitted to circulate in England, they were also moneychangers, acquiring directly the foreign coin and silver plate, which they then reminted into English pennies. After 1066, a small community of Jews from Rouen settled in London. By the 1130s, they too were engaged in a similar combination of moneylending, moneychanging, and merchandizing — although they lacked the advantage of also being minters of the king's coin.

The anarchical conditions of Stephen's reign undermined many of these traditional English moneylending/minting/merchandizing families. In 1158, King Henry II finished them off by ending their monopoly over the minting of coin. By this date, however, moneylending in England was already being conducted on a vastly larger scale than the old Anglo-Saxon merchant moneyers could have handled. Norman and Flemish moneylenders, most famously a Flemish wool merchant and lender named William Cade, made vast fortunes providing capital to the booming economy of mid-twelfth-century England. So too, increasingly, did the Jews of England, still a small community, but one that had now spread outward from London into about a dozen of the larger and more important cities in the kingdom. In the twelfth century, however, the bulk of the moneylending business lay in the hands of Christians, not Jews. When Henry II confiscated the English assets of William Cade's firm, following his death in 1164, it was the Christian merchant/moneylenders of London who benefited most from this unexpected elimination of the competition. But Jews also profited from Cade's removal, especially in the north, where they provided badly needed capital to the booming economies of Lincolnshire and Yorkshire. By the 1180s, Aaron of Lincoln, the greatest of these twelfth-century Jewish financiers, had become the wealthiest man in England after the king.

Twelfth-Century London

One can get an impression of the texture of medieval urban life by looking at London as it existed toward the close of the twelfth century. With a growing population of at least 35,000, London was by far the largest city of its time in the British Isles and one of the leading commercial centers of northwestern Europe. Many of England's bishops, abbots, and barons maintained townhouses there, and the king himself conducted much of his business at a palace, built by William Rufus and standing to this day, in London's western suburb of Westminster. Londoners were served by 139 churches, whose bells pealed over the city and its suburbs to mark the hours of the day.

London's narrow streets were lined with houses and shops, some built of stone in the new fashion, but most still built of wood. Fire was an ever-present danger. The streets were mostly unpaved and during the day were crowded with people, dogs, horses, and pigs. (The French monarchy was launching a major project just then to pave the streets of Paris where, half a century earlier, a crown prince had been killed when his horse

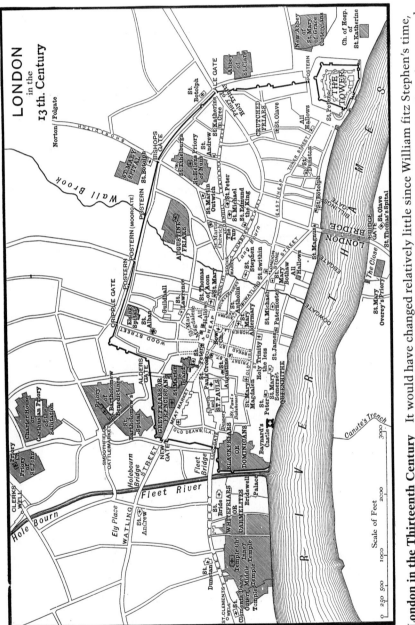

London in the Thirteenth Century   It would have changed relatively little since William fitz Stephen's time, except for the coming of the two great thirteenth-century religious orders, the Grey Friars, or Franciscans, and the Black Friars, or Dominicans. Westminster Abbey and Westminster Palace are just off the map to the left. (*Mansell/Time*)

tripped over a pig.) By today's standards, London was a small, filthy, evil-smelling firetrap. But by twelfth-century standards it was a thriving, progressive metropolis. The old wooden bridge across the Thames River was being replaced by a new London Bridge made entirely of stone. The city employed sanitation workers to clear the streets of garbage. There was a sewer system, consisting of open drains down the centers of streets. There was even a public lavatory — the first of a nationwide network of "public conveniences" that now grace England.

Twelfth-century Londoners were proud of their city. One of them, William fitz Stephen, writing around 1175, described it in these glowing words:

> Among the noble and celebrated cities of the world, London, the capital of the kingdom of the English, extends its glory farther than all others and sends its wealth and merchandise more widely into far distant lands. It lifts its head higher than all the rest. It is fortunate in the healthiness of its air,[9] in its observance of Christian practice, in the strength of its fortifications, in its natural situation, in the honor of its citizens, and in the modesty of its wives. It is cheerful in its sports and the fruitful mother of noble men. . . .[10]
>
> It has on the east the Palatine castle [the Tower of London], very great and strong. The tower and walls rise from very deep foundations and are fixed with a mortar tempered by the blood of animals. On the west there are two castles very strongly fortified, and from these there runs a high and massive wall with seven double gates and with towers along the north at regular intervals. London was once also walled and turreted on the south, but the mighty River Thames, so full of fish, has with the sea's ebb and flow washed against, loosened, and thrown down those walls in the course of time. Upstream to the west there is the royal palace [Westminster Palace] which is conspicuous above the river, a building incomparable in its ramparts and bulwarks. It is about two miles from the city and joined to it by a populous suburb. . . .
>
> Those engaged in business of various kinds, sellers of merchandise, hirers of labor, disperse every morning into their several localities according to their trade. Besides, there is in London on the river bank, among the wines for sale in ships and in the cellars of the vintners, a public cook shop. There daily you may find food according to the season, dishes of meat, roast, fried and boiled, large and small fish, coarser meats for the poor and more delicate for the rich, such as venison and big and small birds. . . .

These delicacies were enjoyed not only by Londoners but also by visitors from afar:

---

[9] In fact, London had a smog problem even in the twelfth century.

[10] Among the noble "men" born in twelfth-century London, William fitz Stephen proudly includes the empress Matilda.

> To this city from every nation under heaven merchants delight to bring their trade by sea. The Arabian sends gold; the Sabaean spice and incense. The Scythian brings arms, and from the rich, fat lands of Babylon comes oil of palms. The Nile sends precious stones; the men of Norway and Russia, furs and sables; nor is China absent with purple silk. The French come with their wines.

William fitz Stephen goes on to describe the entertainments and sports of the metropolis: religious plays showing the miracles of saints and martyrs; the festivities of the annual Carnival Day; cockfights; and ball playing in the fields outside the city, with teams representing various London schools and guilds competing with one another. "On feast days throughout the summer the young men indulge in the sports of archery, running, jumping, wrestling, slinging the stone, hurling the javelin beyond a mark, and fighting with sword and buckler." And in winter,

> swarms of youths rush out to play games on the ice. Some, gaining speed in their run, with feet set well apart, slide sideways over a vast expanse of ice. Others make seats out of a large lump of ice, and while one sits on it, others with linked hands run before it and drag him along behind them. So swift is their sliding motion that sometimes their feet slip, and they all fall on their faces. Others, more skilled at winter sports, put on their feet the shinbones of animals, binding them firmly around their ankles, and, holding poles shod with iron in their hands, which they strike from time to time against the ice, they are propelled as swiftly as a bird in flight.[11]

Not everyone found London so delightful. The twelfth-century chronicler Richard of Devizes put this satiric advice in the mouth of a Jewish merchant from France, giving advice to a boy about to visit England:

> If you come to London, pass through it quickly. . . . Whatever evil or malicious thing that can be found anywhere on earth you will find in that one city. Do not associate with the crowds of pimps; do not mingle with the throngs in eating houses; avoid dice and gambling, the theater and the tavern. You will meet with more braggarts there than in all France. The number of parasites is infinite. Actors, jesters, smooth-skinned lads, Moors, flatterers, pretty boys, effeminates, pederasts, singing and dancing girls, quacks, belly dancers, sorceresses, extortioners, night wanderers, magicians, mimes, beggars, buffooons: all this tribe fill all the houses. Therefore, if you do not want to dwell with evildoers, do not live in London.

The same merchant is equally gloomy about other English towns. At Bristol, "there is nobody who is not or has not been a soap maker" — a particularly noxious-smelling trade at a time when soap was made from animal fats and leached wood ashes. York "is full of Scotsmen, filthy and

---

[11]The description is translated in full in *English Historical Documents, Volume II*, no. 281, pp. 1024–1030.

treacherous creatures — scarcely human." Exeter "refreshes both men and beasts with the same fodder." Bath, lying amid "exceedingly heavy air and sulphurous fumes, is at the gates of hell. . . . Ely stinks perpetually from the surrounding fens."[12] Among all the cities of England, indeed, only Winchester was truly fit for human habitation, and Richard makes clear elsewhere in his account that he has no high opinion of the residents of Winchester either.

The Jews of Angevin England

Jews immigrated to England in the aftermath of the Norman Conquest. The first Jewish settlers came to London from Rouen, and although the Jews of England also had links with the Jews of the Rhineland, the London Jewish community remained essentially an offshoot of the Rouen community until the end of Henry I's reign. Connections between the Jews of England and Normandy would continue until the early thirteenth century, but from the 1140s on, the history of these two Jewish communities began to diverge. During Stephen's reign, Jews began to move from London into some of the other major cities of the kingdom, including Norwich, Lincoln, and Winchester. Because Jews were protected by the crown, their neighborhoods were usually located near the royal castle, where they could retreat for safety if danger threatened them. But although Jewish communities tended to cluster in particular neighborhoods, there were no Jewish ghettos in medieval England. Christians and Jews lived side by side in English towns, sharing the same streets and patronizing many of the same shops and marketplaces, despite the efforts of Christian authorities to segregate the two communities.

With commercial links to Normandy and the Rhineland disrupted by the anarchy, Jews found it increasingly difficult to compete as merchants with their Christian rivals. As a result, they gradually became more dependent upon small- and medium-scale moneylending than they had been prior to 1135, although they continued to perform a variety of craftwork also, including leatherworking, goldsmithing, and silversmithing. After 1154, the trend toward moneylending continued, and by the 1160s a few Jewish entrepreneurs were making substantial fortunes from moneylending. The most successful of these Jewish lenders, Aaron of Lincoln, was the wealthiest man in England when he died in 1186. Aaron's network of agents extended throughout England, but he made the bulk of his fortune by providing capital to the burgeoning economy of northern England, then undergoing an extraordinary expansion driven by population growth and the market for high-quality English wool.

For a fee, the royal government would help Jewish lenders like Aaron collect their debts, as it also aided Christian lenders. Occasionally,

---

[12]*The Chronicle of Richard of Devizes*, ed. John T. Appleby (London, 1963), pp. 65–66.

Henry II borrowed money from Jews, and he periodically imposed taxes upon Jewish communities. It was not until the 1180s, however, that the king acquired a direct stake in the prosperity of the English Jewish community. When Aaron of Lincoln died, Henry II confiscated his entire estate. Most of Aaron's wealth lay in collectible debts from moneylending; the king now began to collect these debts, the vast majority of which were owed by Christians. But the king's officials were much more exacting creditors than Jewish lenders could afford to be, and opposition (both to the crown and to Jewish moneylending) quickly mounted. By the early 1190s, Christian chroniclers in the north were speaking openly of the English Jews as "the king's usurers." In fact, Jewish lenders were no happier with the king's new policy of confiscating and collecting Jewish debts than were their Christian debtors, but predictably the animosity resulting from the king's energetic efforts to collect these debts focused most intensely upon the Jews. In 1189–1190, as King Richard prepared to lead a crusading army to the Holy Land, a series of murderous anti-Jewish riots erupted across England, fueled by a combination of crusading enthusiasm and economic resentment toward Jewish moneylending.

More than economic resentment lay behind the growing hostility of English Christians toward Jews, however. In Norwich during the 1140s, a Christian boy named William was found murdered in the woods outside the city. The boy's relatives alleged that he had been crucified by the Jews, for whom he sometimes worked, in a ritualized display of anti-Christian hatred. The story quickly spread, and although none of the officials of the town gave any credence to the allegations of ritual crucifixion (or indeed, to the claim that Jews had any responsibility at all for William's death), the boy was regarded nevertheless as a martyr to the Christian faith, and his body was entombed in a local monastic house. Miracles of healing now began to be reported around his tomb, bringing publicity, profit, and prestige to the monastic house and establishing the sanctity of St. William of Norwich. The success of this shrine soon brought imitators. By 1290, when the entire Jewish community of England was expelled from the realm, shrines to six more child victims of such alleged "ritual crucifixions" had been established in England. From England, the story also spread abroad, becoming a staple element in Christian anti-Semitism that has lasted until the present day.

The Landholding Aristocracy

The increasing sophistication and wealth of the English economy had a substantial impact on the life of the English aristocracy. Money and commerce made new luxuries available: pepper, ginger, and cinnamon for baronial kitchens; finer and more colorful clothing and jewelry; fur coats for cold winters; grandiose stone manor houses, and — inside them — carpets, wall hangings, and more elaborate furniture. The standards for an appropriately "noble" style of life rose rapidly from the mid-twelfth century on; the costs of these necessary amenities drove some nobles and aspiring nobles into ruinous debt. But neither ostentation nor debt was new in the twelfth and thirteenth centuries. Many aristocrats regarded overspending as a virtue, the mark of a generous spirit, a sentiment encouraged by the followers and supporters who were the principal beneficiaries of their extravagant generosity. Monks might disapprove (unless, of course, noble generosity took the form — as it often did — of extensive grants of land to monastic houses), but conspicuous consumption was an essential element in noble life that no amount of monastic censure could eliminate. The late-eleventh-century magnate, Hugh earl of Chester, may have been more flamboyant than most, but his enthusiasms and his expenditures were typical of his class:

> He was a great lover of the world and its pomp, which he regarded as the greatest blessing of the human lot. He was always in the vanguard in battle, lavish to the point of prodigality, a lover of games and luxuries, entertainers, horses, dogs, and similar vanities. He was always surrounded by a huge following, noisy with swarms of boys, both low-born and high-born. Many honorable men, clerics and knights, were also in his entourage, and he cheerfully shared his wealth and labors with them. . . . He kept no check on what he gave or received. His hunting was a daily devastation of his lands, for he thought more highly of hawkers and hunters than of peasants or monks. A slave to gluttony, he staggered under a mountain of fat, scarcely able to move. He was given over to carnal lusts and sired a multitude of bastards by his concubines.[13]

Knights were affected even more dramatically by the escalating costs of aristocratic luxury than were the great lords like Earl Hugh. As the costs of a knightly lifestyle increased during the twelfth and thirteenth centuries, the numbers of knights declined. Around the year 1100, there were probably about 5,000 knights in England. By the end of the twelfth century, their numbers had been reduced to between 2,000 and 3,000. By 1300, there were only about 1,100 men in England who had formally accepted the distinction of knighthood, which was now seen by many prosperous men as a burden rather than an honor — an obligation to be avoided rather than a privilege to be pursued. Economic changes worked particularly against lesser knights. Inflation was rapid in the years between 1180 and 1220, and again in the years around 1300. Lords who controlled large numbers of dependent peasants could benefit from inflation by holding wages steady and marketing directly the produce of their estates. By contrast, lesser knights, who controlled fewer peasants or whose revenues came primarily from fixed rents and fees, were hit hard by these inflationary conditions. Many such men dropped out of the

---

[13]*The Ecclesiastical History of Orderic Vitalis*, ed. and trans. Marjorie Chibnall, vol. II (Oxford, 1969), pp. 262–263; vol. III (Oxford, 1972), pp. 216–217. Orderic does not explain how the enormously obese Hugh could nonetheless have been in the vanguard of every battle.

knightly ranks altogether as labor costs rose, their revenues stagnated, and the costs of knighthood continued to increase.

The rising costs of knightly equipment also played a role in reducing the number of knights. The high-medieval aristocracy was above all a military class, trained from early youth in the practice of fighting on horseback. Until the last half of the twelfth century, however, the equipment necessary to outfit a knight was relatively modest: an iron helmet, a long shirt of chain mail, a sword, a shield, a lance, and a horse were generally sufficient to qualify a man for knightly combat. From the mid-twelfth century on, however, the standards of knightly training and the costs of knightly equipment escalated dramatically. Horses and armor became vastly more expensive, even before the late-thirteenth-century advent of plate armor sent costs soaring yet again. Fewer and fewer men could manage these increasing costs; and as the numbers of knights diminished, the social prestige of knighthood rose. Although knighthood never became an inheritable legal status in England, from the thirteenth century on knights in England were clearly members of an aristocratic social class. No longer were they merely what they had been in the early twelfth century: members of a military order comprised of all those who fought on horseback in accordance with the laws of war, whose ranks might extend from the prosperous peasantry all the way up to the greatest men of the kingdom.

Wars between nobles could ravage the land, destroying farms and churches, as England learned to its sorrow during Stephen's reign. The destructiveness of medieval warfare could be enormous. In Flanders, for example, it has been calculated that a single afternoon's raid on a single village destroyed the equivalent of 40,000 hours of peasant labor.[14] This destructiveness was increased by the fact that most medieval military commanders tried to avoid pitched battles when they could, preferring instead to plunder the countryside when on attack or to wait for an attacking army to sicken and go home when on defense. As a result, medieval warfare posed less danger to well-armored knights than one might suppose. According to a contemporary report of the one major battle between Henry I and King Louis VI of France:

> I have been told that in the battle between the two kings, in which about nine hundred knights were engaged, only three were killed. All the knights were clad in mail and spared each other on both sides because of their fear of God and their fellowship in arms. They were more concerned to capture fugitives than to kill them.[15]

---

[14]James Campbell, "Was It Infancy in England? Some Questions of Comparison," in *England and Its Neighbours, 1066–1485: Essays in Honour of Pierre Chaplais*, ed. Michael Jones and Malcolm Vale (London, 1989), pp. 1–17, at pp. 1–2.

[15]*Orderic Vitalis*, vol. VI (Oxford, 1978), pp. 240–241.

In peacetime, tournaments took the place of battles. Sometimes, it was difficult to distinguish between the two. Tournaments in the twelfth century typically involved day-long mock battles among groups of one hundred knights or more, in the course of which a participant might be killed, maimed, or taken for ransom. Thirteenth-century tournaments were somewhat better regulated, but continued to be extremely dangerous to participants and destructive to the unfortunate peasants whose crops were trampled by the tournament competitors and their horses. Recognizing the dangers tournaments might pose to public order, English kings prior to King Richard the Lion-Hearted generally prohibited tournaments on English soil. The Church too legislated against tournaments, but to little avail. The aristocracy relished these melees as opportunities to train for war or to collect ransoms — or simply for the sheer joy of fighting, which was, after all, the raison d'être for its existence as a privileged class.

For recreation, aristocrats continued throughout the Middle Ages to enjoy hawking and hunting in their private forests. Besides the sheer fun of it, hunting rid the forests of dangerous beasts — wolves and wild boars — and provided tasty venison for the baronial table. Lords and ladies alike engaged in falconry, a sport that consisted of releasing a trained falcon to soar upward, kill a wild bird in flight, and return it to earth uneaten. Hunting and falconry were both refined into complex arts during the Middle Ages. But hunting in particular never lost its military aspect. As Machiavelli remarked in his famous handbook, *The Prince*:

> [A prince] must never let his mind be turned from the study of warfare and in times of peace he must concern himself with it more than in those of war. . . . [H]e should be fond of hunting and thereby accustom his body to hardships, learning, at the same time, the nature of topography, how mountains slope, how they are cut by valleys, how the plains lie, and the nature of rivers and swamps. And he should give great care to these matters, for such knowledge has two uses: first, he learns to know his own country and can the better understand its defenses; second, through the knowledge and experience of his own country, he can more easily understand other regions when the necessity arises. . . . A prince who does not have this skill lacks the first essential of a good leader. For it is in this way that you learn how to come upon the enemy, secure camping sites, lead armies, prepare battles, and plan sieges to your advantage.[16]

Aristocratic residences also became more refined and luxurious as the Middle Ages progressed. Most baronial castles of the eleventh and early twelfth centuries were nothing more than square towers, often of wood, rising two or three stories up from the ground (see illustration, p. 176). They were usually set atop hills or artificial mounds and surrounded by barracks, storehouses, stables, workshops, kitchen

---

[16]Niccolò Machiavelli, *The Prince*, ed. and trans. Thomas G. Bergin (Arlington Heights, Ill., 1947), Ch. 20, p. 42.

gardens, manure heaps, and perhaps a chapel — all enclosed, along with assorted livestock, within a stockade. The tower, or "keep," was apt to be stuffy, gloomy, and badly heated. Since it was built for defense, not for comfort, its windows were narrow slits for outgoing arrows, and its few rooms accommodated not only the lord and lady and their family but also servants, retainers, and guests. In that world of enforced togetherness, only the wealthier aristocratic couples could enjoy the luxury of a private bedchamber. And no one of any importance went anywhere alone.

By the late thirteenth century, however, rich aristocrats were living in much more commodious dwellings — castles or manor houses built of stone and mortar. Privacy remained rare, for great lords now shared their dwellings with retinues that were much larger than before. But by 1300 the swashbuckling life of the eleventh-century nobility had developed into a new, courtly lifestyle of good manners, troubadour songs, and gentlemanly and ladylike behavior. Handbooks of etiquette became popular in the thirteenth century and remained so long thereafter. They encouraged aristocratic refinement with advice such as this:

> Wash your hands in the morning and, if there is time, your face; use your napkin or handkerchief [not your hands], eat with three fingers only, and don't gorge; don't pick your teeth with your knife or wipe them on the tablecloth; don't butter your bread with your finger; don't spit on the table, or over it.[17]

As the old military elite learned good manners and courtly ways, it was evolving into a "high society," increasingly conscious of itself as a separate class, more exclusive and more rigidly defined than in its earlier, less stylish days.

Women

Women were subordinated to men in virtually all premodern civilizations. Western Christendom was no exception. With respect to property and power, the nuns of the High Middle Ages controlled fewer resources and exercised less political influence than had the aristocratic nuns of the early Middle Ages. The double monasteries of earlier Anglo-Saxon times, ruled over by such royal women as St. Hild of Whitby and St. Etheldreda of Ely, had disappeared long before the Norman Conquest. High-medieval monks tended to regard religious women as threats to male purity and as instruments of diabolical temptation. The canons of a thirteenth-century priory, for example, agreed to avoid all women "as we would avoid poisonous beasts." Nor were religious women accorded any greater respect outside the monastic walls. Women had never been permitted to be priests, but as priesthood became more central to religious life during the High Middle Ages, the exclusion of women from the

---

[17]From Charles Homer Haskins, *Studies in Medieval Culture* (Oxford, 1929), p. 80.

priesthood rankled more deeply than it had in the early Middle Ages, when a wider variety of routes to holiness had been acknowledged. Occasionally, extraordinary women like Christina of Markyate or Hildegard of Bingen might become widely admired for the depth of their holiness and the sanctity of their lives, but for ordinary women the high-medieval Church offered few institutional outlets for the expression of their growing piety. In England, moreover, institutional opportunities for pious women were even more restricted than they were on the Continent. In Cologne and the Low Countries, the thirteenth century saw the emergence of large numbers of residential houses known as *beguinages*, in which lay women who wished to lead lives of extraordinary piety could live and support themselves while engaging in prayer and charitable works. English monks such as the chronicler Matthew Paris had heard of the continental Beguines and admired them from afar. But in England, the Beguine movement never really found a foothold.

Much of the religious culture of the High Middle Ages was flatly misogynistic. But high-medieval Christianity also developed a concept of idealized womanhood through its emphasis on Mary, the virgin mother of Jesus. The cult of Mary was especially strong in late-Anglo-Saxon England, and it re-emerged after the Norman Conquest as a characteristically English form of devotion, a vital religious link between Anglo-Saxon and Norman England.[18] (The renowned Norman abbey of Bec, which produced the first two post-Conquest archbishops of Canterbury — Lanfranc and Anselm — was also dedicated to the Virgin Mary.) As the symbol of maternal compassion, Mary became the subject of countless miracle stories in England and throughout Christendom. Sinners who trembled at the prospect of God's judgment turned their prayers to Mary, confident that she could persuade Christ to forgive them.

The high-medieval troubadour songs and the rise of stylized courtesy in aristocratic households gave rise to another kind of idealization. As romanticized "ladies fair," women were placed on pedestals from which they are only now managing to descend. This idealization of women was itself dehumanizing, for high atop their pedestals women remained objects still. But at least pedestals tended to elevate women from their former lowly status as threats to male purity, or objects of casual knightly seduction and violent rape, or victims of boorish, wife-beating husbands. The courtly lady remained an object, but a more revered and idealized object than she had been before.

Such at least was the position of women in the courtly songs and romances. But social and literary conventions seldom correspond with real life. Medieval lords and ladies did not ordinarily behave like characters from courtly fiction. Wife-beating was common at all social levels of

---

[18]On the Englishness of this cult in the early twelfth century, see R. W. Southern, "The English Origins of the 'Miracles of the Virgin,'" *Medieval and Renaissance Studies* 4 (1958): 176–216

Christian society. Medieval Jews, who prohibited wife-beating by religious law, regarded it as a practice distinctive to their Christian neighbors. Aristocratic women tended to marry relatively young (usually in their teens) and could be immobilized for long periods by the bearing of numerous children, necessary for the preservation of family lines in an era of high childhood mortality rates. Fertility rates among urban and peasant women were probably lower, due to extended periods of nursing (lactation reduces fertility; upper-class women utilized wet nurses, whereas other women nursed their own children), poor nutrition, and rudimentary contraception. Non-aristocratic women's fertility rates were further reduced by their relatively later age at first marriage. Although statistics are better for the fifteenth century than for the thirteenth, it appears that in both centuries most non-aristocratic women married in their mid-twenties to husbands of approximately the same age as themselves. Childbirth, however, was a dangerous experience for women of every age and class. Women who survived their child-bearing years sometimes lived to a ripe old age. Eleanor of Aquitaine was over eighty when she died in 1204. But a combination of high infant mortality rates and deaths in childbirth meant that on average, English women were not likely to live beyond their forties.

The medieval English aristocracy was a warrior class, and women sometimes played prominent roles as military leaders. But first and foremost, the aristocracy was a class of hereditary landholders, and women played a crucial role in the inheritance of land. In the absence of sons, a daughter might become a wealthy, coveted heiress. Even if she had brothers, a well-born daughter might bring a large estate to her husband as a dowry and retain some control over it even as a wife. Women, whether married or single, could sometimes hold and grant fiefs. They could own goods, make contracts and wills, and, under certain conditions, engage in litigation. A widow received by custom a third of her husband's lands (their eldest son received the rest), and since aristocratic wives were often much younger than their husbands, landholding aristocratic widows were common.

A strong king might compel a wealthy maiden or widow to marry some royal favorite. Indeed, the granting of an heiress in marriage to a loyal courtier was an important element in the royal patronage system of medieval England, as well as a source of revenue to the crown. In the financial accounts of Henry I, for example, one encounters items such as these: "Robert De Venuiz renders account to the king for sixteen shillings eightpence for the daughter of Herbert the Chamberlain with her dowry"; and "The sheriff of Hampshire renders account to the king for a thousand silver marks for the office, lands, and daughter of the late Robert Mauduit."[19] One great English heiress, the thrice-widowed Lucy,

---

[19]*The Pipe Roll of 31 Henry I, Michaelmas, 1130,* ed. Joseph Hunter (London, 1833; reprinted 1929), p. 37; translation by C. Warren Hollister.

countess of Chester, was charged a handsome sum simply for the privilege of not having to marry again for five years.

Many a family fortune was built on the strategic marriages of heirs and heiresses. In a landed society such as medieval England's, marriages were crucial to a family's continuing prosperity, and marriages for love alone were luxuries that few families could willingly afford. It has been said that medieval warfare was a game but medieval marriage was a deadly serious business. Sons as well as daughters had their marriages arranged by their parents; frequently, it was the mother who did the arranging. Although medieval canon law demanded that both partners consent to the marriage, in the vast majority of marriages both bride and bridegroom would have been instructed from early childhood to view marriage in the context of family economic and social advancement. This is not to say that women did not have preferences and opinions, but only rarely did their preferences determine their fate. As usual, we know most about aristocratic women. Shortly after the Norman Conquest, William I ordered a young heiress to marry one of his favored barons, who happened to be an elderly hunchback. She refused, and the Conqueror was furious, but the problem was resolved and the desired family alliance achieved when she agreed to marry the hunchback's son. "Love matches" were probably more common among the landless peasantry and urban wage-earners than they were at the upper reaches of aristocratic or urban society. But even peasant families had to calculate carefully the impact of any marriage upon its precious landed resources.

Marriages based on family strategies sometimes did develop into loving relationships. As current divorce statistics suggest, youthful infatuation may not be significantly superior to family arrangement as the basis for a successful lifetime union. But arranged marriages among the upper classes, often pairing teen-age girls with much older men, probably did encourage the emphasis on extramarital romances in courtly literature — and sometimes in the real world as well. We have already encountered the numerous illegitimate children of Earl Hugh and King Henry I. Eleanor of Aquitaine, during her stormy first marriage with King Louis VII of France, was suspected of an extramarital affair with her uncle, and her second husband, King Henry II, was a flagrant and serial adulterer. The Church condemned adultery as a mortal sin for men no less than for women, but aristocratic society tended to look tolerantly on the escapades of well-born husbands. Their wives, however, were judged by a double standard that demanded wifely fidelity to ensure the legitimacy of family lines. Earl Hugh could sire bastards across the Cheshire countryside and beyond, but he expected his wife's children to be his own.

Despite their dowry rights, wives were very much under their husbands' control according to both law and custom. But in real life, a wife might exercise a great deal of power. In the castle and manor house, as in the urban shop-dwelling or the peasant cottage, home and workplace were one. The wife usually governed the castle and barony when her husband was absent — as husbands often were, on wars or crusades. If enemies attacked the castle while the lord was away, his wife frequently commanded its defense. When the earl of Northumberland rebelled against King William Rufus in 1095, he charged his young wife (who bore the highly unoriginal Norman name, Matilda) with defending his chief castle while he scouted the countryside. Matilda defended it courageously against the full force of Rufus's army, surrendering only when Rufus captured her husband, brought him before the castle wall, and threatened to gouge out his eyes.

Even when her husband was at home, a wife might enjoy considerable authority. In medieval marriages, as in modern ones, husband and wife might relate in a wide variety of ways. Some husbands were cruel and domineering. Others were obliging, absent-minded, or senile, in which case — despite social and legal conventions — the wife would rule the household, workshop, or barony. One such person was the Anglo-Norman countess, Avicia of Evreux:

> The count of Evreux's intellect was by nature rather dim as well as being blunted by age. And putting perhaps undue trust in his wife's ability, he left the government of his county entirely in her hands. The countess was distinguished for her wit and beauty. She was the tallest woman in all Evreux and of very high birth. . . . Disregarding the counsels of her husband's barons, she chose instead to follow her own opinion and ambition. Often inspiring bold measures in political affairs, she readily engaged in rash enterprises.[20]

The Anglo-Norman monk who wrote these words, Orderic Vitalis, clearly disapproved of Avicia, not least because he supported the regime of Henry I and resented her policy of rebelling against that king. But Orderic's account discloses an aspect of aristocratic womanhood absent from the arid records of legal custom and the romances of the troubadours, and that must have been at least as common in the unrecorded marriages of the more ordinary residents of medieval England.

Medieval Children

Until recently, scholars of the expanding history of childhood viewed the Middle Ages as pitch dark. Medieval people, they argued, had no conception of childhood as a distinct phase of human life but regarded children simply as unformed "little adults." Childhood thus had to be "invented" at some point in modern history (it was never clear exactly when).

This is nonsense. Even in the early Middle Ages, Gregory of Tours had written of a plague that took a particularly heavy toll on young children. "And so we lost our little ones, who were so dear to us and sweet, whom we had cherished in our bosoms and dandled in our arms, whom we had fed and nourished with such loving care. As I write I wipe away my tears."

---

[20]*Orderic Vitalis*, vol. VI, p. 148.

Young People in School
Mid-fourteenth century.
*(North Wind Picture
Archives)*

With the advent of the High Middle Ages, parents cherished their children even more. The revolutionary high-medieval changes in commerce and social organization required increasing numbers of well-trained specialists in a wide variety of vocations — trading, manufacturing, estate management, ecclesiastical and secular governance — and, hence, much greater emphasis than before on the training and rearing of children. Schools now sprang up on all sides; to the old monastic schools were now added an abundance of urban schools and village schools. It has been estimated that about half the boys and girls of early-fourteenth-century Florence were receiving at least a grammar school education. Other medieval cities probably did not do so well (we lack the figures), and widespread illiteracy continued in the countryside until fairly recent times. But there can be no question that high-medieval society invested heavily in the education of its children.

Aristocratic and urban children, particularly boys, were usually sent away from home at an early age for training in another noble household or urban business. Girls from non-aristocratic families also often left home, either to work as servants in other people's households, or to join the ranks of wage laborers in the towns. We should not conclude from these social and economic patterns, however, that medieval parents were not devoted to their children. Despite (or perhaps because of?) the high rates of infant mortality, parents could love their children dearly and care for them tenderly. Voices began to be raised against the age-old custom of child-beating: the thirteenth-century writer Vincent of Beauvais cautioned that "children's minds break down under excessive severity of correction: they despair, they worry, and finally they hate. And this is most injurious, for where everything is feared, nothing is attempted."

Beginning in the twelfth century, books on the rearing and training of children began to proliferate. One of the most popular of them, by the late-thirteenth-century Spanish writer Raymond Lull, included sections on breast-feeding, weaning, early education, and the care and nourishment of children. "Every person," Lull observed, "must hold his child dear."

Even the traditional Christian doctrine that baptism was necessary to salvation was modified in the twelfth century with respect to unbaptized babies. Previously, they had been condemned to hell; now they were assigned to "limbo," where they could exist for eternity in innocent happiness even though denied the direct apprehension of God. There also emerged in medieval piety a special devotion to the child Jesus, whose beauty and innocence was reflected, to a lesser degree, in all children. "O sweet and sacred childhood," wrote a Cistercian monk, "which brought back humanity's true innocence."

Actual child-rearing practices varied widely from family to family and class to class, and as in most ages they usually fell short of the social ideal. Warnings against child-beating showed not only that it was sometimes frowned upon but also that it continued. And infanticide, although severely condemned by the Church, was never entirely eliminated. Nevertheless, whether we judge from the proliferation of schools, the popularity of books on child-rearing, or the sympathetic literary portrayals of childhood, the people of the High Middle Ages placed a large emotional and material investment in their children. They were by no means blind to the existence of childhood; instead, they idealized it.

The Agrarian Economy of High-Medieval England and the Emergence of Common-Law Villeinage

The growing population of twelfth- and thirteenth-century Europe strained the productive capacity of European agriculture to its limits. To meet the increasing demand for food, new lands were cleared and brought under cultivation, pastures were turned into farmland, and existing farmland was cultivated more intensively than ever before. In the early Middle Ages, it had been common to allow as much as half the arable farmland to lie fallow each year. This fallow period helped to control diseases that might otherwise take root in the soil; and if animals were pastured on the fallow land, their droppings would help to replenish the soil's fertility before another growing season began. In the High Middle Ages, however, many farmers shifted to a three-field crop rotation system, in which only a third of the land was left fallow in any given year. To maintain the fertility of the soil under this more intensive scheme of cultivation, farmers began to grow more leguminous crops, including peas, beans, and vetch (a fodder crop similar to clover). Not only did these new crops provide improved nutrition for both humans and animals, they also (and perhaps even more importantly) helped to restore to the soil the nitrogen that grain crops drained from it. Healthier plow animals, together with iron plowshares, made it possible to plow fields more effectively and more often, controlling weeds and increasing the aeration of the soil, and so improving crop yields. Iron hoes improved the efficiency of hand weeding. Soil additives, including limestone, peat, and manure, also had a positive effect on the ratios of seed harvested to seed sown. Improvements in milling (such as the windmill illustrated on p. 215) and in transportation and marketing also contributed to the increasing efficiency of European, and particularly English, agriculture.

Through these and other improvements, high-medieval Europe man-aged to produce enough food to feed its population during most years. The improvements were not enough, however, to prevent a gradual rise in the prices of agricultural products. One might think that rising prices for agricultural products would have benefited all farmers producing for the market, but in practice the largest landholders seem to have profited most from the new conditions. Great lords were the ones who had the largest surpluses to market — most of the grain produced by peasants was consumed directly by the peasant proprietors or else sold to pay the rent on their landholdings. And great lords (including, of course, monasteries) were also the ones who had the greatest access to unpaid peasant labor. All these new agricultural techniques were extremely labor intensive. Great lords who could command the labor of unpaid (or minimally paid) serfs were therefore better placed than peasants or smaller-scale lords to benefit from the new agricultural technologies.

Only in England, however, did great landholders react to the new eco-nomic circumstances by shifting their estates over to large-scale agricul-tural production for the market. On the Continent, most lords continued to rent out the great bulk of their landholdings to their peasants, drawing off the profits that would otherwise have gone to the peasantry through increased rents and judicial fines. In England, landlords in the late twelfth and early thirteenth centuries began canceling many of the leases by which they had previously granted out land to their peasants in return for fixed rents. Now they began to cultivate these demesne lands directly, paying the costs of cultivation and marketing the resulting crops. To provide labor for their newly recalled demesne lands, lords also began to reimpose labor services on their peasants. This new emphasis on enforcing labor services coincided with the creation of a new class of "villeins" — serfs whose unfreedom was established not merely by cus-tom, but by the categories and criteria of the emerging common law. The resulting system of agriculture, in which great landlords directly culti-vated large tracts of their own land, using a combination of hired and en-forced peasant labor, would last in England until the fourteenth century, when it was finally undermined by the changing economic conditions brought on by the Black Death.

This system of "high farming," as it is sometimes called, was unique to the grain-growing regions of high-medieval England. It was a product both of the high degree of commercialization that twelfth-century Eng-land had already achieved and of the precocious development of the Eng-lish legal system, with its early emphasis upon the protection of free per-sons' property rights.[21] Slavery had disappeared from England in the generation or so following the Norman Conquest. But in the generation around 1200, the English common law succeeded in creating a new class

---

[21]Robert C. Stacey, *Politics, Policy and Finance under Henry III, 1216–1245* (Oxford, 1987), pp. 66–73.

of individuals, villeins, whose unfreedom was more extensive and pro-found than was that of their Anglo-Saxon predecessors or the vast major-ity of peasants elsewhere in Europe. Although they could still bring crim-inal charges if they were assaulted, villeins were explicitly denied the protection of the common law courts for their property rights. Indeed, their inability to sue in the king's courts to protect their property was the most certain proof of their unfreedom. All their property was considered to belong to their lord. Although a lord's right to demand labor services from them or to increase their rents might be limited by the customs of his own manorial court, villeins had no legal protections against a lord who chose to ignore the customs of the manor by imposing additional burdens upon his villeins.[22]

At the same time, however, the creation of common-law villeinage also threw into sharper relief the full extent of the legal freedom enjoyed by all those peasants who were not villeins. Free and unfree peasants con-tinued to live side by side in most English villages. The two groups were often indistinguishable economically and socially, although marriage with a villein would usually reduce a free peasant to villein status. In con-trast to the Continent, however, where peasants tended to be of a single, semi-servile status (freer than English villeins, less free than English free peasants), the English peasantry after c. 1220 was divided into two quite distinct legal categories. Villeins had no legal rights vis-à-vis their lords, although the law tended to regard them as free vis-à-vis all other persons. Free peasants, however, could sue anyone, including their lords, if they believed their property rights had been infringed. Lords who attempted to enforce additional labor services on free peasants, or who tried to raise their rents beyond their customary levels, often found themselves in the king's courts, forced by a royal writ of "customs and services" to answer a group of peasant plaintiffs who had refused to pay the new impositions. In this respect, the property rights of free peasants were not fundamentally different from those of the nobility — an astonishing situation, quite un-paralleled in the legal systems of other European countries.

Why English law should have evolved in this way is not altogether easy to explain. To some extent, these developments are probably acci-dental. When Henry II designed the writ of Novel Disseisin, he restricted its application to "free tenements." His intention, clearly enough, was to make sure that serfs could not bring such cases against their lords. But the popularity of the writ (which could not have been predicted in 1166 when it was designed) soon made it necessary to develop a legally consis-tent definition of a free tenement and a free person. In developing such a definition, however, the king's judges quickly realized that they could not simply exclude all peasants from utilizing the writ. In the first place,

---

[22]Paul R. Hyams, *Kings, Lords, and Peasants: The Common Law of Villeinage in the Twelfth and Thirteenth Centuries* (Oxford, 1980).

there were simply too many free peasants, some of them quite prosperous and important individuals, who played critical roles in the local courts, took oaths of loyalty directly to the crown, and performed military service at the king's summons. To declare such people to be villeins, and so to exclude them from bringing cases in the king's courts, would have been a social revolution on a scale impossible for Henry's judges to contemplate. Second, the judges probably also realized that some of the prosperous peasants of late-twelfth-century England were the descendants of men who, a generation or two before, might even have been knights — and that some of their relatives were probably still knights. In the Middle Ages, unfreedom tended to be contagious: if one of your relatives was declared unfree, the rest of your family might find itself declared unfree also. That relatives of knightly families should be declared unfree was a risk neither the king nor his justices wanted to run. They may or may not have cared about the free peasantry as a class, but they certainly cared about the knights. And the fact was that in Angevin England, no clear dividing line could be drawn between the bottom ranks of the knighthood and the upper ranks of the peasantry. The line, therefore, was drawn much lower down the social scale, resulting in an extraordinary degree of legal protection for the free peasants of medieval England.

Peasant Life in an English Village

Peasant life in the High Middle Ages was tied to the cycle of the seasons and vulnerable to the whims of nature — drought, flooding, epidemics among humans and animals, crop diseases, the summer's heat, and the winter's chill. Today, most inhabitants of the industrialized world are relatively insulated from nature by a screen of modern technological wonders: central heating, air conditioning, a secure food supply, plumbing, modern medicine, and much more. We enjoy the protection of police and fire departments; we defy distance and terrain with our freeways and jets; and we can cure bacterial infections with prescription drugs. All these we take for granted, but they are all products of the very recent past — even penicillin, the first broadly effective antibiotic, did not become widely available to the civilian population until after the Second World War. None of these wonders were dreamt of in the Middle Ages.

A typical peasant's house consisted of a thatched roof resting on a timber framework, with the spaces between the framing filled with webbed branches covered with mud and straw. The houses of wealthier peasants might have two or more rooms, furnished with benches, a table, and perhaps a chest. Some prosperous peasants built stone houses, and archaeological research has shown, from the wear revealed on the cobblestone or flagstone floors of peasant cottages, that the floors were brushed spotlessly clean. But poorer peasants continued to dwell in one-room, half-timbered cottages virtually bare of furniture.

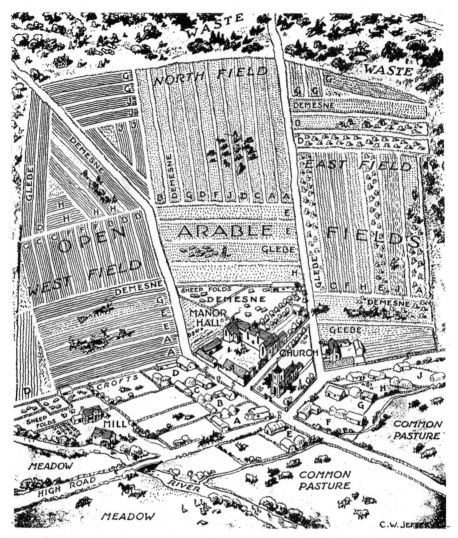

A Modern Reconstruction of a Medieval English Manor   It would be safest to regard this not as a "typical" manor but as a "possible" manor. The *glebe* is the property set aside for the manorial priest, and the capital letters indicate particular fields allotted to families occupying particular cottages. The crofts are small enclosed fields adjoining cottages and used for pasture and small-scale tillage. *(The Granger Collection)*

Fleas, mice, and rats were facts of life in such a world. The smells of sweat and manure were always present, and therefore largely unnoticed. Flies buzzed everywhere. A single cottage might shelter not only a large family but its domestic livestock as well: chickens, dogs, geese, occasionally even cattle. Windows, if any, were small and few, and had no glass. Only wooden shutters kept out the winter cold. Arthritis and rheumatism were common, along with countless other diseases for which there

Spinning and Heating a Fire with a Billows   Early fourteenth century. *(North Wind Picture Archives)*

were no known cures. A simple fire served for cooking and heating, but in the absence of chimneys, smoke filled the room before escaping through holes or cracks in the ceiling. Candles were luxury items, and peasants had to make do with smoky, evil-smelling torches made of rushes soaked in fat. There was always the danger that a stray spark might set the thatched roof afire.

The daily routine of a peasant family began with a pre-dawn breakfast, perhaps of coarse black bread and diluted ale, after which the husband, wife, and post-toddling offspring worked from daybreak to nightfall. Peasants' work involved a close partnership between husband, wife, and children. The father and his sons did most of the heavy plowing. The wife and daughters took primary responsibility for the "inside" work — not only doing domestic chores such as cooking and cleaning, but also manufacturing the family's food and clothing: making cheese and butter, spinning yarn, and sometimes weaving cloth (although weaving was often a male's job). Women milked the cows, fed the livestock, tended the vegetable garden outside the cottage, and joined the men in haymaking, thatching, sheep shearing, sowing and reaping grain, weeding, and sometimes even plowing. In winter, when the fields were frozen, the whole family might stay indoors making and repairing tools. The evening meal might consist of a pot of vegetable broth, more coarse black bread, more ale, and possibly an egg (far smaller than the eggs American shoppers can buy today). Then it was early to bed, to rest for the toils of the next day.

Even this somber picture is a bit idealized. Often one or more members of the peasant family would be immobilized by illness or tormented by injuries, aches, and pains. Wives endured one pregnancy after another in order to ensure the continuation of the family line; childbirth was a mortal danger to mother and baby alike, and infant mortality was very high. We have no accurate figures for child mortality in England, but across medieval and early-modern Europe, it seems likely that two-thirds of all children died before the age of ten, and over one-third died during their first year of life.

In a typical English village, the most substantial buildings were the residence of the lord or his bailiff and the parish church. The lord's residence, the headquarters of the manor, was usually surrounded by a

Manuscript Illumination Showing a Well-Dressed Peasant Woman Milking
(Bodleian Library, Oxford, MS. Bodley 764, f.41v)

walled enclosure that also contained a bakehouse and kitchen, barns, and other structures. The kitchen was normally (but not always) located in a building separate from the main house so that if a fire should start it would not threaten the lord's residence. To the manor house the peasants brought portions of their crops, which they owed as customary dues. There, too, they brought their disputes to be settled at the manorial court. To the parish church, peasants also owed customary dues, usually amounting to a tenth of their produce, known as a "tithe."

The parish church often stood in the center of the village. Its priest was seldom well educated, although he was expected to be literate and to understand enough Latin to recite the prayers and sacraments correctly. He played a central role in the villagers' lives, baptizing infants, presiding at marriages and burials, and celebrating the Mass. Priests were not generally expected to be able to preach sermons; for these, parishioners would usually have to wait for a visit from an itinerant preacher. But by the end of the thirteenth century, most villagers would probably have learned enough about their faith to be able to recite the Lord's Prayer, the "Hail Mary," and a simple statement of theological belief. They would understand the rhythms of the church's liturgical year and might well have participated in a pilgrimage to some local saint's shrine. All would have been baptized, and many would have been confirmed by their bishop at some point in their lives. Church leaders sometimes bemoaned the fact that religious standards were not higher, but at the parish level, the high-medieval English Church can be counted a success.

The church usually doubled as a village meeting hall. And despite canonical prohibitions, the villagers might also use the building on festival days for dancing, drinking, and revelry. The feast days of the Christian calendar — Christmas, Easter, and many lesser holy days (holidays) — provided joyous relief from an otherwise grinding routine. In some parts of England, villages celebrated the feast of Candlemas (February 2) with a candlelight procession followed by a pancake dinner. On the eve of May Day, the young men of some villages would cut branches in the forest and lay them at the doors of houses inhabited by young unmarried women. St. John's Day (midsummer, June 24) brought bonfires and dancing. Throughout the year, villagers found time for the informal sports of wrestling, archery, cockfights, drinking contests, and a rough, early form of soccer. But for most of their days, they labored to raise the food on which their families and social superiors depended for survival.

In examining the lives of the townspeople, aristocrats, and peasant villagers of high-medieval England, we have tried to show not only what their lives were like but also how their lives were changing. Across the generations between 1066 and about 1300, change was most evident among townspeople and aristocrats. The former were participants in a commercial and urban revolution of decisive significance to Western civilization, whereas aristocrats experienced a drastic transformation in taste and style as they moved from grim square towers into elaborate, well-furnished dwellings echoing with the songs of troubadours. Changes in the material lives of peasant villages were less visible to the naked eye but were perhaps no less important. Peasants too were being drawn increasingly into the web of an expanding money economy that provided markets and profits for the surplus production of peasant households. By 1300, most peasant families in England were no longer engaged in "subsistence" farming. Marketing and wage labor were essential elements in the economics of peasant life. At the same time, however, the creation of a legal class of unfree villeins drove a wedge down the middle of English peasant society that would last, in some form, until the end of the Middle Ages.

High-Medieval Christianity

Throughout the Middle Ages, England remained a closely integrated part of a western European religious world united by its allegiance to Catholic Christianity. But the nature of that western religious world changed profoundly during the twelfth and thirteenth centuries. Intellectuals like St. Anselm of Canterbury, Peter Abelard, and St. Bernard of Clairvaux began to reorient western Christian understandings of sin away from a vision of sin as an objective breach of God's honor for which compensation (in the form of penance) had to be paid, toward a view of sin as a psychological reality, the effect of which was to open up a breach between the sinner and God that could be healed through contrition, confession, absolution, and penance. This new, more introspective style of piety, which stressed the love of a suffering, crucified Christ for a world that Christ himself had created good, began in the monasteries of late-eleventh and early-twelfth-century Europe. But it quickly spread beyond the monastic walls, buoyed by a new optimism that held out the hope that all human beings, not just monks and nuns but lay men and women also, could merit salvation through piety, prayer, and good works. What was required for salvation, churchmen now believed, was conversion, and to effect such conversions in the hearts of individual believers the organized Church devoted itself to the pastoral care of the laity to a degree unprecedented in any previous age. From the late-eleventh-century on, the Church made concentrated efforts to raise the moral and spiritual standards of its parish clergy, in the hope that all western Christians would learn not just the rudiments of their faith, but would come to have a lively and intense emotional engagement with religious life. Salvation was now seen as a possiblility for all Christians. But salvation would require nothing less than a remaking of the sinful world in which ordinary men and women lived.

These were ambitious aims. Not surprisingly, they were not always fulfilled. There were still many incompetent priests in the late-thirteenth-century Church, despite two hundred years of effort to improve the educational standards of the parish clergy. And some lay people remained almost wholly ignorant of the most basic elements of Christian belief and practice despite the Church's efforts to teach them. Charms and other forms of thinly Christianized magical practices remained commonplace, and the cult of saints, with its attendant interest in relics, offered plenty of scope for abuse by unprincipled individuals only too happy to sell fake bits of bone or to promise miraculous cures to the gullible or the desperate. But for all of its shortcomings, what the high-medieval Church accomplished during the twelfth and thirteenth centuries was really quite remarkable. Parish churches sprang up everywhere in the twelfth-century countryside, and from 1215 onward all Christians were required to confess their sins and to attend Mass at their local parish church at least once a year. So far as we can tell, this requirement was largely obeyed, and by the end of the thirteenth century, the Mass (at which bread and wine were miraculously transformed into the body and blood of Christ through the ministrations of a priest) had emerged as the liturgical and symbolic center of western European Christianity. Pilgrimages too became common forms of devotion. At their most demanding, such pilgrimages might lead the devout (or sometimes the merely adventurous) on crusades that went all the way to Jerusalem, to fight against Islam for control of the land where Jesus had lived and died. The Virgin Mary also emerged as a particular focus of popular (though perhaps especially male) devotion during these years. Sinners petitioned her ceaselessly to intercede on their behalf with her son Jesus, for what son could refuse his mother if she begged him to forgive a reprobate?

The twelfth and thirteenth centuries also witnessed an extraordinary growth in the administrative authority of the Church hierarchy. The papacy controlled the western Church as never before — through its legates, its authority over bishops and abbots, its sophisticated legal system, and its superbly developed administrative machinery. But despite the Church's theoretically centralized command structure (popes to archbishops to bishops to priests), lines of communication had a way of getting clogged. Ecclesiastical courts were deluged with jurisdictional disputes in which abbots sought exemption from the control of bishops, and bishops from archbishops. The archbishops of York struggled and maneuvered throughout the High Middle Ages to establish their freedom from the jurisdiction of the archbishopric of Canterbury. Nor were bishops and abbots necessarily inclined to accept the papacy's own sweeping view of its authority over them. Resistance to papal attempts to tax the churches of western Europe was sometimes fierce, often with the support of kings. And even when outright resistance was impossible, passive resistance sometimes succeeded in frustrating even the most determined of popes. A bishop who deliberately ignored or "misunderstood" papal commands was difficult to dislodge. And travel and communications were agonizingly slow. It might take half a year for an archbishop of Canterbury to journey to Rome, consult with the pope, and return to England. By the time he returned to England, the situation might have changed so much that a repeat journey would now be necessary. Although the theoretical supremacy of the papacy over the western Church was universally acknowledged by 1300, practical authority over the Church in England continued to rest to a considerable degree in the hands of the English bishops, behind whom stood the king.

The New Orders

The kings and magnates of Norman England had been generous in founding and patronizing Benedictine monasteries, endowing them with numerous productive estates. With the revenues from their manors, Benedictine communities erected enormous abbey churches, dormitories, meeting halls, dining halls, kitchens, and cloisters, joined together in a single architectural configuration that was usually built entirely of stone. Within their abbeys Benedictine monks and nuns lived lives of communal prayer, meditation, and comfort. The better houses admitted only the sons and daughters of aristocratic families, who normally committed one or more of their younger offspring, while they were still children, to a particular monastery or nunnery. Thus, future monks and nuns, like future brides and grooms, found their lives shaped by parental decisions based on family strategy. They themselves had little choice in the matter. Many developed into devoted servants of God; others simply served out their time.

But new, rival orders were emerging in the Anglo-Norman period and continued to proliferate throughout the High Middle Ages. They were founded by reformers dissatisfied with traditional Benedictine monasticism and were peopled by men and women who had chosen their religious vocations for themselves, as adults. In religious life, as in economic life, the increasing range of career choices encouraged a heightened self-awareness. It was not so much a rise of individualism, in the modern and rather lonely sense, as a new freedom to choose among a number of different kinds of communal life — a discovery of self through community.

Perhaps the most popular new order in Norman England was that of the Augustinian Canons (or "Austin Canons"). Breaking sharply from Benedictine tradition, the Augustinian Canons modeled their lives on a rule derived from a set of disciplinary and spiritual directions prepared by St. Augustine of Hippo for his own cathedral clergy back in the fifth century. Although they submitted to the rigor of a strict rule of conduct and devotion, the Augustinian Canons carried on normal ecclesiastical duties in the world, serving in parish churches and cathedrals or doing charitable work in the towns where most of their priories were situated. The founding of Augustinian priories became a favorite form of religious benefaction among the Anglo-Norman aristocracy, in part because of their dedication to serving society in other ways than intercessory prayer, and in part because a priory was far less costly to establish than a great Benedictine house with its elaborate buildings and vast estates. The fusion of monastic discipline and activity in the world culminated in the twelfth-century crusading orders — the Knights Templars, Knights Hospitalers, and similar groups — whose ideal was a synthesis of the monastic and the military life for the purpose of expanding the political frontiers of western Christendom.

The greatest new monastic force of the twelfth century was the Cistercian order, which followed a more austere, more strictly regulated version of the cloistered Benedictine life. The order began in 1098 when a little group of Benedictine dissenters migrated to Cîteaux, in the wilderness of eastern France. For a time, the Cistercians expanded only gradually. But in its early years Cîteaux had the good fortune of being governed by an abbot of extraordinary gifts, the Englishman St. Stephen Harding, who framed the original version of the rule that shaped Cistercian monasticism. Known as the Charter of Divine Love, the Cistercian "constitution" was revised on various subsequent occasions to meet current needs. From the beginning it emphasized a simple life of work, love, prayer, and self-denial.

Although Cistercians regarded themselves as Benedictines — indeed, as the *perfect* Benedictines — they distinguished themselves from the monks of other Benedictine houses by wearing white habits rather than black. Some Benedictine monks of the older tradition regarded this change as showy and affected, and they resented the Cistercians' tendency (as they saw it) to put on puritanical airs. The Cistercians departed from traditional Benedictine monasticism in other ways as well. Their abbeys admitted no children but only adults able to choose their religious vocation for themselves. (Many older Benedictine houses now began to

Ruins of Fountains Abbey   This aerial view of the great Cistercian abbey, built in a Yorkshire wilderness around the mid-twelfth century, shows the bell tower (left), church, and domestic buildings (right). *(Aerofilms Ltd.)*

follow the Cistercians in ceasing to accept children.) Like the Benedictines, the Cistercian order came to include a number of nunneries, but they were established (or incorporated into the order) only with caution. The Cistercians preferred grants of undeveloped land; when, as in some instances, they were given developed land, they relocated its serfs elsewhere. They proceeded to develop their estates by their own labor or, increasingly, by the labor of peasant lay brothers known as *conversi*. Although bound by vows of chastity and obedience to the abbot, the *conversi* were permitted to follow a less demanding form of the Cistercian life. Their incorporation into the order represented a form of spiritual outreach to the peasantry and, concurrently, a solution to the labor shortage on the unmanorialized Cistercian lands.

The Cistercian order began a notable epoch of international expansion when the Frenchman St. Bernard of Clairvaux joined the community c. 1113. A supremely eloquent, strong-willed mystic, St. Bernard was also gifted and effective in the realm of practical affairs. He was to become the most admired churchman of his age, and as his fame grew, the Cistercian movement grew with it. By 1115 Cîteaux had founded four daughter houses, one of which — Clairvaux — had St. Bernard as its first abbot. By 1200 some 500 Cistercian monasteries were scattered across Europe.

Inevitably, the movement spread to England — in the later years of Henry I — and by Stephen's death in 1154 the kingdom had some fifty Cistercian abbeys. They were stark, undecorated buildings, contrasting dramatically with the elaborate churches and conventual buildings of some of the wealthier centers of traditional Benedictine monasticism. Yet even now the beauty of Cistercian ruins such as Fountains and Rievaulx, set in wilderness areas of Yorkshire, is deeply moving. In such remote abbeys, encircled by their fields and pastures, white-clad Cistercian monks lived out their stark and prayerful lives.

Early in the thirteenth century, St. Francis of Assisi and the Spaniard St. Dominic established new religious orders that reinvigorated the spiritual life of western Christendom.[23] Franciscan and Dominican friars lived by a rule, but like their Augustinian predecessors they shunned the walls of the monastery. Instead, they traveled far and wide to preach among the people — especially the people of the rising towns, who were exhibiting a spiritual thirst that the traditional ecclestiastical organization could not quench. The Franciscans directed their energies primarily toward the poor, while the Dominicans preached to the wealthy and powerful — and to heretics. Both orders dedicated themselves to chastity, obedience to their superior, and individual and corporate poverty. In the beginning, the Franciscan and Dominican orders had no property at all, and even though their immense success and popularity soon forced them, in the interest of organizational coherence, to accept jurisdiction over houses, churches, and small parcels of land, they never remotely approached the vast landed wealth of the Benedictines or Cistercians.

The Dominicans came to England in 1221, the Franciscans in 1224. Before long their activities spread to every major town. In England as on the Continent, these orders brought vigorous new life to the Church by their fervent, compassionate preaching, their unpretentious holiness, and their boundless enthusiasm. To these virtues the Franciscans added still another: the joyous, artless simplicity inherited from their remarkable founder, St. Francis of Assisi (d. 1226).

Intellectual Life

Despite their original simplicity, however, the Franciscans were quick to join the Dominicans in enriching the intellectual life of the European

---

[23]On English monasticism see the classic works of David Knowles: *The Monastic Order in England, 940–1216*, 2nd ed. (Cambridge, 1963) and *The Religious Orders in England*, I, *1216–c. 1340* (Cambridge, 1948). A brief, recent account is Janet Burton, *Monastic and Religious Orders in Britain, 1000–1300* (Cambridge, 1994); see, more generally, C. H. Lawrence, *Medieval Monasticism*, 2nd ed. (London, 1989).

universities, which were now rising to great prominence. Several important universities — including Paris and Bologna — had emerged in the vibrant intellectual environment of the twelfth century, but they developed into organized and established educational institutions only in the thirteenth. Bologna was Europe's greatest center for the study of civil and canon law. Paris excelled in philosophy and theology, which were regarded as the supreme intellectual disciplines of the day, and which the scholars of the thirteenth century developed and elaborated in brilliant fashion. Franciscan and Dominican theologians of remarkable ability graced the Paris faculty, which included, at one time or another, the three finest philosophical minds of the age: the Franciscan minister-general St. Bonaventure (1221–1274), and the Dominicans St. Albertus Magnus (1206–1280) and St. Thomas Aquinas (1225–1274). In his rigorously organized, multi-volumed *Summa Theologica* and *Summa Contra Gentiles*, Aquinas created a comprehensive fusion of reason and Christian revelation — a synthesis harmonizing logic with faith. His intellectual system stimulated vigorous controversy in its own time and has done so ever since, but it has also proven remarkably durable. It is an impressive illustration of the profundity of thirteenth-century intellectual life at its best and stands as a major achievement in the history of thought.

England shared in this intellectual revival in a variety of ways. In the tradition of the renowned Northumbrian historian Bede, England produced some of the ablest historians in high-medieval Europe. William of Malmesbury, working in the first half of the twelfth century, wrote histories of the English kings and of important English churchmen with an elegance and insight worthy of Bede himself, and the historical works of William of Newburgh in the late twelfth century and of Matthew Paris in the thirteenth are similarly impressive. A great many other English historians scarcely less talented were writing at the same time.

High-medieval England also witnessed a proliferation of schools — some of them church-related, some private — that trained children and adolescents in reading, writing, and the rudiments of mathematics and other liberal arts. Several hundred such schools were functioning in thirteenth-century England. In the development of centers of higher education, England lagged behind France, and it was common during the twelfth century for bright English students to obtain their university training at French intellectual centers — often at the University of Paris. But by the end of the twelfth century Oxford University was in the process of formation, and in the course of the next century it developed into one of Europe's foremost scholarly institutions. Cambridge soon followed as a center of higher learning, and its schools received a major infusion of talent early in the thirteenth century on the arrival of a colony of intellectual dissidents on strike from Oxford. Archbishop Theobald of Canterbury (1139–1161) had earlier gathered around him an impressive scholarly circle that included such figures as the future archbishop, Thomas Becket, and the eminent twelfth-century humanist and philosopher, John of Salisbury (c. 1120–1180).

John of Salisbury was an Englishman, as his name implies, but his career was international in scope. Having obtained his early schooling in England, he journeyed to France to study under Peter Abelard and other masters at the University of Paris, and at Chartres as well. In the course of his studies in France, John acquired a mastery of the great authors of Roman antiquity and became in later years one of the foremost classical scholars of his generation. In c. 1154, after having served for a time as a papal official, he became Archbishop Theobald of Canterbury's personal secretary, one of his close advisers, and his diplomatic agent at the courts of King Henry II and other princes. After Archbishop Theobald's death in 1161, John remained at Canterbury to serve Theobald's successor and his own good friend, Thomas Becket. John supported Becket against Henry II and absented himself from England during Becket's years of exile, returning to Canterbury in 1170 in time to be an eyewitness of Becket's murder. John spent his final years in high ecclesiastical office in France, as bishop of Chartres (1176–1180).

The writings of John of Salisbury, executed in highly polished Latin, are no less varied than his career. They include histories, a biography of Becket, an important philosophical work (the *Metalogicon*) that defended the correct use of Aristotelian logic, and a very significant treatise on political philosophy, the *Policraticus* (1159). Drawing on the political thought of classical antiquity and the early Middle Ages, the *Policraticus* stresses the divine nature of kingship but emphasizes equally its responsibilities and limitations. The king receives his authority from God, not from the people, yet God commissions him to rule for the good of his subjects rather than for his own good. The king is responsible for giving his subjects peace and justice and for protecting the Church. If he abuses his divine commission and neglects his responsibilities, he loses his God-given authority, ceases to be a king, and becomes a tyrant. He thus forfeits his subjects' allegiance and is no longer their lawful ruler. Under extreme circumstances, and if all else failed, John of Salisbury suggested the possibility of tyrannicide: a good Christian subject, although obliged to obey his king, might assassinate a tyrant. John qualifies his novel doctrine of tyrannicide to such a degree that he may simply be making a rhetorical point — that Christian kings must not tyrannize their subjects. In other respects, the views expressed in the *Policraticus* are in tune with the general political attitudes of the twelfth century: responsible limited monarchy and government on behalf of the governed. These theories, in turn, were idealized reflections of the actual monarchies of the day whose power was held in check — as King John's career so aptly demonstrates — by the nobility, the Church, and ancient custom.

From the Anglo-Norman era to the time of Isaac Newton, Charles Darwin, and on to Stephen Hawking, the English have excelled at science. Adelard of Bath, a younger contemporary of Henry I, pioneered in bringing the Greco-Arabic scientific tradition into western Europe. A great traveler, Adelard came into contact with Greek and Islamic science. He introduced several ancient Greek works of major importance to western Christendom by translating them into Latin — Euclid's *Elements*, for example — and also wrote important scientific treatises of his own. He wrote a treatise on the abacus and may possibly have been associated with the early administration of Henry I's exchequer. Adelard was by no means the only western European of his age with keen scientific interests, nor was he the only English scholar working in the fields of mathematics and science. He and others like him represent the genesis of the rich scientific tradition of medieval and modern England.

It has been argued that the most brilliant scholar-churchman of thirteenth-century England, and the foremost progenitor of modern European science, was Robert Grosseteste (c. 1170–1253). Against all previous scholarly opinion, Robert Grosseteste's most recent and astute biographer, Sir Richard Southern, has argued cogently (although not conclusively) that, unlike many of his gifted contemporaries, Grosseteste obtained his entire education in England.[24] He was born of impoverished parents and could not afford the University of Paris (which did not yet have a scholarship program for needy students). Consequently, so Southern argues, Grosseteste was unacquainted with the best and latest scholastic philosophy of his day, and this deprivation liberated him to blaze a new intellectual trail. Whatever the case, Grosseteste was both an ecclesiastical statesman active in the politics of his day — a chancellor of Oxford University and subsequently bishop of Lincoln — and also a deeply original theologian and scientist and a keen student of the two contending philosophical traditions of his time, those of Plato and Aristotle. Hungry for more and better translations of Greek philosophical texts, he undertook in his sixties to learn the Greek language and then translated important Greek works into Latin.

Grosseteste was the great medieval trailblazer in the area of scientific methodology. As Southern puts it, his works convey "the outline of a scientific method extending from the first fragmentary observations of the senses to the generalities of scientific laws." Grosseteste's attempts to explain such phenomena as comets, tides, rainbows, color, and light (which he regarded as the basic element in the universe) seem primitive by modern standards — as one might well expect of a pioneer. Grosseteste himself was keenly aware of the inadequacies of his scientific conclusions: "I can only hope," he wisely and modestly wrote, "that others may be stimulated to inquire more deeply, and to do better, and to discover more than I have been able to find out." But his belief that mathematics is the key to the secrets of the physical universe, his emphasis on the investigation of nature through innumerable exact observations illuminated by human insight, and his articulation of an experimental method prepared the way for the scientific advances of subsequent centuries. Grosseteste outlined a procedure that anticipated modern scien-

---

[24]R. W. Southern, *Robert Grosseteste: The Growth of an English Mind in Medieval Europe,* 2nd ed. (Oxford, 1992).

tific approaches: carefully observing phenomena, framing a hypothesis, and checking it against the actual behavior of natural phenomena — a process akin to what we would now term experimental verification. Sound methodology is basic to science, and in Grosseteste's work it was set forth in detailed, rational form, although in a terminology strange to modern scientists. Grosseteste cannot be regarded as the father of science, for he drew heavily from his Greek and Islamic predecessors. But from the western European standpoint, there is reason to regard him as its foster father.

Robert Grosseteste exerted a deep influence on his successors, particularly among English scholars of the Franciscan order. Although not a Franciscan himself, Grosseteste became the master teacher of the Franciscans at Oxford. The scientific orientation of English Franciscanism derived from Grosseteste's inspiration, and perhaps also from the profound love of nature exhibited by St. Francis himself.

The most celebrated and controversial scientist of late-thirteenth-century England was the Franciscan friar Roger Bacon. Along with a good deal of superstitious fancy, his extensive writings express a passion for experimentation and for the application of mathematics to scientific investigation reminiscent of Grosseteste: "Reasoning does not disclose these matters," Bacon wrote. "On the contrary, experiments are required, performed on a large scale with instruments and by other necessary means." At times, Roger Bacon assumed the role of scientific prophet: "Experimental science controls the conclusions of all other sciences. It discloses truths which reasoning from general principles (the favored method of the Paris theologians) would never have discovered. Finally, it sets us on the way to marvelous inventions which will change the face of the world." Bacon then goes on to describe telescopes, submarines, automobiles, and airplanes.

Art and Literature

In the course of the High Middle Ages, the Norman Romanesque style of architecture and sculpture gave way to a stunningly beautiful new style described by its later, dull-witted critics as "Gothic" (= "barbaric"; it was described by contemporaries as "modern architecture"). The reign of Henry III, and that of his illustrious French contemporary, Louis IX (St. Louis) marked the zenith of the Gothic style. Originating in the twelfth century in the region around Paris, Gothic architecture, with its radically new principles of design and standards of beauty, reached its culmination in awesome French cathedrals of the thirteenth century such as Chartres, Bourges, Rheims, and Amiens. It was less massive than the Romanesque style that it superseded, and more graceful. The thick walls necessary to the structural stability of Romanesque churches were made superfluous by such Gothic innovations as the flying buttress, pointed arch, and

Westminster Abbey
Henry III rebuilt the abbey in the French High Gothic style, which emphasizes vertical lines and window walls. *(Courtesy of the Royal Commission on the Historical Monuments of England)*

ribbed vault. The new churches were skeletal frameworks of stone in which walls served only as screens and were replaced more and more by huge, lustrous windows of colored glass.

These structural ideas quickly spread to England where, in one instance, they resulted in a nearly perfect imitation. In the thirteenth century, King Henry III, a devotee of French culture, personally directed the rebuilding of Westminster Abbey in the French High Gothic style, much as Edward the Confessor had supervised the building of its predecessor in the Norman Romanesque style. Henry III's Westminster Abbey has survived gloriously to this day, although its original beauty has since been tarnished by the outrageously bad taste of the eighteenth- and nineteenth-century tomb sculptures that creep up its venerable walls like dry rot.

Elsewhere, however, thirteenth-century English builders modified the new French style in accordance with their own tastes into a distinctive variation known as Early English Gothic. The vaulting of Early English churches did not rise to such heights as their French counterparts, nor were their windows quite so large. Their interiors were often painted, and sometimes enlivened by the use of dark stone columns that

Salisbury Cathedral
Approximately contemporary with Westminster Abbey, Salisbury exemplifies the very different style of Early English Gothic, with its smaller windows and strong horizontal lines. *(Courtesy of the Royal Commission on the Historical Monuments of England)*

contrasted with wall surfaces and arches of light-colored stone.[25] The east ends of these churches, behind their high altars, were squared rather than rounded as in France. Strong horizontal lines held the upward thrust of the columns and pointed arches firmly in check, creating a sense of harmonious balance. Early English Gothic was less audacious, less tautly dramatic than French High Gothic but, to some tastes, just as impressive and a good deal more restful. It inspired the building of great cathedrals such as Salisbury, Wells, and Lincoln, as well as countless village and abbey churches, many of which, like the cathedrals, still stand essentially unchanged.[26]

---

[25]The dark stone columns are of what is known as "Purbeck marble" (from the "island of Purbeck"). This would be an apt name for the stone except that it is not marble but a kind of dark, veined limestone, and Purbeck, off the coast of southern England near Bournemouth, is a peninsula, not an island.

[26]Jean Bony, *French Gothic Architecture of the 12th and 13th Centuries* (Berkeley, Calif., 1983), is an excellent work that relates Gothic architecture to the cultural background of the High Middle Ages. For the English styles, see Alec Clifton-Taylor, *The Cathedrals of England*, rev. ed. (London, 1986); David Edwards, *The Cathedrals of Britain* (Andover, England, 1989); and Edwin Smith and Olive Cook, *English Cathedrals* (London, 1989). All these works are beautifully illustrated.

The cathedrals were not, as is sometimes thought, mere monuments to ecclesiastical vainglory, built through the toil and impoverishment of unwilling masses. Our evidence suggests that they were products of a common faith, of a powerful religious culture embodying a Christian world view that was shared by all orders of society. They were the highest artistic achievements of an age of belief in which architects, sculptors, glassmakers, and ordinary builders worked toward the achievement of a shared aspiration to adorn their towns and manifest their faith. The fullest exercise of their creative powers was achieved not in spite of the prevailing ecclesiastical culture but through it. Their finest works, the high-medieval abbey churches and cathedrals, illustrate even today that romantic individualism is not the only path to artistic excellence — that in certain periods of cultural vitality great works of art can emerge from a self-effacing commitment to the ideals of the wider community. In the High Middle Ages these ideals included civic pride, devotion to the Church and its saints, and love of God. High-medieval cathedral builders, although no less human than modern artists, seem to have been less alienated from their society. They did not believe in art for art's sake. Self-expression, rather than being a goal in itself, was a means to a wider goal that artists shared with their contemporaries.

The literature of the High Middle Ages, although perhaps less dazzling than its architecture, is nevertheless impressive. England's conquest and settlement by French-speaking Normans had made Old French the language of polite society, while English remained the common language of the peasantry. And aristocratic children, often reared by English-speaking nannies, tended to grow up bilingual. French, however, was the language of high culture, and in the *romance* it found a congenial form of expression.

The romance is a synthesis of two earlier literary forms: the *chanson de geste* (song of great deeds) and the lyric poem. The *chanson de geste* was popular in northern France and England during the Anglo-Norman era. It was a bellicose narrative poem that stressed the heroic virtues of loyalty and warlike prowess typical of the earlier aristocracy. Its characteristics are splendidly exemplified in the "Song of Roland," an exciting, bloodthirsty tale of a battle between a powerful Muslim army and a small knightly band led by Charlemagne's nephew. The "Song of Roland" is said to have been a favorite of William the Conqueror himself.[27]

The lyric poem, a product of the very different cultural milieu of southern France, was short, sometimes witty, and often romantic. In the course of the later twelfth century, the southern lyric, with its emphasis on idealized love and refined behavior, was transmitted by aristocratic

---

[27]William of Malmesbury alleges that at the onset of the Battle of Hastings, the Normans advanced against the English singing the "Song of Roland." If so, it was probably in an earlier form than the earliest version known to us today, which was transcribed by an anonymous author sometime between c. 1100 and 1130. If the poem had been as long in 1066 as in its earliest manuscript version, the Battle of Hastings would have been much delayed.

southerners such as Eleanor of Aquitaine and her daughter Marie, countess of Champagne, into the courts of northern Europe. There it contributed to the romanticizing of the knightly ideal and to a significant transformation in poetic expression from the epic style of the *chanson de geste* to the thirteenth-century romance. As Bernard de Ventadour, Eleanor of Aquitaine's own troubadour, expressed it:

> Singing isn't worth a thing,
> If the heart sings not the song.
> And the heart can never sing
> If it brings not love along.

In a longer poem for which the music has survived, Bernard de Ventadour poured out his heart, expressing the new sentiments that he and Eleanor of Aquitaine shared:

> When I see the lark beat its wings
> Facing the sun's rays,
> Forgetting itself, letting itself sing
> Of the sweetness that enters its heart —
> Ah! Such a great longing enters me,
> From the happiness I see,
> That only a miracle prevents my heart
> From consuming itself with desire.
> Alas! I thought I knew so much of love
> And I know so little.
> For I can't help loving a lady
> Whom I cannot attain.
> She has all my heart,
> She has me entirely.
>
> .
>
> .
>
> .
>
> She has left me nothing but desire,
> And a foolish heart.

The romance was narrative in form like the *chanson de geste*, but romantic in mood like the lyric poem. For their subject matter, the thirteenth-century romances drew heavily from a series of tales relating to the court of the half-legendary British monarch King Arthur — tales that originated in Wales and were given international publicity by Geoffrey of Monmouth. Geoffrey was a churchman active in England and Wales in the time of Henry I and Stephen, and his fanciful *History of the Kings of Britain* was read widely on both sides of the Channel. In the later twelfth and thirteenth centuries, the Arthurian legends, along with other ancient Welsh tales such as the adventures of Parsifal and Tristan, were beautifully and imaginatively developed by poets in France and Germany. The sensitivity of the twelfth- and thirteenth-century romance, contrasting sharply with the power of the *chanson de geste*, further exemplifies the growing sophistication and international scope of high-medieval civilization.

PART THREE

THE COMMUNITY
OF THE REALM

1216 to 1307

A GIFT OF A RING
(*The Granger Collection*)

CHAPTER 8

The Troubled Reign
of King Henry III
(1216–1272):
Monarchy, Community,
and Parliament

When King John died on October 19, 1216, his heir was his nine-year-old son Henry, whom his father's supporters crowned in a makeshift ceremony at Gloucester only nine days after the old king's death. Henry III was the first child to inherit the English throne since Ethelred "the Unready" in 987. In 1216, however, Henry faced a situation even more dire than the one that had initially confronted, and eventually defeated, King Ethelred. The civil war that had erupted in England in the summer of 1215 continued to rage. By 1216, however, the rebels had gained a new champion and a new political strategy when Prince Louis, son of King Philip of France, declared himself to be the rightful king of England and joined the rebel cause with a contingent of mercenary troops. By October 1216, Prince Louis and the rebels controlled most of northern and southeastern England, including the city of London.

The young king Henry's support lay principally in the midlands and the west. Two great royalist lords, William the Marshal, earl of Pembroke, and Ranulf, earl of Chester, controlled between them the marches of Wales — always a fertile recruiting ground for troops — and kept a check on the ambitions of Llewellyn ap Iorwerth to unite all of Wales under his own rule. In the midlands, King John's military captains also remained steadfastly loyal. These men, most of them born in the old Angevin heartland of Anjou and the Touraine, had lost everything they had on the continent when the Angevin Empire collapsed. Their loyalty to King John had won them a new place in England, but they were unpopular and rapacious lords, whose expulsion from England the Magna Carta rebels had demanded by name. For these "foreign" captains and castellans, the civil war was a life-or-death struggle to retain the place they had won for themselves in England. But although a few royalist strongholds in the north and the southeast continued to hold out (including Dover Castle, held by the king's justiciar, Hubert de Burgh), the prospect that the royalists could defeat Prince Louis and the rebels by military force appeared remote. The old king's death was in that respect a blessing, because it gave his supporters a chance to try to end the civil war through a politically negotiated settlement.

Terms for such a settlement were issued two weeks later, in an assembly of the new king's supporters held at Bristol. In 1215, Magna Carta had been an attempt at peace that had produced a war. In the autumn of 1215, the entire charter had been annulled by the pope, who declared it invalid because it had been extracted from King John by force. In November 1216, however, the new king's supporters, led by William the Marshal and the papal legate Gaula, issued a revised version of the Great Charter as a foundation upon which negotiations between the royalists and the rebels might be reopened. A number of the most sweeping restrictions upon the king's government contained in the 1215 version of Magna Carta were removed from the 1216 charter, including the requirement that the king's subjects must consent before he could levy aids and scutages upon them. But the fundamental claims of the 1215 charter — that the king should rule in accordance with the laws and customs of the land and that the king's justice should be available equally to all free men — survived intact in the 1216 reissue. Nor was the charter issued at Bristol in 1216 conceived by the royalists as unalterable. The final paragraph of the new charter promised further negotiations on the "doubtful and difficult" matters the royalists had deleted from the 1215 charter, if only the rebels would agree to come in and negotiate on these issues.

Only a handful of rebels accepted this offer, a sign of the deep divisions John's tyranny had created in England. Instead, the war dragged on until the spring of 1217, when it ended with a crushing and wholly improbable military victory by the royalists over the rebels at the battle of Lincoln. Their defeat robbed the rebels of the political leverage by which they might have been able to force further revisions in the text of Magna Carta; and so, when the charter was reissued again in 1217 in its final form, it contained only a few, relatively minor alterations from the 1216 version. In one respect, however, the 1217 version of Magna Carta was a very different document, because it was now accompanied by a new set of provisions restricting the king's arbitrary authority to establish forest boundaries and to regulate forested lands. Thereafter, the Charter of the Forests and the Charter of Liberties traveled together. When subsequent generations demanded that kings reconfirm these documents, they spoke sometimes of "the Charters" in the plural and sometimes of "the Charter" in the singular. But the meaning was the same. With only minor modifications thereafter, it was the 1217 version of Magna Carta that thus became the law of the land.

The Government of England during the Minority

There were no real precedents for governing a realm ruled by a child-king.[1] It was not even clear at what age a child-king could claim to rule on his own. In 1180, Philip Augustus of France had been crowned king of France at the age of fourteen, during his father's lifetime; when his father died, in 1181, Philip ruled alone from that date on. A teen-age king might thus be able to rule, but the nine-year-old king Henry clearly could not. Some kind of regency council would be required, but in 1216 the most immediate problem facing the royalist forces was to prosecute and conclude the civil war. In the crisis that confronted the new king and his supporters, how long the king's minority ought to last was not a question that required an immediate answer.

Because King John had granted England as a papal fief in 1213, the guardianship of the king and kingdom belonged legally to the papacy. In practice, however, although papal legates would play an important role in overseeing the political arrangements of the minority, the governance of the realm remained in the hands of the great men who had dominated the final years of King John's reign. From 1216 until his death in 1219, the greatest of these men was the aged earl William the Marshal, whose service to the Angevin cause dated back to his days as a landless household knight during the 1160s. The Marshal had enjoyed a spectacular career, rising through marriage to become earl of Pembroke and Striguil, and so one of the wealthiest landowners in both England and Ireland. That career now culminated with his service as regent (*rector Regis et regni* was the title he sometimes employed) for the young king Henry and his realm. Under the Marshal, Hubert de Burgh continued as justiciar, an office he had held since 1215. Peter des Roches, bishop of Winchester and the man whom de Burgh had replaced in 1215 as justiciar, continued as one of the barons of the exchequer, but now became the young king's personal guardian also. A minority council, composed largely of earls and bishops, provided a degree of consultation and consent to the new government's policies.

Given the degree of disruption the civil war had caused, it is remarkable how quickly the English government resumed functioning after hostilities were concluded in 1217. The exchequer, which had ceased to operate in 1215, began once again to audit, enroll, and collect the king's revenues. New royal justices were appointed, and in 1218 a new kingdomwide visitation (known as a general eyre) by the itinerant justices was launched. If the newly established peace was to be kept, then the innumerable legal cases that had arisen during the civil war had to be

---

[1]David A. Carpenter, *The Minority of Henry III* (London, 1990); Nicholas Vincent, *Peter des Roches: An Alien in English Politics, 1205–1238* (Cambridge, 1996); and Robert C. Stacey, *Politics, Policy, and Finance under Henry III, 1216–1245* (Oxford, 1987), all provide coverage of the king's minority.

resolved speedily and fairly, but the eyre was no less necessary as a way to raise cash for a government whose regular revenues had been reduced to a trickle. The new government moved cautiously, however. The wounds of the war were still fresh, and above all it was important that the war not reignite. Despite the royalist victory, the Marshal's government therefore attempted no significant confiscations or reallocations of land. Most rebels returned to their estates, but at the same time the men who had won the war for the king remained in possession of the castles and estates they had acquired during the war. Such policies would eventually produce conflict, but under the Marshal these were largely kept in check.

After the Marshal's death in 1219, however, a factional struggle for control of the young king's court quickly erupted between Hubert de Burgh and Peter des Roches. Around des Roches were gathered most of the old king's foreign military captains and castellans, as well as Earl Ranulf of Chester and a number of other barons and knights. As justiciar, however, de Burgh controlled both the exchequer and the judiciary, and he also had the support of the English bishops, led by Archbishop Stephen Langton. In the ensuing struggles over offices and property, de Burgh's advantages as justiciar were decisive. By the end of 1224, de Burgh was in undisputed control of the government, and des Roches had lost his position at court. De Burgh now began to use his power to confiscate and redistribute the lands and offices des Roches's supporters had held since the civil war. Several of these men were sent into exile; others made their peace with the new regime, nursed their wounds, and waited for better days. In late 1223, at the height of the political battle between them, des Roches had sworn to have his revenge on de Burgh, "even if it should cost me all that I possess." But in 1227, after three years in the political wilderness, des Roches left the realm to accompany the emperor Frederick II of Germany on a Crusade.

After 1224, de Burgh ruled England as the undisputed head of the minority government. In 1225 he persuaded a great council of earls and barons to grant the king a voluntary tax amounting to one-fifteenth of the value of their moveable property in return for the young king's promise to reconfirm and reissue Magna Carta.[2] Most of the proceeds of this tax went to a futile effort to recapture from King Louis of France the province of Poitou, which Louis had seized from the English during the political wrangling between de Burgh and des Roches in 1224. More important than the failure of this military campaign, however, was the precedent the tax of 1225 established for the future. Although the provi-

---

[2]"Moveable" property included all goods a person intended to sell (whether agricultural produce, trade goods, or craftwork), rents, and other renders in cash or kind. Seed, farm implements, and draft animals were exempt from assessment for such taxes. In the fourteenth century, these taxes came to be known as "subsidies" and were generally assessed at a rate of one-tenth of urban property and one-fifteenth of rural property.

sions of Magna Carta 1215 requiring consent to taxation had been removed from the 1216 and 1217 reissues of the Charter, de Burgh's government made clear that it would not attempt to impose taxation except by consent. And it also made clear that it was prepared to make concessions, including the reconfirmation of the Charters, to obtain consent to the taxation it sought. In both respects, the negotiations of 1225 over taxation established the pattern to which English politics would adhere for the rest of the thirteenth century.

In January 1227, nineteen-year-old King Henry brought his long minority to an end by declaring himself of full age. He was now, for the first time, entitled to make gifts and grants in perpetuity. Almost immediately, Henry used his new authority to elevate Hubert de Burgh to the earldom of Kent. By 1230, however, the young king's enthusiasm for de Burgh was waning. Henry had been stung by the 1224 loss of Poitou, and with the death of the French king Louis VIII in 1227, leaving as his heir a twelve-year-old boy (the future king Louis IX), Henry believed he had a golden opportunity to recover at least Poitou, and possibly the entirety of the Angevin Empire in France. Many of Henry's great men were also keen to attempt the recovery of Normandy, not least because so many of them had claims to family lands there. Hubert de Burgh, however, was a veteran of the campaigns by which King John had lost Normandy. By the late 1220s, he had come to regard Normandy and Anjou as irrecoverable, and Poitou as ungovernable. He also knew that his own control over England depended upon his government's unwillingness to press its fiscal claims too hard. King John's attempts to raise the cash necessary to recover the Angevin lands in France had plunged the realm into civil war and very nearly brought Angevin rule over England to an end. De Burgh had no wish to risk such consequences again by attempting to raise the massive amounts of cash that would be necessary to fight another war in France, which he regarded as unwinnable anyway.

King Henry, however, was insistent. He had hoped to lead an invasion of France in 1229, but the intended expedition never departed, a failure for which the young king blamed de Burgh. In 1230, however, the king and his army, including Hubert de Burgh, finally departed for Brittany, where the count of Brittany had promised his support. Henry's great men had expected that from there he would lead them into Normandy. A number of Norman ports sent ships to support the expedition, and several important Norman barons had promised to join Henry's army when it entered Normandy. Instead, however, the king and de Burgh turned south from Brittany toward Poitou, where Henry believed that his mother Isabella and her husband Hugh de Lusignan, count of La Marche, were prepared to support him. Not for the last time, Henry's trust in his Poitevin relatives was misplaced. The Lusignans never came, and after several expensive and futile months, Henry's army began to dissolve. The king returned home bankrupt, ill, and humiliated, having succeeded only in strengthening his control over Gascony, the last province in France still in English hands.

When Peter des Roches returned to England in 1231, he quickly persuaded the impressionable king that the financial and military failures of the past several years should be laid at the feet of de Burgh. At Christmas 1231, des Roches (whose see of Winchester was the wealthiest of all the English bishoprics) entertained the king at a lavish Christmas feast. The bishop's extravagance contrasted strikingly with the king's poverty. So too did des Roches's stories of the wealth and grandeur of Emperor Frederick II, from whose service in the Holy Land, Italy, and Germany the bishop had just returned. For de Burgh, meanwhile, troubles continued to mount. Wales was on the verge of war, and the king's financial coffers were empty. When de Burgh failed to secure a new grant of taxation from the English magnates in March 1232, his days in power were numbered. In his place, the king now elevated Peter des Roches. By summer, des Roches and his nephew Peter des Rivallis had begun a sweeping consolidation of the king's financial administration into their own hands. For de Burgh, the final blow fell in July 1232, when he was accused of responsibility for a series of assaults upon Italian clerics whom the pope had appointed to Church offices in England. Des Roches was assigned to investigate these charges, and he used the opportunity to dismiss a number of de Burgh's supporters from their offices. De Burgh's own dismissal from the court quickly followed. Des Roches now began a thoroughgoing campaign to restore his own followers to the offices and lands they had lost in 1223–1224.

De Burgh's supporters were systematically hounded from office. Their lands were confiscated, and the charters by which they held them were annulled by the king's will alone, without any legal process whatsoever. The ruthlessness of these measures raised political opposition. But it also raised doubts as to whether King Henry intended to observe the promises contained in Magna Carta. Henry had been a minor in 1216 and 1217 when the Charters were reissued, and he had been a minor still when the Charters were reconfirmed in 1225. By law, however, a minor could make no grant that would permanently alienate any part of his inheritance — and there was a strong case to be made that both the Charter of Liberties and the Charter of the Forests had done precisely that. Might the king, now legally an adult, be preparing to free himself from the Charters altogether?

Nor was 1232 the first time that doubts about the king's allegiance to the Charters had been raised. In 1227, one of Henry's first acts after declaring himself an adult had been to order that the forest boundaries established under the terms of the 1217 Charter of the Forests be annulled and redrawn. Under des Roches's guidance, it now began to appear he might abrogate the Charter of Liberties as well. By the exercise of his own will, Henry had already annulled a number of legally binding charters he had granted to individuals. Might he not just as easily annul the Charters he had granted to the realm as a whole? Rumors began to fly that des Roches was encouraging the king to adopt a whole series of dangerous ideas about kingship, telling him, for example, that a king could not be bound to the law and declaring that because England had no peers comparable to the peers of France, Magna Carta's guarantee of trial by peers was meaningless. Such doctrines were completely contrary to the political understandings that had emerged during the king's minority and threatened to return the realm to the bad old days of King John.

Potentially, such actions were a threat to the property and liberty of every English landholder. But they were particularly offensive to the English bishops, who by the summer of 1233 were united in their opposition to des Roches's regime. These actions were also strongly opposed by the group of professional royal judges that had taken shape during the minority. We can arrive at some sense of the judges' political views during this period from a systematic legal treatise entitled *On the Laws and Customs of England*. This treatise was for long ascribed to the mid-thirteenth-century jurist Henry de Bracton, who did later own a copy of it. It now appears, however, that the bulk of the text was actually compiled during the 1220s and 1230s by a circle of royal judges centered around William de Ralegh, who became chief justice of the king's court in May 1234 when des Roches's regime collapsed. The textual history of the treatise is complex. But many of "Bracton's" most stridently constitutionalist passages belong to the earliest strata of the text, and thus date from the 1220s and 1230s, and not to the later thirteenth century, when the text was revised and many of these provocative passages removed. Perhaps the most famous of these early passages limiting the arbitrary exercise of the king's will is the following:

> The king has a superior, namely, God. Also the law by which he is made king. Also his court (*curia*), namely, the earls and barons, because the earls (*comites*) are called, so to speak, the partners of the king, and he who has a partner has a master. And therefore if the king should be without a bridle, that is without law, the earls and barons ought to put a bridle on him, lest they, like the king, should be without a bridle.[3]

No clearer statement of the supremacy of law and the sanctity of trial by peers can be imagined. That this passage appears in the midst of a discussion about a king's obligations to honor his charters is yet further evidence connecting it with the king's actions during the 1230s while under the influence of Peter des Roches.[4]

In the end, des Roches overreached himself. A breach between des Roches and Richard Earl Marshal (son and heir of William the Marshal) led to a rebellion in Wales and widespread disorder in Ireland. The English bishops, led by Edmund Rich, the archbishop-elect of Canterbury, now united to threaten the king with excommunication from the Church

---

[3]*Bracton: On the Laws and Customs of England*, ed. and trans. Samuel E. Thorne, vol. II (Cambridge, Mass., 1968), p. 110 (folio 34, the so-called *addicio de cartis*). Translation by R. C. Stacey. For Thorne's redating of this text to the 1220s and 1230s, see the introduction to Volume III of this work.

[4]David Carpenter, *The Reign of Henry III* (London, 1996), pp. 37–42.

if he did not dismiss des Roches and his party of "foreigners" from court. Behind the bishops' threats lay their conviction that des Roches and his supporters, including the king, had betrayed their oaths to observe Magna Carta, an act of perjury for which excommunication was the appropriate remedy.

Bowing to the pressure, in April 1234 Henry reluctantly dismissed both des Roches and des Rivallis from court. Almost immediately thereafter, however, it began to appear that des Roches and des Rivallis, acting in the king's name, had been complicit in the treacherous murder of Richard Earl Marshal in Ireland. A wave of revulsion swept the realm, and the frightened king now decisively changed course. Des Roches's status as a bishop saved him from the worst of the king's wrath, but the full weight of Henry's anger fell upon des Roches's nephew, Peter des Rivallis. When the king demanded that he account for all the royal revenues he had handled over the previous two years, des Rivallis fled to sanctuary in Westminster Abbey. Des Roches lived for four more years, but almost half of these he spent abroad, and he took no further part in political affairs in England. Des Rivallis's trial dragged on until 1236, when the king finally pardoned him. But although he would return once again to royal service during the 1240s, he would never again exercise any serious influence on affairs.

Between 1234 and 1236, Henry strove conscientiously to restore his subjects' faith in his commitment to the Charters. In August 1234, he reissued the Charters, ordering that they be read, in their entirety, in every county court.[5] In the same month, he also authorized a new general eyre. Hubert de Burgh was restored to the king's good graces, although only partially to his lands, and not at all to his offices at court. The office of justiciar was left vacant, but Henry now ruled in close cooperation with Archbishop Edmund Rich and William de Ralegh, chief justice of the king's court and now the effective head of the legal system. The royal chancellor, Ralph de Neville, was another key man in Henry's government, in whose commitment to the Charters the realm had confidence; and gradually, the crisis passed. Its consequences, however, were profound. In 1215, Magna Carta had promised that "No free man shall be taken or imprisoned or disseised or outlawed or exiled or in any way ruined, nor will we go or send against him, except by the lawful judgment of his peers or by the law of the land."[6] That promise had been repeated, unaltered, in all subsequent versions of the Charter. It was the events of the minority, however, and particularly of the years between 1232 and 1234, that established that promise, along with the rest of the provisions of Magna Carta, as the law of the land. The kings of England would remain frightening and powerful figures, but after 1234 they would never again be able to rule acceptably by force and will, without reference to

---

[5]Vincent, *Peter des Roches*, p. 443.

[6]James C. Holt, *Magna Carta*, 2nd ed. (Cambridge, 1992), p. 461 (Magna Carta clause 39).

the legal protections enshrined in Magna Carta. Confirmations of the Charters would continue to be demanded after 1234, usually in response to some perceived violation of one or more of their specific provisions. But never again would the very survival of the Charters be in doubt.

The Personal Rule of Henry III (1236–1258)

In 1236, Henry III was twenty-nine years old. Nothing in his performance to date suggested that he was a monarch destined to accomplish great things.[7] He was respectably well-educated; he was usually amiable (though he shared in good measure the famous temper of his Angevin ancestors); he was a man of artistic tastes; and he was genuinely pious. He was generous to his relatives, loyal to his friends, faithful to his wife, and loving toward his children. But he was also mercurial, irresolute, petty, and capricious; he was a poor judge of character; he had no military ability whatsoever; and he was afraid of thunder, along with much else. He did, however, have enormous ambitions. From 1227 until 1243, he worked steadily, though ineffectively, toward the recovery of Poitou, which he saw as the first step toward reconstituting the Angevin Empire in France. But his ultimate aim was much grander than Poitou. He longed to play a role in Europe that would make him the equal of Emperor Frederick II of Germany and King Louis IX of France. His goal was to become a figure in European politics whose influence would stretch from Sicily to Spain, and from Flanders to the Alps.

To promote this aim, Henry took steps to attract continental figures to his court. Among the first to arrive was Simon de Montfort, third son of the leader of the Albigensian Crusade in southern France and a claimant to the English earldom of Leicester. In 1237, the dashing de Montfort wooed and won the king's widowed sister Eleanor, who had come to regret the vow of celibacy she had taken when her first husband died. The resulting scandal quickly passed, however, and de Montfort became a central military and diplomatic figure around Henry's court. Ultimately, he would emerge as the leader of the baronial forces that sought to rule England in the king's name between 1258 and 1265. De Montfort was a man of great ability and even greater self-confidence. He had connections with many of the leading members of the Capetian nobility and with King Louis IX, from whom he held extensive lands in France. He was precisely the sort of man who Henry believed could help him to become a figure of European-wide significance.

---

[7]There is no full narrative history of this period. Stacey, *Politics, Policy, and Finance*, covers the period up to 1245; Carpenter, *Reign of Henry III*, is a valuable collection of essays; and F. M. Powicke, *King Henry III and the Lord Edward: The Community of the Realm in the Thirteenth Century*, 2 vols. (Oxford, 1947), is a classic account, but is difficult to use. The best survey of the entire period 1236–1258 is John R. Maddicott, *Simon de Montfort* (Cambridge, 1994).

In 1235, Henry took another step toward the realization of his continental ambitions by marrying his sister Isabella to Emperor Frederick II of Germany. In 1236, he took a further step in this direction by marrying Eleanor, the second daughter of the count of Provence. Eleanor's eldest sister, Marguerite, was already the wife of King Louis IX of France. By this marriage, Henry and Louis thus became brothers-in-law, a family relationship in which Henry put great stock. The marriage also brought Henry important connections with the counts of Savoy, the family of his wife's mother. Of the queen's six uncles, five came to have links with England. William of Savoy, bishop-elect of Valence, became in 1236 King Henry's chief political adviser, until the opposition of the king's "native" magnates drove him back to the continent. William's brother Peter also came to England, acquired lands, and became one of Henry's most important magnates and advisers. Thomas of Savoy in 1237 became count of Flanders by marriage. Although never resident in England, he was an important ally, who for many years received an annual fee from King Henry. In 1241, Henry arranged to have yet another of these brothers, Boniface of Savoy, elected archbishop of Canterbury. Yet another clerical brother, Philip of Savoy, also acquired a stake in England, but made his career on the Continent, becoming an influential cleric at the papal court and archbishop of Lyons. Other men with Savoyard connections also came to England after 1236 to rise in Henry's service, including Peter of Geneva and Peter d'Aigueblanche, who became bishop of Hereford and one of Henry's most important diplomats.

Although Henry's English-born magnates sometimes grumbled about the "aliens" whom Henry attracted to his court, both de Montfort and the Savoyards made a place for themselves in English society with relative ease, for they were all men of ability, descended from eminent families. Hostility toward "the aliens" grew much more intense after 1247, however, when Henry's own Lusignan half-brothers began arriving in England from Poitou. English sentiments toward Poitevins had never been warm: *Pictavenses* (Latin for "Poitevins") and *proditores* ("traitors") had been virtual synonyms in England since the 1160s. The Lusignans, however, were particularly hated, not only because many people blamed them for the failure of the king's expeditions to recapture Poitou in 1230 and 1242, but also because the Lusignans quickly proved themselves to be arrogant, greedy, and unscrupulous in pursuing their own advantage within England. In 1258, resentment toward the king's Lusignan relations would be one of the important factors behind the baronial reform movement that arose in that year.

How precisely Henry intended to utilize these continental connections is not entirely clear to us and may not have been entirely clear to him. In 1242, he launched a poorly planned invasion of Poitou, but once again his Lusignan relatives betrayed him, and the campaign ended as an expensive and inglorious failure. In 1244, he secured control over several key castles guarding the mountain passes into Provence, perhaps hoping to strengthen his wife's claims to succeed to a portion of the county. But

De reditu Regis in Angliam.
a Wasconia
Rex
Regina

Henry III Sailing Home from Gascony   Mid-thirteenth century line drawing by the historian Matthew Paris. *(North Wind Picture Archive)*

when Queen Eleanor's father died in 1245, the succession to Provence passed to the youngest of the count's four daughters, who married Charles of Anjou, the brother of King Louis IX. Provence thus passed firmly into the orbit of France.

A comparable sense of purposelessness surrounds Henry's attitude toward crusading. In 1248, when Louis IX led perhaps the best-organized of all the Crusades to the Holy Land, King Henry refused to accompany the campaign, and sought unsuccessfully to prevent a contingent of English Crusaders from participating in it. In 1250, however, with Louis already in the Holy Land, Henry suddenly declared himself a Crusader also, and began to organize his own expedition. But almost immediately thereafter, word arrived of the defeat and capture of King Louis IX by the Muslims, and Henry's Crusade preparations were left in abeyance. By the mid-thirteenth century, Europeans had come to expect that their kings would take part in a Crusade. Henry's failure to fulfill this expectation lessened his stature in the eyes of his subjects and helped to lay the groundwork for the baronial opposition that would erupt against him in 1258.[8]

In 1254, however, Henry finally found a foreign policy goal equal to his ambitions. Although Henry's sister Isabella, the wife of Emperor Frederick II, had died in 1243, Henry had remained on good terms with his imperial brother-in-law despite the war that raged between Frederick and the papacy throughout the 1240s. In 1250, however, Frederick died, and the papacy barred any of Frederick's descendants from succeeding to the throne of Sicily. Instead, they sought a new claimant, one who could guarantee that Sicily (which the papacy claimed as a fief) would never again become a part of the Holy Roman Empire. The pope first offered the

---

[8]Robert C. Stacey, "Crusades, Crusaders, and the Baronial *Gravamina* of 1263–1264," in *Thirteenth-Century England, Volume III*, ed. P. R. Coss and S. D. Lloyd (Woodbridge, 1991), pp. 137–150.

Sicilian throne to Henry's brother Richard, earl of Cornwall, a cautious man of enormous wealth who immediately saw the impossibility of the scheme and declined it. But in 1254, Henry III accepted the papal offer of the Sicilian crown on behalf of his second son Edmund, a boy of only ten years of age.

This was an enormous mistake. In accepting the Sicilian crown for Edmund, Henry III was obliged to assume the enormous debt that the papacy had already incurred in its campaigns against Frederick II's family in Sicily. It was a sum in excess of £90,000, almost as much as King Richard the Lion-Hearted's ransom. To make matters worse, the papacy did not actually control the kingdom of Sicily; whoever purchased the Sicilian crown would then have to conquer the kingdom from Frederick II's able, but illegitimate, son Manfred, who quickly consolidated his authority there after the death of Frederick's legitimate son, Conradin, in 1254. Edmund's hopes of winning a kingdom to go with his new crown were never bright, but after 1254 they quickly dimmed. Henry found himself committed to a ruinously expensive venture, which he had no chance of bringing to a successful conclusion.

Once committed to paying the papal debts, however, Henry III could not renege without great difficulty and embarrassment. When he fell hopelessly behind in his payments, the papacy threatened to excommunicate him. Henry was finally obliged to turn to his barons for financial aid, but they agreed to help him only in return for radical political concessions. In 1258, he submitted to their demands and allowed them a significant degree of control over the royal administration. Thus began a seven-year period of baronial reform and rebellion that would shake the political structure of England to its core.

The Problems of Crown Finance (1236–1258)

Under Henry II, Richard, and John, the kings of England had raised large sums of money from their subjects through essentially arbitrary means. Payments to have the king's favor, to encourage the king to hear (or not hear) a judicial case, or to voluntarily limit his feudal rights to exploit wardships, custodies, marriages, and reliefs were both common and profitable. Together, such offerings provided the Angevin kings with a significant proportion of the treasure they had available for war. Magna Carta did not altogether eliminate such payments, but by defining and limiting the king's rights of feudal lordship, and insisting that judgment in legal cases be rendered according to the law of the land, the Charter did reduce substantially the value of these voluntary offerings to the crown. Despite this loss, during the 1230s and 1240s the king's ordinary revenues from justice, the shire farms, and the royal demesne manors sufficed in most years to pay his ordinary expenses. But to meet the costs of war, or even of international diplomacy, Henry III had to seek the permission of his subjects to raise a tax.

As we have seen, the provisions of Magna Carta 1215 that had required the consent of the king's subjects to aids, scutages, or taxation on moveables were deleted from the 1216 and 1217 reissues of the Charter. But in practice, Henry never sought to impose such taxation (except scutages for actual military campaigns) without first securing the consent of his magnates assembled in a "parliament."[9] But the scale of King Henry's ambitions, combined with the limits Magna Carta placed upon his other resources, made it necessary for him to turn frequently to his subjects to ask their consent to taxation. In the resulting negotiations, a new style of political bargaining began to emerge between the king and his subjects, in which his subjects sought to make their grants of taxation conditional upon the king's agreement to respond to their grievances. This relationship between "supply" (as taxation came to be known) and "the redress of grievances" (the king's willingness to respond to his subjects' complaints), forged during the thirteenth century, became a distinguishing feature in the constitutional history of England that would last until the end of the seventeenth century.

In the early years of his reign, Henry generally got the taxation he sought. In 1225, he secured a fifteenth on moveable wealth; in 1232, he got a fortieth; in 1237, a thirtieth. Each time, his subjects sought and received in return a reconfirmation of the Charters. By 1242, however, when Henry stumbled into another war in Poitou, his subjects had lost faith in their king's ability to achieve his goals, and they were also becoming increasingly resentful at his failure to consult them before bungling his way into war. In 1242, the magnates in parliament therefore denied him the taxation he sought, forcing him to pay for the 1242–1243 Poitevin campaign from his own resources. Despite repeated requests, Henry would receive no further grants of taxation on moveable property from his exasperated subjects until 1269. His subjects were not entirely unwilling to grant him the taxation he sought, but in return they were now demanding a voice in Henry's policies and some influence over the men whom Henry appointed to run his administration. Henry refused to grant his magnates the influence they sought, and so they in turn refused to grant him the taxation he requested.

When Henry returned from Poitou and Gascony in 1243, defeated and indebted, he faced almost immediately the threat of hostilities in Wales. This campaign too he financed out of his own regular resources, supplemented by the massive taxation he had now begun to impose upon the Jewish communities of England (discussed more fully below). Remarkably, Henry managed to pay off the debts from both his Gascon and Welsh expeditions during the late 1240s and even to amass a modest surplus, which permitted him to undertake a military campaign to Gascony

---

9"Parliament" is the term that was coming into use from the 1230s on to describe large meetings between the king and his great men. It derives from the French verb *parler*, meaning "to speak."

in 1253–1254. By the end of this Gascon campaign, however, Henry's finances were in a parlous state, from which they never recovered. Between 1248 and 1254, in addition to the costs of war, he had also made expensive promises to pay the dower obligations owing to his sister Eleanor, the wife of Simon de Montfort; to endow his Lusignan half-brothers with English lands and revenues; and to provide Edward, his eldest son and heir, with an annual income of £10,000 per year, approximately a third of Henry's own annual income during these years. When the Sicilian obligations were added on top of these other financial burdens, the king's financial system collapsed, leaving him at the mercy of his exasperated magnates, who in 1258 took over his government in return for their promise to rescue him from his debts.

The King and the Jews

As we have seen, it was not until the reign of King John that arbitrary taxation of the English Jewish community became an important element in the crown's revenues. In 1210, however, John imposed a huge tax, reportedly set at £60,000, upon the Jews of England. Hundreds of Jews were imprisoned for failing to pay this tax, and many Jewish families fled abroad, abandoning their property to the king. Further destruction of Jewish communities resulted from the 1215–1217 civil war, in which Jews were a particular target of the rebel forces. As a result, the Jews of England were, both demographically and financially, a much less significant presence in the realm by 1220 than they had been in 1180. During the 1220s and 1230s, however, the Jewish population of England once again began to increase, and the prosperity of these Jewish communities returned. Overwhelmingly, the prosperity of these revived communities was based on moneylending. Although Jews were never the only money-lenders in the kingdom, during these decades they achieved a dominant position in the credit markets within England. Interest rates were high, averaging around 44 percent per year, and the market for land — the usual collateral for large loans — was buoyant. If Jewish lenders could not collect their bonds directly, they had no trouble finding ready buyers (almost invariably Christians, and frequently powerful figures around King Henry's court) who were willing to purchase these Jewish bonds in hopes of acquiring the lands that guaranteed them. By 1240, the Jews of England numbered perhaps 5,000 men, women and children, but this small community may have been owed, in principal and interest on their loans, as much as a third of the circulating coin in the kingdom.[10]

During the 1220s and 1230s, King Henry taxed the English Jewish communities at a modest, effectively annual rate of between £1,500 and

---

[10]Robert C. Stacey, "Jewish Lending and the Medieval English Economy," in *A Commercialising Economy: England 1086–1300*, ed. R. H. Britnell and B. M. S. Campbell (Manchester, 1995), pp. 78–101.

£2,000 per year. In 1241, however, as the king began to prepare for his Poitevin expedition of the following year, he imposed a massive tax of more than £13,000 upon the English Jews, which he demanded be paid, in cash, within a year. Further taxes on a similarly massive scale quickly followed. Between 1241 and 1258, Henry collected from his Jewish subjects approximately £70,000 of silver. In so doing, he devastated the English Jewish community and permanently reduced its financial value to the crown. But he also created a bitter harvest of political resentment that contributed significantly toward undermining support for his government. In order to pay these massive taxes, Jewish lenders were forced either to raise cash by selling their bonds for a fraction of their real value or else to hand over the bonds themselves to the king for collection. Either way, the bonds tended to fall into the hands of grasping and greedy men at the king's court, who used their positions to acquire the choicest bonds for themselves and who then forced the unfortunate debtors either to pay their bonds in full, or else to surrender the lands they had offered in collateral for the loan. Debtors who lost their property through such means tended to blame the Jews for their predicament, and a wave of anti-Jewish sentiment began to build. But they blamed the king's courtiers also, including of course his Lusignan relations, who were among the royal favorites who profited from this traffic in Jewish bonds.

It is no surprise, then, that when the baronial reformers took over the king's government in 1258, they promised to do something about these consequences of Jewish lending. In the end, however, reforms had to wait until the period of baronial reform and rebellion had ended. And when these reforms came, they took the form of severe restrictions, and then, in 1275, an outright ban, on Jewish moneylending. Jews, however, had few other legitimate sources of employment. After 1275, some Jews eked out a living as craftsmen, while others lived on the assets that remained to them from better times. A few may have been able to shift into the buying and selling of grain and wool. But Jews were banned from membership in merchant guilds, and few any longer had the capital to engage in trade on a large scale anyway.

Anti-Jewish persecution was also becoming more intense. Both Henry III and Edward I mounted campaigns to convert Jews to Christianity. Accusations that Jews ritually crucified Christian children grew more common, especially after 1255, when nineteen Jews were hanged for their alleged involvement in the death, allegedly by ritual crucifixion, of "little St. Hugh" of Lincoln. Then, in 1278–1279, Edward I arrested and executed hundreds of Jews on trumped-up charges of clipping the coinage, in order to sell the resulting silver shards. Finally, in 1290, King Edward ordered the expulsion of the entire Jewish population of England. In return, his Christian subjects granted him in Parliament the largest single tax of the entire Middle Ages. Although negotiations to readmit Jews to England went on fitfully thereafter, no practicing Jew was legally permitted to reside in the kingdom again until the middle of the seventeenth century, when Oliver Cromwell's government readmitted Jews in the hope that, by so doing, they would speed the second coming of Christ.

The Period of Baronial Reform and Rebellion (1258–1267)

Henry's period of personal rule lasted from 1236 until 1258. It was brought to an end by a combination of financial collapse and factional animosities. As Henry's financial situation worsened during the 1250s, his local officials became more and more oppressive, not least because the king himself was pressing these men to pay larger and larger sums from the shires into his own hands. The sense of unfairness was further increased by the unevenness of the resulting burdens. Powerful lords with court connections could generally protect their tenants from the oppressions of the king's sheriffs, but this meant that those who lacked such protection had to pay even more. As the king's debts mounted, splits also began to develop within the circle of magnates at Henry's court. In a period of financial stringency, Henry's generous gifts of lands and revenues to his Lusignan half-brothers were bound to raise the envy of other courtiers. Hostility toward the Lusignans was intensified, however, by their oppressive actions with respect to their own tenants and by their frequently violent relations with other lords. King Henry, however, excused all their activities. Even great men like John fitz Geoffrey, the son of King's John's powerful justiciar Geoffrey fitz Peter, found themselves unable to get cases against the Lusignans heard in court. Simon de Montfort also had grievances against the Lusignans, not least because the Lusignans were acquiring properties from the king that Montfort had hoped would go to him. By 1258, the Savoyards too were lined up against the Lusignans, whom they blamed for having turned Prince Edward against them. Meanwhile, the Welsh had launched a series of successful attacks upon the border regions with England, panicking the Marcher lords. Even the elements seemed to conspire against King Henry. By the spring of 1258, two straight years of famine had reduced thousands of English peasants to near-starvation.

The stage was set for a political revolution, to which the beleaguered king was compelled to give his reluctant consent.[11] In May 1258, King Henry met with his magnates in parliament at Oxford, to plead for their help in resolving his Sicilian debts. The magnates responded, however, by declaring that they would not consider any request for taxation until the government of the realm was reformed. Bowing to their demands, Henry agreed to allow a committee of twenty-four great men (half named by the king, and half by his critics) to appoint a new royal council of fifteen members, whose advice on all matters Henry agreed to follow. The

---

[11]The fullest narrative of the years 1258–1267 is still Reginald F. Treharne, *The Baronial Plan of Reform*, 2nd ed. (Manchester, 1971); but see also the works by Carpenter, Powicke, and Maddicott in note 7 above.

magnates then began to draw up a comprehensive series of reform measures concerning the administration and governance of the kingdom. The Lusignans quickly concluded that these reform measures were specifically directed against themselves and withdrew from the Oxford parliament in an attempt to bring its proceedings to a premature end. This gave their opponents the opportunity to attack them openly, and after a brief show of defiance, the Lusignan brothers were exiled from the realm.

Henry's critics were now in the ascendant, and in the Provisions of Oxford they drew up a radical plan to reform the king's government. A justiciar was appointed for the first time since 1234, who was ordered to do justice to all, rich and poor alike. Almost immediately, he began a kingdomwide visitation, hearing and remedying complaints from local people against the king's officials. A chancellor and a treasurer were also appointed. All three of these great officers were to answer annually for their conduct in office to the royal council. The council, in turn, was to be supervised by three regularly scheduled meetings per year of the magnates in parliament. In all these measures, we see the magnates' insistence that royal government should be a collaborative, consultative enterprise undertaken in the name of the "community of the realm" — a somewhat hazy conception, but one intended to embrace the entire political nation, from the earls and barons at the top down to the politically active free peasantry in the countryside.

The Provisions of Oxford included a number of specific provisions designed to correct abuses by royal officials at both the local and the national level. Fundamentally, however, the Provisions of Oxford were an attempt to place King Henry into a kind of wardship reminiscent of his own minority. Henry's authority to make decisions on his own, without reference to his councilors' advice, was now ended. Instead, he agreed to act only with the consent and approval of the Council of Fifteen, a "continuing council" whose members were to be appointed and dismissed not by the king but by the magnates meeting in parliament. Records of the council's actions over the following year make clear that it was indeed the council that in practice controlled the government. When the king later complained that the council had often met without even informing him of their meetings, the councilors conceded the point and then added that "they do nothing on his [the king's] word alone." And when the king complained that when he did attend council meetings the council did not follow his advice, the councilors responded that they always followed the king's advice, "when he talks sense."[12]

It is easy to see why Henry came to find these arrangements humiliating. Although the appointment of a continuing council, supervised by regular meetings of the magnates in parliament, was a far more sophisticated approach to enforcing limits upon royal authority than anything

---

[12]*Documents of the Baronial Movement of Reform and Rebellion, 1258–1267*, ed. R. F. Treharne and I. J. Sanders (Oxford, 1973), no. 31, pp. 218–239, at pp. 222–225.

the Magna Carta barons had achieved, this solution was still too radical to be lasting. Many of the barons who initially joined in the reform effort in 1258 did so out of a sense of immediate crisis over the Sicilian debts and a deep hostility toward the king's Lusignan relations — not because they desired any fundamental reform of the king's government. With the Lusignans banished and the Sicilian obligations resolved (the new government simply refused to pay, and the pope eventually turned to another candidate), they had no desire to see the king emasculated any further. Other earls and barons became disenchanted as the council itself became more radical. A turning point of sorts was reached in February 1260, when the supporters of the Provisions of Oxford tried to hold the parliamentary session scheduled for that month despite the fact that the king was out of the country and had expressly forbidden the parliament to meet without him. By 1261, support for the Council of Fifteen was withering, and the councilors were increasingly divided amongst themselves. In 1262, Henry III, finding his opponents now hopelessly divided, abolished the Provisions of Oxford altogether. Absolved by the pope of his oaths to obey them, Henry undertook once again to rule by his own authority.

But if Henry's barons had hoped that the king might have learned from his mistakes, they were quickly disappointed. Henry's renewed personal rule was as willful as ever. The Lusignans returned, and abuses by royal officials in the countryside continued. Henry's courtiers continued to enrich themselves through the buying and selling of Jewish bonds. The security situation along the marches of Wales continued to deteriorate. And in the countryside, significant numbers of English knights and free peasants continued to long for a return to the reform arrangements established by the Provisions of Oxford.

Simon de Montfort had been one of the powers behind the Provisions of Oxford in 1258 and had also served as a member of the Council of Fifteen. When King Henry rescinded the Provisions in 1262, Simon left England for his estates in France, declaring that he would not live amongst men who betrayed their oaths. In the spring of 1263, however, he returned to England to lead a powerful new faction of disaffected magnates drawn heavily from amongst the barons and knights of the Welsh march. De Montfort and his partisans attacked the estates of those they blamed for having betrayed the Provisions, whom they characterized as "aliens" in contrast to the king's "native-born" English subjects. So strong was the xenophobia of de Montfort's followers that they regarded as an enemy anyone who did not speak with an English accent. The fact that de Montfort himself had been born and raised in France seems not to have affected his political identification with "Englishness." "Aliens" were a useful target nonetheless.

By the end of 1263, a destructive and dangerous stalemate had been reached between the king's forces and those of de Montfort. The two sides thereupon agreed to submit their dispute to the arbitration of King Louis IX of France. Louis was Henry's brother-in-law, but he was also a

An Equestrian Simon de Montfort, as Depicted on His Personal Seal, c. 1258
(The Granger Collection)

friend of de Montfort's. King Louis's impartiality was famous; what de Montfort did not reckon with, however, was Louis's uncompromising respect for the prerogatives of royalty. Baronial notions of cooperative government, political consultation, and consent were beyond his experience. It was simply inconceivable to him that a king should not be free to name his own officers and councilors and to rule his realm as he alone saw fit. Privately, Louis declared that he would rather be a plowman breaking clods of dirt with his bare feet than be a king in a country ruled by the Provisions of Oxford. Not surprisingly, his arbitration verdict, known as the Mise of Amiens (1264), constituted a ringing denunciation of the baronial cause:

> We suppress and annul all the aforesaid provisions, ordinances, statutes, and obligations, by whatever name, and all that has followed from them. . . . We also decree and ordain that the said king, of his own will, may freely appoint, dismiss, and remove the justiciar, chancellor, treasurer, counselors, lesser justices, sheriffs, and any other officers and ministers of his kingdom and household, as he was used and able to do prior to the time of the aforesaid provisions.[13]

Left without a scrap of their hard-fought program, Henry's opponents now took up arms in a direct rebellion against the king.

---

[13]*Documents of the Baronial Movement*, ed. Treharne and Sanders, no. 38, pp. 286–291, translation by C. Warren Hollister. For Louis's remark about preferring to be a plowman, see Maddicott, *Simon de Montfort*, p. 295.

There were barons on both sides of the dispute between the king and his opponents, not a few of whom switched sides in the midst of the struggle. Most prominent among those who switched were the Welsh marchers, who in 1263 fought for de Montfort, but who in 1264 and 1265 fought for the Lord Edward, Henry III's eldest son and heir, who was now, at the age of twenty-six, the effective head of the royalist forces. Edward was, of course, the coming man, and any attempt by de Montfort to re-impose the Provisions of Oxford on the aging King Henry III would ultimately have to reckon with the eventual succession of his able and assertive son.

The first phase of the rebellion culminated in a pitched battle at Lewes, near the Channel coast, in May 1264. De Montfort's forces were badly outnumbered, but triumphed anyway in a victory their supporters regarded as nothing short of miraculous.[14] Henry III had to submit to the rebels, and Edward was held hostage to ensure the king's cooperation with the new regime. For the following fifteen months Simon de Montfort acted as the de facto ruler in England, ruling in the name of the captive King Henry III.

Simon attempted to govern in the spirit of the Provisions of Oxford, but the narrow base of his support forced him toward an increasingly autocratic style of rule. He summoned parliaments frequently and strove to broaden their representative structure by insisting upon the attendance of knights selected from every shire. In theory, he shared his authority with two colleagues, the young earl Gilbert of Gloucester (whom Simon himself had knighted on the battlefield at Lewes) and Stephen, bishop of Chichester, who were in turn assisted by a permanent, nine-man executive council akin to the former Council of Fifteen. But in fact, de Montfort ruled England by his own authority, and everyone in England knew it. King Henry's authority was a fiction and so too were the ostensible checks on de Montfort's authority established by the restored Provisions. As a result, Simon was never able to legitimize his rule. People expected that kings would use their position to reward their friends and to enrich their families. They were not prepared to accept such conduct from de Montfort when he used his position to enrich himself and his sons. Governance by a magnate through a figurehead monarch was simply too sharp a break from the traditions of the age for it to remain acceptable over the long term — quite apart from all the questions raised by Lord Edward, the heir to a throne now nearly usurped by de Montfort.

As the months went by, de Montfort's party steadily eroded. His colleague, the earl of Gloucester, alarmed by the growing power of de Montfort's family in the Welsh marches, jumped over to the royal cause. In

---

[14]*The Song of Lewes*, ed. and trans. C. L. Kingsford (Oxford, 1890), a fascinating Montfortian propaganda tract dating from late 1264 or early 1265, celebrates de Montfort's victory as a triumph for the rule of law over a king whose self-proclaimed supremacy to the law made him a tyrant.

May 1265, Lord Edward escaped from imprisonment and began to raise an army. When de Montfort allied himself with the Welsh in a desperate bid to shore up his position, he lost most of the credibility he still retained. In August 1265, at the battle of Evesham, Edward routed Simon de Montfort's army. Simon himself was slain and then hideously chopped to pieces. One of his sons was killed with him at Evesham; his other sons fled into exile abroad. The experiment in baronial governance collapsed, and Henry III resumed his authority.

Henry lived on for another seven years, but his power passed more and more into the hands of his able son and heir. Fortunately for the realm, Lord Edward was generous in victory. Although many of the rebels who fought with de Montfort initially lost their lands in the wake of their defeat at Evesham, under the terms of the Dictum of Kenilworth (1266) most of the rebels were eventually permitted to ransom their lands from the victorious royalists in return for stiff fines. The Provisions of Oxford were annulled, but in 1267 the Statute of Marlborough enacted into law a number of legal changes that had been introduced by the baronial reformers. Tensions of course continued between former rebels and the royalists, but with time they began to heal. By 1270, when Lord Edward departed the realm on a Crusade, his army included a number of former Montfortians. Edward was still on crusade when his father died in November 1272. The peace that prevailed in England during the eighteen months between the death of King Henry III and Edward's return to the kingdom in 1274 shows how far England had already come in putting the period of baronial reform and rebellion behind it. Edward had already won the confidence of his new subjects; they were anxious now to see whether he deserved it.

The Emergence of Parliament

From our modern perspective, the rise of Parliament was the most significant development to emerge out of the troubled political history of thirteenth-century England. It is important, however, that we not mistake the nature and functions of these early parliamentary assemblies or assign to them a uniqueness they do not deserve. England was not the only country in thirteenth-century Europe in which consultative assemblies played a role in political life. Nor were parliaments the only, or even necessarily the most important, mechanisms through which medieval kings consulted their great men. The word "parliament" was used in a variety of contexts during the High Middle Ages to refer to meetings of various kinds at which views were exchanged or expressed — in short, a parley. It was used in the early-twelfth-century "Song of Roland" to describe a mere dialogue. But by the later twelfth century, it was starting to acquire the more specialized meaning of a large deliberative meeting. It was used, for example, in connection with Henry II's great dispute with Thomas Becket at the Council of Northampton in 1164 and again to refer to

John's confrontation with his barons on the occasion of Magna Carta. Only from the 1230s on did the term "parliament" come to be applied with any regularity to important meetings of the king's great council, and it was not until the later Middle Ages that the term described an institution rather than an occasion. Until then there was no "Parliament," there were only "parliaments."

As elsewhere in Europe, parliaments emerged not as a counterweight to royal authority but as an extension of it. Parliaments were royal assemblies, summoned by the king to meet in his presence. They were not representative bodies in the modern sense, yet they were assumed to represent the interests of the entire community of the realm and to serve as its voice. The king's council, with its increasingly professional expertise, functioned as the vital core of every parliament and was responsible for initiating and transacting most of its business. In France, professional administrators so dominated the proceedings of the *parlement* that this body came to assume an almost entirely judicial and administrative aspect. In England, however, earls, magnates, and prelates also attended parliaments, most in response to a personal summons. From the 1250s on, English parliaments also frequently included representatives of the towns, the shires, and sometimes the lower clergy. As a result, English parliaments inevitably had an important political and consultative aspect that one does not always find elsewhere. In retrospect, the presence of these representative elements, especially when taxation was to be discussed, was a constitutional development of enormous significance. It must not be imagined, however, that members of the lower social orders — unfree peasants or landless workers or urban journeymen — were included. It was the prosperous middle group of landholding shire knights, well-to-do free peasants, and established merchants and artisans who sent their representatives to parliament when the king ordered them to do so. But the prominent role these groups had played during the troubled years between 1258 and 1267 made clear that the voices of these shire and borough representatives could not be ignored. They spoke for a much larger political nation, the support of which was now essential to successful monarchical rule in England.

The functions of these parliamentary assemblies were as varied as their composition. They sat as the high court of England to hear judicial pleas that were too delicate or too controversial for the king to wish to hear on his own. They settled thorny issues of law and administration. They advised the king on great matters of state, such as undertaking war or concluding peace, and they declared their support in moments of crisis. From Edward I's reign onward, they entertained petitions from subjects and local groups for the redress of grievances — particularly those arising from the misconduct of royal officials. In turn, parliaments provided the king with an important means by which to communicate his own concerns to the countryside and to have the concerns of the countryside communicated to him. And from the beginning — or at least from

Parliament of Edward I   Edward I presides over a parliament, flanked by the king of Scots, the prince of Wales, and, beyond them, the archbishops of York and Canterbury. Churchmen are seated to the left and barons to the right, with royal judges seated between them on sacks of wool. *(Society of Antiquaries, London)*

1215 onwards — they were empowered to grant the king voluntary taxation of various kinds.

Ultimately, Parliament's role in approving extraordinary taxes would become the key to its power, but in the thirteenth century that role was still developing. "Scutage and aid shall be levied in our kingdom only by the common counsel of our kingdom." Such was John's promise in Clause 12 of Magna Carta 1215. The clause itself was dropped from all subsequent reissues of the Charter. But the sentiment it expressed was not forgotten, and as the thirteenth century progressed, the claim that subjects must be asked for their consent to taxation became increasingly accepted. In 1297, Edward I made the concession explicit: no extraordinary taxes would be levied without the assent of the whole community of the realm. Not until Edward III's reign would the assent of the community of the realm be identified necessarily with a properly summoned parliament to which shire and borough representatives had been summoned. But by the end of the thirteenth century, parliament was already regarded as not only the most convenient and effective means of obtaining the realm's consent to taxation, but as the proper and correct body to assent to such taxation.

From their beginnings, however, parliaments were regarded by the king's great men as far more important assemblies than their merely fiscal functions would suggest. Throughout the thirteenth and fourteenth centuries, parliaments remained, in essence, supreme political and legal tribunals, which wise kings approached with a carefully calculated mixture of majesty and deference. Kings like Henry III, who summoned parliaments to ask for taxes but ignored their advice on matters of policy, quickly ran into trouble. The great men of the kingdom regarded themselves as the king's "natural counselors." Prudent kings respected this claim and learned to benefit from it.

Even representatives from the towns and shires performed important consultative functions. Shire knights were summoned by John to meet with the king and his great men in 1213 and again by Henry III in 1254. On both occasions their chief function was to speak for their shires in approving an aid. In 1261, however, when Henry summoned them again, it was as much for their moral support in his struggle with the baronial reformers as for the financial help they might be able to provide. Simon de Montfort summoned shire knights to a parliament in 1264, and in 1265 he summoned yet another assembly that included, in addition to the magnates and prelates, two knights from every shire and two burghers from every town or city. Simon's chief purpose was to broaden the base of his support by appealing to the urban elite and the shire gentry to support his cause. No taxation was proposed at this assembly, and none was collected.

King Edward, in turn, experimented constantly with the composition of his parliaments. Burghers and shire knights were present at only four of the thirty parliaments held during the first quarter-century of his reign, but during his final decade, when he faced almost continuous war, the king summoned representatives frequently to serve alongside the great lords in parliament. Edward's most famous parliament — the so-called Model Parliament of 1295 — included not only the lords, burghers, and shire knights, but also representatives of the lower clergy. But despite its name (assigned to it by nineteenth-century historians), the Model Parliament did not serve as a model for the future. In 1295, the knights and barons met together in one group, the clergy in a second group, and the townsmen in a third — on the pattern of the later French

Estates General, rather than of the Lords (earls and barons) and Commons (knights and townsmen) familiar to us from later medieval English parliaments. In the fourteenth century, the lesser clergy chose to exclude themselves from parliaments altogether, preferring to meet separately and deal with the king in ecclesiastical convocations. By the 1320s, however, the burghers and shire knights were meeting regularly together as a separate group that would become the nucleus of the modern House of Commons. The magnates and highest prelates, left to themselves, evolved into the House of Lords.

The increasing participation of burghers and shire knights in thirteenth-century parliaments was a reflection of the growing power and importance of the broad political community that Angevin fiscal, judicial, and administrative policies had helped to create. Shire knights played an indispensable role in assessing and collecting taxes, carrying out surveys, arraying troops, staffing local administrative offices, and fulfilling a wide variety of other, mostly unpaid, administrative tasks. They played an equally critical role in the judicial system as jurors, inquisitors, and local justices. Without their ready cooperation with the king's commands, Angevin government would quickly grind to a halt, as unpopular kings like Edward II would discover to their cost. Angevin government in the twelfth and thirteenth centuries thus rested fundamentally upon consultation and consent: not only the formal consent of the earls, barons, and prelates as expressed in parliaments, but also the practical consent of knights, townsmen, and free peasants, whose opinions were expressed and whose voices were heard through their willingness to undertake the thousands of administrative tasks that made it possible for the kings of England to rule their country, as opposed to merely reigning over it. A very broad range of English aristocratic society was already part of the "political nation" by 1215, as the events of the Magna Carta rebellion proved. But the scope of political society in England became much wider as the thirteenth century progressed. This new and vastly larger political society came of age in England between 1258 and 1265, as both the king and his opponents began to appeal directly to the lesser knights and free peasants of the shires for their political support, and as even peasants began to take an active and informed role in the political rebellions of the period.[15] The influence of the "commons" in the parliaments of Edward I and his successors reflects the growing resources and the increasing political consciousness of these "middling orders" of English society.

The political events of thirteenth-century England were not alone responsible for the evolution of Parliament. In the course of the High Middle Ages, parallel institutions were emerging throughout western

---

[15]David Carpenter, "English Peasants in Politics, 1258–1267," *Past and Present* 136 (1992): 3–42.

Christendom: the French Estates General, the Cortes of Castile and Aragon, and similar representative bodies in Italy, Sicily, Germany, and the Low Countries. Townspeople were represented in the Cortes of Aragon, for example, as early as 1164, and in 1232 two representatives from every town were summoned to a royal assembly of the kingdom of Sicily.[16] Underlying all these developments was the old and widely shared tradition that kings and lords should consult with their great men and should be bound by custom and law. These views owed something perhaps to early Germanic procedures and something also to feudal custom. They are reflected in the opinions of contemporary philosophers such as John of Salisbury in the twelfth century and St. Thomas Aquinas in the thirteenth — both of whom asserted that a king must rule in accordance with good law and in the interests of his people; otherwise he need not be obeyed. This idea was in no sense democratic — St. Thomas was a dedicated monarchist — but it contained the seed of constitutionally limited government.

Most of the representative assemblies that emerged in western Europe during the Middle Ages succumbed to the rising royal absolutism of the early modern era, but the English parliament endured. It derived its strength from the unique character of medieval English political experience. More than any other such assembly, the English parliament was a national body — not a fusion of regional groups, nor a rival to the royal government, but an integral part of it. Parliament in England rose on the solid foundation of vigorous local government. Representatives of shire and town came to parliaments with valuable political experience gained from their local administrative activities. Ever since Henry II's time, shire knights had been handling judicial, financial, and administrative affairs in the counties. Town representatives were equally rich in political experience, having served in their borough or shire courts, or in the various structures of municipal self-government. Parliament, therefore, evolved out of a political system in which the middle ranks of the social order shared administrative responsibility with kings and magnates and were accustomed to participating in their own governance.

There is obviously nothing democratic about thirteenth-century parliaments, nor can it really be said that they were instrumental in limiting royal power. Most of the parliaments of the age were summoned on royal initiative for the purpose of doing the king's business, whether by granting him an aid, hearing a judicial case, or otherwise supporting his policies. Rather than limiting the monarchy, they served it. Simon de Montfort notwithstanding, the parliamentary idea emerged in thirteenth-century England because the monarchy — particularly under Edward I — regarded parliaments as useful instruments of royal policy. We know

---

[16]For a good discussion and thought-provoking reinterpretation of high-medieval assemblies, see Susan Reynolds, *Kingdoms and Communities in Western Europe*, 2nd ed. (Oxford, 1997), pp. 262–331.

that many centuries later Parliament did become a deeply significant democratic institution — that in the broadest sense it served as a bridge between medieval feudal monarchy and modern representative democracy. But the kings and magnates of the thirteenth century, who would have despised democracy had they known about it, hadn't the slightest notion of engaging in institutional bridge building to the twenty-first or any other century. They were much too absorbed in problems of their own.

CHAPTER 9

The Reign of Edward I

Edward I's reign (1272–1307), a crucial epoch in the development of parliamentary custom, was significant in other ways as well.[1] The new king had demonstrated his ability long before his father's death by his victory over Simon de Montfort at Evesham and by his intelligent exercise of power during Henry III's final years. Contemporaries regarded him as a skillful and highly competent leader, although extraordinarily ambitious and occasionally devious. Whatever his shortcomings, he was seen as a spectacular improvement on his father. When Henry III died in 1272, Edward was away on a Crusade, but as a mature, self-confident man of thirty-five, he had no worries about his succession. He returned in a leisurely fashion, settling affairs in Gascony on his way and reaching England only in 1274.

Edward was the first king since the Norman Conquest to bear an English name, the result of his father's devotion to the cult of Edward the Confessor. In the words of a modern historian, the Confessor displayed some of Henry III's own qualities of piety and incompetence. But Edward I ruled in a style radically different from that of his father, for Edward was a king whom the nobles could admire. He was a courageous warrior, a man of chivalrous instincts, an aristocrat among aristocrats. His presence was almost awesome: he was so tall that he stood head and shoulders above an ordinary crowd. His hair was dark but turned snowy white as he grew old, making him all the more striking in appearance. His handsome features were marred only by a drooping left eyelid, like his father's. And his long, powerful arms and legs enabled him to excel at swordsmanship, riding, and jousting. One contemporary called him "the best lance in the world." Despite a tendency to lisp, he was a fluent, persuasive talker. At times, he could terrify his adversaries with his explosive temper: when an ecclesiastical synod objected to his levying a tax

---

[1] The best biography is Michael C. Prestwich, *Edward I*, new ed. (New Haven, 1998). On Edward I's legal achievements, see (in addition to the works by Pollock and Maitland and by Brand noted in Chapter 8) T. F. T. Plucknett, *The Legislation of Edward I* (Oxford, 1949); J. M. W. Bean, *The Decline of English Feudalism, 1215–1540* (Manchester, 1968); and Paul Brand, *The Origins of the English Legal Profession* (Oxford, 1992).

A Manuscript Illumination of King Edward I
(Reproduced with permission of The British Museum)

against the Church, he flew into such a rage that the dean of St. Paul's of London dropped dead on the spot.

Law and Administration

Although Edward's great passions were fighting and hunting, he could, when necessary, devote himself to the less robust pursuits of law and administration. Edward respected the law, but he also took a sweeping and peremptory view of his legal rights as king. He did not deny that others too possessed legal rights, but as king he claimed the right to decide what everyone else's legal rights should be. Edward was in this respect a characteristic figure of the age that produced the legal treatise ascribed to Bracton and the works of Thomas Aquinas. Like those authors, he had an intense desire for system and definition, which led him to bring to completion the legal achievements of Henry II, Hubert Walter, and the administrators of Henry III.

In the admiring words of a seventeenth-century chief justice, "The very scheme, mold and model of the common law was set in order by King Edward I, and so, in a very great measure, it has continued the same in all succeeding ages to this day." Edward I's regime gave structure and system to the common law, but in doing so it rendered the law less flexible than before. No longer could monarchs extend their jurisdiction merely by deciding to create new writs. No longer would the legal system develop principally through the precedents established by individual judicial decisions. The extensive series of statutes under Edward I limited the latitude and individual interpretation previously exercised by royal judges. Customary law began to give way to enacted law; thereafter, when the royal government sought to effect significant legal changes, it generally did so by issuing new statutes.

It was under Edward I that "statute" became a widely understood concept. The ancient notion that law was traditional and unchanging had long been inconsistent with the realities of legal development. As far back as Alfred the Great, the promulgation of law had depended on the king's judgment. Many of the provisions in the legal codes of Edmund, Edgar, and Ethelred "the Unready" constituted new law, and the possessory assizes of Henry II unquestionably bore the mark of original legislation. Nevertheless, when Anglo-Saxon kings issued new laws, they tended to present them as clarifications or interpretations of existing custom. Even the Angevin assizes were seen by contemporaries as new administrative procedures rather than legislative statutes — one reason why no "official" texts of these assizes were ever issued. By Edward I's time, however, the English were coming to understand more clearly that the king, with baronial consent, might indeed change old laws and create new ones. But they still regarded original legislation as an act of such unusual significance and solemnity that it should properly be enacted in the form of a statute, which in formal, written form ought to be approved by the realm in Parliament.

The issuing of statutes per se long antedated Edward I's reign. Later jurists came to regard Magna Carta as the first statute, and the term is used to describe several acts of Henry III. Even under Edward I, a great deal of statutory law continued to do no more than summarize earlier practice. But under Edward it does begin to be possible to distinguish statutes from the more routine royal ordinances, even though contemporary lawyers continued to treat as statutes numerous measures that had never received any sort of parliamentary approval. In the fourteenth century, the definition of a statute would become progressively sharper:

whereas an ordinance might be issued by the king and his council, a statute could only be enacted by the king in Parliament. Adding to the importance of Parliament in the process of statute-making was the fact that so many of the legislative provisions contained in Edward I's statutes were intended to rectify complaints presented to the king in petitions of grievance brought to Parliament by the shire and borough representatives. This developing association between parliaments and statutory law was of enormous importance, for it led eventually to Parliament's power to legislate. In Edward's time, however, parliaments were relatively subservient, and the king and his council (a body that included the royal judges) took the initiative in drafting statutes.

"Bracton's" treatise declared that the king was the fountainhead of all justice and that magnates and prelates who operated courts of their own did so only by royal permission. Edward I undertook to translate this theory into reality. The royal administration insisted that private franchises[2] would be recognized only if they had been granted by royal charter. As early as Henry III's reign, the monarchy had tried to enforce this principle through writs of *quo warranto* ("by what warrant?"), which initiated investigations of the legal foundations of private franchises. Between 1278 and 1294, Edward I initiated *quo warranto* proceedings on a large scale. His Statute of Gloucester (1278) stipulated that

> all those who claim rights of jurisdiction by charters of the king's predecessors as kings of England, or by any other title, shall come before the king or the itinerant justices on a certain day and at a certain place to show what sorts of franchises they claim to have, and by what warrant. . . . And if those who claim to have such franchises fail to come on the aforesaid day, those franchises shall be taken into the king's hand by the local sheriff.

Predictably, these royal efforts evoked a baronial furor. The *quo warranto* proceedings proved largely ineffective, because Edward's administration lacked the capacity to implement a new policy of such massive scope against stiff baronial resistance. Most magnates had no charters to authenticate their jurisdictional claims. Baronial families had exercised their franchises for generations without royal challenge and, understandably, had no intention of surrendering them now. A fourteenth-century chronicler tells a story that, whether accurate or embroidered, catches the outraged spirit of Edward I's nobility. The elderly earl Warenne, summoned to defend his jurisdictional rights, waved a rusty sword before the royal justices:

> Here, my lords, here is my warrant. My forefathers came over with William the Bastard and conquered their lands with this sword. And I

---

[2]Private franchises were districts in which a great private landholder operated the legal machinery. For the *Quo Warranto* enquiries, see Donald W. Sutherland, *Quo Warranto Proceedings in the Reign of Edward I, 1278–1294* (Oxford, 1963).

will defend them with the same sword against anyone who tries to take them from me. The king did not conquer and subdue this land alone. Our ancestors were his comrades and confederates.

The confrontation between royal initiative and baronial opposition gave rise to a bevy of complex disputes. The monarchy continued to press its jurisdictional claim in principle, but with sufficient restraint to avoid widespread hostility. In the Statute of *Quo Warranto* of 1290, Edward modified his policy: his administration would recognize franchises backed not only by royal charter but by ancient privilege as well. By endorsing unchartered franchises that could be shown to date back to at least the time of Richard I, Edward was in fact submitting to Earl Warenne's argument of the rusty sword. The potency of immemorial custom in medieval legal thought left him no choice. Thereafter, Edward's government continued to tread softly, often confirming franchises unsupported by either criterion. But while doing so, the king's officials held to their basic principle that a landholder might exercise private justice only by royal delegation. As a consequence, the primacy of royal jurisdiction gained ever-wider acceptance.

Edward's statutes also contributed much to property law, clarifying and simplifying some of the bewildering issues arising from the labyrinth of feudal tenures. By the later thirteenth century, William the Conqueror's original land distributions had become hopelessly tangled by many generations of disputes over rights, inheritances, marriage settlements, "temporary" grants, forfeitures, and subinfeudations. Unwieldy chains of lord-vassal relationships, running down through many degrees of subordination, created considerable confusion regarding rights to land and resulted in endless buck passing when it came to performing feudal obligations. A certain Roger of St. German, for example, held an estate in Huntingdonshire in fief from Robert of Bedford, who held it of Richard of Ilchester, who held it of Alan of Chartres, who held it of William le Boteler, who held it of Gilbert Neville, who held it of Devorguil Balliol, who held it of the king of Scotland, who held it of King Edward I. Such a situation could hardly have commended itself to Edward's orderly administration, and it would have been similarly frustrating to magnates trying to exact services and aids from their tenants.

Consequently, Edward strove to bring some degree of coherence to the tangled feudal relationships of his day. The Statute of Westminster of 1285 undertook, first, to specify conditions under which a lord might confiscate the land of a tenant who failed to perform his required services and, second, to establish clear rules governing conditional and temporary land grants. The Statute of Mortmain ("dead hand") of 1279 prohibited land grants to the Church without the license of the grantor's lord; for once an estate was granted to the Church — which never "died" — the land passed permanently from lay control. Most significant of all was the Statute of *Quia Emptores* (1290), which established an absolute prohibition against further subinfeudation.[3] Thereafter, if a tenant sold a part of his land, he could no longer retain any claim of lordship over the buyer. The buyer would hold the land directly from the seller's lord, and the seller himself dropped out of the feudal chain altogether. This concession to lords was matched by a guarantee to their tenants that hereafter tenants could buy and sell their land freely, with or without the consent of the lords from whom they held it. *Quia Emptores* by no means abolished feudal tenures, but it did, in time, diminish the importance of lord-vassal relationships below the level of the king and his tenants-in-chief. It was an important partial step away from the feudal concept of dependent landholding toward the modern practice of outright ownership of land.

The same passion for system that infused Edward's statutes prompted him to institute major administrative reforms. The assertion of royal legislative supremacy in the statutes of Gloucester and *Quo Warranto* mirrored the growth and systematization of the king's own legal machinery. The highest tribunal in the land consisted of the king himself sitting in Parliament or passing judgment with the advice of the royal council. But unless a legal case involved particularly important persons or raised some unusually difficult legal subtlety, it passed to one of the three royal courts sitting at Westminster, or to itinerant judges working in the shires. At Westminster were the common-law courts of Exchequer, Common Pleas, and King's Bench. All three were staffed with professionals — trained lawyers or, at the Exchequer, skilled accountants. The King's Bench handled cases of special royal concern, the Exchequer dealt with cases involving royal revenues, and the remaining cases went to Common Pleas.

The exchequer was of course not only a court but also, and preeminently, the key institution in the royal fiscal system. Exchequer, chancery, council, and household were the four chief organs of royal administration under Edward I. The exchequer, usually supervised by the treasurer, continued to serve as the central accounting office for royal revenues. By Edward's time it was responsible not only for the accounts of the sheriffs but also for those of numerous other local officials who collected money for the king.

By the end of Edward I's reign in 1307, the chancery was becoming increasingly independent of the royal household. It was evolving from a mere royal record-keeping office into a separate department of state that, like the exchequer, had become permanently stationed at Westminster. There, it carried on and expanded its traditional work of issuing royal documents and judicial writs under the Great Seal and preserving copies of them in ever-increasing numbers and types of chancery records. The chancellor and his clerks were by now professional, salaried administrators.

---

[3]*Quia Emptores* means, literally, "Because Buyers." Like papal bulls, English statutes often took their names from their opening words.

The king's council, a small group of royal advisers including judges, administrators, bishops, and baronial cronies, was the vital center of the king's administration. This group remained flexible and ill-defined in membership and continued to accompany the king as he traveled through his lands. In 1258, the magnates had tried to assert control over the council, and they would make further attempts in the course of the fourteenth century. But in Edward I's reign, the council remained an obedient and increasingly professional instrument of the royal will.

The household, too, accompanied the royal person. It had evolved considerably since late-Anglo-Saxon and Norman times, but it retained its essential character as a body of royal servants whose tasks ranged from menial duties to high administrative responsibilities. Because the chancery and exchequer had become separate departments, the king now had to maintain smaller parallel institutions in his own household so that he could transact business quickly, no matter where he was. The Great Seal stayed in the chancery at Westminster, but the traveling household included its own staff of writing clerks and a keeper of the Privy Seal. In the late thirteenth and early fourteenth centuries, the king's household used the Privy Seal ("private seal") with increasing frequency as a means of authorizing the chancery to issue documents under the Great Seal. In this way, chancery authentication of household documents became a more or less automatic procedure. Similarly, some of the financial duties formerly performed by the exchequer passed to the clerks of the royal wardrobe. They supervised receipts and disbursements in the king's household and sometimes paid the wages of troops and met other expenses when the king was engaged in military campaigns. Thus, considerable tax revenues went directly into the wardrobe without being received or recorded by the exchequer.

In the twelfth century, the sheriffs and itinerant justices had been the chief connecting links between crown and countryside. Both continued to function in Edward I's reign, but in the meantime many new shire officials had emerged. Cases in the shires were sometimes handled by royal judges sent with special commissions. Increasingly, these smaller groups of justices on special assignment were taking over the work previously done by the itinerant justices on general eyres. The general eyres had become slow and cumbersome. They were also unpopular, being regarded as a way for the king to drain money from the countryside. Efforts to limit them had begun during Henry III's reign and would continue under Edward I. In the fourteenth century, popular opposition forced the monarchy to abandon the general eyres altogether and to hand responsibility for judging most cases over to justices of the peace — members of the local aristocracy appointed by the crown, but who were more sensitive to the interests of their locality than were the itinerant justices sent out from Westminster.

Royal administration in the counties entailed a delicate balance between central authority and local initiative. This balance was a matter of immense importance in the evolution of English government, for it meant that the royal administration could function effectively at the local level without suppressing the political vigor of the local shire communities. Rather than resisting the royal administration or being crushed by it, local notables could participate in it, protecting their own interests and gaining political experience in the bargain. Magnates and gentry thus became involved not only in their own regional affairs but also in the affairs of the realm. Their sense of community and local responsibility increased accordingly.

One can best appreciate this phenomenon by contrasting Edward I's England with contemporary France.[4] Much more than in England, the French government ruled its provinces through royal ministers sent from the king's household — officials without local roots, whom the monarchy might transfer from one district to another. English kings, too, sometimes shuffled their local and regional officials in and out of offices, but less frequently than the kings of France. Important local personages worked actively in the administration of the English shires. They accompanied the royal judges on circuits of the counties, often served as the king's sheriffs, came in large numbers to sessions of the shire courts, and filled numerous offices charged with maintaining peace and collecting royal revenues. The coroners, who investigated murders and other felonies, normally came from the local gentry. So too did the keepers of the peace, who saw to the maintenance of order and apprehended criminals. Local men also abounded among the host of assessors, customs officials, and tax collectors who served the king in shire and town.

Edward I's reign also witnessed important developments in military administration.[5] Mounted knights still formed the core of Edward's armies, but the growing use of the longbow and increasingly complex and effective siege engines made archers, engineers, and infantry critically important contributors to military campaigns. Edward's Statute of Winchester in 1285 defined the military responsibilities of the English population along the lines of Henry II's Assize of Arms (1181; see pp. 182–83), which had already been amended and expanded more than once under Henry III. The monarchy began to grant "commissions of array" to regional notables, licensing them to raise forces from among the inhabitants of their shires, whose military obligations were set forth in the Statute of Winchester. The king could still summon his tenants-in-chief to bring their knights to the royal host, but the knights now expected wages for their services. More important was the use of mercenaries under contract. Edward I employed the policy — which his fourteenth-century successors developed much more fully — of entering into contracts with important lords, binding them to supply mercenary contingents for the army in

---

[4]Richard W. Kaeuper, *War, Justice and Public Order: England and France in the Later Middle Ages* (Oxford, 1988), develops this comparison in a stimulating way.

[5]See Michael C. Prestwich, *Armies and Warfare in the Middle Ages: The English Experience* (New Haven, 1996).

return for regular retaining fees. This arrangement — known as the *indenture* system — was extended to contracts between the lord and his own military followers. Just as the lord undertook to supply troops to the king in return for regular payments, so the lord's own men undertook to follow him into battle in return for similar payments. Since the contracts were frequently for life, the relationships created by the indenture system tended to be stable and permanent, and the subordination of man to lord that the system entailed gradually took the place of the older lord-vassal bonds. The vastly expanded indenture system of the fourteenth century has sometimes been called "bastard feudalism." It created, in effect, a social hierarchy bound together by money.

Under Edward I, the indenture system was still in its infancy, but it was already becoming a burden on the royal treasury. Indeed, by medieval standards, the numerous wars of Edward I were immensely expensive. His military ambitions far outran the normal resources of the monarchy, and he was obliged to exploit every conceivable source of revenue. His desperate need for money was an important motive for his summoning of numerous parliaments and for including in them, with increasing frequency, representatives from the shire gentry and the towns. Edward's parliaments often granted him authority to collect a substantial percentage of his subjects' chattels or annual rents — although they sometimes did so only after considerable persuasion. He taxed the clergy with similar severity and thereby aroused vigorous opposition from the Church. He collected heavy customs dues, particularly from Italian merchant-banking companies to which he had granted a monopoly on English wool exports. He turned to these same Italian merchant-bankers for large loans when his tax revenues failed to meet his expenses, and in return he took the Italian financiers under his special protection. Yet for all his skillful and sometimes cruel ingenuity, Edward failed to balance his books. When his favorite Italian merchant-banking house, the Riccardi Company of Lucca, went bankrupt in 1294, Edward found himself facing some of the most serious military crises of his reign with inadequate financial backing. Later in the reign, he replaced the Riccardi with another company of Italian merchant-bankers, the Frescobaldi, who continued to serve the English monarchy into the early years of Edward II's reign.

The Wars of Edward I

The reign of Edward I splits into two distinct periods. Between his return from the Crusade in 1274 and the beginning of his war with France in 1294 — coinciding with the collapse of the Riccardi Company — his foreign policy was highly successful, and he pursued his domestic policies of administrative and legal centralization without significant opposition from his subjects. But from 1294 until his death in 1307, his wars were inconclusive, and his relations with his subjects were stormy.

Edward reigned in an age when older concepts of feudal monarchy were gradually giving way to a new concept of national sovereignty. Edward had considerable respect for the traditional aristocratic ties between lord and vassal, but his conception of such feudal relationships often took the form of exploiting his own rights of lordship to the full, while undermining those of other lords. This was particularly true in his relations with Wales and Scotland, over which English kings had long claimed a vague suzerainty. Edward, however, tried to turn this overlordship into a claim of sovereignty over all of Britain. Ironically, Edward's troubles with France arose from the fact that his French contemporary, King Philip IV "the Fair" (1285–1314), shared this same policy of exploiting rights of lordship over vassal states and turned it against Edward. Edward, as duke of Aquitaine, was Philip's vassal for his lands in Gascony, and he resented Philip's behaving toward Gascony as he himself behaved toward Wales and Scotland.

Edward's greatest military triumph was his conquest of Wales. The Anglo-Welsh controversy had been going on ever since the Anglo-Saxon invasions. The aggressions of the Anglo-Norman frontier lords, although periodically subjected to Welsh counterattacks, had resulted ultimately in a significant westward extension of English authority at Welsh expense. Still, despite innumerable royal expeditions into Wales, Welsh independence endured. Previous English kings had sought to enforce their claims to lordship over the princes of Wales, but none had sought to conquer Wales and amalgamate it to England, as Edward I sought to do.

Edward's Welsh campaigns began in 1277 when the Welsh prince Llywelyn refused to do him homage. Marching into Wales, Edward succeeded in winning Llywelyn's homage and restricting his authority. But in 1282, when Llywelyn and other Welsh princes rose in rebellion once again, Edward raised a large army and invaded for a second time. In the course of the struggle, Llywelyn was killed (December 1282). By the spring of 1283, all Wales was in Edward's hands. Thereafter, it became a province of the kings of England. "Prince of Wales" no longer referred to an independent Welsh ruler but became the title for the reigning monarch's eldest son. And so it has remained.

Considering the antiquity of the Anglo-Welsh conflict, Edward's conquest was remarkably swift and easy. The Welsh rebelled in 1287 and again in 1294–1295. But although the latter rebellion succeeded in embarrassing Edward and delaying a projected expedition against France, neither uprising threatened seriously to undo the conquest of 1282–1283. Edward tightened his hold on Wales — at staggering expense — by building a network of enormous castles of the most advanced design to awe the Welsh and discourage further resistance. Edward's Welsh castles were perhaps the greatest system of fortifications in medieval Europe. Their ruins haunt Wales to this day.

Edward's struggle with Scotland promised for a time to bring him an even more notable victory, but in the end Scotland eluded Edward and

Ruins of Beaumaris Castle, North Wales   A superbly designed fortification built under Edward I. *(Aerofilms Ltd.)*

defeated his son. Again, the issue turned on Edward's claims to suzerainty. As overlord of Scotland, he was called upon by the Scottish nobility in 1290 to adjudicate a disputed royal succession. He began his task by demanding and receiving the allegiance of the Scottish magnates and thereupon took temporary possession of Scotland while pondering at leisure the relative merits of the two royal claimants: Robert Bruce and John Balliol. At length, late in 1292, he decided in Balliol's favor. But he then enraged the Scots by asserting his overlordship over Balliol in a heavy-handed and altogether unprecedented fashion. He violated custom by hearing judicial claims of Balliol's Scottish subjects at Westminster and even summoned Balliol himself to answer a complaint by one of his Scottish countrymen (much as Philip Augustus, long before, had summoned King John to the French royal court to answer a complaint by Hugh de Lusignan). The Scottish nobility was divided in its attitude toward Balliol, but the English king's imperious behavior created a dangerous legacy of resentment that united them in opposition to Edward. In 1295, when Edward was deeply involved in French affairs, the Scots rebelled.

Abandoning for the moment his plan to invade France, Edward turned his attention northward and in 1296 led a brilliantly successful expedition against the Scots. Forcing Balliol to abdicate, Edward assumed direct control of Scotland and declared the independent kingship of Scotland at an end. He dramatized his achievement by bringing back to England as a souvenir of his campaign the Stone of Scone, on which by ancient custom the Scottish kings were crowned. Edward ordered that an elaborately carved "coronation chair" be built to enclose the Stone of Scone. On perpetual display in Westminster Abbey, the chair continues to be used in English coronation ceremonies to this day. The Stone, however, was returned to Scotland in 1996, seven hundred years after it was stolen by Edward I.

Edward's conquest of 1296 did not last. Scotland was too big to control through a campaign of castle building, and in any event, Edward lacked the resources to attempt such a solution. In 1297, a new Scottish insurrection broke out, led by a member of the lesser nobility named William Wallace, who became the heart and soul of Scottish resistance for the next eight years. The rebellion alternately flared and simmered as repeated English campaigns failed to re-establish Edward's power in its former fullness. At length, in 1304, most of the Scottish nobles submitted to Edward, and the uprising collapsed with the capture of Wallace in the following year.

But in 1306 the Scots rebelled once again, led this time by Robert Bruce, grandson of the former claimant to the Scottish throne. Crowned king of Scots by his followers in 1306, he lost a battle to Edward but carried on the struggle. Edward I died in 1307 on the road to Scotland, still seeking the tantalizing but elusive prize. His son Edward II, perhaps the most incompetent king ever to sit on the English throne, proved no match for Robert Bruce, and Scotland was able to consolidate its independence. Not until the seventeenth century would the two crowns be joined in the person of King James VI (of Scotland) and I (of England). And even then, it was a Scottish king who became king of England.

Scottish independence was won by the tenacity of the Scots themselves, but their cause was aided immeasurably by the fact that at crucial moments in the conflict Edward I was preoccupied with his struggle against King Philip "the Fair" of France. The Anglo-French controversy had begun long before with the Norman Conquest, when the English monarchy first became involved in the preservation and extension of French territories. The rivalry persisted off and on into the nineteenth century. Over this vast span of time, the two countries fought numerous wars separated by peaceful intermissions, sometimes of long duration. When Edward I ascended the throne, England and France had not engaged in serious hostilities for a generation. The outstanding issues between the two monarchies had been resolved by the Treaty of Paris of 1259, which provided that the English king should hold Gascony as a vassal of the king of France while surrendering his claims to the rest of the former Angevin Empire in France.

In the course of the thirteenth century, England and Gascony developed a considerable degree of economic interdependence. England exchanged cloth, grain, and other products for large quantities of Gascon wine, for which the English had developed a special fondness. The trade between the two lands gradually assumed such importance that Gascony's prosperity came to hinge on its English connection. Edward himself valued Gascony highly. He spent a number of months establishing order there in 1273–1274, on his return journey to England from the Crusade, and in the later 1280s he devoted the better part of three years to strengthening his authority over the Gascons. Edward was touchy about his rights in Gascony and could not be expected to relinquish them without a stiff fight.

Philip "the Fair" rekindled the Anglo-French conflict by insisting on enforcing to the full his overlordship over Gascony. For the first two decades of Edward's reign, England and France were at peace, but in 1293, Philip, on the pretext of a dispute between English and Gascon pirates, summoned Edward to his court. Like his grandfather King John, Edward refused the summons. Philip responded in 1294 by undertaking to conquer Gascony and by supporting the Scots in their resistance to Edward's attempts to conquer them. This "auld alliance" between Scotland and France would last until the end of the sixteenth century.

Philip's hostile actions prompted Edward to take expensive countermeasures. He wove a network of alliances against France — much as Richard and John had done earlier — and prepared for a large-scale invasion. But in undertaking the daunting task of holding distant Gascony, Edward presented a tempting opportunity to his previous victims. The Welsh rebellion of 1294–1295 forced him to delay his expedition to France, and the Scottish uprising of 1295–1296 necessitated still another postponement. By 1297, when his French expedition was ready at last, Edward's alliance system had broken down, his prestige was damaged, and his finances were in disarray. He had not yet found another banking company willing to provide him credit on the scale of the now-defunct Riccardi Company, and the more he taxed his subjects, the more they grumbled.

When Edward crossed to France in the summer of 1297, he left England in a state of unrest and disaffection. He returned in the early fall after an inconclusive campaign. After several years of warfare and complex negotiations, France and England concluded a peace in 1303 on the basis of the *status quo ante bellum.* Edward gained nothing and, apart from a heavy outflow of money, lost nothing. The pact was sealed by marriages between Edward I and Philip "the Fair"'s sister Margaret, and between Edward's son (the future Edward II) and Philip's daughter, Isabella. The latter marriage was not a happy one. But it would provide future English kings with a claim to the French throne, thereby contributing to the outbreak of the Hundred Years' War in the fourteenth century.

Edward succeeded in retaining Gascony. But the struggle with France, together with concurrent campaigns in Scotland and Wales, clouded the king's relations with his English subjects. The great problem was money. The normal royal revenues were grossly inadequate to meet the costs of these widespread military enterprises. Between 1294 and 1298, Edward's military expenses alone ran to something like £750,000. Over these same years, the crown's ordinary income — from demesne lands, justice, the forests, customs revenues, and other sources — came to roughly £250,000. Taxation probably added an additional £280,000 to Edward's coffers. He collected a tenth of the income of all his lay land-holders in 1294, an eleventh in 1295, a twelfth in 1296, and a ninth in 1297. He won similar substantial grants of taxation from his burghers and clergy, as well as special taxes on exports over and above the normal customs dues. But each of these special taxes required the acquiescence of the groups being taxed, and they acquiesced with increasing reluctance. The years between 1294 and 1298 marked the most intense period of taxation since Ethelred's reign. Even so, Edward's revenues did not suffice to meet his expenses. When he died in 1307, he left several hundred thousand pounds of debts to his son.[6] In short, the year 1294 marked the end of a long political honeymoon.

The great domestic crisis of Edward I's reign occurred in 1297. By then his foreign policy was straining English resources dangerously. The Gascon threat, the bribes to allied princes on the Continent, and the nearly concurrent uprising of William Wallace in Scotland constituted a military and diplomatic crisis of major proportions. Moreover, Edward's heavily taxed subjects resisted additional exactions for a foreign policy of questionable outcome. The gentry opposed Edward's effort to make everyone with an annual landed income of £20 or more take up the burdensome responsibilities of knighthood. Some of Edward's magnates refused to serve abroad. And the Church, led by the archbishop of Canterbury, Robert Winchelsey (1294–1313), declined to pay additional taxes without express papal approval. In taking this stand, English churchmen were following the policy of the pope himself. In 1296, Pope Boniface VIII issued the bull *Clericis Laicos*, which specified that the clergy could only be taxed by laymen, including kings, with the prior permission of the papacy. Although Pope Boniface's stand was justified in canon law, it was contrary to the custom of recent years and aroused violent royal opposition in both England and France. On the arrival of the bull in England, Archbishop Winchelsey undertook to promulgate it throughout the kingdom. Edward responded promptly with a writ of prohibition, thereby generating a royal-archiepiscopal showdown.[7]

Threatened from many directions, Edward handled the crisis of 1297 with great skill and emerged without serious wounds. He managed to coax from the clergy and laity the taxes he needed to continue his campaigning, and although his relations with his subjects were thereafter more troubled than before, he remained in control. His conflict with the Church subsided toward the end of 1297 when Pope Boniface modified *Clericis Laicos*. Earlier that year, Edward had soothed the laity by

---

[6]These figures are drawn from Prestwich, *Edward I*, pp. 398–412. See also John R. Maddicott, "The English Peasantry and the Demands of the Crown, 1294–1341," *Past and Present Supplement 1* (1975): 1–75.

[7]J. H. Denton, *Robert Winchelsey and the Crown, 1294–1313: A Study in the Defence of Ecclesiastical Liberty* (Cambridge, 1980), is the standard biography of Winchelsey.

confirming Magna Carta and granting further concessions. He promised, among other things, that extraordinary taxes would thereafter be levied only by consent of the community of the realm assembled in a parliament.

Historians have traditionally interpreted this last concession as a major setback for the crown, but Edward probably did not regard it as such. He controlled his parliaments, as we have seen, and used them to advance the royal interest. Because they were his most convenient means of obtaining consent for voluntary taxes, his promise to employ them for that purpose cannot have troubled him deeply. From the constitutional standpoint, the concession was a milestone in the growth of Parliament; from Edward's standpoint, parliaments were his tools.

During the final decade of the reign, as before, Edward I continued to assert his royal prerogatives. On the election of a docile pope in 1305, Edward obtained papal authorization to repudiate some of his earlier concessions on royal forest rights and to have his old antagonist, Archbishop Winchelsey, suspended from office and forced into exile. Edward was a determined monarch, and events seemed once again to be tilting in his favor. It is possible that he might have won Scotland, too, for at his death in 1307 he was on his way northward with a powerful military expedition. But in his closing years the obedience of his subjects depended more on force from above than affection from below. His remorseless insistence on his self-styled rights at home and abroad severely strained the resources of his realm. By 1307, a great many people with grievances were simply waiting for the old king to die, so that they could press their grievances upon his more malleable son. Despite Edward's severity, however, and despite the inconclusive outcome of his Gascon and Scottish wars, his reign remains one of the most productive in the annals of England. It was a period of immense legal and administrative accomplishment and decisive constitutional development. Under Edward I, the royal administration became truly professional, the common law reached maturity, voluntary taxation and customs duties became an accepted part of the crown's revenues, and Parliament became an indispensable component of English government. These were the foundations upon which the political history of later medieval and early modern England would be built.

PART FOUR

THE REALM
IN TRANSITION

1307 to 1399

THE BATTLE OF CRÉCY, AUGUST 26, 1346
Detail of an illustration from a fourteenth-century manuscript
of Froissart's Chronicles. *(The Granger Collection)*

CHAPTER 10

The Bloom Fades: England in the Age of Edward II

T he adjective "transitional" can be applied with some justice to any historical epoch, but it is particularly appropriate to the fourteenth century. On the Continent no less than in England, the prosperity and relative social cohesion of the thirteenth century were giving way to a new mood of violence and unrest, as a series of economic, demographic, and climatic changes swept across European society. In the eleventh, twelfth, and thirteenth centuries, the population had been rising rapidly on the wings of a burgeoning economy, and the frontiers of Christendom had widened significantly. Within Europe, vast new areas of farmland had been created out of forests and swamps, while at the same time Latin Christendom had advanced far beyond its earlier boundaries, into Spain, Sicily, Syria, and the Baltic lands. As the fourteenth century opened, however, these external and internal frontiers had ceased to expand, and after a time they began to shrink. The Christian reconquest of Spain came to a halt in the 1260s; Granada — the last Muslim foothold on the Iberian Peninsula — remained under Islamic control until 1492. The Teutonic Knights, who had pushed German-Christian power far eastward and northward along the Baltic shore, were gradually driven back. In 1291, Acre, the last important bridgehead of the Crusaders in the Holy Land, fell to the Muslims, and by the mid-fourteenth century an aggressive new Islamic people, the Ottoman Turks, were moving into the Balkans.

Economic and Social Change in Fourteenth-Century England

The fourteenth century also saw the onset of a widespread agrarian and commercial depression, although its impact varied from year to year and from place to place. The clearing of forests and draining of marshes continued on a minor scale in certain parts of England, but the process of opening new fields to cultivation had generally reached completion by the later thirteenth century. The medieval system of strip fields and heavy plow had by then expanded to its limits. What new lands were cleared tended to be only marginally productive, especially for growing grain. As the population continued to expand, it either spilled onto these marginal lands or made do with smaller holdings. In either case, the result was a decline in the peasants' standard of living and a precarious situation in which one or two bad crop years could cause widespread misery and near-starvation.[1]

These conditions of agricultural saturation were aggravated by increasingly burdensome royal taxes necessitated by the wars of Edward I and Edward III. Taxation and purveyance (the forced requisitioning of food and supplies for the king's armies) brought severe hardship to many peasant communities. So too did population growth. By 1300, England's population probably numbered around five million, a figure it would not regain until the seventeenth century. The country had reached the effective limit of its food supplies. During the first half of the fourteenth century, the population held static or perhaps began to decline. When the Black Death hit in the mid-fourteenth century, however, the population decline suddenly became cataclysmic. By the end of the fourteenth century, the English population had been reduced to around three million people: a 40 percent decline over the course of the century, most of which occurred between 1348 and 1380.

Land revenues fell in the wake of the plague, and the peasantry abandoned marginal fields and villages on a large scale. Adding to the resulting sense of agricultural crisis were a series of climatic changes. The climate of the entire Northern Hemisphere was gradually becoming cooler and rainier, reducing the length of the growing season in countries like England and giving rise to a devastating series of crop failures and animal diseases that caused widespread devastation, especially between 1316 and 1322, during the "Great Famine" when 10 to 15 percent of the English population may have died.

Famine and plague caused unimaginable suffering among the English peasantry of the fourteenth century. By reducing the population of farmers and wage-earners, however, these disasters created a labor shortage that worked ultimately to the advantage of the wealthier peasant families, who extended their holdings, built more commodious homes, and ascended into the class of yeoman farmers. Wage-earners in the towns also benefited from the rising wages. The nobility, by contrast, now suffered from reduced land revenues and rising production costs. As a result, they began to shift away from the direct exploitation of their own estates through servile labor and began instead to lease out their lands in smaller parcels to independent peasant proprietors. As this process picked up steam, lords had less incentive to insist upon the unfree legal status of their serfs. By the end of the fifteenth century, serfdom in England had effectively disappeared.

---

[1]Christopher Dyer, *Standards of Living in the Later Middle Ages: Social Changes in England, c. 1200–1520* (Cambridge, 1989), is excellent.

As income from agricultural land dropped, England's commercial structure changed dramatically. During the first half of the fourteenth century, Italian merchants continued by and large to serve as the chief royal bankers, and Italians, Flemings, and Germans from the cities of the Hanseatic League controlled about two-thirds of the wool trade. But English merchants were struggling to take more of the trade into their own hands. They sought to concentrate the selling of English wool in one foreign trading center under English control — a single town to which the king granted a monopoly on wool exportation. Such a center was called a "staple."

During the 1290s, Edward I established the first staples at Dordrecht and Antwerp in the Low Countries. Anxious to build up his war chest, he found it advantageous to concentrate the wool trade so that it could be easily supervised and efficiently taxed. In 1314, Edward II set up the first compulsory staple at St. Omer in Flanders. And Edward III, responding to the financial squeeze of the Hundred Years' War, established staples at one time or another at Antwerp and Bruges. Foreign merchants still played an important role in the trade, but now, unless specially privileged, they were obliged to buy their wool at the staple from English traders.

The monarchy began to favor English merchants more wholeheartedly after the collapse in 1339 of the Bardi and the Peruzzi — the two Italian merchant firms on which Edward III had particularly depended for loans and whose fall resulted in part from his failure to repay. For a time, Edward turned for credit to merchants of the German Hansa towns. Beginning in the 1350s, however, he depended primarily on domestic loans and subsidies, and granted favors in return. In 1363, the king established a staple at Calais — in northern France but under English occupation — and gave control of it to a group of English merchants known as the Company of the Staple. This company acquired a monopoly of the wool trade, the one exception being that wool could still be shipped by sea from England to Italy. The wool monopoly enabled the Company of the Staple to dominate the trade for many years thereafter.

During these years, however, the wool trade as a whole was declining as a result of the steady rise of the English cloth industry. From about 1200 onward, English textile workers were consuming more and more wool in the manufacture of English cloth, so that the amount remaining for export decreased.[2] English weavers were exempt from the high royal duties on wool, and as relative newcomers on the economic scene they were less tightly bound by cumbersome guild regulations. The crown, moreover, never succeeded in imposing a significant customs duty on the export of wool cloth. As a result, English cloth producers were able to undersell their continental rivals, and, in time, they won large markets for

---

[2]A. R. Bridbury, in *Medieval English Clothmaking: An Economic Survey* (London, 1982), argues persuasively for this early beginning of large-scale cloth manufacturing in England.

their cloth, not only in England but all across Europe. As the fourteenth century closed, English merchants of all kinds were beginning to penetrate deep into the Continent, competing successfully in areas long dominated by the merchants of Flanders and the Hanseatic League. No longer merely a source of raw materials, England was now a great textile producer. Its merchants were beginning to demonstrate the sort of initiative that in later centuries would make their kingdom the commercial nexus of the world.

English towns also underwent fundamental changes. The economic forces of the fourteenth century brought about the decline of many towns — Oxford and Lincoln, for example — that were agricultural markets or centers of the faltering wool trade. But at the same time, the rise of cloth manufacturing transformed towns such as Norwich, York, and Coventry into thriving textile centers. The profits from cloth production enabled many villages to build lavish churches in the late-medieval Gothic style that are sources of local pride to this day. The intensification of the cloth trade made London more prosperous than ever, but it also assisted in the rise of Bristol, which was emerging as London's chief commercial rival. Relatively few new towns were established in the later Middle Ages, however. Whereas some 265 boroughs appear for the first time in records of the thirteenth century, fifteenth-century records disclose only seventeen.

The labor shortages resulting from the post-plague population decline presented new opportunities to the lesser urban classes, journeymen, and minor artisans, whose services were now much in demand. But the wealthy and privileged merchant guilds, along with the important craft associations that controlled the cloth industry, maintained their long-standing control of urban economic life and town government. They clung to their valuable monopolies, repressed the rising organizations of journeymen and the guilds of the lesser crafts, and did everything in their power to keep wages down. Consequently, the later fourteenth century witnessed a series of severe urban riots, which terrified the ruling merchants but did not dislodge them. Although winning ever-wider privileges and increasingly generous charters from the monarchy, the towns also remained firmly under the control of the crown. Independent city-states of the sort that abounded in contemporary Italy and northern Germany were unknown in England.

In the countryside also, the post-plague labor shortage gave agricultural wage-earners the advantage of being in great demand. The dominant groups in town and country alike reacted by attempting to preserve the status quo, suppressing lower-class associations, and, through Parliament, procuring royal statutes that fixed wages at artificially low, pre-plague levels. The unrest that resulted from these policies culminated in the Great Revolt of 1381, known traditionally as the "Peasants' Revolt," which will be discussed in the final chapter. Similar popular uprisings occurred on the Continent as well. A particularly savage revolt known as the Jacquerie Rebellion broke out in France in 1358, and between 1378 and 1382 popular insurrections afflicted Germany, Italy, and the Netherlands. Fourteenth-century Europe suffered a surge of violence, rebellion, and murder; a sharpening of class conflict; and increased factionalism among the nobility. Added to these misfortunes were the twin horrors of plague and war. France was devastated by contending armies and rampaging bands of ill-disciplined mercenary soldiers. England suffered little from direct military violence except in the north, where invading Scottish armies wreaked havoc on the countryside, and it took ten armed men to deliver a single letter. But England's inhabitants endured severe taxation to support their armies and allies on the Continent, and at times the English monarchy teetered on the brink of bankruptcy.

Changes in architecture accompanied the shifts in social and economic conditions. The Early English Gothic style of the thirteenth century — balanced, graceful, and restrained — gave way in the late thirteenth and early fourteenth centuries to a new English variation known as Decorated Gothic. Buildings in the new style — the stunning "Angel Choir" of Lincoln Cathedral, for example, and the exuberantly sculpted chapter house at Southwell Minster — were rich in naturalistic carving

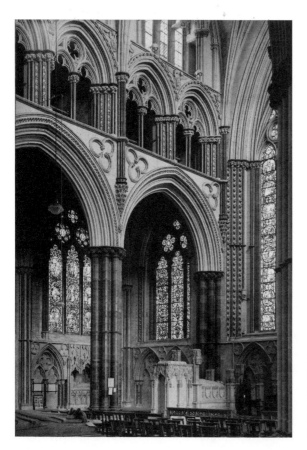

The Angel Choir, Lincoln Cathedral (1256–1320) An example of English Decorated Gothic architecture. *(Dr. Martin Hürlimann)*

Decorated Gothic Carving in the Chapter House, Southwell Minster
(C. M. Dixon)

and elaborate vault ribbing. Stone tracery in windows and on walls became increasingly complex, as simple arcs and circles evolved around 1290 into twisting serpentine curves. Capitals and choir screens displayed marvelously lifelike stone foliage, attesting to the artists' keen perception of the natural world and their skill with the chisel.

In the 1330s there emerged the last great style of English medieval architecture, Perpendicular Gothic, which spread gradually across the kingdom and remained in vogue for the next two centuries. The style remained a distinctively English achievement. The contemporary French "Flamboyant Gothic" was closer in spirit to the English Decorated style than to the Perpendicular and probably developed through English inspiration. Exemplified by the cloister and remodeled choir of Gloucester Cathedral and by the vast "chapel" of King's College, Cambridge, Perpendicular Gothic architecture features richly sculpted walls, uninterrupted upward lines, vertical bar tracery in its windows and choir screens, and intricately patterned "fan vaulting." A progressive thinning of columns and arches resulted in a new feeling of plasticity — a flowing unity of overall design. Immense windows flooded spacious interiors with light;

Choir, Gloucester Cathedral   The Norman Romanesque choir was remodeled during the mid-fourteenth century in the Perpendicular Gothic style, with elaborate ribbed vaulting and unobstructed vertical lines. *(National Monuments Record)*

the Gothic dream of window walls set in a slender framework of stone had seldom been so completely realized. The stately harmony of earlier Gothic architecture, based on the principle of horizontal-vertical equilibrium, gave way to the aspiring upward thrust — the passionate verticality — of Perpendicular Gothic.

In intellectual life, the fourteenth century witnessed a series of powerful attacks against the fusion of reason and revelation that thirteenth-century scholastic philosophers such as Thomas Aquinas had achieved. Criticism of Aquinas had not been lacking even in his own day, but it accelerated under the influence of the English Franciscan John Duns Scotus (d. 1308) and climaxed with another English Franciscan, William of Ockham (d. 1349). Duns Scotus was far more than a mere critic; he constructed an elaborate philosophical system of his own, of such marvelous complexity as to captivate some later scholars, repel others, and bewilder the rest. His system of thought tended to place narrow limits on humanity's ability to approach God and religious truth through reason. In the tradition of the Franciscan scientists, he taught that the most appropriate object of human reason was the natural world rather than the supernatural, and he maintained that a number of Christian dogmas that Aquinas had regarded as rationally verifiable could be accepted only on faith.

William of Ockham went much further, insisting on a radical disjunction between empirical facts and Christian doctrine. He believed in both but concluded that the dogmas of the Catholic religion transcended reason. The existence of God had to be taken on faith. It could not be proven, and because the scope of human reason was limited to the world of visible phenomena, all efforts to infer knowledge about God from empirical observation of the created world were therefore futile. Ockham's separation of reason from faith severed the age-long bond between theology and natural science, freeing science to follow its own independent course.

The most striking intellectual achievement of the thirteenth century had been the welding of faith and logic into a single coherent system of thought, and the fourteenth-century philosophers subjected that system to intense logical criticism. In doing so, they were accomplishing on an intellectual level what late-medieval civilization was achieving concurrently on the social, economic, and cultural levels: the erosion of an old ethos and the first tentative, uncertain steps toward a new one.

The Reign of Edward II (1307–1327)

Three kings ruled England through most of the fourteenth century: Edward II (1307–1327), Edward III (1327–1377), and Richard II (1377–1399). Of these three, two had their reigns cut short by rebellion and deposition. Edward II was the most despised and least successful of them.[3] His inadequacies stand out in particularly sharp relief against the iron strength of his father, Edward I, and the success and popularity of his son, Edward III. He has been described, not unjustly, as "one of the most incompetent men to sit on the throne of England," and the history of his reign as "one of successive political failures punctuated by acts of horrific violence."[4]

Edward II inherited from his father an ambitious foreign policy, an empty treasury, and a restive nobility. But Edward I failed to pass on to him the intelligence and resolution necessary to cope with these problems. Even as a youthful Prince of Wales, the future Edward II had demonstrated his willfulness and incapacity, and before accepting him as their king the barons forced him to take a coronation oath of extraordinary scope. The oath took the form of a series of questions posed to the prospective king by Robert Winchelsey, archbishop of Canterbury, who had returned from exile on the death of Edward I. Significantly, the oath was neither in Latin nor in French but in English, which was by now overtaking French as the language of English aristocratic society:

---

[3]Excellent surveys of Edward's reign are available in Michael C. Prestwich, *The Three Edwards: War and State in England, 1272–1377* (London, 1980); John R. Maddicott, *Thomas of Lancaster, 1307–1322: A Study in the Reign of Edward II* (Oxford, 1970); and Natalie Fryde, *The Tyranny and Fall of Edward II, 1321–1326* (Cambridge, 1979). The most important contemporary history of Edward II's reign is the *Vita Edwardi Secundi*, ed. and trans. Noel Denholm-Young (London, 1957).

[4]Prestwich, *The Three Edwards*, pp. 295, 79.

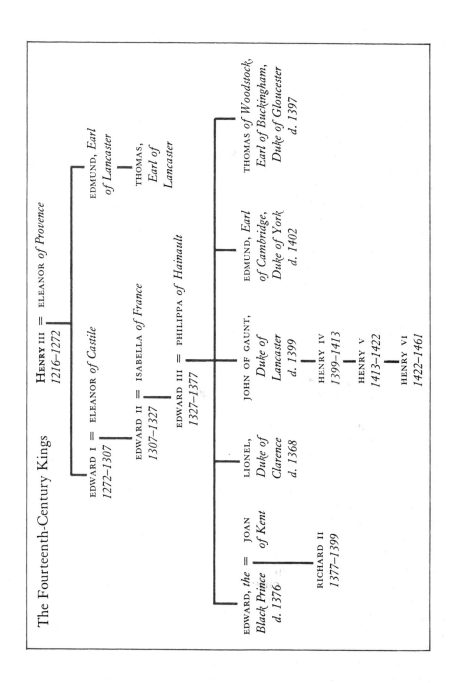

The Fourteenth-Century Kings

HENRY III = ELEANOR of Provence
1216–1272

EDWARD I = ELEANOR of Castile
1272–1307

EDMUND, Earl
of Lancaster

THOMAS,
Earl of
Lancaster

EDWARD II = ISABELLA of France
1307–1327

EDWARD III = PHILIPPA of Hainault
1327–1377

EDWARD, the = JOAN
Black Prince   of Kent
d. 1376

LIONEL,
Duke of
Clarence
d. 1368

JOHN OF GAUNT,
Duke of
Lancaster
d. 1399

EDMUND, Earl
of Cambridge,
Duke of York
d. 1402

THOMAS of Woodstock,
Earl of Buckingham,
Duke of Gloucester
d. 1397

RICHARD II
1377–1399

HENRY IV
1399–1413

HENRY V
1413–1422

HENRY VI
1422–1461

"Sire, will you grant and keep and confirm to the people of England by your oath the laws and customs given them by the previous just and God-fearing kings, your ancestors, and particularly the laws, customs, and liberties granted the clergy and people by the glorious king, the sainted Edward,[5] your predecessor?"

"I grant and promise them."

"Sire, will you in all your judgments, to the best of your ability, preserve to God and the Holy Church and to the clergy and people full peace and concord before God?"

"I will preserve them."

"Sire, will you, to the best of your ability, have justice rendered rightly, fairly, and widely, in compassion and truth?"

"I will do so."

"Sire, do you grant to be held and kept the laws and just customs which the community of your realm shall choose, and, to the best of your ability, will you defend and enforce them to the honor of God?"

"I grant and promise them."

The last of these four promises was the most novel and doubtless the most important, embodying as it did the concept of community that had provoked such contention in the thirteenth century. By now it was coming to be understood that Parliament was the instrument through which the community of the realm expressed its will, and of necessity Edward II summoned parliaments frequently. The new king was as willing to make promises as his predecessors had been, and as ready to break them. The coronation oath discloses in very general terms what the political community expected of its king, but more than an oath would be required to bridle the obstinate Edward II.

At the time of his coronation, Edward was twenty-four years old. A contemporary described him as "fair of body and great of strength." But in character he was mercurial and unknightly. Bishop William Stubbs, writing well over a century ago, admirably described Edward's many-faceted personality:

He was a trifler, an amateur farmer, a breeder of horses, a patron of playwrights, a contriver of masques, a smatterer in mechanical arts; he was, it may be, an adept in rowing and a practiced whip; he could dig a pit or thatch a barn; somewhat varied and inconsistent accomplishments, but all testifying to the skillful hand rather than the thoughtful head.

In short, Edward II was an eccentric. He was "a weakling and a fool," who was deficient "not only in military capacity, but also in imagination, energy, and common sense."[6] Because he lacked the chivalric and military virtues of the knight, he could not win the respect of his barons, who preferred that their kings be warriors, not cart drivers. His corona-

---

[5]Edward the Confessor, not Edward I (whom Archbishop Winchelsey loathed).

[6]May McKisack, *The Fourteenth Century, 1307–1399* (Oxford, 1959), p. 95.

tion ushered in a generation of civil strife that would leave a lasting mark on the political consciousness of the fourteenth-century nobility.

Throughout his career, Edward II demonstrated a dangerous and self-defeating tendency to engage in emotionally charged relationships with ambitious young men and to fall hopelessly under their influence. The first such man, undoubtedly the great love of Edward's life, was Piers Gaveston, a Gascon knight of modest birth whose courage and ability were tainted by arrogance. Gaveston had been exiled by Edward I as a bad influence on his impressionable son, but when Edward II inherited the throne, he immediately brought Gaveston back to England and made him earl of Cornwall, a title that had traditionally been assigned to the king's brother.

Edward's relationship with Gaveston caused endless difficulties. As one contemporary expressed it:

> [Baronial antagonism toward Piers] mounted day by day, for Piers was very proud and haughty in bearing. All those whom the custom of the realm made equal to him, he regarded as lowly and abject, nor could anyone, he thought, equal him in valor. On the other hand the earls and barons of England looked down upon Piers because, as a foreigner and formerly a mere man-at-arms raised to such distinction and eminence, he was unmindful of his former rank. Thus he was an object of mockery to almost everyone in the kingdom. But the king had an unswerving affection for him.[7]

With the king's affection went also great influence around the court, and it soon became clear that Gaveston was the man who, more than any other, could convince the king to grant a petitioner's request for favor. As a result, Gaveston began to become politically influential in the countryside. To the earls and barons, however, it must have seemed that the bad old days of Henry III had returned with a vengeance. Edward II ignored the will of the community, scorned the advice of his nobles, and listened only to the vainglorious Gaveston. Meanwhile, the Scots were raiding northern England, and neither Edward nor Gaveston seemed inclined to mount any sort of effective military campaign against them. Predictably, the disgruntled magnates began to conspire against the king, led by one of the wealthiest and most powerful magnates that England had ever known: Thomas, earl of Lancaster, grandson of King Henry III and first cousin (and, until 1313, heir) of Edward II.

A magnate of Thomas's vast resources would have been unthinkable under the Norman and early Angevin kings, whose wealth and lands far exceeded that of their greatest vassals. But over the generations the disparity in landed wealth between king and magnates had been reduced by the alienation of royal demesne lands, the awarding of lavish territorial endowments to younger royal sons (thereby establishing them as

---

[7]*Vita Edwardi Secundi*, p. 3.

magnates of surpassing wealth), and the consolidation of baronial estates through intermarriage. And no magnate was more formidable than Thomas of Lancaster. At the height of his power, Thomas held five earldoms — Lancaster, Leicester, Derby, Salisbury, and Lincoln — together with vast estates in northern and central England. He defended his lands and interests with a large private army. His impact on English history would have been greater still had not his policies been short-sighted, capricious, and limited by and large to the satisfaction of his personal ambitions. Recent attempts to present his career in a more favorable light do not dispel the impression that he was a grasping, stupid blunderer.

Nevertheless, Earl Thomas's royal opponent was at least as stupid and blundering as he. Edward II's lack of interest in his father's Scottish war had been known even before his accession; in 1306, he and Gaveston had deserted the English army as it marched north in Edward I's last great campaign. After his accession, Edward showed no greater interest in the war with Scotland. Although he summoned several military expeditions, they dissolved in muddle and incompetence before they ever succeeded in engaging the Scots. Failed campaigns, however, were almost as expensive as successful ones. Edward I had left his son a mounting pile of debt, to which Edward II and Gaveston added further. Edward exploited every possible source of tax revenue and borrowed heavily from Italian bankers, particularly the Frescobaldi of Florence, who had been the monarchy's principal creditors since Edward I's later years. Ultimately, however, the king was obliged to seek extraordinary financial support from his barons in Parliament.

This provided the magnates with an opportunity to establish a degree of control over the unwilling king. In 1310, they forced him to accept a committee of notables empowered to draw up a series of ordinances to reform the governance of the realm. The fruits of their work, the Ordinances of 1311, echoed the Provisions of Oxford of half a century earlier but were even more thoroughgoing. They provided that both Gaveston and Edward's chief banker, Americo dei Frescobaldi, be exiled from England. Parliaments were to be summoned at least twice a year and were empowered to endorse or reject the appointment of high administrative officers such as the chancellor and treasurer. More than that, parliaments could veto the appointments of important officials in the king's household itself — the master of the wardrobe and the keeper of the Privy Seal. Finally, and perhaps most humiliating of all, the king could declare war only with parliamentary approval; while between parliaments, he was obliged to follow the advice of a continuing royal council appointed by Parliament and dominated by Thomas of Lancaster.

In 1311, as in 1258, the magnates forced the monarchy to accept a comprehensive series of limitations on royal power. And as before, the king soon disavowed his concessions, sparking a baronial uprising. Within a year, Edward II brought Gaveston back from his Irish exile, declaring that he would never hereafter be parted from him. The exasperated magnates responded by taking up arms, seizing the royal favorite, and murdering him. With Gaveston's execution, Edward II's reign entered a new phase of brutality and revenge.

Gaveston's murder cost the insurgents much support. Several magnates, restive anyway under Thomas of Lancaster's self-seeking leadership, felt that opposition to the king had grown too extreme. The kingdom was on the verge of civil war when, in 1313, king and magnates arranged a reconciliation. For the moment, the Ordinances of 1311 dropped from view, as the king and his great men turned their attention at last to the disasters occurring along their northern border with Scotland. Lancaster, however, refused to participate in the planned campaign against the Scots, fearing that the king would use the opportunity to take vengeance upon him for the murder of Gaveston. He was therefore not present when, at Bannockburn in 1314, an overwhelming victory by Robert Bruce and his Scottish army over the largest army of Edward II's reign shattered the entire northern policy of the first two Edwards.

This spectacular Scottish triumph was so complete as to doom for a generation all further English efforts to subdue the northern kingdom. In the years that followed, the Scots would take the offensive against England, sometimes with the support of dissident English nobles, until Edward II finally arranged a truce with them in 1323. A formal treaty of peace followed in 1328. Scotland had regained its independence, and Robert Bruce ruled his kingdom unchallenged. In England, however, enthusiasm for renewing the Scottish war would remain high, and under Edward III the war would begin again. For so long as Edward II ruled over them, however, the English nobility saw little hope of reversing the military verdict rendered against them at Bannockburn.

Meanwhile, the king continued to quarrel with his magnates and his parliaments. Thomas of Lancaster returned to power in the wake of the Bannockburn disaster. In a parliament held in the autumn of 1314, he succeeded in reestablishing the Ordinances of 1311. He remained the dominant figure in the king's government until 1317. But he never won Edward's confidence, nor indeed did he even try. Not only Edward II but many of his magnates as well were becoming alarmed at Lancaster's immense authority. In 1317, the personal armies of the earls of Lancaster and Surrey clashed openly. By 1318, Lancaster's influence was waning, as a new and more conciliatory group of earls rose to power at court. These men were suspicious of Lancaster and less interested than he in forcing royal government into the rigid framework of the ordinances. This group included a youthful nobleman of intelligence and ruthless ambition, Hugh Despenser the Younger, who soared to power much as Gaveston had done at the beginning of Edward II's reign, and with much the same results.

Despenser was the son and namesake of a royal official who had rendered good service to Edward I. Hugh Despenser the Elder continued to serve the monarchy under Edward II, and father and son both profited prodigiously from the royal favor. Being a well-born Englishman, the

Detail of the Tomb Effigy of Edward II, Gloucester Cathedral   *(A. F. Kersting)*

Younger Despenser could not be denounced as an upstart foreigner like Gaveston. But he was even more ambitious, and ultimately more danger-ous to the rest of the English nobility. With Edward II's ardent backing, he and his father acquired vast landed wealth through advantageous mar-riages, outright extortion, and the shameless manipulation of the legal system. By 1321, he had ascended to a position of overwhelming author-ity at the royal court. It was now the Younger Despenser, rather than Ed-ward II or his other magnates, who ran the government.

Once again, the magnates formed a coalition against the king and his favorite, led by notables such as Thomas of Lancaster and the Morti-mers — a family of marcher lords who resented Despenser's brazen pol-icy of collecting lordships for himself in the Welsh marches. The struggle between king and insurgent nobles now broke into open warfare, but at the crucial battle of Boroughbridge in March 1322, Thomas of Lancaster's forces were routed by a royal army. The earl surrendered and was sum-marily tried and condemned for treason. His captors mounted him on a skinny white nag, placed a ragged old hat on his head, led him through a jeering crowd that pelted him with snowballs, and had him beheaded. This was a shocking development: no English earl had been executed for treason since Waltheof in 1075. But with Thomas of Lancaster's humiliating death, the king and the Younger Despenser had won unchallenged dominion over the kingdom. The result was a reign of terror for the English nobility.

In the aftermath of Boroughbridge, Edward and Despenser, disregarding law and custom, executed their major opponents right and left, confiscated their lands, and imprisoned their kinfolk, including their children and elderly relations. These acts of royal tyranny spawned an era of violence and plundering, and a breakdown of law and order unparalleled since the reign of King Stephen.[8] The memory of this period would last until the end of the fourteenth century and would haunt the reign of King Richard II, whose policies came increasingly to resemble those of Edward II.

The years following the king's military triumph at Boroughbridge, 1322–1326, were marked by peace abroad and terror at home. Wales had been won, Scotland lost, and Gascony remained at peace. The dramatic reduction in military and diplomatic expenses, combined with a heavy influx of cash from frightened, browbeaten subjects, replenished the royal treasury and made Edward II the wealthiest English monarch in living memory. Edward I had left his son a debt of some £200,000, whereas Edward II, at the close of his reign in 1327, had a surplus of over £60,000 — nearly a year's income in reserve. There had been nothing like it since Henry I, nearly two centuries earlier in 1135, had left nearly £100,000 to his luckless successor, Stephen. But Edward II, while enriching himself and his few friends, had earned the passionate hatred of his subjects.

With Thomas of Lancaster dead, the Younger Despenser ruled imperiously over king and kingdom, amassing estates and enemies. But his power and success made him overconfident — as so often happens with successful people — and he carelessly allowed a new coalition to develop that would ultimately prove fatal to his ambitions. The Welsh marcher lord Roger Mortimer, imprisoned during the crackdown after Boroughbridge, escaped from the Tower of London in 1323 and took refuge in France. Two years later, the long-neglected Queen Isabella was sent across the Channel to negotiate with her brother, King Charles IV, on the long-standing Anglo-French dispute over Gascony. Once in France, Isabella broke with her husband and became the mistress of Roger Mortimer. In 1326, Mortimer and Isabella returned to England with an army. With them came the young Prince Edward, son of Edward II and Isabella, and heir to the throne.

Mortimer and Isabella at once became the center of a general uprising of English magnates against the hated Despenser and the tyrannical

---

[8]Scott L. Waugh, *England in the Reign of Edward III* (Cambridge, 1991), has a particularly good description of Despenser's land grabbing during these years and of the lawlessness to which it gave rise.

Queen Isabella Returning from France to Dethrone Her Husband, Edward II
From a fourteenth-century manuscript. *(Bibliothèque Nationale, Paris)*

Edward. Late in 1326, the rebels captured and imprisoned the king and executed Despenser after first chopping off his genitals and burning them before his eyes. In January 1327, a parliament formally deposed King Edward in favor of his fourteen-year-old heir, Edward III. To avoid any possibility of a royal comeback, Edward II's enemies forced him to abdicate, imprisoned him in Berkeley Castle, and apparently had him murdered. About a decade later, a letter from a papal notary to Edward III related a beguiling but unlikely tale of Edward II escaping from the castle just ahead of his would-be killers. On his way out, he is said to have murdered a porter, whose body was alleged by the bumbling assassins to be that of the king. Afterwards, Edward supposedly wandered in disguise through England, Ireland, and the Continent, paying a secret visit to the pope in Avignon and ending his days in an Italian hermitage.

The deposition of a king, unprecedented in English history, was an awesome event. Although a parliament was the formal instrument of the deposition, the real agents of Edward II's downfall were Mortimer and Isabella, aided by the unwillingness of the English people to fight on his behalf. Edward II was defeated and imprisoned by means of armed rebellion. The parliament of 1327 was controlled by the insurgents and ratified their wishes. Nevertheless, the fact that the formalities of the royal deposition were carried out in a parliament is itself significant. It was through parliaments that the community of the realm spoke, and in 1327 the community gave its legal sanction to what otherwise would have been an act of high treason. Never before had it been asserted so straightfor-

The Execution of Hugh Despenser the Younger at Hereford in 1326 *(Bibliothèque Nationale, Paris)*

wardly that royal authority was based on the assent of the community. The English had at last found a constitutional means of justifying the removal of a king who refused to abide by customary laws and the community's will: the representatives of the English community, acting in Parliament, could cast him from the throne. No subsequent king of England could safely ignore or forget that lesson.

Throughout the Middle Ages, the monarchy remained the central force in English politics. For that very reason, the reign of a king like Edward II robbed the kingdom of its political balance and brought on a state of civil turmoil. Despite the ever-growing importance of English political and administrative institutions, the strength and wisdom of the monarch remained essential to the well-being of the realm. Kingship was simply too important in England for the great men of the country to allow it to remain in the hands of a dangerous incompetent like Edward II. This did not make them revolutionaries; rather, it made them hanker for a return to the traditional understandings between a king and his people. Under Edward III, this is what they would get.

The immediate effect of the revolution of 1327, however, was to renew the bitterness and disaffection from which England had suffered so long. Although Edward III inherited the kingdom, he was still too young to rule. Actual power passed to Mortimer and Isabella, who dominated the regency government. Mortimer proceeded to enrich himself handsomely from the lands of Edward II's defeated associates, while the baronial faction that had supported Mortimer's deposition of Edward II dissolved into internal bickering. The new government's 1328 treaty of peace with the Scots was widely unpopular, and the sexual relationship between Mortimer and Queen Isabella was a national scandal. The two were well on their way to making as many enemies as Despenser when, in 1330, they were suddenly brought to ruin by a court conspiracy led by the young king himself. Mortimer was seized in his room in Nottingham Castle by Edward III's followers, tried by a parliament, and hanged. Isabella was permitted a generous allowance but was deprived of power. Seventeen-year-old King Edward III, having thus emphatically proclaimed his coming of age, now turned to the essential work of healing England's divisions by restoring vigorous royal leadership to his troubled kingdom.

CHAPTER 11

Edward III and the Hundred Years' War

Like Richard the Lion-Hearted, Edward III was a warrior-king.[1] Chivalrous and magnanimous, he was immensely popular — except during a brief stand-off with some dissident barons in 1341 and in his final, senile years. Some historians have dismissed him as a grandiose fool, addicted to extravagance, dissipation, ostentatious display, and spectacular but ultimately fruitless military campaigning. Yet he succeeded to a remarkable degree in maintaining the loyalty of his magnates and his six sons. Earlier kings of England — William I and Henry II in particular — had been tormented by the revolts of ambitious offspring. But the sons of Edward III respected and supported him, and at no time in his entire fifty-year reign did his barons raise the standard of rebellion.

One key to Edward's success was his cheerful, amiable disposition. As one contemporary observed, he was "not accustomed to be sad," and he never pushed his royal prerogatives to the point of openly challenging the laws and customs of the realm. More important was his taste for chivalry and his triumphant military campaigns — which some historians have too quickly dismissed. The magnates held pageantry and military victories in the highest regard, and Edward III's theatrical behavior and soldierly exploits won him the admiring loyalty of his barons and the obedience of his subjects. To contemporaries he was "our comely king," "the famous and fortunate warrior," under whom "the realm of England

---

[1]There are two excellent recent biographies of Edward III: W. M. Ormrod, *The Reign of Edward III: Crown and Political Society in England, 1327–1377* (New Haven, 1990), and Scott L. Waugh, *England in the Reign of Edward III* (Cambridge, 1991). An excellent older survey of the Hundred Years' War is Edouard Perroy, *The Hundred Years War*, trans. W. B. Wells (London, 1951). See, more recently, Christopher Allmand, *The Hundred Years War: England and France at War, c. 1300–c. 1450* (Cambridge, 1988). See also Richard Barber, *Edward, Prince of Wales and Aquitaine: A Biography of the Black Prince* (New York, 1978), and Juliet Vale, *Edward III and Chivalry: Chivalric Society and Its Context, 1270–1350* (Woodbridge, Suffolk, 1982). On Edward's parliaments, see Sir Goronwy Edwards, *The Second Century of the English Parliament* (Oxford, 1979); G. L. Harriss, *King, Parliament and Public Finance in Medieval England to 1369* (Oxford, 1975); and George Holmes, *The Good Parliament* (Oxford, 1975).

has been nobly improved, honored, and enriched to a degree never seen in the time of any other king." His victories abroad kindled a glow of national pride by creating an international reputation for English military prowess: "When the noble Edward first gained England in his youth," a French writer observed, "nobody thought much of the English, nobody spoke of their prowess or courage. . . . Now, in the time of the noble Edward, who has often put them to the test, they are the finest and most daring warriors known to man."[2]

The Reign of Edward III (1327–1377)

Reversing the political equation of Edward II's final years, Edward III's reign was characterized by peace at home and war abroad. Between 1333 and 1336, the king led a series of successful, though brutal and inconclusive, expeditions into Scotland. Later, in 1346, the English won a decisive victory over the Scots at the battle of Neville's Cross, taking King David II of Scotland into captivity and devastating the Scottish countryside. But Edward III directed his chief military efforts against France, and it was there that he won his greatest renown.

Edward's French campaigns mark the opening phase of a protracted military struggle known as the Hundred Years' War. The name is inappropriate for several reasons. For one thing, the "war" lasted not for 100 years but for 115 — from 1338 to 1453. For another, the campaigns waged during this time span were separated by prolonged truces, some of them lasting a number of years. One might, in fact, reasonably regard the Hundred Years' War as a series of much shorter wars. Moreover, as should be obvious by now, the conflict between the kings of England and France began not in 1338 but shortly after 1066. Almost every English king since the Norman Conquest had campaigned against the French at one time or another, and the Hundred Years' War was in many respects a continuation of these earlier struggles. Nevertheless, the term has been hallowed by custom and will be used here for the sake of convenience.

One theme that links the various campaigns of the Hundred Years' War and separates them from previous Anglo-French conflicts is the English monarchy's claim to the French throne. When Charles IV, the last of the Capetian kings, died childless in 1328, Edward III became a serious contender for the French royal succession through his mother Isabella, Charles's sister. But the French, purporting to be guided by an "ancient" (and most convenient) custom — that the royal succession could not pass down through the female line — gave the crown to the Frenchman Philip VI (1328–1350), a first cousin of Charles IV and founder of the long-lived Valois dynasty. Edward did not at first dispute this decision, but later,

---

[2]Jean le Beau, *Chroniques,* I, 155–156, quoted in May McKisack, *The Fourteenth Century, 1307–1399* (Oxford, 1959), p. 150.

Edward III's Tomb Monument in St. Stephen's Chapel, Westminster
(Mansell/Time)

when other matters prompted him to take up arms against the French, he revived his claim and used it to justify his invasions. Subsequent kings of England would also claim the throne of France, and the Valois succession was not finally recognized in England until after the war's end in 1453.

In the middle and later 1330s Anglo-French relations were severely strained by several other disputes as well. The two kingdoms were at odds over Flanders, which France had long endeavored to control but which England prized as a market for its wool. Moreover, Edward III objected strongly to the French policy of supporting the Scots in their warfare with England. Finally, the old dispute over the remaining English holdings in southern France continued to simmer. It boiled over in 1337 when Philip VI, after having canceled his plans for a large-scale Crusade to the Holy Land, ordered the confiscation of Gascony. Underlying these issues was the fact that the young king Edward and the chivalrous knights and nobles he had gathered around him hungered for the glory and the booty arising from military adventure. Encouraged by an astute campaign of royal propaganda, they became increasingly enthusiastic about the opportunity of winning fame and fortune by taking up arms against the French.

So it was that in 1338, after elaborate preparations, Edward III led a glittering and hopeful army southward across the English Channel. His plan was to invade France through the Low Countries — to attack on a huge scale not only with his own soldiers but with those of his continental allies as well. For Edward III, like John and Edward I before him, had forged a system of alliances with important princes in the Netherlands and Germany. Such a system required staggeringly heavy expenditures for subsidies and bribes to these allies, imposing a considerable strain on English resources. Edward attempted to finance his soldiers and diplomats by means of heavy taxes on wool and by various complex but ineffective schemes to create artificial wool shortages and thereby raise prices and customs revenues. But Edward found that his allies' thirst for money was unquenchable and that, when the time came for action, they demanded more than he could pay them. Accordingly, the campaigning between 1338 and 1340 accomplished little except to drive the English monarchy into debt. Edward salvaged one military triumph from the early phase of the war when in 1340 his fleet annihilated a French armada at the battle of Sluys, off the Flemish coast. The victory at Sluys enabled the English to control the Channel for the next several years. But Edward's initial land campaigns were both frustrating and expensive.

During the 1340s and afterward, Edward altered his military strategy. Concluding that an alliance system was both inefficient and much too costly, he undertook to invade France with English armies that were lightly supplied but prepared to forage off the land. The new policy proved its worth in 1342, when a series of English raids succeeded in establishing English control over Brittany. Again in 1345 Edward sent armies into France — one to Brittany, another to Gascony. In 1346 the king himself crossed the Channel with an army of ten thousand men — immense by the standards of the age. Campaigning in Normandy, he plundered the important town of Caen and from there led his force first southeastward toward Paris, then northward into Ponthieu. At Crécy, a few miles from the Channel, he encountered the French royal army, and the two forces clashed in the first great land battle of the Hundred Years' War (see the map on the facing page).

The battle of Crécy, fought on August 26, 1346, ended in an overwhelming victory for Edward III. It was, indeed, the most stunning military triumph of his career. Edward's longbowmen decimated the mounted French nobles and thereby crippled their military capability for

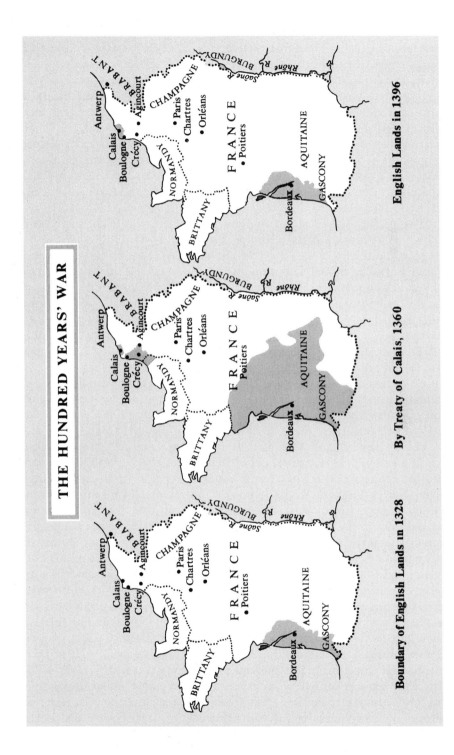

THE HUNDRED YEARS' WAR

Boundary of English Lands in 1328

By Treaty of Calais, 1360

English Lands in 1396

years to come. The triumph enabled Edward, a year later, to take the key Channel port of Calais, which would remain in English hands for the next two centuries. The successful campaign of 1346–1347 cemented Edward's popularity at home and brought him European-wide prestige.

A decade after Crécy the English, again depending heavily on their longbowmen, won another major victory over the French at Poitiers. Edward III was not present at the battle; his eldest son, Edward the "Black Prince," led the English army. Although badly outnumbered, the English put the French to rout, captured their king, John the Good, and returned to England with the royal prisoner. English arms had triumphed dramatically once again, and the Black Prince won acclaim as "the most valiant prince that ever lived in this world, throughout its length and breadth, since the days of Julius Caesar or Arthur."

The battles of Crécy and Poitiers were separated by the cataclysmic arrival of the Black Death in Europe. Shattered by two military disasters, the plague, the loss of its king, and the harrying of mercenary companies, France in the later 1350s lay prostrate. In 1358 the French monarchy and aristocracy suppressed a large-scale rebellion of peasants only after a savage struggle, and in 1359 the Black Prince led his army across France from the Channel to Burgundy virtually unopposed. At length, in 1360, the two kingdoms concluded a truce on terms exceedingly favorable to the English. Edward III temporarily dropped his claim to the French throne but in return acquired vast territories in southern France for which he would no longer owe homage to the French crown. And the French ransomed King John the Good for the staggering sum of half a million pounds, five times the ransom of Richard the Lion-Hearted in the late twelfth century.

Yet all that the English had won in these French campaigns they would lose over the next two decades. This reversal in military fortunes resulted from a revival of French royal authority, ineffective political leadership in England, and the dogged, unrelenting pressure of French armies against the overextended English positions. England prospered during most of the 1360s; Edward III basked in the prestige of his earlier victories, and the royal treasury drew rich nourishment from French ransom payments. But as the 1360s drew to a close, the balance of quality in French and English leadership tipped in France's favor. Edward III's high living — primarily drinking and chasing women — had driven him into an early dotage; he became senile in his late fifties and passed his later years as a tool of unscrupulous courtiers and of his mistress at the time, Alice Perrers. His eldest son, the Black Prince, fell victim to a lingering illness. On the French side, the inept King John died in 1364, leaving the kingdom to his intelligent and energetic son, Charles V (1364–1380). King Charles was served by an astute military commander, Bertrand du Guesclin, reputed to be the ugliest man in France and the best general in Europe. Charles V and du Guesclin adopted a military policy of relentless harassment. They avoided major battles but won many skirmishes. From

1369 on, England's French possessions dissolved steadily until, at Edward III's death in 1377, the English held only Calais, Cherbourg, a little territory around Bordeaux, and a few Breton harbors. Two generations would pass before England, under the bold leadership of Henry V, made any serious attempt to recover its losses and resume its quest for the throne of France.

Parliament in the Fourteenth Century

Against the backdrop of foreign military campaigning that characterized much of the fourteenth century, Parliament developed significantly. Huge military expenditures forced the monarchy to depend increasingly on extraordinary taxation, and the revenues that the kings so desperately needed could be obtained only by parliamentary consent. Hence, the parliaments of the fourteenth century were in an ideal bargaining position. The magnates, sharing Edward III's chivalric tastes, generally supported his French wars and were not inclined to be stingy in backing them financially. But fourteenth-century parliaments included classes other than the nobility, and although the townspeople and gentry also supported Edward's wars, hard bargaining over subsidies ensured that it was they who gained the most politically from the king's dependence on parliamentary grants.

As the fourteenth century dawned, Parliament remained ill-defined in membership and function. But by the close of the century it had assumed something of its modern form. It had split into Lords and Commons, and the Commons had acquired a crucial role in taxation and legislation. By 1399 the parliamentary tradition had become etched indelibly into the English political system.

The fourteenth century, therefore, was a crucial epoch in the development of Parliament and, more specifically, in the rise of the Commons. By the time of Edward I's death, the summoning of representatives of townspeople and gentry was becoming common practice, and although they were present at only three of the first seven parliaments of Edward II, they attended all but two of the parliaments between 1310 and 1327. They became a normal component of Edward III's parliaments and were invariably present from the mid-fourteenth century onward.

Just when representatives of town and shire were becoming an integral part of Parliament, the two groups were also coalescing into a single political body. Gradually they came to realize that they shared many interests. The shire knights remained more assertive than the burghers in fourteenth-century parliaments. But the economic resources of the urban elites, relative to those of other classes, expanded throughout this period, and both gentry and townspeople discovered that they could accomplish more by cooperating than by defending their interests alone. Frequent intermarriages between members of the two classes cemented their community of interest. Before the fourteenth century was half over they had fused politically into a single parliamentary group: the Commons.

This process of fusion began under Edward II and reached its completion under Edward III. Representatives of town and shire may have met together in 1332, and they unquestionably did so in 1339 to deliberate jointly over a royal grant. They were described in the rolls of Parliament at that time as "men of the Commons." Thereafter, joint meetings became customary, and the Commons took its place as a normal element in the government of England.

Because Commons developed as a separate parliamentary group, the members of Parliament who were not included in the Commons became, in effect, a separate group themselves. These men — the great magnates and prelates of the realm — evolved into a distinct body known as the House of Lords. The term *house of lords* does not actually appear in documents until the sixteenth century, but the institution itself was in existence by the mid-fourteenth.

In the thirteenth century many notables had regarded attendance in parliaments as a burden, but as the fourteenth century progressed they began to consider it a privilege. Eligibility for attendance in parliaments was now much more rigorously defined than before. Under Edward II there evolved a fixed list of barons who alone and invariably received parliamentary summonses. This select group came to be known as the peerage. And although the term *peer* literally means "social equal," the peers were in fact, to paraphrase George Orwell, more equal than anyone else in the realm. Fourteenth-century barons who were eligible for a parliamentary summons fell into two groups: first, the greatest magnates and prelates, who received individual summonses to Parliament; and second, lesser lords, whose tenures were regarded by custom as "baronial" rather than merely "knightly" and who were called by a general parliamentary summons (but often failed to attend). The right of a lord to attend Parliament became hereditary and was passed down, like a great baronial estate, from father to eldest son. Thus, the peerage became a permanent and clearly defined group at the apex of the social order.

The process of selecting particular individuals to represent their shires or towns in Commons was more fluid and complex, and many details of the process are hidden from us. Normally, the shire representatives were chosen at a meeting of the shire court, which was usually attended only by the more substantial men of the district. The sheriff was the chief figure at these meetings and was sometimes able to manipulate the elections in his own favor or on behalf of the monarchy. Indeed, the electoral procedures were frequently so ill defined that the sheriff could simply name his own slate of representatives. Similarly, a powerful local magnate might overawe the court with his private army of retainers and secure the election of his own henchmen. In the later fourteenth century, John of Gaunt exerted virtually absolute control over the selection of shire knights from his vast palatinate of Lancaster, and the great mag-

The Payment of Tithes, Fifteenth Century   In addition to the taxes they paid to the crown, English men and women also owed a tenth of their produce or revenues (a tithe) to the Church. *(E. T. Archive)*

nates of Yorkshire appear to have dominated the elections of Commons representatives from their county. Such manipulation increased sharply in the fifteenth century, when the local power of the great lords reached its height. But manipulation of county elections by sheriffs or magnates, although widespread, was by no means universal. Left to themselves, the county courts were apt to elect knights or squires of wealth and substance. The same was true of the towns, where electoral arrangements were so varied as to defy generalization. Whatever the details, the Commons representatives were generally pillars of their community (unless they were paid royal or baronial agents), and one will look in vain in the fourteenth-century Commons for lower-class protest or revolutionary ferment.

Nevertheless, the emergence of Commons and the progressive extension of its power is a matter of immense significance in the development of the unwritten English "constitution." In the crisis of 1297 the royal government of Edward I had conceded that all uncustomary taxes must be approved by the community of the realm. It was assumed by then that the community was embodied in parliaments. Under Edward III this power to approve taxes passed gradually into the hands of Commons. It was to be the key to all of that body's future power, and the members of

Commons seem to have understood this. When they approved a particular grant, they would often demand and receive greater control over grants in general. Commons was in a strong position, for the increasingly affluent classes that it represented were supplying the monarchy with much of its tax revenues. Accordingly, by the end of the fourteenth century the Commons was coming to exercise the exclusive right to originate parliamentary taxation. In 1395 a parliamentary grant was made "by the Commons with the advice and assent of the Lords." This was the first time these exact words were used, but they became the standard formula in years thereafter.

Thus, by 1399 the approval of Parliament, more specifically the Commons, was required for all extraordinary taxes, direct or indirect, even tolls and customs from merchants. Parliament even supervised and audited tax revenues and was beginning to specify the uses to which particular taxes could be put. Profiting from the military dangers and general unrest of Richard II's reign (1377–1399), Parliament used its fiscal power to establish an ever-greater control over government policies. In 1377 it insisted on overseeing the use to which its grant was put and succeeded in obtaining the appointment of two London merchants as treasurers of war. And in 1382 the parliamentary representatives imposed their own foreign policy on the royal government by insisting on a military campaign in Flanders. The right to grant or refuse taxes, they were discovering, was an effective avenue to political power.

The relationship between taxation and power is nowhere better illustrated than in the gradual growth of Commons' role in eliciting legislation. This function, undreamed of at the close of the thirteenth century, was well established a hundred years later. Edward III's first Parliament, meeting in 1327, introduced for the first time a Commons petition — a list of grievances that Parliament expected the monarchy to consider seriously in return for the granting of taxes. Parliaments had long been accustomed to receiving and passing on to the king petitions from individuals or groups. The Commons petition differed from these earlier requests in that it dealt with matters of general interest to the community of the realm. The Commons petition of 1327 concerned such issues as the reaffirmation of Magna Carta, the soundness of English currency, and the size of cloths sold in English markets. Coming at a time of grave political crisis, it received the sympathetic attention of the royal government and gave rise to two statutes and several ordinances and decrees. More important, it set a precedent. Similar petitions were introduced in the parliaments of 1333 and 1337, and they appeared regularly from 1343 onward. Fourteenth-century parliaments used the Commons petition repeatedly as a device to put pressure on the king to grant their wishes, and as time went on it became customary for a Commons petition to give rise to royal statutes. Thus the Commons petition was a significant step in the direction of parliamentary legislation. In later years the Commons petition evolved into the Commons bill, and thus the will of the

House of Commons became the law of England. Indeed, after the mid-fourteenth century, most statutes resulted directly from Commons petitions or bills rather than from royal initiative, as in the days of Edward I. The mechanism for Commons legislation was thereby established. It remained only to refine the process.

Originally, the procedure consisted of Commons presenting a petition and voting a grant. The king would then approve the petition, and it would be translated into a statute. But if some item in the petition was offensive to the king, he might ignore it or alter its meaning. To prevent this sort of royal tampering, and to achieve complete identity between petition and statute, the Commons developed the principle of "redress before supply." Only if and when the king satisfied their petition, both in matter and spirit, would Commons make the requested grant. Redress before supply, which had become a normal procedure by the early fifteenth century, was a key factor in transforming Parliament's privilege to petition into its power to make law.

Law and Administration

The evolution of other branches of the fourteenth-century English government was less spectacular than that of Parliament. The functions of the council — now a fixed body of sworn royal councilors — became steadily more elaborate and varied. It remained the organizational core of every parliament. It supervised the entire system of royal justice and functioned, although on a diminishing scale, as a court of equity to settle cases unadaptable to the common-law courts. It counseled the king (as before), kept watch over the departments of chancery and exchequer, handled affairs of diplomacy, and enacted royal ordinances, many of which gave rise to royal statutes in Parliament. As the fourteenth century progressed, the council became increasingly an executive body, authorizing under the Privy Seal, without direct royal mandate, most of the ordinary business of state. These activities and responsibilities had by now become much too complex for direct royal supervision, and as time passed, the council operated more and more on its own initiative. By the century's close, it had achieved sufficient independence to keep separate records of its meetings.

Baronial attempts to control council and household had begun, as we have seen, under Henry III and were revived under Edward II, but never with lasting success. Edward III, a friend of the barons, normally made it a point to fill his council with nobles or men acceptable to them. This was not invariably the case, however, and on two occasions the barons in parliament sought to intervene in the make-up of the royal council and household. In 1341 Edward III submitted very briefly to a degree of parliamentary control over his officers of state. And again in his old age, the "Good Parliament" of 1376 crippled Edward's regime for a time by refusing to grant subsidies. It challenged his authority by forcing the appointment of a new royal council and dismissing from court — through the novel process of impeachment — the king's chamberlain and the king's mistress. But within months the impeachments were quashed. The crises of 1341 and 1376 proved to be isolated, momentary disturbances in a long and otherwise placid era of royal-baronial harmony.

The two departments of chancery and exchequer continued to drift further away from direct royal control. Each had acquired its own seal; both had now gone out of court and were carrying on their functions at Westminster. In the course of the fourteenth century the chancery's administrative independence declined as it came to share more and more of its authority with the household departments of wardrobe and chamber. By the end of the century, the chancery's initiative was largely limited to the automatic issuing of judicial writs, and the drafting and authenticating of royal documents already authorized elsewhere. The chancellors themselves — most of whom were churchmen as in earlier times — devoted less and less attention to supervising the chancery and its clerks and more and more to great matters of state. Throughout much of the period the chancellor was the dominant figure in the council, and as time went on he assumed the further task of presiding over a special tribunal responsible for hearing cases in equity.

Such cases, as we have seen, had traditionally been heard by the full council. But now the council's administrative burdens were growing to such a point that it could no longer serve with much effectiveness as a tribunal. The chancellor, as chief officer in the council, was particularly well equipped to take equity cases under his own jurisdiction. He was likely to be an expert jurist, and his responsibilities included the channeling of pleas into the appropriate common-law courts — King's Bench, Common Pleas, or Exchequer. He was therefore in a strategic position to identify cases that were appropriate to none of these courts — cases requiring special, equitable treatment in a court unhampered by the hardening rules and procedures of the common law. Such a court developed in the course of the fourteenth century — a group of learned justices and lawyers selected by the chancellor to aid him in judging cases. Not until later did this tribunal disentangle itself completely from the council to become the official Court of Chancery. But by the end of Edward III's reign it was already, for all practical purposes, functioning on its own and draining off most of the pleas formerly heard by the council. Its development illustrates once again the growing professionalization and departmentalization of the royal government, and the steady drift of its components farther and farther away from direct royal supervision.

Meanwhile, the judicial structure evolved slowly along the general lines established by Edward I. The lords in Parliament continued to function as the highest tribunal. The common-law courts grew increasingly specialized — and increasingly jealous of one another. The court of King's Bench was now primarily responsible for criminal cases, Common Pleas for civil cases, and the Exchequer for royal revenue cases. The role of the itinerant justices had been declining since the 1290s, as the volume of local judicial business became greater than the eyres could handle, and as the traveling justices grew increasingly unpopular. Edward III abolished the eyres altogether in 1361, at Commons' insistence, and thereafter the king's justice in the countryside was handled by a new group of officials — usually drawn from the local gentry — known as justices of the peace. The rise of these new officers meant that the gentry had, in effect, won control of the local courts.

Justices of the peace would remain dominant in the administrative and judicial organization of the counties for centuries to come. The office evolved out of Edward I's keepers of the peace, who exercised police functions under the authority of the sheriff. A statute of 1330 gave them the responsibility to indict criminals as well as apprehend them, and this new judicial function was broadened greatly when a statute of 1360 empowered the keepers of the peace to try felons and trespassers. In effect, the statute of 1360 transformed the keepers of the peace into justices of the peace. Their judicial functions were further elaborated in 1362, when they were directed to hold courts four times a year. These "quarter sessions" gave the justices of the peace preeminence in legal affairs over all other county officials, including sheriffs. By the century's close, their jurisdictional supremacy had ripened into a general supervision of the county administration, and the quarter sessions had virtually superseded the older shire courts. By then the justices had also assumed the obligation of supervising military recruitment within their counties. In short, justices of the peace had replaced sheriffs as the primary links between crown and shire.

Edward III and the Decline of Royal Authority

The Hundred Years' War and concurrent warfare against the Scots placed a tremendous burden on the royal administration. The staggering expenses of foreign campaigns left Edward III even more dependent on parliamentary grants than his predecessors had been, and he won the financial backing of the community only by acceding to most of its demands. He soothed Parliament by consulting with it on important matters of policy and appointing no high-handed royal ministers of the sort that Parliament found offensive. His pliancy contributed much, as we have seen, to the growth of the power of Commons. And by transferring local judicial responsibility to the justices of the peace, he speeded the decline of royal authority in the countryside. In the absence of justices from the royal court, magnates could often dominate law and administration in their regions, bribing the local justices of the peace or intimidating them with private armies.

Overall, Edward III was splendidly successful in restoring the prestige of the crown after the disasters of his father's reign and in working harmoniously with his subjects — but at a cost. All was well as long as

England remained under the spell of a victorious, politically adroit king. But Edward's less pliant and less adept successors would quickly discover that they could no longer rule successfully without the skills of political management that Edward III had possessed. The Commons, through their control of taxation, could hamstring royal policies with which they disagreed. And in the next century, the magnates' unprecedented power in the shires would drive England toward political chaos. Not until the coming of the Tudors would the crown regain the supremacy over the nobility that it had enjoyed in the twelfth and thirteenth centuries. And never again could it safely ignore the Commons.

C H A P T E R   1 2

Death, Disorder, and Creative Flowering

During the second half of the fourteenth century, England's foreign struggles and constitutional transformations unfolded against a background of plague, cultural change, and growing social upheaval. The Black Death of 1348–1349 and its periodic recurrences served as the somber backdrop to a deepening economic crisis, a bitter popular insurrection in 1381 known as the "Peasants' Revolt," mounting social tensions, and a growing restlessness toward the institutional Church, and especially the papacy. These problems cannot be bracketed within an arbitrary date range such as historians too often impose on them. They continued to characterize English society well after 1399, the terminal point of this book, and many of them are discussed more fully in the next volume of this series.

For all its difficulties, however, the later fourteenth century was also one of the most brilliantly creative periods in English history. For the first time since the Norman Conquest, English re-emerged as the primary language of high culture in England. Geoffrey Chaucer and William Langland, two of the greatest poets in the English language, produced masterpieces of vernacular literature during these years, each reflecting, in very different ways, the tensions and contradictions of their period. Architectural developments were equally rapid, not only in the great cathedrals, but also in the numerous parish churches that were lavishly rebuilt in stone and glass from the late fourteenth century on. The English philosophers William of Ockham and John Wycliffe produced the most influential logical works of the fourteenth century. English scientists performed ground-breaking studies of optics. And English mystics pioneered a style of lay piety that would have repercussions across all of Europe.

Behind the creativity of this period lay the growing wealth of the English people. The massive population reduction caused by the Black Death led to a period of extraordinary prosperity for the English peasantry. This prosperity did not come as quickly as many small farmers, artisans, and urban wage-earners hoped. The frustrations created by this delay, combined with heavy taxation to support a failing war in France, led to the 1381 rebellion. Thereafter, however, the taxation pressure eased. During the fifteenth century, a substantially smaller percentage of peasant incomes went to the government in taxation than had been the case a century before.[1] Peasants were wealthier, and their taxes lower, than at any time since the tenth-century. These developments were just beginning as the fourteenth century ended, and they were purchased at the price of enormous misery. But they laid the foundations upon which the prosperity of fifteenth-century England would rest.

The Black Death

As the fourteenth century opened, the economic conditions that had characterized the High Middle Ages came to an end. The ever-increasing pressure of population on resources and the shift to a colder, rainier climate caused widespread hunger and malnutrition. Poor harvests and crop failures brought famine to peasants and townspeople alike. Towns suffered particularly, for they depended upon the prosperity of the surrounding countryside not only for food, but also to provide a market for their goods. The population of England may already have been leveling off when a series of terrible floods and famines struck the country between 1315 and 1317, followed by an equally devastating cattle disease in 1319–1321 and a disastrous crop failure in 1321. Together, these catastrophes provoked a kingdomwide agrarian crisis. Agricultural production rebounded during the 1330s, but by the 1340s land was again going out of cultivation. All this pales, however, by comparison with the consequences of the plague. The Black Death reached Europe at the end of 1347 and began to spread rapidly during the winter of 1347–1348. In England, it struck hardest in 1349, when it carried off at least a quarter of the population of the country. Further outbreaks occurred during the 1360s and 1370s. By the end of the century, the total population of England had been reduced by approximately 40 percent from its pre-plague levels.

There is much dispute among scholars over the demographic effects of the various factors that affected English agriculture before the Black Death: weather, soil exhaustion, sheep and cattle disease, the extension of cultivation into marginal districts, and the overpopulation of fertile lands. Kingdomwide population figures for the first half of the fourteenth century do not exist. Studies of particular agrarian communities provide more exact information, but it is not clear how far such case studies reflect general trends. A particularly rigorous analysis of the West

---

[1]W. M. Ormrod, *Political Life in Medieval England, 1300–1450* (New York, 1995), p. 132. This splendid study is the best short account of its subject.

Midlands parish of Halesowen, near Birmingham, shows the population growing through the late thirteenth and early fourteenth centuries, until the calamities of 1317–1321 reduced it by some 15 percent. Growth resumed during the 1320s, reaching a maximum in the late 1340s, but then the Black Death reduced the number of inhabitants of Halesowen by nearly half.[2] The crisis of 1315–1322 and the Black Death probably affected vast areas of England in much the same way that they affected Halesowen. Yet it remains uncertain whether England's entire population grew slowly, declined slowly, or held even during the half-century before 1348.[3] On the appalling demographic impact of the Black Death, however, there is no disagreement. England's population, which in the year 1300 probably numbered around five million people, was reduced by 1400 to no more than three million.

The Black Death traveled in three forms. Bubonic plague, the most common form, was carried by black rats and by the fleas that rode on their backs. To contract bubonic plague, one had to be bitten either by an infected rat or by an infected flea. Bubonic plague attacked the lymphatic system, producing huge swellings ("buboes") in the lymph nodes, especially in the groin, armpits, and neck. Although excruciatingly painful, bubonic plague was not directly infectious. Mortality rates in the late nineteenth century (when doctors were able to observe it firsthand, but still could not cure it) were between 60 percent and 90 percent, with death coming in four to seven days.

Pneumonic plague, by contrast, was highly contagious. It resulted when a bubonic plague sufferer also had (or developed) pneumonia, and the plague bacillus invaded the pneumococcus cells in the lungs. Water droplets sprayed from the lungs by coughing, sneezing, or even breathing could thus communicate the plague bacillus to another person. This form of the disease was nearly always fatal, and killed within two to five days. The third form, septicemic plague, was the rarest, but also the most deadly and the most terrifying. Like bubonic plague, septicemic plague was born by fleas, but instead of attacking the lymphatic system, the bacillus went directly into the victim's blood stream, producing death in a matter of hours, before buboes could even form. This is the form of plague that caused people in apparently perfect health at bedtime to be dead by morning.[4]

---

[2] See Zvi Razi, *Life, Marriage and Death in a Medieval Parish: Economy, Society and Demography in Halesowen, 1270–1400* (New York, 1980).

[3] Barbara Harvey's introductory essay in *Before the Black Death: Studies in the "Crisis" of the Early Fourteenth Century*, ed. B. M. S. Campbell (Manchester, 1991) is the best account of current thinking on the demographic history of the period between 1270 and 1349.

[4] Philip Ziegler, *The Black Death* (New York, 1969), remains an excellent account of the plague.

Entering southern and eastern Europe during the winter of 1347–1348, the plague moved quickly into Germany and France. One French chronicler described it as causing

> so great a mortality of people of both sexes . . . that it was scarcely possible to bury them. They were only ill for two or three days and died suddenly, their bodies almost sound. And he who was in good health one day was dead and buried the next. They had swellings in the armpits and groin, and the appearance of these swellings was an unmistakable sign of death. . . . In many towns, great and small, the priests were terrified and fled, but some monks and friars, being braver, administered the sacraments. Soon, in many places, of every twenty inhabitants only two remained alive. The mortality was so great at the hospital in Paris that for a long time more than 500 bodies were carried off on wagons each day, to be buried at the cemetery of the Holy Innocents. And the holy sisters of the hospital, fearless of death, carried out their task to the end with the most perfect gentleness and humility. These sisters were all wiped out by death.

In the summer of 1348, the Black Death reached England. It first broke out at the port of Melcombe Regis in Dorset, then spread through the southwestern shires. By winter, it was in London, and in the following summer it reached its peak, ravaging the heavily populated counties of central and eastern England. "So great a pestilence," wrote a Lincolnshire monk, "had never been seen, heard, or written of before this time. . . . Even the flood of Noah's days had not, it was thought, swept away so great a multitude." The fourteenth-century historian Henry Knighton described it in these words:

A Physician and His Assistants Provide Care for a Plague Victim   *(The Granger Collection)*

In Leicester, in the little parish of St. Leonard, more than 380 people died; in the parish of the Holy Cross more than 400; and in the parish of St. Margaret in Leicester more than 700. And so in each parish they died in great numbers. . . . And the sheep and cattle wandered about through the fields and among the crops, and there was nobody to go after them or to collect them. They perished in countless numbers everywhere, in secluded ditches and hedges, for lack of watching, since there was such a lack of serfs and servants that nobody knew what he should do. . . . Meanwhile there was such a lack of priests everywhere that many widowed churches had no divine services — no masses, matins, vespers, sacraments, or sacramentals. . . . Likewise many small villages and hamlets were completely deserted; not a single house remained in which any inhabitants were still alive. Many such hamlets will probably never again be inhabited.

Contemporary writers, suffering from shock and terror, may have exaggerated, but modern studies make it clear that the plague's toll was heavy. Some 35 percent of the population of Bristol succumbed. About 44 percent of the clergy perished in the dioceses of York and Lincoln, and nearly 50 percent in the dioceses of Exeter, Winchester, Norwich, and Ely. It has been estimated that half the English clergy may have died of plague. And yet the surviving population endured the calamity without general panic or widespread flight. Life went on, agriculture and commerce continued, and the war with France persisted.

By the end of 1349, the Black Death had run its course in England. There is evidence of unusually numerous marriages and births in the years just following, as the English endeavored to preserve family lines and repopulate the land. But in 1361–1362 the plague returned, striking especially hard at the young people born since 1349. This "children's plague" was only the first of a long series of epidemics. The plague struck again in 1369, 1374–1375, 1379, 1390, 1407, and periodically throughout the fifteenth and sixteenth centuries and far into the seventeenth. For many generations, plague was a recurring hazard, keeping the people in a state of perpetual anxiety for their lives and the lives of their families. The population of England and the Continent dropped drastically in the wake of the Black Death and appears to have continued its decline well into the fifteenth century. England's population would not recover to its pre-plague levels until the seventeenth century.

It is impossible to measure the grief brought by the plague, but one can comprehend its effects in more tangible ways — in the deserted villages, the temporary decline of the European wool market, and the severe shortage of labor. The Black Death vastly accelerated the breakdown of the high-medieval economy. Among other things, it hastened the demise of the old manorial regime. Because of rising wages brought about by the labor shortage and the declining grain market resulting from the population drop, land profits and land values plummeted. Demesne farming became increasingly profitless and gradually disappeared almost entirely. Landlords abandoned direct farming, preferring to divide their old demesne lands into individual peasant plots and to live entirely off the rents, or, in some instances, to convert their lands to sheep raising. But the nobility did not enter an economic crisis. Governmental efforts to fix wages and prices in the immediate aftermath of the plague helped to protect landlords from the worst economic consequences of the labor shortage, at least for a decade or two. During the 1350s, the profits of war in France also helped to cushion the impact of the changing economic conditions upon the nobility. The real turning point came in 1381, with the Great Revolt. Thereafter, wage and price controls were eased, and landlords largely ceased trying to enforce unpaid labor services upon their peasantry. To maintain their incomes, noblemen now looked increasingly toward the marriage market, hoping to marry themselves or their heirs to wealthy heiresses.

The effects of plunging population on the English peasantry were mixed, but many of the plague's peasant survivors profited from a more open, fluid society and from the dramatic transformation of the previous land shortage into a labor shortage. A wealthy class of yeoman farmers began to emerge, whose properties extended over sixty acres or more, and whose annual revenues averaged between £5 and £10 per year. Villeins too were able to acquire larger holdings, and as lords began to abandon the direct exploitation of their own demesne lands, villeins were less often forced to perform unpaid work services for their lords. By the end of the fifteenth century, royal courts were beginning to recognize and enforce villeins' legal rights to their customary lands. With the rise of copyhold (as such formerly customary holdings were known), serfdom in England effectively came to an end. As one historian put it, for the peasantry the economic effects of the Black Death were, in the long run, more purgative than toxic.

Political Conflict

None of these changes occurred easily. Although historians can look back and see that much good would come of them, for people at the time the sense of social and economic crisis was quite real. This sense of crisis was further heightened by the political malaise that settled around the royal court during the last decade of Edward III's reign. Edward's death brought no relief to this sense of "drift" in royal policy. When Edward finally passed from his long dotage in 1377, he was succeeded by his ten-year-old grandson, Richard II (1377–1399), son of the Black Prince, (who had died the previous year). For the next decade, England was ruled by a minority government dominated by contending baronial factions. Plague, social disorder, and inept royal leadership all contributed to the general gloom, as did the series of military humiliations that England was suffering in France. Fear that the French would invade England darkened the years between 1377 and 1380 and ended only with the death of the able French monarch, Charles V. But France had been suffering, too, and the succession of a child to the French throne in 1380 — the fitfully insane Charles VI — brought on a long era of strife centering on the rivalry of two royal uncles: the dukes of Burgundy and Orleans. Long battered by invading English armies and marauding mercenary companies, France now suffered the further torment of civil war. But England gained no immediate advantage. The duke of Burgundy managed to maintain military pressure against the English, and Richard II had no taste for large-scale campaigning in France.

Religious Ferment

The turmoil of the later fourteenth century was accompanied by an increasing alienation from the ecclesiastical hierarchy of the Church. Outcries against the wealth and spiritual shortcomings of the clergy were centuries old, but they grew more strident as plague and social upheaval created a mood of religious radicalism. At the same time, however, the loyalty of most English men and women to their parish churches was growing. During the twelfth and thirteenth centuries, the medieval Church had put tremendous effort into improving pastoral care for the laity. Problems of course remained; like any human institution, the Church can never be better than the imperfect human beings who constitute it. By the fourteenth century, however, the English parish clergy were better educated and more attentive to their pastoral duties than ever before. Pilgrimages, saints cults, and prayers for the dead all came under attack from rigorists, but for the broad mass of the English laity, the rituals and devotions of late medieval Catholicism remained deeply meaningful expressions of their religious faith. Criticisms of the papacy and of the bishops for their worldliness should not obscure the deep attachment most English men and women felt to their local churches and to their faith.[5]

The papacy's situation was perhaps the most scandalous. Early in the century, the papacy had abandoned faction-ridden Rome for Avignon, in what is today southern France. There it remained for seven decades, under the shadow of the French monarchy, devoting itself more and more to administration and to collecting its revenues with ever-greater efficiency. Although at the time Avignon was a papal city, outside the boundaries of France, in practice the French king maintained a considerable degree of diplomatic control over the Avignon popes, not least because so large a percentage of their revenues derived from the kingdom of France. For the English, at war with France during much of the fourteenth century, having to pay taxes to a pope controlled by the king of France aroused growing hostility. The situation worsened after 1378 when the Church split into two fragments — one led by a pope at Avignon

---

[5]Eamon Duffy, *The Stripping of the Altars: Traditional Religion in England, 1400–1540* (New Haven, 1992), is a thorough account.

(supported by France), the other by a pope at Rome (supported by England and much of Germany). This tragicomic schism persisted to the end of the fourteenth century and beyond, provoking mutual excommunications and charges of heresy on both sides.

Opposition to the papacy and the church hierarchy proceeded along several lines. The English Franciscan philosopher William of Ockham contended not only against the faith-reason synthesis of St. Thomas Aquinas, but also against the complacency, greed, and corruption he saw in the contemporary Church. An avowed enemy of papal authority, he argued that the Church should be governed and reformed through ecclesiastical councils, the selection of which ought to begin at the parish level. Some continental writers were expressing similar and even more radical views. The clergy, they suggested, should renounce its wealth or be deprived of it, and the pope should withdraw from politics and restrict his attention to spiritual matters.

As confidence in the established ecclesiastical order waned, however, piety at the parish level continued to deepen. In England, the later fourteenth century witnessed an upsurge of mysticism in such works as *The Revelations of Divine Love* by the hermit mystic Dame Juliana of Norwich. The medieval Church had always found room for mystics but had never been entirely comfortable with them. Mysticism involved a direct relationship between the believer and God that — although rarely questioning the sacraments or the priesthood — seemed to bypass them and diminish their importance. The Church served its members as mediator between God and humanity, but mystics claimed an immediate link with God that had the potential to undermine the authority of the hierarchical Church. In practice, however, most mystics, including Juliana of Norwich, remained faithful and devoted adherents of the Church. Juliana, for example, acted frequently as a spiritual counselor to pious laymen and laywomen such as Margery Kempe, whose spiritual autobiography is among the most remarkable works of this period.[6]

The Flowering of English Literature

The alienation of individual believers from the ecclesiastical hierarchy is illustrated in quite different ways in the writings of two towering literary figures of the late fourteenth century: William Langland and Geoffrey Chaucer. Their works mark the emergence of the English language as a dominant literary vehicle after centuries of French linguistic supremacy. During this interim, when English was primarily a *spoken* language of the lesser social orders, it evolved from the *Old English* of pre-Conquest times (virtually a foreign language to modern readers) to the more immediately comprehensible *Middle English* of Langland and Chaucer. Both these writers are very widely read and studied to this day. And both dis-

---

[6]*The Book of Margery Kempe*, ed. and trans. Barry A. Windeatt (New York, 1985).

close — each in his own manner — the growing popular hostility toward the ecclesiastical establishment of their era.

Langland (d. after 1388), unlike the mystics of his time, was a moralist, not a contemplative. Like many late-medieval critics, he loved the Church as it should be but despised it as it was. Perhaps one might more properly say that his love for the essential Church — the Body of Christ — prompted him to condemn the corrupt behavior of contemporary clergy all the more severely. Langland was neither a revolutionary nor a heretic. He revered the Church as the agent of human salvation and the vehicle of divine love. But he denounced the Franciscan and Dominican friars of his era for their greed, the theologians for their hair-splitting complexity, and the papacy for its malign influence on simple Christian believers. More than anything else, Langland condemned the avarice and arrogance of the wealthy and the selfish cruelty of those in power, whether clergy or laity. To Langland, wealth hardened people's hearts and made them uncharitable, and the Church should therefore return to a condition of apostolic poverty. In his masterpiece, *Piers Plowman*, he wrote:

> Ah, well it may be with poverty, for he may pass untroubled,
> And in peace among the pillagers if patience follow him.
> Our prince, Jesus, and his apostles chose poverty together,
> And the longer they lived the less wealth they mastered. . . .
> If possession is poison and makes imperfect orders,
> It would be well to dislodge them for the Church's profit
> And purge them of that poison before the peril is greater.

Not only the Church but all society was corrupted by wealth:

> As weeds run wild on ooze or on the dunghill,
> So riches spread upon riches give rise to all vices.
> The best wheat is bent before it ripens,
> On land overlaid with marl or the dungheap.
> And so are surely all such people.
> Overplenty feeds the pride which poverty conquers.

Langland was bitterly critical of his society, but like a Hebrew prophet he softened his protests with a strain of hope — hope for a purified humanity moved by love rather than greed.

William Langland's morose moral sensitivity contrasts sharply with the mood of his genial and worldly-wise contemporary, Geoffrey Chaucer (c. 1343–1400). Chaucer's literary genius derived in part from his ability to portray with remarkable insight the personalities and motivations of his characters. He entered into their minds, displayed them for all to see, yet was able to remain personally aloof from them. He was neither a conscious reformer nor a prophet crying out against the sins of his age but an acute observer of human character. In that role, he was able to illuminate vividly the vices and virtues of contemporary clerics. The pilgrims depicted in his *Canterbury Tales* include the Parson — a compassionate and well-intentioned village priest — and the Oxford Clerk, absorbed in his devotion to scholarship. They also include less attractive ecclesiastical

Chaucer on Horseback
This illustration is taken
from the Ellesmere manu-
script, which was nearly
contemporary with
Chaucer. *(Henry E. Hunt-
ington Library)*

types: the superficial, mannered Prioress, the Pardoner who was essentially a salesman of indulgences, the lecherous Summoner, the Monk
who was addicted to the pleasures of the hunt, and the corrupt Friar:

> Highly beloved and intimate was he
> With country folk wherever he might be,
> And worthy city women with possessions;
> For he was qualified to hear confessions,
> Or so he said, with more than priestly scope;
> He had a special license from the pope.
> Sweetly he heard his penitents at shrift
> With pleasant absolution, for a gift.[7]

Political Anticlericalism

Criticism and resentment of the contemporary Church also found forceful expression at the political level. During the later thirteenth and early

---

[7]*The Canterbury Tales,* trans. Nevill Coghill (Baltimore, 1952). Langland's *Piers Plowman*
is rendered into modern English by, among others, J. F. Goodridge (Baltimore, 1959).

fourteenth centuries, the papacy had considerably expanded its right of "provision" — to directly appoint clerics to Church offices at all levels, from parish and canonry to archdiocese, bypassing the rights of local electors and officials to nominate and select appropriate candidates. The right of papal provision — which reflected the growing tendency toward ecclesiastical centralization — gave the papacy the power to appoint a large number of clergy in fourteenth-century England, some of whom were foreigners interested solely in the revenues such offices could provide. Resentful of such control being exercised over the English Church by the Avignon popes, Parliament in 1351 issued the Statute of Provisors, which succeeded in limiting papal provisions — but only slightly. A second Statute of Provisors in 1390 was more effective, but the popes retained considerable influence on English ecclesiastical appointments until the sixteenth century. By and large, the late-medieval papacy exercised its powers of provision with the support of the English crown, which found it easier to secure the appointment of its own favored candidates through papal provisions than through the time-consuming process of browbeating individual clerical electors to support the king's candidate.

The old issue of appeals to the pope from the Church courts of England was another lightning rod for antipapal hostility during the later fourteenth century. In 1353, Parliament set out to limit such appeals to a "foreign" pope through its first Statute of Praemunire, just as it had sought to limit papal provisions two years before. It was not until the third Statute of Praemunire in 1393, however, that the practice was seriously curtailed. Papal taxation of the English Church was another fertile ground for complaint. Parliament protested vehemently against papal taxation in 1375 and 1376, and on two occasions Richard II refused it altogether. These struggles, although inconclusive, diminished the popes' hold on the English Church. They constituted a political expression of the rising anticlericalism that affected society at all levels.

John Wycliffe

Fourteenth-century anticlericalism found its most eloquent spokesman in John Wycliffe (d. 1384), an Oxford philosopher of broad and deep learning. Wycliffe's thought was rooted in the tradition of medieval scholastic philosophy. It was also tinged with anticlerical protest such as had already manifested itself in many ways — in popular opposition to ecclesiastical wealth and corruption, in hostility between the English government and the papacy, and in scholarly attacks on medieval theology and the Church hierarchy by writers such as Ockham. Wycliffe first attained repute as a gifted and orthodox Oxford logician and theologian. In the mid-1370s, however, he came under the protection of the most powerful magnate of the age, John of Gaunt, duke of Lancaster, a younger son of Edward III, who used Wycliffe's inflammatory anticlerical sermons to frighten the English clergy into granting taxation to the government. After 1378, however, Wycliffe's increasingly heterodox doctrinal views made it impossible for him to continue his political career, and he devoted his final years to writing.

In these years of retirement, his opposition to the established Church deepened. He condemned the Church's vast landed wealth and suggested that the king had the right to seize it. He questioned the doctrine of the Eucharist as it was explained by previous Catholic philosophers. He also cast doubt on the entire priestly sacramental system. To Wycliffe, the organized Church was not the essential mediator between God and humanity. Rather, it was an agency responsible for guiding individual Christians on their spiritual quests. The true Church comprised only those individuals whom God had already chosen for salvation. The sacramental ministrations of clerics who were not themselves holy were therefore of no spiritual value whatsoever to those true believers whom God had predestined for heaven. Prayers for the dead, the cult of the saints, and the belief in purgatory were similarly unnecessary or misguided, in Wycliffe's view. They were simply ways for an avaricious and unworthy clergy to steal money from the laity.

John Wycliffe, from a Copy of Wycliffe's Bible in The British Museum   The text is from the opening of the Gospel of John and is written in English, reflecting the importance Wycliffe and his followers placed upon vernacular translations of the Bible. *(North Wind Picture Archives)*

Such, in brief, were John Wycliffe's new religious doctrines. Most of his English contemporaries found them repellent. William Langland's longing for a purification of the old order was more congenial to the mood of the times than Wycliffe's more fundamental objections to the sacramental system of the late-medieval Church. Yet Wycliffe's scholarly influence was great; in an atmosphere of growing hostility toward the Church hierarchy, there were some who adopted his views. His followers were known as Lollards (from the Middle English word *lollaerd*, meaning *mumblers* [of prayers]). The Lollards included a handful of Oxford scholars, but most were independent-minded lay people with enough education to read Lollard tracts, or at least to understand them when they were read aloud by others. To some of them, Wycliffe's religious views carried strong overtones of social revolution; armed Lollard rebellions in 1415 and 1431 would do much to discredit the movement. Within a few years, however, Wycliffe's philosophical and theological ideas had spread to the Continent, where they influenced the views of the Bohemian reformer John Hus. In 1415, the fathers of the Council of Constance burned John Hus at the stake after Hus had been lured to the council on an imperial promise of safe conduct. But Hus's doctrines, like Wycliffe's endured to influence the Protestant reformers of the sixteenth century.

England had not produced a major heretic since the fifth century, when Pelagius had so annoyed St. Augustine of Hippo. Having enjoyed nearly a millennium of untroubled orthodoxy, the English Church was caught off guard by Wycliffe. In time, however, churchmen reacted against his teachings and had little difficulty in enlisting the support of the lay establishment. Wycliffe himself enjoyed John of Gaunt's protection to the end, and he therefore had the pleasure of dying a natural death in 1384. But his doctrines had already been officially condemned, and during the later part of Richard II's reign it became royal policy to hunt down Lollards. This policy of repression was strengthened by a statute of 1401 bearing the forthright title, the Statute on the Burning of Heretics. By the early fifteenth century the immediate crisis was over, but the seeds of religious protest were planted and continued to germinate.

The Great Revolt of 1381

Ecclesiastical wealth evoked powerful protest in the later fourteenth century,[8] but as the poetry of William Langland demonstrates, popular

---

[8] J. Ambrose Raftis, "Social Change versus Revolution: New Interpretations of the Peasants' Revolt of 1381," in *Social Unrest in the Late Middle Ages*, ed. Francis X. Newman (Binghamton, 1986), pp. 3–22, is a useful survey. See also *The English Rising of 1381*, ed. R. H. Hilton and T. H. Aston (Cambridge, 1984); W. M. Ormrod, "The Peasants' Revolt and the Government of England," *Journal of British Studies* 29 (1990): 1–30; and the collection of documents compiled by R. B. Dobson, *The Peasants' Revolt of 1381,* (2nd ed. (London, 1982).

opposition was directed not only against wealthy prelates but against wealthy nobles as well:

> The poor may plead and pray in doorways,
> They may quake for cold and thirst and hunger.
> None receives them rightfully and relieves their suffering;
> They are hooted at like hounds and shooed away.

These words illustrate a profound sense of grievance that ripened into increasing social antagonism. In 1381, the tension burst in an uprising of peasants, urban workers, and other laborers — a rebellion known traditionally (if not quite accurately) as the Peasants' Revolt. This tragic episode was in part the product of the growing conflict between landlord and tenant that arose from the Black Death, the falling population, and the resulting shortage of labor. As the labor supply diminished, wages rose and landlords faced an economic squeeze, caught between rising labor costs and shrinking markets. Working through the Commons, they quickly obtained the legislation they desired: an ordinance of 1349 that froze wages at pre-plague levels, followed in 1351 by the first of a series of Statutes of Laborers. These measures succeeded in limiting wage increases but failed to halt them altogether. Landlords often found themselves competing with one another for peasants' services, and a black market in labor resulted. Nevertheless, tenants and wage-earners felt wronged by this legislation, and many reached the conclusion, not unfounded, that the ruling orders were conspiring against them.

This conviction received powerful confirmation from a series of poll taxes levied between 1377 and 1381. Traditionally, parliamentary subsidies on moveable wealth had fallen primarily on the well-to-do, but the poll taxes were assessed on rich and poor alike, by head count. The Commons, hard-pressed by declining land revenues and convinced that the peasants and wage-laborers were having things too much their own way, seized on the idea of reducing their own tax burden at their workers' expense. The most severe poll tax, that of 1381, was intended to help fund military campaigns in the seemingly endless war with France. There was massive tax evasion, however, and the government's heavy-handed efforts to enforce collection lit the fuse of the Great Revolt.

Beyond the economic grievances of the peasantry, however, lay a widespread popular concern with the recent failures in the French war. Edward III had succeeded in persuading the English populace that their own best interests were involved in the successful prosecution of the war effort. But under the minority government of the young king Richard II, the war had gone from bad to worse. The government's new taxes might not have been quite so inflammatory if the taxpayers had been able to see that they were doing some good. But with defeats abroad, French attacks on English coastal towns, and the minority government apparently incapable of mounting any effective response, the peasants, artisans, and demobilized soldiers of eastern and southern England took up arms and marched to London to petition their young king for redress of their grievances.

The uprising lasted scarcely a month — from late May 1381 to the end of June. By then, the government had suppressed the rebels, and the old social order was everywhere restored. The revolt was a hopeless endeavor, but for a brief time it shook society to its foundations, and for many years thereafter it was remembered with dread. It was a violent protest against the miserable conditions resulting from war, depression, taxation, and plague. But it was also a telling demonstration of the extent to which English political society had grown by the end of the fourteenth century to include within it the common people of England.

The Great Revolt began in Essex and quickly spread to neighboring Kent. As news of the rebellion spread, further revolts erupted across much of central and southeastern England. Its participants included a wide spectrum of rural and urban society, including men of some wealth and experience in local affairs. Among its many leaders, the most prominent were the Kentishman Wat Tyler and a former priest named John Ball, whose memorable couplet symbolizes the radical egalitarianism of at least some of the rebels:

> When Adam dug and Eve spun,
> Who then was the gentleman?

The Great Revolt of 1381   This illustration from the *Chronicles* of Jean Froissart shows John Ball preaching on social injustice. *(Mansell/Time)*

The rebels converged on London in mid-June. For the most part, they were remarkably disciplined. Looting was rare, and the men whom they murdered — Simon Sudbury, archbishop of Canterbury who, as chancellor, headed the royal government, and Sir Robert Hales, the king's treasurer and prior of the wealthy crusading order of Knights Hospitalers — were both prominently identified with the government's taxation policies and its failures in the French war. They must have been deliberately chosen. The man most directly identified with these failures, John of Gaunt, was another particular target of the rebel forces, but fortunately for him, he was out of the country, so the rebels were forced to content themselves with blowing up his London palace (the Savoy) with gunpowder. The remainder of the court — "marvelously discouraged" as one eyewitness aptly put it — took refuge in the Tower of London. Then, according to a contemporary observer, the rebel leaders proclaimed

> that anyone who could catch any Fleming or other alien of any nation might cut off his head, and so they did forthwith. Then they took the heads of the archbishop and of the others and put them on wooden poles and carried them before them in procession as far as the shrine of Westminster Abbey. . . . Then they returned to London Bridge and set the head of the archbishop above the gate, with eight other heads of those they had murdered, so that all could see them who crossed over the bridge. Thereupon they went to the church of St. Martin's in the Vintry, and found within it thirty-five Flemings, whom they dragged out and beheaded in the street. On that day there were beheaded about 140 or 160 people in all. Then they made their way to the houses of Lombards and other aliens and broke into their dwellings and robbed them of all their goods that they could lay hands on. This continued all that day and the night following, amidst hideous cries and horrid tumult.

Although hostile to the gentry, nobility, and foreign merchants, the rebels remained respectful of the monarchy. The terrified court, barricaded in the Tower, had no recourse but to send out the fourteen-year-old king, Richard II, to negotiate. On two successive days, the young monarch and the rebel leaders parleyed. The rebels demanded above all the abolition of legal villeinage. They further demanded a ceiling on rents, not to exceed fourpence per acre. Beyond these specific concessions, some chroniclers report (and it is well to remember that all the chroniclers were hostile to the rebels) that the rebels demanded a series of even more radical reforms that would have overturned the entire late-medieval social order: equality of all men before the law, abolition of all lordship except the king's, confiscation and redistribution of all ecclesiastical property not essential to the direct sustenance of the clergy, and the elimination of all English bishoprics but one. We have no way of knowing whether these were actual rebel demands or the fevered imaginings of chroniclers who saw their world being turned upside down and presumed that this was precisely the sort of thing such men would want. Most fundamentally, however, the rebels demanded inclusion in the "community of the realm." They sought a voice in the kingdom's politics, a role in what one rebel leader called "the great society."

Richard II, having no real choice, submitted to the rebels — for the moment. At the first of his two parleys with them he agreed to some of their demands, including total amnesty and freedom from villein status. The jubilant rebels spent the evening in wild celebration. On the following day, at the second parley, the rebel force was considerably reduced by widespread and very severe hangovers, and by the desertion of many who thought that their cause was won. Their leader, Wat Tyler, for reasons unknown, threatened one of the king's followers by brandishing a dagger, and the Lord Mayor of London responded by mortally wounding him. The young king, showing great presence of mind, quieted Tyler's followers by offering to be their leader. He led them out of London, and they then dispersed. Perhaps they were under the illusion that they had triumphed. In fact, however, once they withdrew from London their revolt was doomed. Although they continued to terrorize the countryside for another week or two — pillaging monasteries, burning manors, and plundering towns — the rebellion quickly lost its momentum. By the end of June, the rebel bands had been suppressed and the old social order restored. The concessions were of course forgotten, but the rebels had gained one thing: out of fear of another such rising, the government dropped the idea of a poll tax on the entire population, and it was not revived until the very late twentieth century. Its revival under Prime Minister Margaret Thatcher in 1989–1990 was one of the causes of her being driven from office, not by peasants but by the members of her own Conservative Party.

In 1381, however, Richard II remained in office and crushed the Peasants' Rebellion:

> Afterwards the king sent out his messengers into divers parts to capture the evildoers and put them to death. And many were taken and hanged in London, and they set up many gallows around the city of London and in other cities and boroughs of the south country. At length, as it pleased God, the king saw that too many of his faithful subjects would be undone, and too much blood spilled, and he took pity in his heart and granted them full pardon, on condition that they should never rise again, under penalty of death or mutilation, and that each of them should get his charter of pardon, and pay the king, as a fee for sealing the charter, twenty shillings for his enrichment. And so finished this wicked war.

The Great Revolt had no real chance to overturn fourteenth-century society. Yet some of its goals were realized in the next few decades through the operation of basic economic forces. The old demesne economy was no longer paying its way, and English villeinage was rapidly disappearing of its own accord. A villein was bound to perform work services for his lord, and as demesne lands were divided more and more into tenants' plots, work service became unnecessary. By the early fifteenth century, the old manorial regime was all but dead, and villeinage was dying with it.

The Reign of Richard II (1377–1399)

Richard II owed his succession to the fact that his father, Edward the Black Prince, was Edward III's eldest son. The Black Prince died in 1376 after a prolonged illness, Edward III died in 1377, and Richard II thereupon ascended the throne at the age of ten[9] (see the genealogical chart on p. 311). In the kingdom he inherited, the political balance among crown, magnates, and gentry had shifted substantially since the days of Edward I. The ongoing expenses of war had long ago forced the crown to turn to Parliament for help, and in the course of Edward III's reign the Commons had come to demand an ever-greater voice in royal policy in return for its subsidies. The ennobling and enriching of kings' younger sons, the consolidation through marriage and stricter inheritance customs of existing baronial estates, and the growing practice of nobles paying fees to "retain" country knights in their service had raised a handful of magnates to positions of formidable wealth and power. Parliament's efforts to control the royal council had culminated, during the Good Parliament of 1376, in the development of a process by which the Commons could remove unpopular royal ministers by impeachment. And Edward II's fall in 1327 had demonstrated that, as a last resort, Parliament might formally depose the king.

Throughout his reign, Richard II strove to reverse the decline of royal power and to restore the monarchy to what he believed was its rightful position of authority over the realm. But by pursuing this goal with such blatant disregard for the political and constitutional changes that had taken place in England during the preceding half-century, Richard so alienated the magnates and gentry of his kingdom that he ultimately provoked his own deposition in 1399.

Richard himself possessed courage and determination, as his behavior during the Peasants' Revolt makes clear. He was small in stature and perhaps slightly hunchbacked; his portraits disclose a sensitive, anxious face. He was a thoughtful, moody man, a connoisseur of the arts and a devotee of the cult of kingship. Particularly during his last years, he preoccupied himself with the symbols and ceremonies of monarchy: he stressed the sacred qualities of the royal anointing, displayed the sun on his banners, and turned ordinary court procedures into elaborate and colorful pageants. In these and other ways, he gave visible expression to his lofty notions of royal authority. No monarch had ever surrounded himself with so much regal display as Richard II. And none had pursued so thoroughgoing a royalist policy under such unfavorable circumstances.

In 1380, Parliament dismissed the council that had ruled during the opening years of Richard's reign. In the years immediately following,

---

[9]On Richard II, see Nigel Saul, *Richard II* (New Haven, 1997); Anthony Tuck, *Richard II and the English Nobility* (London, 1973); F. R. H. Du Boulay and Caroline M. Barron, eds., *The Reign of Richard II: Essays in Honour of May McKisack* (London, 1971); and Gervase Matthew, *The Court of Richard II* (London, 1968).

Richard surrounded himself with loyal friends, thereby creating a "court party" faithful to the crown. He favored these friends by granting them earldoms, duchies, and high offices at court, and with their advice and support he embarked on his policy of rebuilding royal power — heedless of the opinion of magnates and gentry outside his small inner circle. The more successful of the Norman and early Angevin kings would never have made such a blunder.

The barons were in no sense a monolithic force. If anything, they were even more faction-ridden than in earlier times. They were at odds not only with one another but also with the gentry and townspeople, who now exercised considerable power in the Commons. But all classes were alarmed at the young Richard's independent course, and his standing was further undermined by a continuing series of military reverses abroad. Rumors circulated that some of Richard's court favorites were pocketing revenues intended for warfare and plotting with foreign enemies. In 1381 and 1382, members of Parliament unsuccessfully demanded investigations of what they regarded as the king's extravagant household expenses. In 1384, two royal favorites were accused of financial irregularities. Richard, showing none of Edward III's wise pliancy, charged the accusers with defamation of character and punished them harshly. In 1385, Parliament requested an annual review of the household accounts, and although the king permitted the drawing up of an ordinance to that effect, he never implemented it. Instead, he continued his hazardous policy of isolating his court and household from the meddling of outsiders.

In 1386, Parliament's dissatisfaction intensified. Thus far, relations between crown and community had been tempered by the moderating influence of Richard's uncle, John of Gaunt, duke of Lancaster and patron of John Wycliffe. Although some contemporaries regarded John of Gaunt as a haughty, tactless, thoroughly unlikeable man, he nevertheless commanded respect. As England's wealthiest magnate — master of the immense Lancastrian inheritance through marriage — he was a political figure of formidable influence. But in 1386 he departed for a military adventure in Spain, and in his absence both court and community acted with less restraint. The Parliament of autumn 1386 demanded the dismissal of Richard's chancellor and favorite, Michael de la Pole, a merchant's son whom the king had elevated to the earldom of Suffolk. Richard retorted that he would not dismiss even one of his kitchen scullions at their request. Thereupon, Parliament reminded him that if a king refused to govern with the assent of his people, a clear precedent existed "for deposing the king himself from the throne and elevating some close relative of the royal line." Abashed, Richard gave in, and the Commons impeached Michael de la Pole on charges of graft and maladministration, misdeeds of which de la Pole was by no means entirely innocent.[10] Even

---

[10]On this issue, see J. S. Roskell's meticulous analysis, *The Impeachment of Michael de la Pole, Earl of Suffolk, in 1386 in the Context of the Reign of Richard II* (Manchester, 1984).

more important, Parliament appointed a new royal council to govern for a year in the nineteen-year-old king's name, and authorized it to control revenues, supervise household expenses, and reform the royal government.

Early in 1387, Richard departed from Westminster, where the council was sitting, taking with him his household and court favorites including de la Pole. Ruling once again through his inner circle, he ignored the parliament-appointed council and did not return to Westminster until its year of power had almost expired. Meanwhile, he had a series of constitutional questions placed before a group of England's chief justices, and they answered exactly as the king wished: they judged that the Parliament-appointed continuing council offended the royal prerogative and was therefore illegal, and that those who had forced it on the king were guilty of treason — for which the customary penalty was death. The judges proclaimed further that it was treason to hinder in any way the king's exercise of his royal power, that Parliament had no right to make demands on the king prior to granting him requested subsidies, and that the king was empowered to dissolve any parliament at his pleasure. Finally, they stated that no parliament could lawfully impeach any minister of the king without royal consent and that it was an act of treason to view the deposition of Edward II as a legal precedent.

These judgments represented an unqualified assertion of the royal prerogative — a firm statement of the political viewpoint that Richard cherished. According to this view, royal councilors were to be chosen by the king alone and were responsible to the king alone; Parliament, too, was to be a royal tool, summoned and dismissed at the king's will; and anyone who acted contrary to these rules was subject to condemnation for treason. King Edward I would have nodded in his tomb. But by expanding the definition of treason (which Edward III had severely restricted), Richard was raising once more the dangerous spectre of King Edward II's disastrous reign.

The judges' rulings had no effect on the king's enemies. Instead, Richard's defiance united the opposition against him. In November 1387, a group of magnates approached the king at Westminster and brought charges of treason against several of his favorites. Seeming to comply, Richard promised to arrest those accused and hold them until the next parliament, when the "appeal" of treason would be judged. In reality, he was merely playing for time, and permitted his accused favorites to remain at liberty. But in February 1388, the dissident magnates routed a royalist army at Radcot Bridge in Oxfordshire, leaving Richard with no adequate means of defending himself. Lacking the necessary military power, he submitted to the magnates and accepted their "appeals" against his favorites.

The so-called "Merciless Parliament" met in 1388 to hear the appeals of five of its leading members, who numbered among the wealthiest magnates in England. These "lords appellant" entered the assembly "arm in arm, clad in cloth of gold," to prosecute their case. Dominated by them and their supporters, the Merciless Parliament convicted the accused councilors and executed several others as well. Michael de la Pole was sentenced to hang, but he had already fled to France, never to return. The offending royal judges, meanwhile, were exiled to Ireland. Richard's court circle disintegrated, and for the king there now remained no choice but to cooperate with his magnates and his parliaments. The barons appointed a new royal council whose members swore to support all acts of Parliament. And the five lords appellant requested and received £20,000 for their efforts and expenses "in procuring the salvation of the realm and the destruction of the traitors." Not everyone in the realm appreciated being saved in this costly fashion.

The Merciless Parliament was the central political event of Richard II's reign. It marks the zenith of parliamentary power and the nadir of the royal prerogative in fourteenth-century England. The lords appellant themselves justified their actions on legal and constitutional grounds, but their acts betrayed cruelty and vindictiveness. Like so many victorious magnates before them, they went too far. The magnitude of their triumph evoked a reaction of venomous factionalism and widespread dissent. Moreover, England's wars abroad fared no better under the new government than before. The French campaigns remained hopelessly bogged down, and in 1388 an invading Scottish army inflicted a crushing defeat on the English. In 1389, John of Gaunt returned from Spain, and in the years that followed Richard II seems to have enjoyed his tacit support. With the situation thus turning in his favor, Richard was able in 1389 to dismiss his baronial council and rule once more through councilors of his own choosing. Having lost much of its support, the baronial council withdrew without protest, and Richard was again master of his court.

For the next eight years, the king bided his time and mended his fences. In the style of Edward III, he cooperated with barons and Parliament in the governance of his realm. If he did not abandon his dreams of royal absolutism, at least he pursued them more cautiously than before. Gritting his teeth, he showed honor and favor even toward the lords appellant. And slowly he built around him a new circle of trustworthy supporters. Meanwhile, he sought to free himself from total financial dependence on Parliament by ending the war with France. A definitive peace eluded him, but he did succeed in arranging a truce that was intended to last for twenty-eight years. He sealed it by taking as his royal bride the princess Isabella, eldest daughter of the half-mad king of France, Charles VI. Isabella was a child of nine, but Richard himself was still in his twenties and could seemingly afford to wait a few years for an heir. And Isabella brought with her a dowry of 800,000 francs.

Accordingly, when Richard returned to England with his child-bride late in 1396 his financial position was vastly improved. The dowry helped, and the freedom from war expenses helped still more. No longer did he have to go begging to Parliament or permit his need for parliamentary subsidies to hamper his exercise of the royal prerogative. Working through his sheriffs and other local administrators, he packed the spring parliament of 1397 with his own supporters and overawed it with his military retainers. The parliamentarians found themselves encircled, quite literally, by royal archers. When a member of the Commons demanded a reduction in the royal household expenses, he was arraigned for treason and convicted. And the lords in Parliament ratified the king's declaration that anyone who "shall move or excite the Commons of Parliament or any other person to make remedy of any matter which touches our person, our government, or our regality, shall be considered a traitor."

With the situation so encouraging, Richard took his long-awaited vengeance on the lords appellant. The autumn parliament of 1397, again packed with royalists, moved savagely against the king's former enemies — depriving them of their lands and liberty, forcing some into exile and executing others. Three of the lords appellant now suffered the irony of being themselves "appealed" in Parliament for treason. One of the three was murdered, a second legally executed, and a third banished from the realm. Lands were confiscated on an immense scale and redistributed among a new group of magnates, some of them close friends of the king. A parliament of 1398 formally revoked all the acts of the Merciless Parliament, and everyone involved in antiroyalist activity during 1387 and 1388 was obliged to seek the royal pardon. The royalist opinions of the judges in 1387 were now resurrected and, with Parliament's assent, declared to be the law of the realm. And Richard, anxious to secure still greater independence from annual parliamentary grants, demanded and received a lifetime privilege of collecting the customs duties on wool exports. Financially and politically, the English throne had never stood higher.

Intoxicated by these triumphs, Richard pressed on. He forced huge loans from townspeople and assessed heavy fines on a number of shires for failing to support him in his struggle against the lords appellant ten years before. In autumn 1398, he banished the two remaining lords appellant, one of whom was Henry Bolingbroke, son and heir of the wealthy and aged John of Gaunt, duke of Lancaster. When Gaunt died early in 1399, the king refused to consider the claims of the banished heir, despite his previous promise to allow Bolingbroke to inherit his father's lands should Gaunt die while his son was in exile. Instead, Richard now extended Henry Bolingbroke's sentence of exile from ten years to life and seized the vast Lancastrian lands for himself.

Henry Bolingbroke had been a very considerable landholder in his own right. The addition of the Lancastrian patrimony would have made him a magnate of almost kingly wealth, and it is understandable that Richard would fear the concentration of such prodigious resources in the hands of any single magnate, particularly a former enemy. Nevertheless, the king's seizure of the Lancastrian inheritance kindled the fear of the landholding aristocracy. Security of inheritance had always been of vital concern to the great noble families, and they now found themselves

The Capture of Richard II
From a manuscript of Jean
Froissart's *Chronicles of
France and England*
(c. 1460–1480). *(Repro-
duced with permission of
The British Library)*

ruled by a king who rode roughshod over the rights of noble heirs.
Richard's throne had never seemed as secure as it was in early 1399, but
in fact the king could count on little support outside his immediate circle. Supremely confident, he led an expedition into Ireland in the summer of 1399, leaving a weak regency government to safeguard his interests back home. While he was away, Henry Bolingbroke returned to
England to claim his Lancastrian inheritance by force.

As the eldest surviving son of John of Gaunt and a grandson of Edward III, Henry Bolingbroke possessed the necessary royal blood, and
when he landed in Yorkshire and moved southward, one magnate after
another rallied to him. Some of Bolingbroke's supporters sought only to
install him in his father's Lancastrian estates, but others were determined to make him king of England in Richard's stead. Richard returned
from Ireland to find his cause abandoned. In August 1399 he negotiated
with Henry's supporters and agreed to restore the Lancastrian patrimony.
On his departure from the meeting, Richard was ambushed, forced to abdicate, and hauled off to a prison room in the Tower of London. Parliament

received his abdication in September and recognized Henry Bolingbroke as King Henry IV of England.[11]

Richard died in captivity early in 1400 — he was probably murdered — and the new Lancastrian dynasty stood virtually unchallenged. But Richard II's deposition, which reinforced the precedent of Edward II's, left the Lancastrians an uncertain legacy and a tottering throne.

Whereas Edward II had been deposed because of his weakness, Richard fell because of his strength. He had pitted himself against a long and potent trend toward shared power between crown and community, a trend that by the late fourteenth century had progressed too far to be easily reversed. The magnates were by then very powerful, and the burghers and gentry had become politically articulate. Neither could be ignored. In his final years Richard tried to control them by fear and failed. A century thereafter, when the Tudors succeeded at last in rebuilding royal authority, they did so on a sturdy foundation of popular support. The idea does not seem to have occurred to Richard II.

Conclusion

The fall of Richard II marks an appropriate end to a century of violence and turmoil, a fundamental turning point in English politics. A king had been deposed in 1327 but was succeeded by his eldest son and unquestioned heir. With Richard II's forced resignation in 1399, however, the very concept of hereditary succession was thrown into doubt. For Richard was the last of the Plantagenet kings. He had no son. The succession was irregular for the first time in two hundred years. Legitimate succession was basic to the politics and aristocratic social order of the Later Middle Ages, and the compromising of that principle in 1399 rocked English society. For the next century, rival families contended for the throne, afflicting England with misrule and civil war. Not until the establishment and consolidation of the Tudor dynasty generations later was the destructive work of 1399 repaired — as the Tudors themselves, and their propagandists, were pleased to announce to any who would listen.

The transition from medieval to modern England was far from complete in 1399. The English continued to suffer from recurring plagues, social unrest, and political turmoil. In emphasizing this change of dynasty in 1399, we must not ignore more subtle changes that were still in process and would remain so for generations. As our period closes, England's population was still falling, its struggle with France remained unresolved, its economy was still adjusting to the enormous mortality of the preceding half-century, and its countryside remained turbulent. Yet for all that, England in 1399 was by no means a society in decline. There

---

[11]*Chronicles of the Revolution, 1397–1400: The Reign of Richard II*, trans. and annotated by Chris Given-Wilson (Manchester, 1993), is the best collection of documents with commentary on these events.

was anxiety and suffering, but there was also tremendous creativity. People such as Chaucer, Langland, and Wycliffe displayed originality to a degree that would ornament any age. Like their fellow countrymen and women, all three also demonstrated a heightened sense of a distinctively English national identity. Chaucer and Langland were crucial figures in the development of English as an important literary vehicle. Wycliffe dreamed of an English translation of the whole Bible and accorded the king a central position in the governance of the English Church. Richard II's reign was also a great creative age in the development of Perpendicular Gothic architecture — witness the naves of Canterbury and Winchester and the choir of York. The new architectural style was not only profoundly impressive in itself but also less cosmopolitan, more distinctly English, than earlier Gothic styles had been. At this same time, English merchants, who had once allowed their foreign rivals to dominate English trade, were creating lucrative new markets for themselves across northern Europe.

As the fourteenth century closed, western Europe was beginning to make a slow transition from a world of multi-ethnic medieval kingdoms toward a discernibly modern world of political nationalism in which kingdoms would be regarded as embodiments of the unique characteristics of a single people. With respect to this emerging identification between ethnic identity and the state, England in 1399 was clearly the most precocious nation-state in Europe. Traditions of political unity in England developed in the Anglo-Saxon period and continued without interruption until the end of the Middle Ages and beyond. To an extraordinary degree, therefore, modern England rests upon medieval foundations. Monarchy, council, household, Parliament, shires, aristocracy, and the common law are all, in England, securely rooted in the developments of the Middle Ages. So too is the development of a socially extensive political nation, with wide responsibility for its own local self-government.

In marked contrast to most of the modern nation-states of Europe and the Western Hemisphere, English identity has never rested upon a revolutionary moment in which all things were suddenly made new. English identity has rested instead upon a perceived coincidence of interest between an ancient and continuously evolving state and a population that, from an equally early date, conceived of itself as comprising a single people. As we have seen, this conviction that the English were indeed a single people began with Augustine of Canterbury, Theodore of Tarsus, and Bede. King Alfred and his successors linked this conception of the *gens Anglorum* (the English people) to the political domination of the West Saxon monarchy over all, or almost all, of the ancient Roman province of Britain. In this politicized form, the idea of the English nation survived the Norman Conquest to become the foundation upon which Edward I and Edward III would base their attempted conquests of Wales, Scotland, and France.

As the fourteenth century ended, many Englishmen were frustrated by the reverses that their imperial dreams had suffered over the previous generation. But their conviction that England was indeed a chosen nation, destined by God to rule in foreign lands, remained unaltered and would soon be strengthened again by the extraordinary military victories won by King Henry V in France.[12] This tension — between a vision of Englishness as unique to England and yet of the English as a people destined to rule an overseas empire — is a theme that would continue to characterize English life for centuries after the Middle Ages ended. But like so many of the themes discussed in this book, it powerfully illuminates the essential medieval contribution to the making of England.

---

[12]On this sense of English election, see the introduction to *Henry V: The Practice of Kingship*, ed. Gerald L. Harriss (Oxford, 1985).

Appendix

The English Kings from Alfred to Henry IV

The Anglo-Saxon Kings

Alfred 871–899
Edward (the Elder) 899–924
Athelstan 924–939
Edmund 939–946
Eadred 946–955
Eadwig 955–959
Edgar (the Peaceable) 959–975
Edward (the Martyr) 975–978

Ethelred (the Unready) 978–1016
Edmund (Ironside) 1016
Cnut 1016–1035
Harold (Harefoot) 1035–1040
Harthacnut 1040–1042
Edward (the Confessor) 1042–1066
Harold (Godwineson) 1066

The Norman Kings

William I (the Conqueror)
   1066–1087
William II (Rufus) 1087–1100

Henry I 1100–1135
Stephen 1135–1154

The Angevin (Plantagenet) Kings

Henry II 1154–1189
Richard I (the Lion-Hearted)
   1189–1199
John 1199–1216
Henry III 1216–1272

Edward I 1272–1307
Edward II 1307–1327
Edward III 1327–1377
Richard II 1377–1399

The Lancastrian Kings

Henry IV 1399–1413

Bibliography

Bibliographies

Altschul, Michael. *Anglo-Norman England, 1066–1154*. Conference on British Studies Bibliographical Handbooks. Cambridge, 1969.

Bates, David. *A Bibliography of Domesday Book*. Woodbridge, Suffolk, 1986.

Berger, Sidney E. *Medieval English Drama: An Annotated Bibliography of Recent Criticism*. New York, 1990.

Boyce, Gray C. *Literature of Medieval History, 1930–1975*. 5 vols. Millwood, N.Y., 1981.

Elton, Sir Geoffrey, and others, eds. *Royal Historical Society: Annual Bibliography of British and Irish History*. London, 1976ff. (Annual volumes for 1975 ff.)

Graves, Edgar B. *A Bibliography of English History to 1485*. Oxford, 1975.

Guth, DeLloyd J. *Late Medieval England, 1377–1485*. Conference on British Studies Bibliographical Handbooks. Cambridge, 1976.

Keynes, Simon. *Anglo-Saxon History: A Select Bibliography*. Binghamton, N.Y., 1987.

Mullins, E. L. C. *A Guide to the Historical and Archaeological Publications of Societies in England and Wales, 1901–1933*. London, 1968.

———. *Texts and Calendars, I: An Analytical Guide to Serial Publications*. Royal Historical Society. London, 1958.

———. *Texts and Calendars, II: An Analytical Guide to Serial Publications, 1957–1982*. Royal Historical Society. London, 1983.

Rosenthal, Joel T. *Anglo-Saxon History: An Annotated Bibliography, 450–1066*. New York, 1985.

Wilkinson, Bertie. *The High Middle Ages in England, 1154–1377*. Conference on British Studies Bibliographical Handbooks. Cambridge, 1987.

Reference Works

Cokayne, Geroge E. *The Complete Peerage of England, Scotland, Ireland, Great Britain, and the United Kingdom*, ed. Vicary Gibbs et al. 13 vols. London, 1919–1959, reprinted 1984, and again, Gloucester, 1987.

Fryde, E. B., D. E. Greenway, S. Porter, and I. Roy, eds. *Handbook of British Chronology*. 3rd ed. Royal Historical Society, London, 1986.

Gilbert, Martin. *An Atlas of British History*. 2nd ed. Oxford and New York, 1993.

Hill, David. *An Atlas of Anglo-Saxon England*. Toronto, 1981.

Jones, Barri, and David Mattingly. *An Atlas of Roman Britain*. Toronto, 1990.

Knowles, David, C. N. L. Brooke, and Vera London, eds. *The Heads of Religious Houses, England and Wales, 940–1216*. Cambridge, 1972.

Knowles, David, and R. N. Hadcock. *Medieval Religious Houses: England and Wales*. 2nd ed. London, 1971.

Loyn, Henry. *The Middle Ages: A Concise Encyclopedia*. New York, 1989.

Manley, John. *An Atlas of Prehistorical Britain*. Oxford, 1989.

Sanders, I. J. *English Baronies: A Study of their Origin and Descent, 1086–1327.* Oxford, 1960.

Spufford, Peter, with Wendy Wilkinson and Sarah Tolley. *Handbook of Medieval Exchange.* Royal Historical Society. London, 1986.

Stephen, Leslie, and Sidney Lee, eds. *The Dictionary of National Biography from the Earliest Times to 1900.* 22 vols. Oxford, 1921–1922.

Szarmach, Paul E., M. Teresa Tavormina, and Joel T. Rosenthal. *Medieval England: An Encyclopedia.* New York and London, 1998.

Williams, Ann, Alfred Smyth, and David Kirby. *A Biographical Dictionary of Dark Age Britain: England, Scotland and Wales from c. 500–c. 1050.* London, 1991.

Woodcock, Thomas, and John Martin Robinson. *The Oxford Guide to Heraldry.* Oxford, 1988.

General and Political History

General Medieval

Barrow, Geoffrey W. S. *Feudal Britain: The Completion of the Medieval Kingdoms, 1066–1314.* London, 1956. Paperback ed. London, 1972.

Bartlett, Robert. *The Making of Europe: Conquest, Colonization and Cultural Change, 950–1350.* Princeton, 1993.

Bartlett, Robert, and Angus Mackay, eds. *Medieval Frontier Societies.* Oxford, 1990.

Bloch, Marc. *The Royal Touch: Sacred Monarchy and Scrofula in England and France.* London, 1973.

Brown, R. Allen, H. M. Colvin, and A. J. Taylor. *A History of the King's Works.* Vols. I and II, *The Middle Ages.* London, 1963.

Clanchy, Michael T. *England and Its Rulers, 1066–1272: Foreign Lordship and National Identity.* 2nd ed. Oxford, 1998.

———. *From Memory to Written Record: England, 1066–1307.* 2nd ed. Oxford, 1993.

Crouch, David. *The Image of Aristocracy in Britain, 1000–1300.* London, 1992.

Davies, R. R. *Conquest, Coexistence, and Change: Wales, 1063–1415.* Oxford, 1987.

———. *Domination and Conquest: The Experience of Ireland, Scotland and Wales, 1100–1300.* Cambridge, 1990.

Dickinson, W. C. *Scotland from the Earliest Times to 1603.* 3rd ed. London, 1977.

Douglas, David C., and George Greenaway, eds. and trans. *English Historical Documents.* Vol. II, *1066–1189.* 2nd ed. London, 1981.

Duncan, Archibald A. M. *Scotland: The Making of the Kingdom.* New York, 1975.

Frame, Robin. *The Political Development of the British Isles, 1100–1400.* Oxford, 1990.

Gillingham, John, and Ralph A. Griffiths, *The Oxford History of Britain.* Vol. II, *The Middle Ages.* Oxford, 1992.

Given-Wilson, Chris, ed. *An Illustrated History of Late Medieval England.* London, 1996.

Jones, Michael, and Malcolm Vale, eds. *England and Her Neighbours, 1066–1453: Essays in Honour of Pierre Chaplais.* London, 1989.

Keen, Maurice. *England in the Later Middle Ages.* London, 1973.

King, Edmund. *Medieval England, 1066–1485.* Oxford, 1988.

Lloyd, J. E. A. *A History of Wales from the Earliest Times to the Edwardian Conquest.* 3rd ed. 2 vols. London, 1967.

Maddicott, John R., and David M. Palliser, eds. *The Medieval State: Essays Presented to James Campbell.* London, 2000.

Myers, A. R., ed. and trans. *English Historical Documents*. Vol. IV, *1327–1485*. London, 1969.

Owen, D. Huw, ed. *Settlement and Society in Wales*. Cardiff, 1989.

Reeves, A. C. *The Marcher Lords*. A New History of Wales. Llandybie, Dwfed, 1983.

Richardson, H. G. *The English Jewry Under Angevin Kings*. London, 1960.

Roth, Cecil. *A History of the Jews in England*. 3rd ed. Oxford, 1964.

Rothwell, Harry, ed. and trans. *English Historical Documents*. Vol. III, *1189–1327*. London, 1975.

Saul, Nigel, ed. *The Oxford Illustrated History of Medieval England*. Oxford, 1997.

Southern, Richard W. *Medieval Humanism and Other Studies*. Oxford, 1970.

Walker, David. *Medieval Wales*. Cambridge, 1990.

———. *The Norman Conquerors*. A New History of Wales. Llandybie, Dyfed, 1977.

Whitelock, Dorothy, ed. and trans. *English Historical Documents*. Vol. I, *c. 500–1042*. 2nd ed. London, 1979.

Celtic, Roman and Anglo-Saxon

An outstanding annual publication, *Anglo-Saxon England*, Cambridge, 1972 ff., is devoted to the history, archaeology, literature, and culture of this era.

Abels, Richard. *Alfred the Great: War, Culture and Kingship in Anglo-Saxon England*. London, 1998.

Alcock, Leslie. *Arthur's Britain: History and Archaeology*, A.D. *367–634*. New York, 1971.

Arnold, C. J. *Roman Britain to Saxon England*. Beckenham, Kent, 1984.

Barlow, Frank. *Edward the Confessor*. Berkeley, 1970.

Bassett, Steven, ed. *The Origins of Anglo-Saxon Kingdoms*. Studies in the Early History of Britain. London, 1989.

Blair, Peter Hunter. *Anglo-Saxon Northumbria*. London, 1984.

———. *An Introduction to Anglo-Saxon England*. 2nd ed. Cambridge, 1977.

———. *Northumbria in the Days of Bede*. London, 1976.

———. *The World of Bede*. Cambridge, 1990.

Bowman, A. K. *Life and Letters on the Roman Frontier*. London, 1994.

Bowman, A. K., and J. D. Thomas, *The Vindolanda Writing Tablets*. London, 1994.

Campbell, James, ed. *The Anglo-Saxons*. Oxford, 1982.

———. *Essays in Anglo-Saxon History*. London, 1986.

———. *The Anglo-Saxon State*. London, 2000.

Chadwick, Henry M. *Studies on Anglo-Saxon Institutions*. Cambridge, 1905.

Chadwick, Nora K., ed. *Studies in Early British History*. Cambridge, 1954.

———, ed. *Celt and Saxon: Studies in the Early British Border*. Cambridge, 1963.

Clemoes, Peter, and Kathleen Hughes, eds. *England Before the Conquest: Studies in Primary Sources Presented to Dorothy Whitelock*. Cambridge, 1971.

Collingwood, R. G., and I. A. Richmond. *The Archaeology of Roman Britain*. Rev. ed. London, 1969.

Crossley-Holland, Kevin, ed. *The Anglo-Saxon World*. Woodbridge, Suffolk, 1982.

Cunliffe, Barry. *Iron-Age Communities in Britain*. 3rd ed. London, 1991.

Davies, Wendy. *An Early Welsh Microcosm*. Studies in the Llandaff Charters. London, 1978.

———. *Patterns of Power in Early Wales*. Oxford, 1990.

———. *Wales in the Early Middle Ages*. Studies in the Early History of Britain. Leicester, 1982.

Driscoll, Stephen T., and Margaret R. Nieke, eds. *Power and Politics in Early Medieval Britain and Ireland.* Edinburgh, 1988.

Dumville, David, and Gillian Jondorf. *France and Britain in the Early Middle Ages.* Woodbridge, Suffolk, 1990.

Dumville, David, and Michael Lapidge, eds. *Gildas: New Approaches.* Woodbridge, Suffolk, 1984.

Esmonde Cleary, A. S. *The Ending of Roman Britain.* Savage, Md., 1990.

Farmer, D. H., ed. *The Age of Bede.* Rev. ed. New York, 1983.

Frere, Sheppard S. *Britannia: A History of Roman Britain.* 3rd ed. London, 1987.

Frey, O. H., V. Kruta, B. Raftery, and M. Szabo, *The Celts.* New York, 1991.

Green, Miranda J., ed. *The Celtic World.* London, 1995.

———. *The World of the Druids.* London, 1997.

Hanson, W. S. *Agricola and the Conquest of the North.* London, 1987.

Hines, John, ed. *The Anglo-Saxons from the Migration Period to the Eighth Century: An Ethnographic Perspective.* Studies in Historical Archaeoethnology. Vol. 2. Woodbridge, Suffolk, 1997.

Hodges, Richard. *The Anglo-Saxon Achievement: Archaeology and the Beginnings of English Society.* London, 1989.

Howe, Nicholas. *Migration and Mythmaking in Anglo-Saxon England.* New Haven, 1990.

Hudson, Benjamin T., and Vickie Ziegler, eds. *Crossed Paths: Methodological Approaches to the Celtic Aspect of the European Middle Ages.* Lanham, Md., 1991.

John, Eric. *Orbis Britanniae and Other Studies.* Leicester, 1966.

———. *Reassessing Anglo-Saxon England.* Manchester, 1996.

Johnson, Stephen. *Later Roman Britain.* London, 1980.

Keynes, Simon, and Michael Lapidge, eds. and trans. *Alfred the Great: Asser's Life of King Alfred and Other Contemporary Sources.* New York, 1983.

Kirby, D. P. *The Earliest English Kings: Studies in the Political History of the Anglo-Saxon Heptarchy, c. 575–875.* London, 1990.

Laing, Lloyd. *Celtic Britain.* New York, 1979.

Laing, Lloyd, and Jennifer Laing. *Anglo-Saxon England.* New York, 1979.

Lawson, M. K. *Cnut: The Danes in England in the Early Eleventh Century.* London, 1993.

Levison, Wilhelm. *England and the Continent in the Eighth Century.* Oxford, 1946.

Loyn, Henry R. *The Vikings in Britain.* New York, 1977.

Millett, Martin. *English Heritage Book of Roman Britain.* London, 1995.

Nash-Williams, Victor E. *The Roman Frontier in Wales.* 2nd ed. Cardiff, 1969.

Richards, Julian D. *English Heritage Book of Viking Age England.* London, 1991.

Richmond, I. A. *Roman Britain.* 3rd ed. London, 1995.

Ritchie, R. L. Graeme. *The Normans in England Before Edward the Confessor.* Exeter, 1948.

Ronay, Gabriel. *The Lost King of England: The East European Adventures of Edward the Exile.* Woodbridge, Suffolk, 1990.

Salway, Peter H. *Roman Britain.* The Oxford History of England. Oxford, 1981.

Sawyer, Peter H., and John Blair. *The Oxford History of Britain.* Vol. I, *Roman and Anglo-Saxon Britain.* Rev. ed. Oxford, 1992.

Sawyer, Peter H. *From Roman Britain to Norman England.* 2nd ed. London, 1998.

———. *Kings and Vikings.* London, 1982.

———, ed. *The Oxford Illustrated History of the Vikings.* Oxford, 1997.

Smyth, Alfred P. *King Alfred the Great.* Oxford, 1995.

———. *Scandinavian Kings in the British Isles, 850–880.* Oxford, 1977.

Stafford, Pauline. *Unification and Conquest: A Political and Social History of England in the Tenth and Eleventh Centuries.* London, 1989.

Stanley, E. G., ed. *British Academy Papers on Anglo-Saxon England.* Oxford, 1990.

Stenton, Frank M. *Anglo-Saxon England.* 3rd ed. The Oxford History of England. Oxford, 1971.

———. *Preparatory to Anglo-Saxon England*, ed. Doris M. Stenton. Oxford, 1970.

Thompson, E. A. *St. Germanus of Auxerre and the End of Roman Britain.* Dover, N.H., 1984.

Todd, Malcolm. *Roman Britain.* 3rd ed. Oxford, 1999.

Wacher, J. S. *The Towns of Roman Britain.* 2nd ed. London, 1995.

Wallace-Hadrill, J. M. *Bede's Ecclesiastical History of the English People: A Historical Commentary.* Oxford, 1988.

———. *Early Germanic Kingship in England and on the Continent.* Oxford, 1971.

Webster, Graham. *Boudica: The British Revolt Against Rome, A.D. 160.* Totowa, N.J., 1978.

———, ed. *Fortress into City: The Consolidation of Roman Britain, First Century A.D.* London, 1988.

———. *The Roman Invasion of Britain.* London, 1980.

Welch, Martin. *English Heritage Book of Anglo-Saxon England.* London, 1992.

Whittock, Martyn J. *The Origins of England, 410–600.* London, 1986.

Williams, Ann. *Kingship and Government in Pre-Conquest England.* New York, 1999.

Wilson, David. *The Anglo-Saxons.* 3rd ed. New York, 1981.

Woods, J. Douglas, and David A. E. Pelteret, eds. and trans. *The Anglo-Saxons: Synthesis and Achievement.* Waterloo, Ont., 1985.

Wormald, Patrick, with Donald Bullough and Roger Collins, eds. *Ideal and Reality in Frankish and Anglo-Saxon Society: Studies Presented to J. M. Wallace-Hadrill.* Oxford, 1983.

Norman Conquest to Magna Carta

Two excellent annual periodicals focus on the history and culture of the Anglo-Norman world and its neighbors: *Anglo-Norman Studies* (Woodbridge, Suffolk, 1979 ff.) and *The Haskins Society Journal: Studies in Medieval History* (London, 1989 ff.).

Appleby, John T. *England Without Richard, 1189–1199.* Ithaca, N.Y., 1965.

Barlow, Frank. *The Feudal Kingdom of England, 1042–1216.* 4th ed. London, 1988.

———. *The Norman Conquest and Beyond.* London, 1983.

———. *William I and the Norman Conquest.* London, 1965.

———. *William Rufus.* Berkeley, Cal., 1983.

Bates, David, *William the Conqueror.* London, 1989.

Bernstein, David J. *The Mystery of the Bayeux Tapestry.* London, 1986.

Brown, R. Allen. *Castles, Conquest, and Charters: Collected Papers.* Woodbridge, Suffolk, 1989.

———. *The Norman Conquest, Documents of Medieval History.* London, 1984.

———. *The Normans.* Woodbridge, Suffolk, 1984.

———. *The Normans and the Norman Conquest.* 2nd ed. Woodbridge, Suffolk, 1985.

Chibnall, Marjorie. *Anglo-Norman England, 1066–1166.* Oxford, 1987.

———. *The Debate on the Norman Conquest.* Manchester, 1999.

———. *The Empress Matilda: Queen Consort, Queen Mother and Lady of the English.* Oxford, 1991.

Cronne, H. A. *The Reign of Stephen, 1135–54: Anarchy in England.* London, 1970.

Crouch, David. *The Beaumont Twins: The Roots and Branches of Power in the Twelfth Century.* Cambridge, 1986.

————. *William Marshal: Court, Career, and Chivalry in the Angevin Empire, 1147–1219.* Harlow, Essex, 1990.

David, C. W. *Robert Curthose, Duke of Normandy.* Cambridge, Mass., 1920.

Davis, R. H. C. *From Alfred the Great to Stephen.* London, 1991.

————. *King Stephen, 1135–1154.* 3rd ed. London, 1990.

Douglas, David C. *The Norman Achievement, 1050–1100.* Berkeley, Cal., 1969.

————. *The Norman Fate, 1100–1154.* Berkeley, Cal., 1976.

————. *William the Conqueror: The Norman Impact upon England.* Berkeley, Cal., 1964.

Flanagan, Marie Therese. *Irish Society, Anglo-Norman Settlers, Angevin Kingship: Interactions in Ireland in the Late Twelfth Century.* Oxford, 1990.

Fleming, Robin. *Kings and Lords in Conquest England.* Cambridge, 1991.

Gameson, Richard, ed. *The Study of the Bayeux Tapestry.* Woodbridge, Suffolk, 1997.

Gibbs-Smith, Charles H. *The Bayeux Tapestry.* New York, 1973.

Gillingham, John. *Richard Coeur de Lion: Kingship, Chivalry and War in the Twelfth Century.* London, 1994.

————. *Richard the Lionheart.* 2nd ed. London, 1989.

————. *Richard I.* New Haven, 1999.

Green, Judith A. *The Aristocracy of Norman England.* Cambridge, 1997.

Harper-Bill, Christopher, Christopher J. Holdsworth, and Janet L. Nelson, eds. *Studies in Medieval History Presented to R. Allen Brown.* Wolfeboro, N.H., 1989.

Hollister, C. Warren, ed. *The Impact of the Norman Conquest.* New York, 1969.

————. *Monarchy, Magnates, and Institutions in the Anglo-Norman World.* London, 1986.

Holt, J. C. *The Northerners: A Study in the Reign of King John.* Rev. ed. New York, 1992.

Kapelle, William E. *The Norman Conquest of the North: The Region and Its Transformation, 1000–1135.* Chapel Hill, 1979.

Le Patourel, John. *Feudal Empires, Norman and Plantagenet.* London, 1984.

————. *The Norman Empire.* Oxford, 1976.

Loyn, Henry R. *The Norman Conquest.* 3rd ed. London, 1982.

Maund, K. L. *Ireland, Wales and England in the Eleventh Century.* Woodbridge, Suffolk, 1990.

Mortimer, Richard. *Angevin England, 1154–1258.* Oxford, 1994.

Nelson, Lynn H. *The Normans in South Wales, 1070–1171.* Austin, Tex., 1966.

Newman, Charlotte. *The Anglo-Norman Nobility in the Reign of Henry I: The Second Generation.* Philadelphia, 1988.

Owen, D. D. R. *Eleanor of Aquitaine: Queen and Legend.* Oxford, 1993.

Painter, Sidney. *The Reign of King John.* Baltimore, 1949.

Poole, Austin Lane. *From Domesday Book to Magna Carta, 1087–1216.* 2nd ed. Oxford History of England, 1955.

Powicke, F. M. *The Loss of Normandy, 1189–1204.* 2nd ed. Manchester, 1961.

Ritchie, R. L. Graeme. *The Normans in Scotland.* Edinburgh, 1954.

Round, John Horace. *The Commune of London and Other Studies.* Westminster, 1899.

————. *Geoffrey de Mandeville, A Study of the Anarchy.* London, 1892.

Searle, Eleanor. *Predatory Kinship and the Creation of Norman Power, 840–1066.* Berkeley, Cal. 1988.

Stringer, Keith J. *The Reign of Stephen.* Lancaster Pamphlets. 1993.

Thorpe, Lewis, ed. *The Bayeux Tapestry and the Norman Invasion.* London, 1973.

Turner, Ralph V. *King John.* London, 1994.

_____. *Men Raised from the Dust: Administrative Service and Upward Mobility in Angevin England.* Philadelphia, 1988.

Warren, W. L. *Henry II.* Berkeley, Cal., 1973.

_____. *King John.* Berkeley, Cal., 1978 (first published in London, 1961).

Whitelock, Dorothy, et al. *The Norman Conquest: Its Setting and Impact.* New York, 1966.

Wilkinson, Donald, and John Cantrell, eds. *The Normans in Britain.* Houndmills, Basingstoke, Hampshire, 1987.

Wilson, David M. *The Bayeux Tapestry: The Complete Tapestry in Colour.* London, 1985.

Thirteenth Century

Carpenter, D. A. *The Minority of Henry III.* London, 1990.

_____. *The Reign of Henry III.* London, 1996.

Clifford, E. R. A. *A Knight of Great Renown: The Life and Times of Othon de Grandson.* Chicago, 1961.

Coss, P. R., and S. D. Lloyd, eds. *Thirteenth-Century England.* Vols. I–V. Woodbridge, Suffolk, 1986–1996; Vols. VI–, ed. R. Britnell, R. Frame, and M. C. Prestwich. 1998–.

Cuttino, George P. *English Diplomatic Administration, 1259–1339.* 2nd ed. New York, 1971.

_____. *English Medieval Diplomacy.* Bloomington, 1985.

Denholm-Young, N. *Richard of Cornwall.* Oxford, 1947.

Harding, Alan. *England in the Thirteenth Century.* Cambridge, 1993.

Herbert, Trevor, and Gareth Elwyn Jones. *Edward I and Wales.* Cardiff, 1988.

Howell, Margaret. *Eleanor of Provence.* Oxford, 1997.

Lloyd, S. D. *English Society and the Crusades, 1216–1307.* Oxford, 1988.

Maddicott, John R. *Simon de Montfort.* Cambridge, 1994.

Ormond, Mark, ed. *England in the Thirteenth Century: Proceedings of the 1984 Harlaxton Symposium.* Woodbridge, Suffolk, 1986.

Parsons, John C. *Eleanor of Castile: Queen and Society in Thirteenth-Century England.* New York, 1994.

Powicke, F. M. *King Henry III and the Lord Edward: The Community of the Realm in the Thirteenth Century.* 2nd ed. 2 vols. Oxford, 1947.

_____. *The Thirteenth Century, 1216–1307.* 2nd ed. The Oxford History of England. Oxford, 1962.

Prestwich, Michael. *Edward I.* Berkeley, Cal., 1988.

_____. *English Politics in the Thirteenth Century.* London, 1990.

_____. *War, Politics, and Finance under Edward I.* Totowa, N.J., 1972.

Stacey, Robert C. *Politics, Policy, and Finance Under Henry III, 1216–1245.* Oxford, 1987.

Treharne, R. F. *The Baronial Plan of Reform, 1258–1263.* Rev. ed. New York, 1971.

_____. *Simon de Montfort and Baronial Reform: Thirteenth-Century Essays.* ed. E. B. Fryde. London, 1986.

Vincent, Nicholas. *Peter des Roches: An Alien in English Politics, 1205–1238.* Cambridge, 1996.

Fourteenth Century

Allmand, C. T. *The Hundred Years War: England and France at War, c. 1300–c. 1450.* Cambridge, 1988.

Barber, Richard. *Edward, Prince of Wales and Aquitaine: A Biography of the Black Prince.* New York, 1978.

Barrow, G. W. S. *Robert Bruce and the Community of the Realm of Scotland.* 3rd ed. Edinburgh, 1988.

Bruce, Marie Louise. *The Usurper King: Henry of Bolingbroke, 1366–1399.* London, 1986.

Curry, Anne. *The Hundred Years War.* London, 1993.

Denton, Jeffrey H., and John P. Dooley. *Representatives of the Lower Clergy in Parliament, 1295–1340.* Woodbridge, Suffolk, 1987.

DuBoulay, F. R. H., and C. M. Barron, eds. *The Reign of Richard II: Essays in Honour of May McKisack.* London, 1971.

Fowler, Kenneth. *The Age of Plantagenet and Valois: The Struggle for Supremacy, 1328–1498.* New York, 1967.

———, ed. *The Hundred Years War.* London, 1971.

———. *The King's Lieutenant: Henry of Grosmont, First Duke of Lancaster, 1310–1361.* New York, 1969.

Fryde, Natalie. *The Tyranny and Fall of Edward II, 1321–1326.* Cambridge, 1979.

Given-Wilson, Chris. *The English Nobility in the Late Middle Ages: The Fourteenth Century Political Community.* London, 1987.

Goodman, Anthony. *John of Gaunt: The Exercise of Princely Power in Fourteenth-Century Europe.* London, 1992.

Hamilton, J. S. *Piers Gaveston, Earl of Cornwall, 1307–1312: Politics and Patronage in the Reign of Edward II.* Detroit, 1988.

Kaeuper, Richard W. *War, Justice, and Public Order: England and France in the Later Middle Ages.* Oxford, 1988.

Keen, Maurice. *England in the Later Middle Ages.* London, 1973.

Lander, J. R. *The Limitations of English Monarchy in the Later Middle Ages.* Toronto, 1989.

McKisack, May. *The Fourteenth Century, 1307–1399.* The Oxford History of England. Oxford, 1959.

Maddicott, J. R. *The English Peasantry and the Demands of the Crown, 1294–1341.* Oxford, 1975.

———. *Law and Lordship: Royal Justices as Retainers in Thirteenth- and Fourteenth-Century England.* Oxford, 1978.

———. *Thomas of Lancaster, 1307–1322.* London, 1970.

Mathew, Gervase. *The Court of Richard II.* London, 1968.

Nicholson, Ranald. *Edward III and the Scots: The Formative Years of a Military Career, 1327–1335.* London, 1965.

Ormrod, W. M. *Political Life in Medieval England, 1300–1450.* New York, 1995.

———. *The Reign of Edward III: Crown and Political Society in England, 1307–1377.* New Haven, 1991.

Packe, Michael. *King Edward III,* ed. L. C. B. Seaman. London, 1983.

Palmer, J. J. N. *England, France, and Christendom, 1377–1399.* London, 1972.

Perroy, Edouard. *The Hundred Years War.* Trans. W. B. Wells. London, 1951.

Phillips, J. R. S. *Aymer de Valence: Earl of Pembroke, 1307–1324.* New York, 1972.

Prestwich, Michael. *The Three Edwards: War and State in England, 1272–1377.* London, 1981.

Roskell, J. S. *The Impeachment and Trial of Michael de la Pole, Earl of Suffolk, in 1386 in the Context of the Reign of Richard II.* Manchester, 1984.

Russell, P. E. *The English Intervention in Spain and Portugal in the Time of Edward III and Richard II.* Oxford, 1955.

Saul, Nigel. *Richard II.* New Haven, 1997.

Sumption, Jonathan. *The Hundred Years War.* Vol. I, *Trial by Battle.* Philadelphia, 1992; Vol. II, *Trial by Fire.* Philadelphia, 1999.

Taylor, John, and Wendy Childs. *Politics and Crisis in Fourteenth-Century England.* Wolfeboro Falls, N.H., 1990.

Tuck, Anthony. *Crown and Nobility, 1272–1461: Political Conflict in Late-Medieval England.* London, 1985.

———. *Richard II and the English Nobility.* New York, 1974.

Vale, Juliet. *Edward III and Chivalry: Chivalric Society and Its Context, 1270–1350.* Woodbridge, Suffolk, 1982.

Vale, M. G. A. *The Angevin Legacy: The Hundred Years' War, 1250–1340.* Oxford, 1990.

Walker, Simon. *The Lancastrian Affinity, 1361–1399.* Oxford, 1990.

Waugh, Scott L. *England in the Reign of Edward III.* Cambridge, 1991.

Wilkinson, Bertie. *The Later Middle Ages in England, 1216–1485.* London, 1969.

Local and Regional Studies

An extremely valuable series of regional histories of England is being published in 21 volumes by Longman, London and New York (1985 ff.) under the general editorship of Barry Cunliffe and David Hey. They include: J. V. Beckett, *The East Midlands from AD 1000*; J. H. Betty, *Wessex from AD 1000*; Peter Brandon and Brian Short, *The South East from AD 1000*; Peter Drewett, David Rudling, and Mark Gardiner, *The South East to AD 1000*; David Hey, *Yorkshire from AD 1000*; Nick Higham, *The Northern Counties to AD 1000*; Marie B. Rowlands, *The West Midlands from AD 1000*; and Malcolm Todd, *The South West to AD 1000.* Other valuable local and regional studies include the following works.

Biddick, Kathleen. *The Other Economy: Pastoral Husbandry on a Medieval Estate.* Berkeley, Cal., 1989.

Biddle, Martin. *Crafts and Industries of Medieval Winchester: Objects of Medieval Winchester.* 2 vols. Oxford, 1990.

———, ed. *Winchester in the Early Middle Ages: An Edition and Discussion of the Winton Domesday.* Oxford, 1976.

Brooke, Christopher, with Gillian Kier. *London, 800–1216: The Shaping of a City.* Berkeley, Cal., 1975.

Crawford, Barbara E. *Scandinavian Scotland. Scotland in the Early Middle Ages, 2.* Leicester, 1987.

Coleman, M. Clare. *Downham-in-the-Isles: A Study of an Ecclesiastical Manor in the Thirteenth and Fourteenth Centuries.* Woodbridge, Suffolk, 1984.

Dalton, Paul. *Conquest, Anarchy and Lordship: Yorkshire, 1066–1154.* Cambridge, 1994.

Douglas, David C. *The Social Structure of Medieval East Anglia.* Oxford, 1927.

DuBoulay, F. R. H. *The Lordship of Canterbury: An Essay on Medieval Society.* New York, 1966.

Dyer, Christopher. *Lords and Peasants in a Changing Society: The Estates of the Bishopric of Worcester, 680–1540.* Cambridge, 1980.

Everitt, Alan. *Continuity and Colonization: The Evolution of Kentish Settlement.* Leicester, 1986.

Finberg, H. P. R. *Tavistock Abbey: A Study in the Social and Economic History of Devon.* 2nd ed. Newton Abbot, 1969.

Harvey, Barbara. *Westminster Abbey and Its Estates in the Middle Ages.* Oxford, 1977.

Hill, J. W. F. *Medieval Lincoln.* Cambridge, 1948.

Hinton, David A. *Alfred's Kingdom: Wessex and the South, 800–1500.* London, 1977.

Hoskins, William G. *The Midland Peasant: The Economic and Social History of a Leicestershire Village.* London, 1957.

Keene, Derek. *Survey of Medieval Winchester.* 2 vols. Oxford, 1985.

Miller, Edward. *The Abbey and Bishopric of Ely: The Social History of an Ecclesiastical Estate from the Tenth Century to the Early Fourteenth Century.* Cambridge, 1951.

Morgan, Philip. *War and Society in Medieval Cheshire, 1277–1403.* Manchester, 1987.

Raftis, J. Ambrose. *The Estates of Ramsey Abbey: A Study in Economic Growth and Organization.* Toronto, 1957.

———. *Warboys: Two Hundred Years in the Life of an English Medieval Village.* Toronto, 1964.

Razi, Zvi. *Life, Marriage and Death in a Medieval Parish: Economy, Society and Demography in Halesowen, 1270–1400.* New York, 1980.

Rosser, Gervase. *Medieval Westminster, 1200–1540.* Oxford, 1989.

Rubin, Miri. *Charity and Community in Medieval Cambridge.* Cambridge, 1987.

Searle, Eleanor. *Lordship and Community: Battle Abbey and Its Banlieu, 1066–1538.* Toronto, 1974.

Williams, Gwyn A. *Medieval London: From Commune to Capital.* London, 1963.

Legal, Constitutional, and Governmental History

General Medieval

Baker, John Hamilton. *An Introduction to English Legal History.* London, 1990.

Bean, J. M. W. *The Decline of English Feudalism, 1215–1540.* Manchester, 1968.

———. *From Lord to Patron: Lordship in Late Medieval England.* Philadelphia, 1989.

Bellamy, John G. *Bastard Feudalism and the Law.* London, 1989.

Butt, Ronald. *A History of Parliament: The Middle Ages.* London, 1989.

Cam, Helen Maud. *Law-Finders and Law-Makers in Medieval England.* London, 1962.

———. *Liberties and Communities in Medieval England.* Cambridge, 1944.

Chaplais, Pierre. *Essays in Medieval Diplomacy and Administration.* London, 1981.

Chrimes, S. B. *An Introduction to the Administrative History of Medieval England.* 3rd ed. New York, 1980.

Cockburn, J. S., and Thomas A. Green, eds. *Twelve Good Men and True: The Criminal Trial Jury in England, 1200–1800.* Princeton, 1988.

Davies, Wendy, and Paul Fouracre, eds. *The Settlement of Disputes in Early Medieval Europe.* Cambridge, 1986.

Edwards, J. G. *Historians and the Medieval English Parliament.* Glasgow, 1960.

———. *The Second Century of the English Parliament.* Oxford, 1979.

Fryde, E. B., and Edward Miller, eds. *Historical Studies of the English Parliament.* Vol. I, *Origins to 1399.* Cambridge, 1970.

Harriss, G. L. *King, Parliament and Public Finance in Medieval England to 1369.* Oxford, 1975.

Hearder, H., and Henry R. Loyn, eds. *British Government and Administration: Studies Presented to S. B. Chrimes.* Cardiff, 1974.

Helmholz, Richard H. *Canon Law and the Law of England.* London, 1987.

Hicks, Michael. *Bastard Feudalism.* London, 1995.

Howell, Margaret. *Regalian Right in Medieval England.* London, 1962.

Hoyt, Robert S. *The Royal Demesne in English Constitutional History, 1066–1272.* Ithaca, N.Y., 1950.

Hunnisett, R. F. *The Medieval Coroner.* Cambridge, 1961.

Jewell, Helen M. *English Local Administration in the Middle Ages.* New York, 1972.

Jolliffe, J. E. A. *The Constitutional History of Medieval England from the English Settlement to 1485.* 4th ed. New York, 1961.

Lyon, Bryce. *A Constitutional and Legal History of Medieval England.* 2nd ed. New York, 1980.

———. *From Fief to Indenture.* Cambridge, Mass., 1957.

Milsom, S. F. C. *Studies in the History of the Common Law.* London, 1985.

Mitchell, Sydney Knox. *Taxation in Medieval England.* New Haven, 1951.

Morris, William A. *The Medieval English Sheriff to 1300.* Manchester, 1927.

Palmer, Robert C. *The County Courts of Medieval England, 1150–1350.* Princeton, 1982.

Plucknett, T. F. T. *Early English Legal Literature.* Cambridge, 1958.

———. *Studies in English Legal History.* London, 1983.

Pollock, Frederick, and Frederic William Maitland. *The History of English Law Before the Time of Edward I.* Rev. reissue of 2nd ed. 2 vols. Cambridge, 1968.

Poole, Austin Lane. *Obligations of Society in the XII and XIII Centuries.* Oxford, 1946.

Reynolds, Susan. *Fiefs and Vassals: The Medieval Evidence Re-interpreted.* Oxford, 1994.

Richardson, H. G., and G. O. Sayles. *The English Parliament in the Middle Ages.* London, 1981.

———. *Parliaments and Great Councils in Medieval England.* London, 1961.

Sayers, Jane E. *Law and Records in Medieval England: Studies on the Medieval Papacy, Monasteries and Records.* London, 1988.

Sayles, G. O. *The Functions of the Medieval Parliament of England.* London, 1988.

———. *The King's Parliament of England.* New York, 1974.

———. *Scripta Diversa.* London, 1982.

Schramm, Percy E. *A History of the English Coronation.* Oxford, 1937.

Stubbs, William A. *The Constitutional History of England.* 6th ed. 3 vols. Oxford, 1897; abridged ed., Chicago 1979.

Thorne, Samuel E. *Essays in English Legal History.* London, 1985.

Tout, T. F. *Chapters in the Administrative History of Medieval England.* 6 vols. Manchester, 1920–1933.

Wolffe, B. P. *The Royal Demesne in English History: The Crown Estate in the Governance of the Realm from the Conquest to 1509.* London, 1971.

Young, Charles R. *The English Borough and Royal Administration, 1130–1307.* Durham, N.C., 1961.

———. *The Royal Forests of Medieval England.* Philadelphia, 1979.

Roman and Anglo-Saxon

Abels, Richard. *Lordship and Military Obligation in Anglo-Saxon England.* Berkeley, Cal., 1988.

Harmer, Florence E. *Anglo-Saxon Writs.* Manchester, 1952.

Hollister, C. Warren. *Anglo-Saxon Military Institutions on the Eve of the Norman Conquest.* Oxford, 1962.

John, Eric. *Land Tenure in Early England: A Discussion of Some Problems.* Leicester, 1960.

Keynes, Simon. *The Diplomas of King Aethelred "The Unready" 978–1016: A Study in Their Use as Historical Evidence.* Cambridge, 1980.

Loyn, H. R. *The Governance of Anglo-Saxon England, 500–1087.* London, 1984.

Oleson, Tryggvi J. *The Witenagemot in the Reign of Edward the Confessor.* Toronto, 1955.

Wormald, Patrick. *The Making of English Law, King Alfred to the Twelfth Century,* Vol. I: *Legislation and Its Limits.* Oxford, 1999.

Norman Conquest to Magna Carta

Brown, R. Allen. *Origins of English Feudalism.* London, 1973.

Cheney, C. R. *Hubert Walter.* London, 1967.

Fleming, Robin. *Domesday Book and the Law: Society and Legal Custom in Early Medieval England.* Cambridge, 1998.

Galbraith, V. H. *Domesday Book: Its Place in Administrative History.* Oxford, 1974.

———. *The Making of Domesday Book.* Oxford, 1961.

Garnett, George, and John Hudson, eds. *Law and Government in Medieval England and Normandy: Essays in Honour of Sir James Holt.* Cambridge, 1994.

Green, Judith A. *The Government of England under Henry I.* Cambridge, 1986.

Hallam, Elizabeth M. *Domesday Book through Nine Centuries.* London, 1986.

Holdsworth, Christopher, ed. *Domesday Essays.* Exeter Studies in History, no. 14. Exeter, 1986.

Hollister, C. Warren. *The Military Organization of Norman England.* Oxford, 1965.

Holt, J. C. *Magna Carta.* 2nd ed. Cambridge, 1992.

———. *Magna Carta and Medieval Government.* London, 1985.

———, ed. *Domesday Studies: Papers Read at the Novocentenary Conference of the Royal Historical Society and the Institute of British Geographers, Winchester, 1986.* Woodbridge, Suffolk, 1987.

———, ed. *Magna Carta and the Idea of Liberty.* New York, 1972.

Hudson, John. *Land, Law and Lordship in Anglo-Norman England.* Oxford, 1993.

———. *The Formation of the English Common Law: Law and Society in England from the Norman Conquest to Magna Carta.* London, 1996.

Jolliffe, J. E. A. *Angevin Kingship.* 2nd ed. London, 1963.

Kealey, Edward J. *Roger of Salisbury, Viceroy of England.* Berkeley, Cal., 1972.

Keefe, Thomas K. *Feudal Assessments and the Political Community Under Henry II and His Sons.* Berkeley, Cal., 1983.

Milsom, S. F .C. *The Legal Framework of English Feudalism.* Cambridge, 1976.

O'Brien, Bruce R. *God's Peace and King's Peace: The Laws of Edward the Confessor.* Philadelphia, 1999.

Poole, Reginald Lane. *The Exchequer in the Twelfth Century.* Oxford, 1912.

Richardson, H. G., and G. O. Sayles. *The Governance of Mediaeval England from the Conquest to Magna Carta.* Edinburgh, 1963.

_____. *Law and Legislation from Aethelberht to Magna Carta.* Edinburgh, 1966.

Round, John Horace. *Feudal England.* London, 1895.

Sawyer, Peter, ed. *Domesday Book: A Reassessment.* London, 1985.

Stenton, Doris M. *English Justice between the Norman Conquest and the Great Charter, 1066–1215.* Philadelphia, 1964.

Stenton, F. M. *The First Century of English Feudalism, 1066–1166.* 2nd ed. Oxford, 1961.

Sutherland, Donald W. *The Assize of Novel Disseisin.* Oxford, 1973.

Turner, Ralph V. *The English Judiciary in the Age of Glanvill and Brackton, c. 1176–1239.* Cambridge, 1985.

_____. *The King and His Courts: The Role of John and Henry III in the Administration of Justice, 1199–1240.* Ithaca, N.Y., 1968.

Van Caenegem, R. C. *The Birth of the English Common Law.* 2nd ed. Cambridge, 1988.

_____. *Royal Writs from the Conquest to Glanvill.* Selden Society. London, 1959.

_____. ed. *English Lawsuits from William I to Richard I.* 2 vols. Selden Society. London, 1990–1991.

Warren, W. L. *The Governance of Norman and Angevin England, 1086–1272.* London, 1987.

West, Francis J. *The Justiciarship in England, 1066–1232.* Cambridge, 1966.

Young, Charles R. *Hubert Walter, Lord of Canterbury and Lord of England.* Durham, N.C., 1968.

Thirteenth Century

Brand, Paul. *The Making of the Common Law.* London, 1992.

_____. *The Origins of the English Legal Profession.* Oxford, 1992.

Cam, Helen Maud. *Studies in the Hundred Rolls.* Oxford, 1921.

Ellis, Clarence. *Hubert de Burgh.* London, 1952.

Hyams, Paul R. *Kings, Lords, and Peasants in Medieval England: The Common Law of Villeinage in the Twelfth and Thirteenth Centuries.* Oxford, 1980.

Meekings, C. A. F. *Studies in Thirteenth-Century Justice and Administration.* London, 1981.

Plucknett, T. F. T. *Edward I and Criminal Law.* Cambridge, 1960.

_____. *The Legislation of Edward I.* Oxford, 1949.

Powicke, Michael. *Military Obligation in Medieval England: A Study in Liberty and Duty.* Oxford, 1962.

Waugh, Scott. *The Lordship of England: Royal Wardships and Marriages in English Society and Politics, 1217–1327.* Princeton, 1988.

Fourteenth Century

Bellamy, J. G. *The Law of Treason in England in the Later Middle Ages.* Cambridge, 1970.

Booth, P. H. W. *The Financial Administration of the Lordship and County of Chester, 1272–1377.* Manchester, 1981.

Brown, Alfred L. *The Governance of Late-Medieval England, 1272–1461.* London, 1989.

Buck, Mark. *Politics, Finance, and the Church in the Reign of Edward II: Walter Stapeldon, Treasurer of England.* Cambridge, 1983.

Edwards, J. G. *The Commons in Medieval English Parliaments.* London, 1958.

———. *The Second Century of the English Parliament.* Oxford, 1979.

Given-Wilson, Chris. *The Royal Household and the King's Affinity: Service, Politics and Finance in England, 1360–1413.* New Haven, 1986.

Hewitt, Herbert I. *The Organization of War under Edward III, 1338–1362.* Manchester, 1966.

Holmes, George. *The Good Parliament.* Oxford, 1975.

Lapsley, G. T. *Crown, Community, and Parliament in the Later Middle Ages: Studies in English Constitutional History.* Helen Maud Cam and Geoffrey Barraclough, eds. Oxford, 1951.

Palmer, Robert C. *The Whilton Dispute, 1264–1380: A Social-Legal Study of Dispute Settlement in Medieval England.* Princeton, 1984.

Powell, J. Enoch, and Keith Wallis. *The House of Lords in the Middle Ages: A History of the English House of Lords to 1540.* London, 1968.

Raban, Sandra. *Mortmain Legislation and the English Church, 1279–1500.* Cambridge, 1983.

Roskell, J. S. *The Commons and Their Speakers in English Parliaments, 1376–1523.* Manchester, 1965.

Roskell, J. S., Linda Clark, and Carole Rawcliffe, eds. *The History of Parliament: The House of Commons 1386–1421.* 4 vols. Stroud, Engl., 1993.

Willard, J. F., et al., eds. *The English Government at Work, 1327–1336.* 3 vols. Cambridge, Mass., 1940–1950.

Economic and Social History

General Medieval

Arnold, Ralph. *A Social History of England, 55 B.C. to A.D. 1215.* New York, 1967.

Aston, Michael, David Austin, and Christopher Dyer, eds. *The Rural Settlements of Medieval England: Studies Dedicated to Maurice Beresford and John Hurst.* Oxford, 1989.

Aston, T. H., ed. *Landlords, Peasants, and Politics in Medieval England.* Cambridge, 1987.

Ault, Warren O. *Open Field Farming in Medieval England: A Study of Village By-Laws.* New York, 1972.

Baker, A. R. H., and R. A. Butlin, eds. *Studies of Field Systems in the British Isles.* Cambridge, 1973.

Barraclough, Geoffrey. *Social Life in Early England.* London, 1960.

Bartlett, Robert. *The Making of Europe: Conquest, Colonization and Cultural Change, 950–1350.* Princeton, 1993.

Bennett, Judith M. *Women in the Medieval English Countryside: Gender and Household in Brigstock Before the Plague.* Oxford, 1987.

Beresford, Maurice. *The Lost Villages of England.* New York, 1954.

———. *New Towns of the Middle Ages: Town Plantation in England, Wales and Gascony.* New York, 1967.

Beresford, Maurice, and J. K. S. St. Joseph. *Medieval England: An Aerial Survey.* 2nd ed. Cambridge, 1979.

Beresford, Maurice, and John Hurst, eds. *Deserted Medieval Villages.* Gloucester, 1989.

Bolton, J. L. *The Medieval English Economy, 1150–1500.* Totowa, N.J., 1980.

Britnell, Richard H. *The Commercialisation of English Society.* 2nd ed. Manchester, 1996.

Brooke, George C. *English Coins from the Seventh Century to the Present Day.* 3rd ed. London, 1950.

Bush, M. L. *The English Aristocracy: A Comparative Synthesis.* Manchester, 1984.

Cornfield, Penelope J., and Derek Keene, eds. *Work in Towns, 850–1850.* New York, 1990.

Dyer, Christopher. *Standards of Living in the Later Middle Ages: Social Change in England, 1200–1520.* Cambridge, 1989.

Hallam, H. E. *Rural England, 1066–1348.* Brighton, Sussex, 1981.

Hanawalt, Barbara A. *The Ties That Bound: Peasant Families in Medieval England.* New York, 1986.

Harding, Alan. *A Social History of English Law.* Baltimore, 1966.

Harvey, P. D. A., ed. *The Peasant Land Market in Medieval England.* Oxford, 1984.

Hilton, R. H. *Class Conflict and the Crisis of Feudalism: Essays in Medieval Social History.* London, 1985.

Hinton, David A. *Archaeology, Economy and Society: England from the Fifth to the Fifteenth Century.* London, 1990.

Holt, J. C. *Robin Hood.* Rev. ed. London, 1989.

Holt, Richard, ed. *The Medieval Town: A Reader in English Urban History, 1200–1540.* London, 1990.

Jewell, Helen. *Women in Medieval England.* Manchester, 1996.

Kanner, Barbara, ed. *The Women of England from Anglo-Saxon Times to the Present.* Hamden, Conn., 1979.

Keen, Maurice. *Chivalry.* New Haven, 1984.

_____. *English Society in the Later Middle Ages, 1348–1500.* London, 1990.

_____. *The Outlaws of Medieval England.* Rev. ed. Toronto, 1977.

King, Edmund. *England, 1175–1425.* London, 1979.

_____. *Peterborough Abbey, 1086–1310: A Study in the Medieval Land Market.* New York, 1973.

Langdon, John. *Horses, Oxen and Technological Innovation: The Use of Draught Animals in English Farming from 1066 to 1500.* Cambridge, 1986.

Leyser, Henrietta. *Medieval Women: A Social History of Women in England, 450–1500.* London, 1995.

Lloyd, T. H. *Alien Merchants in England in the High Middle Ages.* Brighton, 1982.

Longworth, Ian, and John Cherry, eds. *Archaeology in Britain since 1945: New Directions.* London, 1986.

Lucas, Angela M. *Women in the Middle Ages: Religion, Marriage, and Letters.* New York, 1983.

Lunt, William E. *Financial Relations of the Papacy with England to 1327.* Cambridge, Mass., 1939.

_____. *Financial Relations of the Papacy with England, 1327–1534.* Cambridge, 1962.

Miller, Edward, and John Hatcher. *Medieval England: Rural Society and Economic Change, 1086–1348.* New York, 1978.

_____. *Medieval England: Towns, Commerce and Crafts.* London, 1995.

Moore, Ellen. *The Fairs of Medieval England: An Introductory Study.* Toronto, 1985.

Platt, Colin. *The Castle in Medieval England and Wales.* London, 1982.

_____. *The English Medieval Town.* London, 1976.

_____. *Medieval England: A Social History and Archaeology from the Conquest to 1600.* New York, 1978.

Pollard, S., and D. W. Crossley. *The Wealth of Britain, 1085–1966.* London, 1968.

Postan, M. M. *Essays on Medieval Agriculture and General Problems of the Medieval Economy.* Cambridge, 1973.

———. *The Medieval Economy and Society: An Economic History of Britain, 1100–1500.* Berkeley, Cal., 1972.

———. *Medieval Trade and Finance.* Cambridge, 1973.

Power, Eileen. *Medieval Women,* ed. M. M. Postan. Cambridge, 1975.

———. *The Wool Trade in English Medieval History.* Oxford, 1941.

Pugh, Ralph B. *Imprisonment in Medieval England.* New York, 1968.

Raftis, J. Ambrose. *Tenure and Mobility: Studies in the Social History of the Medieval English Village.* Toronto, 1964.

Reynolds, Susan. *An Introduction to the History of English Medieval Towns.* New York, 1977.

———. *Kingdoms and Communities in Western Europe, 900–1300.* 2nd ed. Oxford, 1984.

Rigby, Stephen H. *English Society in the Later Middle Ages: Class, Status and Gender.* London, 1995.

Roberts, Brian K. *The Making of the English Village: A Study in Historical Geography.* Harlow, Essex, 1987.

———. *Rural Settlements in Britain.* Hamden, Conn., 1977.

Rodwell, Warwick. *The Archaeology of Religious Places: Churches and Cemeteries in Britain.* Rev. ed. Philadelphia, 1990.

Rosenthal, Joel, and Colin Richmond, eds. *People, Politics and Community in the Later Middle Ages.* Gloucester, 1987.

Sawyer, P. H., ed. *English Medieval Settlement.* London, 1979.

Tait, James. *The Medieval English Borough.* Manchester, 1936.

Vinogradoff, Paul. *The Growth of the Manor.* 3rd ed. London, 1920.

———. *Villainage in England.* Oxford, 1892.

Roman and Anglo-Saxon

Alcock, Leslie. *Economy, Society, and Warfare Among the Britons and Saxons.* Cardiff, 1987.

Birley, Anthony Richard. *Life in Roman Britain.* New ed. London, 1981.

———. *The People of Roman Britain.* Berkeley, Cal., 1980.

Blackburn, Mark, ed. *Anglo-Saxon Monetary History: Essays in Memory of Michael Dolley.* Leicester, 1986.

Blunt, C. E., B. H. I. H. Stewart, and C. S. S. Lyon. *Coinage in Tenth-Century England: From Edward the Elder to Edgar's Reform.* Oxford, 1989.

Dolley, R. H. M., ed. *Anglo-Saxon Coins: Studies Presented to Sir Frank Stenton.* London, 1961.

———. *Anglo-Saxon Pennies.* London, 1964.

Edwards, Nancy. *The Archaeology of Early Medieval Ireland.* Philadelphia, 1990.

Fell, Christine, with Cecily Clark and Elizabeth Williams. *Women in Anglo-Saxon England and the Impact of 1066.* Oxford, 1986.

Finberg, H. P. R., ed. *The Agrarian History of England and Wales.* Vol. I, pt. 2 (A.D. 43–1042). Cambridge, 1972.

Hooke, Della, ed. *Anglo-Saxon Settlements.* Oxford, 1988.

Jackson, Kenneth. *Language and History in Early Britain: A Chronological Survey of the Brittonic Languages, First to Twelfth Century A.D.* Cambridge, Mass., 1953.

Maitland, Frederic W. *Domesday Book and Beyond.* Cambridge, 1897.

Margary, I. D. *Roman Roads in Britain.* 3rd ed. London, 1973.
Merrifield, Ralph. *The Archaeology of Ritual and Magic.* New York, 1988.
_____. *London, City of the Romans.* Berkeley, 1983.
Richards, Julian D. *The English Heritage Book of Viking Age England.* London, 1991.
Whitelock, Dorothy. *The Beginnings of English Society.* Baltimore, 1952.

Norman Conquest to Magna Carta

Darby, H. C. *Domesday England.* Cambridge, 1977.
Dolley, R. H. M. *The Norman Conquest and the English Coinage.* London, 1966.
Finn, R. Welldon. *Domesday Book: A Guide.* London, 1973.
_____. *The Domesday Inquest and the Making of Domesday Book.* London, 1961.
_____. *The Norman Conquest and Its Effects on the Economy, 1066–86.* London, 1971.
Kealey, Edward J. *Harvesting the Air: Windmill Pioneers in Twelfth-Century England.* Berkeley, 1987.
_____. *Medieval Medicus: A Social History of Anglo-Norman Medicine.* Baltimore, 1981.
Lennard, Reginald V. *Rural England, 1086–1135: A Study of Social and Agrarian Conditions.* Oxford, 1959.
Logan, F. Donald, ed. *Norman London* (the description by William fitz Stephen). New York, 1990.
Mc Donald, John, and G. D. Snooks. *Domesday Economy: A New Approach to Anglo-Norman History.* Oxford, 1986.
Painter, Sidney. *Studies in the History of the English Feudal Barony.* Baltimore, 1943. Reprinted New York, 1980.
Rowley, Trevor. *The Norman Heritage, 1055–1200.* London, 1983.
Thomas, Hugh M. *Vassals, Heiresses, Crusaders and Thugs: The Gentry of Angevin Yorkshire, 1154–1216.* Philadelphia, 1993.

Thirteenth Century

Altschul, Michael. *A Baronial Family in Medieval England: The Clares, 1217–1314.* Baltimore, 1965.
Hilton, R. H. *A Medieval Society: The West Midlands at the End of the Thirteenth Century.* New York, 1966.
Homans, George C. *English Villagers of the Thirteenth Century.* Cambridge, Mass., 1941.
Kaeuper, Richard W. *Bankers to the Crown: The Riccardi of Lucca and Edward I.* Princeton, 1973.
Lloyd, S. D. *English Society and the Crusades, 1216–1307.* Oxford, 1988.
Titow, J. Z. *English Rural Society, 1200–1350.* New York, 1969.
Treharne, R. F. *Essays on Thirteenth-Century England.* London, 1971.

Fourteenth Century

Barnie, John. *War in Medieval English Society: Social Values in the Hundred Years War, 1337–99.* Ithaca, N.Y., 1974.
Bellamy, John. *Crime and Public Order in England in the Later Middle Ages.* London, 1973.

Bridbury, A. R. *Economic Growth: England in the Later Middle Ages.* Rev. ed. Brighton, 1975.

Campbell, Bruce M. S., ed. *Before the Black Death: Studies in the "Crisis" of the Early Fourteenth Century.* Manchester, 1991.

Dobson, R. B. *The Peasants' Revolt of 1381.* 2nd ed. London, 1983.

DuBoulay, F. R. H. *An Age of Ambition: English Society in the Late Middle Ages.* New York, 1970.

Fryde, E. B. *The Great Revolt of 1381,* The Historical Association. London, 1981.

Hanawalt, Barbara A. *Growing Up in Medieval London: The Experience of Childhood in History.* Oxford, 1993.

Hilton, R. H. *Bond Men Made Free: Medieval Peasant Movements and the English Rising of 1381.* New York, 1973.

————. *The Decline of Serfdom in Medieval England.* 2nd ed. London, 1983.

————. *The English Peasantry in the Later Middle Ages.* Oxford, 1975.

Hilton, R. H., and T. H. Aston, eds. *The English Rising of 1381.* New York, 1984.

Holmes, G. A. *The Estates of the Higher Nobility in Fourteenth-Century England.* Cambridge, 1957.

Hybel, Nils. *Crisis of Change: The Concept of Crisis in the Light of Agrarian Structural Reorganization in Late-Medieval England.* Aarhus, 1989.

Jordan, William C. *The Great Famine: Northern Europe in the Early Fourteenth Century.* Princeton, 1996.

McFarlane, K. B. *The Nobility of Later Medieval England.* Oxford, 1973.

Maddicott, J. R. *The English Peasantry and the Demands of the Crown, 1294–1341.* Past and Present Supplements. Oxford, 1975.

Shrewsbury, J. F. D. *A History of Bubonic Plague in the British Isles.* Cambridge, 1970.

Thrupp, Sylvia. *The Merchant Class of Medieval London, 1300–1500.* Chicago, 1948.

Ziegler, Philip. *The Black Death.* London, 1969.

Ecclesiastical History

General Medieval

Bettey, J. H. *Church and Community: The Parish Church in English Life.* New York, 1979.

Blair, John, ed. *Minsters and Parish Churches: The Local Church in Transition, 950–1200.* Oxford, 1988.

Burton, Janet. *Monastic and Religious Orders in Britain, 1000–1300.* Cambridge, 1994.

Butler, Lionel. *Medieval Monasteries of Great Britain.* London, 1987.

Colvin, H. M. *The White Canons in England.* Oxford, 1951.

Dickinson, John C. *An Ecclesiastical History of England: The Later Middle Ages, From the Norman Conquest to the Reformation.* London, 1979.

————. *Monastic Life in Medieval England.* London, 1961.

Finucane, Ronald C. *Miracles and Pilgrims: Popular Beliefs in Medieval England.* Totowa, N.J., 1977.

Harvey, Barbara F. *Living and Dying in England, 1100–1540: The Monastic Experience.* Oxford, 1993.

————. *Monastic Dress in the Middle Ages: Precept and Practice.* Oxford, 1988.

Kemp, E. W. *An Introduction to Canon Law in the Church of England.* London, 1957.

Knowles, David. *The English Mystical Tradition*. New York, 1961.

———. *The Monastic Order in England, 940–1216*. 2nd ed. Cambridge, 1963.

———. *The Religious Orders in England*. 3 vols. Cambridge, 1948–1959.

———. *Saints and Scholars: Twenty-Five Medieval Portraits*. Cambridge, 1962.

Lawrence, C. H., ed. *The English Church and the Papacy in the Middle Ages*. New York, 1965.

———. *Medieval Monasticism: Forms of Religious Life in Western Europe in the Middle Ages*. 2nd ed. London, 1989.

Moorman, J. R. H. *The Grey Friars in Cambridge, 1225–1538*. Cambridge, 1952.

Rodes, Robert E., Jr. *Ecclesiastical Administration in Medieval England: The Anglo-Saxons to the Reformation*. Notre Dame, 1977.

Roth, Francis. *The English Austin Friars, 1249–1538*. Vol. I., *History*. New York, 1966.

Southern, R. W. *Western Society and the Church in the Middle Ages*. Baltimore, 1970.

Tyerman, Christopher. *England and the Crusades, 1095–1588*. Chicago, 1988.

Warren, Ann K. *Anchorites and Their Patrons in Medieval England*. Berkeley, Cal., 1985.

Roman and Anglo-Saxon

Barley, M. W., and R. P. C. Hanson, eds. *Christianity in Britain, 300–700*. Leicester, 1968.

Barlow, Frank. *The English Church, 1000–1066*. 2nd ed. London, 1979.

Blair, John, and Richard Sharpe, eds. *Pastoral Care Before the Parish*. Leicester, 1992.

Bonner, Gerald, David Rollason, and Clare Stancliffe, eds. *St. Cuthbert, His Cult and Community to A.D. 1200*. Woodbridge, Suffolk, 1989.

Brooks, Nicholas. *The Early History of the Church of Canterbury: Christ Church from 597 to 1066*. Leicester, 1984.

Chadwick, Nora. *The Age of the Saints in the Early Celtic Church*. London, 1961.

Clayton, Mary. *The Cult of the Virgin Mary in Anglo-Saxon England*. Cambridge, 1990.

Dales, Douglas. *Dunstan: Saint and Statesman*. Cambridge, 1988.

Deanesly, Margaret. *The Pre-Conquest Church in England*. 2nd ed. London, 1963.

———. *Sidelights on the Anglo-Saxon Church*. London, 1962.

Edwards, Nancy, and Alan Lane, eds. *The Early Church in Wales and the West*. Oxbow Monographs 16. Oxford, 1992.

Godfrey, John. *The Church in Anglo-Saxon England*. Cambridge, 1962.

Henig, Martin. *Religion in Roman Britain*. New York, 1984.

Hutton, Ronald. *The Pagan Religions of the Ancient British Isles: Their Nature and Legacy*. Oxford, 1991.

Mayr-Harting, Henry. *The Coming of Christianity to Anglo-Saxon England*. 3rd ed. University Park, Pa., 1991.

Owen, Gale R. *Rites and Religions of the Anglo-Saxons*. New York, 1981.

Ramsay, Nigel, Margaret Sparks, and Tim Tatton-Brown, eds. *St. Dunstan: His Life, Times and Cult*. Woodbridge, Suffolk, 1992.

Ridyard, Susan J. *The Royal Saints of Anglo-Saxon England: A Study of West Saxon and East Anglian Cults*. Cambridge, 1988.

Rollason, D. W. *Saints and Relics in Anglo-Saxon England*. Oxford, 1989.

Sims-Williams, Patrick. *Religion and Literature in Western England, 600–800*. Cambridge, 1990.

Thomas, Charles. *Christianity in Roman Britain to A.D. 500*. Berkeley, Cal., 1981.

Watts, Dorothy. *Christians and Pagans in Roman Britain*. London, 1991.

Webster, Graham. *Celtic Religion in Roman Britain*. Totowa, N.J., 1987.

Whitelock, Dorothy, Martin Brett, and C. N. L. Brooke, eds. *Councils and Synods with Other Documents Relating to the English Church*. Vol. I, A.D. *871–1204*, Part 1, *871–1066*. Oxford, 1981.

Norman Conquest to Magna Carta

Barlow, Frank. *The English Church, 1066–1154: A History of the Anglo-Norman Church*. London, 1979.

_____. *Thomas Becket*. London, 1986.

_____. *Thomas Becket and His Clerks*. Canterbury, 1987.

Brooke, Z. N. *The English Church and the Papacy from the Conquest to the Reign of King John*. Cambridge, 1931; reprinted with a new Foreword by C. N. L. Brooke, Cambridge, 1989.

Cheney, C. R. *English Bishops' Chanceries, 1100–1250*. Manchester, 1950.

_____. *From Becket to Langton: English Church Government, 1170–1213*. Manchester, 1956.

Cheney, Mary G. *Roger, Bishop of Worcester, 1164–1179*. Oxford, 1980.

Chibnall, Marjorie. *The World of Orderic Vitalis*. Oxford, 1984.

Crosby, Everett U. *Bishop and Chapter in Twelfth-Century England: A Study of the Mensa Episcopalis*. Cambridge, 1994.

Dickinson, J. C. *The Origins of the Austin Canons and Their Introduction into England*. London, 1950.

Elkins, Sharon K. *Holy Women of Twelfth-Century England*. Chapel Hill, 1988.

Gibson, Margaret, *Lanfranc of Bec*. Oxford, 1978.

Hill, Bennett D. *English Cistercian Monasteries and Their Patrons in the Twelfth Century*. Urbana, Ill., 1968.

Knowles, David. *The Episcopal Colleagues of Archbishop Thomas Becket*. Cambridge, 1951.

_____. *Thomas Becket*. London, 1970.

Mason, Emma. *St. Wulfstan of Worcester*. Oxford, 1990.

Matthew, D. J. A. *The Norman Monasteries and Their English Possessions*. London, 1962.

Morey, Adrian, and C. N. L. Brooke, eds. *Gilbert Foliot and His Letters*. 2 vols. Cambridge, 1965.

Nicholl, Donald. *Thurstan, Archbishop of York (1114–1140)*. York, 1964.

Powicke, F. M. *Stephen Langton*. Oxford, 1928.

Saltman, Avrom. *Theobald, Archbishop of Canterbury*. London, 1956.

Scammell, G. V. *Hugh du Puiset, Bishop of Durham*. Cambridge, 1956.

Smalley, Beryl. *The Becket Conflict and the Schools: A Study of Intellectuals in Politics in the Twelfth Century*. Totowa, N.J., 1973.

Southern, R. W. *Saint Anselm and His Biographer: A Study in Monastic Life and Thought, 1059–c. 1130*. Cambridge, 1963.

_____. *St. Anselm: A Portrait in a Landscape*. Cambridge, 1991.

Squire, Aelred. *Aelred of Rievaulx: A Study*. London, 1969.

Vaughn, Sally N. *The Abbey of Bec and the Anglo-Norman State, 1034–1136*. Woodbridge, Suffolk, 1981.

_____. *Anselm of Bec and Robert of Meulan: The Innocence of the Dove and the Wisdom of the Serpent*. Berkeley, Cal., 1987.

Whitelock, Dorothy, Martin Brett, and C. N. R. Brooke, eds. *Councils and Synods with Other Documents Relating to the English Church.* Vol. I, A.D. *871–1204,* Part II, *1066–1204.* Oxford, 1981.

Wilks, Michael, ed. *The World of John of Salisbury.* Studies in Church History, Subsidia 3. Oxford, 1984.

Thirteenth Century

Brentano, Robert J. *Two Churches: England and Italy in the Thirteenth Century.* Princeton, 1968; new ed. with an additional essay by the author, Berkeley, 1988.

———. *York Metropolitan Jurisdiction and Papal Judges Delegate, 1279–1296.* Berkeley, Cal., 1959.

Denton, J. H. *Robert Winchelsey and the Crown, 1294–1313: A Study in the Defence of Ecclesiastical Liberty.* Cambridge, 1980.

Douie, D. L. *Archbishop Pecham.* Oxford, 1952.

Hinnebusch, W. A. *The Early English Friars Preachers.* Rome, 1951.

Moorman, J. R. H. *Church Life in England in the Thirteenth Century.* Reprint with corrections. Cambridge, 1955.

Powicke, Frederick Maurice, and Christopher Cheney, eds. *Councils and Synods with Other Documents Relating to the English Church,* Vol. II, *1205–1307,* 2 Parts. Oxford, 1962.

Sayers, Jane E. *Papal Government in England during the Pontificate of Honorius III (1216–1227).* New York, 1984.

Wood, Susan. *English Monasteries and Their Patrons in the Thirteenth Century.* New York, 1955.

Fourteenth Century

Aston, Margaret. *England's Iconoclasts.* Vol. I, *Laws Against Images.* Oxford, 1988.

———. *Lollards and Reformers: Images and Literacy in Late-Medieval Religion.* London, 1984.

———. *Thomas Arundel: A Study of Church Life in the Reign of Richard II.* Oxford, 1967.

Dahmus, Joseph H. *William Courtenay, Archbishop of Canterbury, 1381–1396.* London, 1966.

Haines, Roy Martin. *Archbishop John Stratford: Political Revolutionary and Champion of the Liberties of the English Church, ca. 1275/80–1348.* Toronto, 1986.

———. *The Church and Politics in Fourteenth-Century England: The Career of Adam Orleton, c. 1275–1345.* Cambridge, 1978.

Hudson, Anne. *Lollards and Their Books.* London, 1985.

———. *The Premature Reformation: Wycliffite Texts and Lollard History.* Oxford, 1988.

Hudson, Anne, and Michael Wilks, eds. *From Ockham to Wyclif.* Studies in Church History; Subsidia 5. Oxford, 1987.

McFarlane, K. B. *John Wycliffe and the Beginnings of English Nonconformity.* London, 1952.

Pantin, W. A. *The English Church in the Fourteenth Century.* Cambridge, 1955.

Robson, J. A. *Wyclif and the Oxford Schools.* Cambridge, 1961.

Thompson, A. Hamilton. *The English Clergy and Their Organization in the Later Middle Ages.* 2nd ed. Oxford, 1966.

Wright, J. Robert. *The Church and the English Crown, 1305–1334.* Toronto, 1980.

Intellectual and Cultural History

General Medieval

Archer, Michael, Sarah Crewe, and Peter Cormack. *English Heritage in Stained Glass: Oxford.* Oxford, 1988.

Bannon, W. R. J. *English Medieval Romance.* London, 1987.

Brewer, Derek, ed. *Studies in Medieval English Romances: Some New Approaches.* Cambridge, 1988.

Catto, J. I., ed. *The History of the University of Oxford.* Vol. I, *The Early Oxford Schools.* Oxford, 1984.

Clifton-Taylor, Alec. *The Cathedrals of England.* New York, 1970.

Clucas, Philip. *England's Churches.* Guildford, 1984.

Cobban, Alan B. *The Medieval English Universities: Oxford and Cambridge to c. 1500.* Aldershot, 1988.

Coote, Stephen. *English Literature of the Middle Ages.* London, 1988.

Craig, Hardin. *English Religious Drama of the Middle Ages.* Rev. ed. Oxford, 1964.

Crewe, Sarah. *Stained Glass in England, c. 1180–c. 1540.* London, 1987.

Denvir, Bernard. *From the Middle Ages to the Stewarts: Art Design, and Society Before 1689.* New York, 1988.

Gardner, Arthur. *English Medieval Sculpture.* Rev. ed. Cambridge, 1951.

Gransden, Antonia. *Historical Writing in England c. 550 to c. 1307.* London, 1974.

———. *Historical Writing in England c. 1307 to the Early Sixteenth Century.* London, 1982.

Harrison, F. L. *Music in Medieval Britain.* New York, 1958.

Heffernan, Thomas J. *Sacred Biography: Saints and Their Biographers in the Middle Ages.* New York, 1988.

Jack, Ronald D. S. *Patterns of Divine Comedy: A Study of Medieval English Drama.* Cambridge, 1989.

Leader, Damian R. *A History of the University of Cambridge.* Vol. I, *The University to 1546.* Cambridge, 1988.

Oakeshott, Walter F. *The Sequence of English Medieval Art.* London, 1950.

Orme, Nicholas. *Education and Society in Medieval and Renaissance England.* London, 1989.

———. *English Schools in the Middle Ages.* London, 1973.

———. *From Childhood to Chivalry: The Education of the English Kings and Aristocracy, 1066–1530.* London, 1984.

Patterson, Lee. *Negotiating the Past: The Historical Understanding of Medieval Literature.* Madison, 1987.

Rickert, Margaret J. *Painting in Britain: The Middle Ages.* 2nd ed. Baltimore, 1965.

Salter, Elizabeth. *English and International Studies in the Literature, Art, and Patronage of Medieval England,* Derek Pearsall and Nicolette Zeeman, eds. Cambridge, 1988.

Stone, Lawrence. *Sculpture in Britain: The Middle Ages.* 2nd ed. Baltimore, 1972.

Swanton, Michael James. *English Literature Before Chaucer.* London, 1987.

Talbot, Charles H. *Medicine in Medieval England.* London, 1967.

Webb, Geoffrey. *Architecture in Britain: The Middle Ages.* Baltimore, 1956.

Williamson, Paul. *Medieval Sculpture and Works of Art.* New York, 1987.

Woodforde, Christopher. *English Stained and Painted Glass.* Oxford, 1954.

Roman and Anglo-Saxon

Brooks, Nicholas. *Latin and the Vernacular Languages in Early Medieval Britain.* Leicester, 1982.

Brown, George Hardin. *Bede the Venerable.* Boston, 1987.

Clapham, A. W. *English Romanesque Architecture Before the Conquest.* Oxford, 1930.

Damico, Helen, and Alexandra Hennessy Olsen, eds. *New Readings on Women in Old English Literature.* Bloomington, 1990.

Duckett, Eleanor S. *Alcuin, Friend of Charlemagne.* New York, 1951.

———. *Anglo-Saxon Saints and Scholars.* New York, 1947.

Greenfield, Stanley B. *A Critical History of Old English Literature.* New York, 1965.

———. *Hero and Exile: The Art of Old English Poetry,* ed. George H. Brown. London, 1989.

Hanning, Robert W. *The Vision of History in Early Britain: From Gildas to Geoffrey of Monmouth.* New York, 1966.

Henderson, George. *From Durrow to Kells: The Insular Gospel Books, 650–800.* New York, 1987.

Kennedy, Charles W. *The Earliest English Poetry: A Critical Survey of the Poetry Written before the Norman Conquest.* London, 1943.

Lapidge, Michael, and H. Gneuss. *Learning and Literature in Anglo-Saxon England.* Cambridge, 1985.

Nordenfalk, Carl. *Celtic and Anglo-Saxon Painting: Book Illumination in the British Isles, 600–800.* New York, 1977.

Rice, D. Talbot. *English Art, 871–1100.* Oxford, 1952.

Stanley, E. G., ed. *Continuations and Beginnings: Studies in Old English Literature.* London, 1966.

Stoll, Robert. *Architecture and Sculpture in Early Britain: Celtic, Saxon, Norman.* New York, 1967.

Toynbee, J. M. C. *Art in Britain under the Romans.* Oxford, 1964.

Webster, Leslie, and Janet Backhouse. *The Making of England: Anglo-Saxon Art and Culture, A.D. 600–900.* London, British Museum, 1991.

Whitelock, Dorothy. *From Bede to Alfred: Studies in Early Anglo-Saxon Literature and History.* London, 1980.

Norman Conquest to Magna Carta

Boase, T. S. R. *English Art, 1100–1216.* Oxford, 1953.

Clapham, A. W. *English Romanesque Architecture after the Conquest.* Oxford, 1934.

Darlington, R. R. *Anglo-Norman Historians.* London, 1947.

Evans, Gillian R. *Anselm and a New Generation.* Oxford, 1980.

Forde, Helen. *Domesday Preserved.* London, 1986.

Henry, Desmond P. *The Logic of St. Anselm.* Oxford, 1967.

Legge, M. Dominica. *Anglo-Norman in the Cloisters: The Influence of the Orders upon Anglo-Norman Literature.* Edinburgh, 1950.

———. *Anglo-Norman Literature and Its Background.* Oxford, 1963.

Liebeschütz, Hans. *Medieval Humanism in the Life and Writings of John of Salisbury.* London, 1950.

Partner, Nancy F. *Serious Entertainments: The Writing of History in Twelfth-Century England.* Chicago, 1977.

Tatlock, J. S. P. *The Legendary History of Britain.* Berkeley, Cal., 1950.

Williams, G. H. *The Norman Anonymous of 1100 A.D.* Cambridge, Mass., 1951.

Zarnecki, George. *Later English Romanesque Sculpture, 1140–1210.* London, 1953.

Thirteenth Century

Bony, Jean. *The English Decorated Style: Gothic Architecture Transformed, 1250–1350.* Ithaca, N.Y., 1979.

Brieger, Peter H. *English Art, 1216–1307.* Oxford, 1957.

Callus, D. A. P., ed. *Robert Grosseteste, Scholar and Bishop.* Oxford, 1955.

Crombie, A. C. *Robert Grosseteste and the Origins of Experimental Science, 1100–1700.* Oxford, 1953.

Hunt, Tony. *Popular Medicine in Thirteenth-Century England.* Woodbridge, Suffolk, 1990.

Leff, Gordon. *Paris and Oxford Universities in the Thirteenth and Fourteenth Centuries: An Institutional and Intellectual History.* New York, 1968.

McEvoy, James. *The Philosophy of Robert Grosseteste.* Oxford, 1982.

Southern, Sir Richard. *Robert Grosseteste: The Growth of an English Mind in Medieval Europe.* 2nd ed. Oxford, 1995.

Swanson, Jenny. *John of Wales: A Study of the Works and Ideas of a Thirteenth-Century Friar.* Cambridge, 1989.

Vaughan, Richard. *Matthew Paris.* Cambridge, 1958.

Fourteenth Century

Aers, David. *Community, Gender, and Individual Identity: English Writing: 1360–1430.* London, 1988.

Brewer, Derek S. *Chaucer.* 3rd ed. London, 1973.

Bullock-Davies, Constance. *Register of Royal and Baronial Domestic Minstrels, 1272–1327.* Woodbridge, Suffolk, 1986.

Courtenay, William J. *Schools and Scholars in Fourteenth-Century England.* Princeton, 1987.

Evans, Joan. *English Art, 1307–1461.* Oxford, 1949.

Hussey, S. S. *Chaucer: An Introduction.* 2nd ed. London, 1981.

Kenny, Anthony. *Wyclif.* Oxford, 1985.

Leff, Gordon. *Bradwardine and the Pelagians.* Cambridge, 1957.

Morse, Ruth, and Barry Windeatt, eds. *Chaucer Traditions: Studies in Honor of Derek Brewer.* Cambridge, 1990.

Norton-Smith, John. *Geoffrey Chaucer.* London, 1974.

Phillips, Helen, ed. *Langland, the Mystics, and the Medieval English Religious Tradition: Essays in Honour of S.S. Hussey.* Cambridge, 1990.

Robbins, Rossell H. *Historical Poems of the Fourteenth and Fifteenth Centuries.* New York, 1959.

Saul, Nigel, ed. *The Age of Chivalry: Art and Society in Late Medieval England.* New York, 1992.

Taylor, John. *English Historical Literature in the Fourteenth Century.* Oxford, 1987.

Military History

Beeler, John. *Warfare in England, 1066–1189*. Ithaca, N.Y., 1966.

Birley, Eric B. *Roman Britain and the Roman Army*. Kendal, Engl., 1953.

Bradbury, Jim. *The Battle of Hastings*. London, 1997.

———. *The Medieval Siege*. Woodbridge, Suffolk, 1992.

———. *Stephen and Matilda: The Civil War of 1139–1153*. London, 1995.

Breeze, David John. *Roman Forts in Britain*. Aylesbury, Bucks., 1983.

Brown, R. Allen. *Castles from the Air*. Cambridge, 1989.

———. *English Castles*. 3rd ed. London, 1976.

Burne, A. H. *The Agincourt War: A Military History of the Latter Part of the Hundred Years War from 1369 to 1453*. London, 1956.

———. *The Crecy War: A Military History of the Hundred Years War from 1337 to the Peace of Bretigny, 1360*. London, 1955.

Carpenter, David. *The Battles of Lewes and Evesham, 1264/65*. Staffordshire, 1987.

Davidson, H. R. E. *The Sword in Anglo-Saxon England*. Oxford, 1962.

Davis, R. H. C. *The Medieval Warhorse: Origin, Development and Redevelopment*. London, 1989.

DeVries, Kelly. *Medieval Military Technology*. Peterborough, Ontario, 1992.

Hawkes, Sonia Chadwick, ed. *Weapons and Warfare in Anglo-Saxon England*. Oxford, 1990.

Haywood, J. *Dark Age Naval Power: A Reassessment of Frankish and Anglo-Saxon Seafaring Activity*. London, 1991.

Hewitt, Herbert J. *The Black Prince's Expedition of 1355–1357*. Manchester, 1958.

Humphries, P. H. *Castles of Edward I in Wales*. London, 1983.

Kenyon, John R., and Richard Avent, eds. *Castles in Wales and the Marches: Essays in Honour of D. J. Cathcart King*. Cardiff, 1987.

King, David James Cathcart. *The Castle in England and Wales: An Interpretive History*. London, 1988.

Marcus, Geoffrey J. *A Naval History of England*. Vol. I, *The Formative Centuries*. Boston, 1961.

Morillo, Stephen. *Warfare under the Anglo-Norman Kings*. Woodbridge, Suffolk, 1994.

Oakeshott, Ewart. *Records of the Medieval Sword*. Woodbridge, Suffolk, 1990.

Platt, Colin. *The Castle in Medieval England and Wales*. London, 1982.

Renn, Derek F. *Norman Castles in Britain*. 2nd ed. New York, 1973.

Seward, D. *The Hundred Years War*. London, 1982.

Simpson, W. Douglas. *Castles in England and Wales*. London, 1969.

———. *Hermitage Castle*. 3rd ed. Edinburgh, 1987.

Strickland, Matthew, ed. *Anglo-Norman Warfare*. Woodbridge, Suffolk, 1992.

Index